**Evening Standard**

# The London
# Pub & Bar
## Guide 1998

GW00542666

## Edward Sullivan

ESB

With thanks to Angus McGill

First published in Great Britain in 1997 by
EVENING STANDARD BOOKS
Northcliffe House, 2 Derry Street, London W8 5EE

ISBN 1 900625 75 X

Text © Edward Sullivan 1997

Design © Evening Standard 1997
Jacket illustration © Philip Mount
Maps © The Clever Map Company Limited

The moral right of the author has been asserted

Additional reporting by:

Robert Jennings, Alexander Robinson, David Mears, Jo Stubbs,
Nick Gill, Jemima Maxwell,  Martin Barnes.

| Publishing Manager: | Joanne Bowlby |
| Editorial Manager: | Charlotte Coleman-Smith |
| Production Manager: | Roger Hall |
| Typesetting by: | Sally Blackmore |
| Copy-editing by: | Tracey Beresford |
| Proof-reading by: | Terry Blackmore and Helen Ridge |

Printed and bound in Great Britain by Redwood Books Ltd, Trowbridge, Wilts.

A CIP catalogue record of this book is available from the British Library.

This book may be ordered by cheque or credit card on: 0171 538 2345.

*Also published in the series:*

The London Restaurant Guide, The London Fashion Guide,
Children's London

# Contents

4 **Foreword**

6 **Eros Awards**

8 **Reviews**

208 **Maps**

226 **Indices**

By area

Late-openers

With outside seating

With accommodation

Gay venues

Waterside venues

With dartboards

Name changes

With pool tables

With bar billiards

With strippers

Best places for food

Places to pull

Top ten cool, naff and pulling venues

Top ten for wine lovers, terrific views and other greats

International bars

EVERY year in the UK, we drink around 864 million litres of wine, 20 million litres of spirits and almost 1300 million gallons of beer. This makes the drinks business one of the most lucrative industries in the country today, fuelled by our seemingly insatiable appetite to part with our disposable income in pubs and bars. London, as we know, is the coolest place on earth and residents of, and visitors to the capital are indeed privileged to imbibe in the swinging social scene. Pubs have come a long way in recent years, these days you can get better food in some pubs than you can in many restaurants and they are drastically transforming themselves to meet our ever-changing demands. Bars have brought new dimensions to the drinks world and have dragged it stratospherically upmarket. It seems there's a bar for almost any occasion, function and purpose.

There's a growing trend for some of the finer drinking venues to employ rather curious door policies which are strictly enforced, although without explanation when you are refused admission. A hundred years ago, when I was a lad, we'd call them bouncers but the people in charge of access rights these days are given the rather unkind name of Door Whores. This Guide explores the wealth of London's drinking venues and suggests ways to get around those tedious clipboards. Dress codes are becoming more prominent again and in the course of research for this Guide I have been asking the management of various establishments why they use them.

The Cocktail Bar at The Connaught and The American Bar at The Savoy require gentlemen to wear ties. The Dog House in Soho asks men to remove their ties as a matter of policy and insist that it makes for a more comfortable atmosphere. When I asked a director of the Kemia Bar why they operate a no-suits policy, he suggested that I wouldn't be happy to go to a night club in a suit so why should I wear one here? When I pointed out that Kemia is not a club and that I am surely the best person to say what I'd be comfortable wearing, he terminated the telephone call. Similar no-suit policies are apparently operated at Saint and Riki Tik. The interesting thing is when you eventually get in to these places, there are more suits than you can poke a coat hanger at. So there must be something more sinister afoot, and there is! A door whore who works at several London venues finally told me the truth. 'It's got nothing to do with what you're wearing – they just hide behind that –– we just allow in the good-looking people or those who are dressed in the Glam fashion.' Babushka, who operate Glam

Sundays at their venues in Blackfriars Road and Caledonian Road openly admit this. 'We just pick the people who look the best' said one of the owners. So there you have it.

One of the aims of this book is to describe the atmosphere you are likely to experience during a visit to any one of these pubs and bars. Criticisms, where appropriate, are based on repeat poor performances rather than the occasional slip and all observations are made by bona-fide reporters of this Guide. There are some truly excellent venues in London and the indices at the back of the book should assist you to locate the type of place you're looking for in any given area. Enjoy it – I did.

EDWARD SULLIVAN

October 1997

Northcliffe House
2 Derry Street
London W8 5EE

## HOW TO USE THIS GUIDE
Although every effort has been made to obtain accurate information for inclusion in this Guide some details may change.

## OPENING HOURS
Throughout the life of this Guide legislation is likely to be introduced allowing an extra hour's drinking on Friday and Saturday.

## CREDIT CARDS
As so few places seem to take Diners, we have not included this card in the listings but credit cards are now an acceptable way of paying for drinks in most venues.

## BANK HOLIDAYS
Despite what the pubs and bars tell us, we have noticed that on bank holidays, opening hours and food service hours alter drastically so it is worth calling a venue before planning your day.

# Eros Awards

## Pubs

**Bread & Roses, SW4**     32
Eat with a conscience and drink to the cause

**Duke of Cambridge, SW11**     67
Dramatic conversion with great food and decent ales

**Enterprise, NW3**     73
Is there a better Irish pub in London?

**Legless Ladder, SW6**     123
Fulham at its best

**Lord's Tavern, NW8**     125
Not just for cricket days

**Paradise, W10**     150
A good place to celebrity spot

**Sun & Doves, SE5**     184
Yuppies come out in Camberwell

**Sun & Thirteen Cantons, W1**     185
Worth any number of visits

**Westbourne, W2**     196
Great food, a truly good pub!

**White Cross, Richmond**     201
Very traditional pub but beware of the Thames!

# Eros Awards

## Bars

**All Bar One, EC4**    12
Very hard to match this excellent chain

**Alphabet, W1**    13
Some of the best places to be found are in West Soho

**Babushka, W11**    18
A cool and trendy find in West London

**The Collection, SW3**    49
Beautiful, opulent clientele in stylish surroundings

**Kemia Bar at Momo, W1**    117
Moroccan theme, beautifully designed

**Mondo, W1**    133
Very trendy late night drinking spot in Soho

**Oblivion, SW4**    139
Popularity unmatched in Clapham

**La Perla, WC2**    151
Mexican theme – possibly the best service in London

**Rupert Street, W1**    170
Well designed, openly attractive gay bar

**Saint, W1**    170
Glam venue but difficult to get past the clipboards

## Adam and Eve

81 Petty France, SW1. Tel: 0171 222 4575

When you go to apply for your passport you will be given a delicatessen-style number that usually means that there is time enough to pop along the street to the Adam and Eve. They're used to all that form-filling in here. Scottish & Newcastle turned it into one of their real ale houses several years ago and there are nine cask beers on the hand pumps to sample before your number comes up back at the Passport Office. Should you have missed your turn, go back to the Adam and Eve and this time stick to halves! Food, luckily, is served all day.

*Open: 11.00–23.00 (Mon–Sat), 12.00–15.00 (Sun)*
*Food: 11.00–23.00 (Mon–Fri), 12.00–15.00 (Sat & Sun)*
*Credit cards: all major cards*
*Draught beers: Courage Best, Courage Directors, John Smith's Extra Smooth, Theakston Best, Theakston Old Peculier, Theakston XB, three guest ales, Beck's, Foster's, Gillespie's, Strongbow*
*Wheelchair access to venue*
*Nearest tube station: St James's Park*

## Admiral Codrington

17 Mossop Street, SW3. Tel: 0171 581 0005

Throughout the seventies and eighties the Admiral Codrington had an air of excitement about it. It was fun, it was happening – it was, quite simply, the place to be. This was where trust funds were frittered away and City bonuses celebrated, the very first mobile phone rang in a pub (probably), Fergie and Prince Andrew met to discuss their wedding arrangements, a young slip-of-a-lass by the name of Lady Diana Spencer enjoyed her favourite tipple and, I hear, where both her ladies-in-waiting met their future spouses. During Thatcher's reign (and almost exactly to those dates) the Cod was in the safe hands of Mel Barnett and his wife, model Irene Dunford. For many a social season they encouraged the young, the beautiful and the rich to whoop it up, and whoop it up they did. Such was their success that when the lease came up for renewal in 1990, jealous Bass wanted it back. The Marquess of Bath – Viscount Weymouth as he was then – led a long campaign, gathered 3,000 or so names and pleaded with the brewers to leave it alone. The campaign failed. Mel stormed out of the pub declaring, 'I will never set foot in that pub again – unless I own it.' The customers left along with the Barnetts, and Bass struggled with the place for years, so much so that at the end of 1996 they decided to sell the lease again. Guess who bought it? Correct. Mel and Irene returned to the Cod and described it as a 'homecoming'. Sitting there today it's hard to imagine such a rich and colourful history. It is an average Victorian boozer with a rather pleasant conservatory, but I'm pleased to report that things seem to be gathering pace once again. The Yuppies of its hey-day may well be taking the sea air at Eastbourne this year, but luckily, there is always another generation waiting to take over….

*Open: 11.00–23.00 (Mon–Sat), 12.00–22.30 (Sun)*
*Food: 12.00–15.00 (Mon–Sun), 18.30–21.00 (Mon–Thurs)*
*Credit cards: all major cards*
*Draught beers: Bass, Fuller's London Pride, Greenall's IPA, Carling Black Label, Grolsch, Guinness, Dry Blackthorn*
*Wheelchair access to venue*
*Private room: conservatory with cocktail bar, seats 30*
*Nearest tube station: South Kensington*

## The Albert

52 Victoria Street, SW1. Tel: 0171 222 5577

The Albert is the very model of a high Victorian public house with its fine engraved windows, rich decorations, gleaming bar and a noble staircase. It takes a staff of 28 to keep the place running, and even more in the summer. With the Houses of Parliament just up the road, it is well frequented by MPs; a division bell in the upstairs restaurant provides a timely reminder of important matters to attend to. The portraits on the staircase reflect every Prime Minister from the Marquis of Salisbury in 1885; one of Tony Blair is being prepared as I write. Mr Blair has apparently been in on a number of occasions, although not as yet in his new role. Mrs Thatcher unveiled her own portrait. Maybe this is a good opportunity for Mr Blair to revisit?

*Open: 11.00–23.00 (Mon–Sat), 12.00–22.30 (Sun)*
*Food: bar 12.00–23.00 (Mon–Sat), 12.00–22.00 (Sun); carvery 12.00–21.30 (Mon–Sun)*
*Credit cards: all major cards*
*Draught beers: Courage Best, Courage Directors, Theakston Old Peculier, one guest ale, Foster's, Holsten, Kronenbourg, Miller, Guinness, Strongbow*
*Wheelchair access to venue*
*Private room seats 24*
*Nearest tube station: St James's Park*

## Albertine

1 Wood Lane, W12. Tel: 0181 743 9593

This is a bar for the connoisseur of wines rather than the session drinker, with a wide-ranging list that has some good value, quality offerings. The success of Albertine is down to its having resisted the temptation to become a restaurant. You can eat, of course – the menu includes Greek salad (£4.60) and leek and mushroom quiche (£4.30) – but food isn't the prime motive of this bar. It has the appearance of a musty eighties wine bar, with dark wooden tables and candle-wax-coated bottles. Table service is all that's lacking to make this an almost perfect place for the wine lover.

*Open: 11.00–23.00 (Mon–Fri)*
*Food: 12.00–22.45 (Mon–Fri)*
*Credit cards: all major cards except AmEx*
*Wheelchair access to venue*
*Private room: 30 seated, 40–50 standing*
*Nearest tube station: Shepherd's Bush*

## The Albion

10 Thornhill Road, N1. Tel: 0171 607 7450

This graceful ivy-covered coaching inn belongs to a quieter, more rural time. The delightful Thornhill Road is lined with Georgian houses, and if going to The Albion means making a detour, then make it. It is an elegant, prosperous pub. The roomy bar used to have a restaurant area but the demand for the hearty cooked lunches and suppers has grown to such an extent that they now serve them throughout the pub. The star turn at The Albion, though, is the beer garden at the back – big, quiet and extraordinarily pleasant in the summer with its trellis and roses and picnic tables.

*Open: 11.00–23.00 (Mon–Sat), 12.00–22.30 (Sun)*
*Food: bar 12.00–15.00 and 18.00–21.30 (Mon–Fri), 12.00–22.30 (Sun); brunch 12.00–17.00 (Sun)*
*Credit cards: all major cards*
*Draught beers: Courage Best, John Smith's Extra Smooth, Theakston Best, Theakston XB, Foster's, Holsten, Lowenbrau, Guinness, Strongbow*
*Wheelchair access to venue*
*Private room seats 60*
*Nearest tube stations: Angel, Highbury & Islington*

# G. E. Aldwinkles

154 Fleet Road, NW3. Tel: 0171 485 2112

G. E. Aldwinkles, you may remember, is the former home of The White Horse in Hampstead which was smartened up a bit (quite a lot, actually) when Regent Inns took it over a few years ago. The renovation programme involved uncovering its original floor tiles, restoring its enamel plate ceiling and nice horseshoe bar, replacing gloomy windows with clear glass, and improving the food. It is now famous for its Tex-Mex specialities which include spicy beanburgers, nachos and burritos (from £4.95) and a wide range of ciabatta sandwiches (from £2.95). The cellar bar hosts Saturday comedy nights, known as The Hampstead Clinic, and is also available for private parties should you have your own brand of entertainment in mind.

*Open: 11.00–23.00 (Mon–Thurs), 11.00–01.00 (Fri–Sat), 12.00–22.30 (Sun)*
*Food: 12.00–15.00 and 18.00–21.30 (Mon–Fri), 12.00–21.30 (Sat), 12.00–17.00 (Sun)*
*Credit cards: all major cards*
*Draught beers: Brakspear, Courage Directors, Theakston Best, Theakston XB, Foster's, Holsten Export, Kronenbourg, Beamish, Dry Blackthorn*
*Wheelchair access to venue*
*Private room: 50 seated, 60 standing*
*Nearest tube station: Belsize Park*

# Alexandra

14 Clapham Common Southside, SW4. Tel: 0171 627 5102

This tall, impressive, tile-fronted building is handy as the first port of call when leaving the tube at the south side of Clapham Common. The exterior disguises a vast barn-like interior, with a combination of low and high-beamed ceilings, wooden floors, tables, chairs and walls, and the occasional step in the floor where you least expect it. The crowd is mostly young. Although it's a large bar, it fills up quickly at weekends.

*Open: 12.00–23.00 (Mon–Sat), 12.00–22.30 (Sun)*
*Food: 12.00–15.00 and 18.30–22.30 (Tues–Fri), 12.00–16.00 and 18.30–22.30 (Sat–Sun)*
*Credit cards: none taken*
*Draught beers: Courage Best, Courage Directors, John Smith's Extra Smooth, Foster's, Kronenbourg, Miller, Guinness, Scrumpy Jack*
*Private room: 150 seated, 250 standing*
*Nearest tube station: Clapham Common*

# The Alexandra

33 Wimbledon Hill Road, SW19. Tel: 0181 947 7691

The Alex is a busy town-centre pub, classically Victorian, which has been very carefully refurbished by Young's over recent years. The old public bar is the Wine and Ale Bar now, all beams and brickwork, with a log fire spit-roasting beef and turkey on cold winter days. A staircase leads to the new roof garden, where in the winter you will encounter Wimbledon's first rooftop marquee. In the summer you will find a barbecue. A no-smoking bar gives on to the Green Bar (now predominantly red, actually). Go past the counter where pub meals are served and you are in the wine bar, the brewery's first, where you can eat and drink till 1am on Friday and Saturday nights.

*Open: 11.00–23.00 (Mon–Sat), 12.00–22.30 (Sun), Wine bar to 01.00 (Fri & Sat)*
*Food: 12.00–22.00 (Mon–Thurs), 12.00–21.00 (Fri–Sun)*
*Credit cards: all major cards*
*Draught beers: Ramrod Smooth, Young's Bitter, Young's Special, Young's Wheatbeer, Castlemaine, Grolsch, London Lager, Premium Lager, Oatmeal Stout, Guinness, Dry Blackthorn*
*Wheelchair access to venue*
*Nearest tube station: Wimbledon*

# All Bar One

The growth of All Bar Ones continues at a steady pace following a year of site acquisitions, new openings and teams of people scurrying around spending money on even more prime sites. There are 20 in London at the moment, and that figure will continue to grow as the programme of openings rolls on. Some people criticise and say they are all the same wherever you go. Others praise and say they are all the same wherever you go. What you do get is consistency – wherever you find an All Bar One you know that it will be a spacious bar with library-style wine racks, a high standard of catering, a good range of beers and wines, and friendly, efficient staff. This is the All Bar One standard offer. It is what they call a retail brand in the Bass portfolio of eating and drinking venues, and it has proved so successful that Bass are going to expand it throughout the country as well as increasing its London presence. This is not to be sighed at. All Bar Ones are a very welcome addition to any high street, and the crowds who pile into them bear testament to this.

The blackboard-driven food menus offer a range of modern British fare, and on all my visits the dishes have been excellent, although they can be somewhat heavy on the salad greens. They come in small plates and large plates but even the small ones are much more substantial than many pub and bar 'starters'. All Bar Ones are food-focused, but you don't have to eat there, and large groups of people can easily gather around the big wooden tables to drink and enjoy the atmosphere. All branches are air-conditioned and offer table service, and the staff check the tables regularly to ensure that everything is as you would want it to be.

There are a few peculiar quirks to All Bar One. I'm not convinced that the own-label branding of wines is a good idea. Own-labels in supermarkets imply cheapness and I'm always suspicious about their origin. At All Bar One the cheaper wines (£9.50) bear the brand name as does the champagne (£18.50). All the branches carry a rather curious sign on the windows – it reads 'Sorry, no children under 14 years of age. Over 21s only.' If anyone can work that out, I'd be grateful if they'd let me know. A couple of branches are reviewed separately below – if there's one near you, you're in for a treat.

*Branches at:*

**Canary Wharf**: 42 Mackenzie Walk, South Colonnade, E14. Tel: 0171 512 9495. Nearest railway station: Canary Wharf (DLR)

**Chiswick**: 197–199 Chiswick High Road, W4. Tel: 0181 742 3339. Nearest tube station: Turnham Green

**City (EC2)**: 34 Threadneedle Street, EC2. Nearest tube station: Bank

**City (EC4)**: 103 Cannon Street, EC4. Tel: 0171 929 5162. Nearest tube station: Cannon Street

**City (EC4)**: 44–46 Ludgate Hill, EC4. Tel: 0171 248 1356. Nearest tube stations: Blackfriars, St Paul's

**City (SE1)**: 28–30 London Bridge, SE1. Nearest tube station: London Bridge

**Clapham:** 32–38 Northcote Road, SW11. Nearest railway station: Clapham Junction

**Fulham**: 587–591 Fulham Road, SW6. Tel: 0171 385 6668. Nearest tube station: Fulham Broadway

**Highgate**: 1–1a Highgate, N6. Nearest tube station: Highgate

**Islington**: 1 Liverpool Road, N1. Tel: 0171 278 5906. Nearest tube station: Highbury & Islington

**Notting Hill**: 126–128 Notting Hill Gate, W11. Nearest tube station: Notting Hill Gate

**Richmond**: 9–11 Hill Street, Richmond, TW9. Tel: 0181 332 1121. Nearest tube station: Richmond

**St John's Wood**: 60 St John's Wood High Street, NW8. Tel: 0171 722 6144. Nearest tube station: St John's Wood

**Soho**: 36–38 Dean Street, W1. Tel: 0171 287 4641. Nearest tube station: Tottenham Court Road

**Sutton**: 2 Hill Road, SM1. Tel: 0181 642 6510. Nearest railway station: Sutton
**Wandsworth**: Old York Road, SW18. Nearest railway station: Wandsworth Town
**West End**: 3–4 Hanover Street, W1. Tel: 0171 495 2216. Nearest tube station: Oxford Circus
**West End**: 48 Leicester Square, WC2. Tel: 0171 839 0972. Nearest tube station: Leicester Square
**West End**: 289–293 Regent Street, W1. Tel: 0171 636 6554. Nearest tube station: Oxford Circus
**Wimbledon**: 37–39 Wimbledon Hill Road, SW19. Tel: 0181 947 8654. Nearest tube station: Wimbledon

*Telephone numbers for some of the newer branches were not available at the time of going to press. The All Bar One head office is contactable on 0171 278 5847.*

## All Bar One

48 Leicester Square, WC2. Tel: 0171 839 0972

This All Bar One occupies the primest of sites in London, with a long glass frontage on the west side of Leicester Square. Sit at a window table and the entire square is spread before you with what might seem like the entire world milling about. It is an exceptionally roomy, lofty bar with a new mezzanine floor in the middle. During the day it moves into its brasserie mode, but in the evening the nation turns to drink and people queue to get into the All Bar One, now a bar again. There is any amount of standing room but, at about six in the evening, never enough. Mr Todd Slaughter, the splendidly named general manager, says that his lunchtime customers are suits at work. In the evening, he says, they are suits at play.

*Open: 11.00–23.00 (Mon–Sat), 12.00–22.30 (Sun)*
*Food: 12.00–22.00 (Mon–Thurs), 12.00–21.00 (Fri–Sun)*
*Credit cards: all major cards*
*Draught beers: Bass, Caffrey's, London Pride, Carling Black Label, Grolsch, Red Rock*
*Wheelchair access to venue*
*Nearest tube station: Leicester Square*

## All Bar One                          EROS AWARD WINNER

44–46 Ludgate Hill, EC4. Tel: 0171 248 1356

If you walk up Ludgate Hill towards St Paul's, you'll find plenty of wine bars and pubs on the way, some busy, some quiet, some empty. When you reach the corner of Old Bailey, and reach it you must, you'll come across All Bar One. It will be buzzing. I've walked past many times, and popped in far too many more times. It is irresistible. The classic All Bar One characteristics apply: large windows, big wooden tables, polished wooden floors, air conditioning, table service, high quality food ... the list of positives goes on. Big- spending City types like it, lesser paid office workers like it, and I think I agree.

*Open: 11.30–23.00 (Mon–Fri), 12.00–18.00 (Sat)*
*Food: 12.00–22.00 (Mon–Thurs), 12.00–21.00 (Fri), 12.00–17.00 (Sat)*
*Credit cards: all major cards*
*Draught beers: Bass, Caffrey's, London Pride, Carling Black Label, Grolsch, Red Rock*
*Wheelchair access to venue and loo*
*Nearest tube stations: St Paul's, Blackfriars*
*Nearest railway station: City Thameslink*

## The Alma Tavern

499 York Road, SW18. Tel: 0181 870 2537

The Alma Tavern stands directly opposite Wandsworth Town station, and after victory or defeat at Twickers, rugger buggers bound for Waterloo see the Alma's elegant Frenchified dome, pour off the train and head straight into the bar where you can be promised a lively night all right. The Alma is a prosperous pub faced by shiny bright green glazed tiles, and inside there are painted mirrors, gold mosaic medallions, a classical plaster frieze and a fine mahogany staircase leading out of the bar. All these have been scrupulously restored. In winter a fire blazes in the Art Deco fireplace and a handsome 1920s range heats the separate dining room. The place gets packed for Sunday lunches and pretty much stays that way throughout the week.

*Open: 11.00–15.00 and 17.30–23.00 (Mon–Sat), 12.00–15.00 and 19.00–22.30 (Sun)*
*Food: 12.00–22.30 (Mon–Sat), 12.00–16.00 and 19.00–22.00 (Sun)*
*Credit cards: all major cards*
*Draught beers: Ramrod Smooth, Young's Bitter, Young's Special, Young's Wheatbeer, Castlemaine, Grolsch, Young's London Lager, Young's Premium Lager, Guinness, Oatmeal Stout, Beamish, Scrumpy Jack*
*Wheelchair access to venue*
*Private room seats 70*
*Nearest railway station: Wandsworth Town*

## Alphabet    EROS AWARD WINNER

61–63 Beak Street, W1. Tel: 0171 439 2190

If I were a brave man, I'd make glowing predictions for the place. Soho nightlife is definitely moving to West Soho and beyond, and this post-modernist bar is going to be smack bang in the middle of it. The last time I spoke to the managers Andrew Maillard and 'Spike' (who doesn't have a spike) Marchant, they had already changed the menu to suit the burgeoning crowds. Alphabet is attracting a large eclectic following of street-fashionable twentysomethings along with the usual, earthy Soho set. There's no draught beer so it's a bottle-sucking joint, and it also has a decent range of 20 New World wines, all under £20 a bottle, with champagne at £21. There's a downstairs bar with adjustable car seats and a street map of Soho on the floor. Alphabet seems to be achieving the level of activity occasionally lacking at Notting Hill Arts Club (qv). It's early days yet, but here's my brave prediction: Alphabet is about to become one of the hippest places in town.

*Open: 11.00–23.00 (Mon–Sat)*
*Food: 11.00–23.00 (Mon–Sat)*
*Credit cards: all major cards*
*Wheelchair access to venue*
*Nearest tube station: Piccadilly Circus*

## The American Bar

Savoy Hotel, Strand, WC2. Tel: 0171 836 4343

This bar is much more relaxed of late, but the dress code of jacket and tie should be observed – certainly no denims. Spirits are served as doubles for around £5 and bottled beers start at £4. Stylish, sophisticated surroundings make this a place where business people can happily punish their expense accounts. Service is somewhat stilted but friendly and efficient, and the kettle chips, almonds and olives are constantly replenished. All in all it is rather a good deal.

*Open: 11.00–15.00 and 17.30–23.00 (Mon–Sat), 12.00–15.00 and 18.00–22.30 (Sun)*
*Credit cards: all major cards*
*Nearest tube station: Temple*

## Anchor, Bankside

234 Park Street, SE1. Tel: 0171 407 1577

Based on the riverside walk on Bankside, the Anchor is a fine old pub with five bars, a minstrels' gallery, a private 18th-century dining room, a new riverside terrace with serried ranks of picnic tables, a garden terrace, a barbecue and a most superior restaurant. As I write there are plans to expand even further, making this already Tardis-like building able to hold even more people. The individual rooms circumnavigate the bar and are all cosy and compact, some with their own fireplaces, some with snug-hole access to the bar. The floorboards creak with every step and seem to grow more lopsided by the day. It's a fine stop on a riverside walk, a good tourist attraction and a delightful local.

*Open: 11.00–23.00 (Mon–Sat), 12.00–22.30 (Sun)*
*Food: bar 12.00–21.00 (Mon–Sun); restaurant 12.00–14.30 and 18.00–21.30 (Mon–Sun)*
*Credit cards: all major cards*
*Draught beers: Bass, Flowers, Thomas Greenall's Original, plus nine cask-conditioned bitters changed on a weekly basis, Foster's, Kronenbourg, Stella Artois, Murphy's, Dry Blackthorn*
*Private room seats 50*
*Nearest tube station: London Bridge*

## The Angel

101 Bermondsey Wall East, SE16. Tel: 0171 237 3608

There has been an inn here in Rotherhithe since the 17th century when there were at least four little bars on the ground floor, the haunt of sailors, pirates, smugglers, press gangs and bawds. There is still a balcony, narrow but with a bench to sit on, and a new flagged terrace with tables and chairs and the river passing by. The Angel has been rebuilt a few times in its day but it has done well to survive at all, what with hard times and the Blitz. Even the dockers have gone now, but old Rotherhithe meets new Rotherhithe in the bar, and business lunchers from the City use the restaurant upstairs, a serious eatery with formally dressed waiters and a fine view of Tower Bridge and the City. It is open in the evenings too.

*Open: 11.00–23.00 (Mon–Sat) during summer months, 11.30–15.00 and 17.00–23.30 (Mon–Fri) during winter months; 12.00–15.00 and 19.00–22.30 (Sun)*
*Food: bar 12.00–14.30 and 18.30–21.00 (Mon–Sun); restaurant: 12.00–14.00 and 19.00–21.30 (Mon–Fri), 19.00–21.30 (Sat), 12.00–14.30 (Sun)*
*Credit cards: all major cards*
*Draught beers: Caffrey's, Thomas Greenall's Original, Worthington's Best, Foster's, Kronenbourg, Stella Artois, Murphy's, Strongbow*
*Private room seats 50*
*Nearest tube station: Rotherhithe*

## Anglesea Arms

215 Selwood Terrace, SW7. Tel: 0171 373 7960

The Anglesea is an early Victorian free house, an integral part of a prosperous South Kensington terrace. There is a large saloon bar and a smaller bar down some steps, which is known as the cubby and very cosy with a fire in winter. The Anglesea has only just started to open all day and there are plans to improve the food. It has a stretch of forecourt that some would say was the jewel in its crown. A hugely popular place to drink in the summer.

*Open: 11.00–23.00 (Mon–Sat), 12.00–22.30 (Sun)*
*Food: 12.00–16.00 (daily)*
*Credit cards: all major cards except AmEx*
*Draught beers: Adnams, Boddingtons, Brakspear, Brakspear Original, Harvey Sussex, London Pride, Marston's Pedigree, Carlsberg Export, Foster's, Grolsch, Heineken, Stella Artois, Murphy's, Guinness, Dry Blackthorn*
*Nearest tube stations: South Kensington, Gloucester Road*

# The Antelope

22 Eaton Terrace, SW1. Tel: 0171 730 7781

This 200-year-old snug little pub with low ceilings sits in the heart of Sloaneland and attracts the residents of the Eatons, who pop in for a power-drink, peruse the financial pages and ponder over the state of their portfolios. Lunch is a comfortable and sedate affair but after six in the evening the floppy haired, pin-striped suits meet up with power-dressed women wearing Alice bands for beers, beers and more beers. If you're not one of the privileged few to get pride of place on the bar stools, you may struggle to be noticed. The scene can resemble that of a trading floor, with outstretched arms clutching handfuls of money trying to catch the eye of the bar person. They used to spill out onto the pavement in the summer, but that's all changed now – it apparently upsets those neighbours who don't use the pub. Fanny Cradock (remember her?) once said its little panelled restaurant recaptured the flavour of the old chop-house, and that is still the aim – good plain cooking.

*Open: 11.00–23.00 (Mon–Sat), 12.00–15.00 and 19.00–22.30 (Sun)*
*Food: 12.00–14.30 (Mon–Sat)*
*Credit cards: all major cards*
*Draught beers: Adnams, Kilkenny, Tetley, Marston's Pedigree and two guest ales, Carlsberg, Castlemaine, Lowenbrau, Guinness, Dry Blackthorn*
*Wheelchair access to venue*
*Private room seats 40*
*Nearest tube station: Sloane Square*

# The Archery Tavern

4 Bathurst Street, W2. Tel: 0171-402 4916

This is a deeply traditional, attractive little pub tucked away in a side street behind the Bayswater Road. It wouldn't be out of place in a country village and has a most charming seating area outside, bedecked with flowers and hanging baskets. The pinball and satellite TV seem slightly incongruous but these appear to be the ubiquitous features of a Hall & Woodhouse pub.

The Archery Tavern took its name from Thomas Waring's archery range which previously occupied the site. He was a famous toxophilite (archer to you and me), and the Royal Toxophily Society was founded in the pub in 1871. Bows aren't the usual pull around here these days, however.

*Open: 11.30–23.00 (Mon–Fri), 10.30–22.30 (Sat–Sun); early opening at the week-end for breakfast*
*Food: 12.00–22.00 (Mon–Fri), 10.30–22.00 (Sat–Sun)*
*Credit cards: Mastercard, Visa*
*Draught beers: Badger's Best, Badger IPA, Blackadder, Tanglefoot, Hofbrau lagers, Guinness, Dry Blackthorn*
*Private room seats 40*
*Nearest tube station: Lancaster Gate*

# The Argyll Arms

18 Argyll Street, W1. Tel: 0171 734 6117

Tucked away behind Oxford Circus tube station en route to the London Palladium is this spectacular Victorian pub which attracts hordes of local business workers and a fair smattering of tourists. A glittering mirrored corridor with etched glass partitions opens on to small numbered bars, a larger saloon bar and a dining room. Up the massive mahogany staircase is another big bar which can be used for private functions. The Argyll has been kept in splendid nick by Nicholson's, who are constantly giving it some tender loving care. An 'acceptable standard of dress' is required and the big man on the door on Saturday nights enforces this.

*Open: 11.00–23.00 (Mon–Sat), 12.00–21.00 (Sun)*
*Food: 11.00–19.00; hot salt-beef sandwiches up to 21.00 (Mon–Sun)*
*Credit cards: all major cards*
*Draught beers: Adnams, Calder's Cream Ale, Kilkenny, Lowenbrau, Tetley, plus guest ales which change on a regular basis, Carlsberg, Castlemaine, Holsten Export, Guinness, Dry Blackthorn*
*Wheelchair access to venue*
*Private room: 30 seated, 70 standing*
*Nearest tube station: Oxford Circus*

## Atlantic Bar and Grill

20 Glasshouse St, W1. Tel: 0171 734 4888

The design is that of a thirties cruise liner gliding gently across the Atlantic in search of the rich spoils of the New World. Going down the wide sweeping staircase into the bar and restaurant area, you will encounter Harry's Bar (presumably the first-class lounge); the calm atmosphere here is mainly due to the man on the door controlling the numbers. The main bar is vast, with high ceilings, a large island bar and plenty of deck space for drinking cocktails. There is a bar menu with sandwiches (starting at £6.50), steak and chips (£15) and beluga caviar (£40 for 27.5g). The City boys on the pull and office party girlies who look like they might have a long train journey home in an easterly direction seem to enjoy the vibrant, chatty environment and opportunistic atmosphere. This is not the place to arrange to meet a large gathering as you can bet your last jar of beluga you won't all get in. The admission policy – 'at the discretion of the door' – is quite extraordinary in its design and implementation, making this an unreliable venue for a special occasion.

*Open: 12.00–03.00 (Mon–Sat), 18.00–22.30 (Sun)*
*Food: bar 12.00–03.00 (Mon–Sat), 18.30–22.00 (Sun); restaurant 12.00–15.00 and 18.00–midnight (Mon–Fri), 18.00–midnight (Sat & Sun)*
*Credit cards: AmEx, Mastercard, Visa, Switch*
*Draught beers: Mash, plus a guest ale, Hoegaarden*
*Wheelchair access to venue*
*Private room seats 60*
*Nearest tube station: Piccadilly Circus*

## The Audley

41 Mount Street, W1. Tel: 0171 499 1843

Pubs do not come much grander than The Audley, with Mount Street – the heart of Mayfair – and Berkeley Square at one end, and Park Lane at the other. Its style is high Victoriana, and its pink terracotta is enhanced by such a colourful floral display that it is almost impossible to pass. Like all pubs of its generation, The Audley mirrored the class divisions of the world outside. It was cut up into a parish of separate bars, each with its own social nuances. Mahogany and glass partitions hid each group of customers from each other, while narrow hinged screens hid customers from staff. The screens and partitions have long gone, of course, and we can see, as the original customers could not, the whole of the superb, deep-red painted plaster ceiling and the splendid bar. The original chandeliers have survived, and so have the clocks and The Audley's general air of being rather a cut above – which, indeed, while here, we all are. Suited business people like it very much, and the panelled dining room upstairs is popular with overseas visitors.

*Open: 11.00–23.00 (Mon–Sat), 12.00–15.00 and 19.00–22.30 (Sun)*
*Food: bar 11.00–21.15 (Mon–Sun); restaurant 12.00–15.00 and 17.30–21.30 (Mon–Sat), 12.00–15.00 (Sun)*
*Credit cards: all major cards*
*Draught beers: Courage Best, Courage Directors, John Smith's Extra Smooth,*

*Theakston Best, Becks, Foster's, Kronenbourg, Guinness, Strongbow*
*Wheelchair access to venue*
*Private room: jazz-theme room seats 120*
*Nearest tube stations: Green Park, Marble Arch*

# The Australian

29 Milner Street, SW3. Tel: 0171 589 3114

Standing in the middle of Chelsea today it's hard to imagine that there was a cricket field here at some point. In fact it was a very important cricket field, where, in 1878, Australia, on only its second tour, played two matches on the smart new pitch on Prince's Green, now occupied by Lennox Gardens. The first was against the Gentlemen of England and this saw all three Grace brothers turning out for the Gentlemen, who won by an innings and one run. The Australians then played the Players of England in a match that was unfinished. The Australian cricketers used this pub as a refreshment stop and the pub eventually adopted the new name in honour of the overseas visitors. Over the years, the collection of memorabilia has built up to the extent that this is now almost a perfect museum of cricket. It is an extraordinarily pretty pub with Virginia creeper crawling over all three storeys and a handsome floral display of hanging baskets and tubs. The rickety interior is a comfortable place to sip on the Pimms and enjoy the fine real ales and good quality English fare.

*Open: 11.00–23.00 (Mon–Sat), 12.00–22.30 (Sun)*
*Food: bar 11.00–21.15 (Mon–Sun); restaurant 12.00–15.00 (Mon–Sat) and 18.00–21.00 (Mon–Thurs), 12.00–14.30 (Sun)*
*Credit cards: all major cards except AmEx*
*Draught beers: Adnams, Marston's Pedigree, Tetley, plus guest ales, Carlsberg, Carlsberg Export, Castlemaine, Guinness, Dry Blackthorn*
*Nearest tube stations: Knightsbridge, Sloane Square*

# Babushka

173 Blackfriars Road, SE1. Tel: 0171 928 3693

Gary Hibberd and John O'Donnell, a couple of guys from the rag trade, spotted a gap in the market for providing decent quality bars and eateries in previously unpopular areas. This bar – the old King's Head – was their first venture. They gutted it, reopened it, and in a matter of weeks it was necessary to make bookings for lunch – the modern British cuisine was clearly an instant hit. The assembly of small rooms was knocked through to create one large bar stripped down to its bare brick and girders with a Dali-esque mural along one wall. There's a lounge area at the back with a grand piano, and an enormous beer garden for barbecues. In the evenings they whip off the napery and play host to a throng of after-work drinkers. At weekends the volume rises even more as pre-clubbers prepare for a long night at the nearby Ministry of Sound. Sundays have become a bit of an event, featuring Enigma, a daytime club scenario organised with the Ministry, who bring in five DJs for a glam, mostly gay event. They have a picker on the door (a new name for bouncer) and the more glam you are, the more likely you are to be picked.

*Open: 12.00–23.00 (Mon–Wed), 12.00–midnight (Thurs–Fri), 20.00–midnight (Sat), 11.00–17.30 (Sun)*
*Food: 12.00–16.00 (Mon–Fri)*
*Credit cards: all major cards*
*Draught beers: Caffrey's, London Pride, Carling Black Label, Carling Premier, Grolsch, Guinness, Dry Blackthorn*
*Private room: 200 seated, 350 standing*
*Nearest tube stations: Waterloo, Blackfriars*

# Babushka

125 Caledonian Road, N1. Tel: 0171 837 1924

An even better conversion style-wise than its sister in Blackfriars Road (see above), this branch is split over three levels with a long ground-floor bar, an upstairs lounge filled with chesterfields, and a restaurant on the next level with views over the Regent's Canal. The food is really of a very high standard: pan-fried tuna with sweet and sour tomatoes (£7.25), and ricotta and leek strudel with tomato jam (£5.75). Extras are extra. If you live near the Caledonian Road you're quite lucky; if you don't, it's worth a trip. Not many people seem to know about the restaurant and, as with many a quiet place, the service can be slow. Things really get going on Sunday nights with a glam club, Pushka, where you're likely to find trannies dancing on the bar.

*Open: 12.00–23.30 (Mon–Fri), 17.00–23.30 (Sat), 17.00–22.30 (Sun)*
*Food: bar 12.00–22.30 (Mon–Fri), 17.00–23.30 (Sat); restaurant 12.00–22.30 (Mon–Fri), 17.00–23.30 (Sat)*
*Credit cards: all major cards*
*Wheelchair access to venue*
*Private room: dining room for hire, seats 40*
*Nearest tube station: King's Cross*

# Babushka                              **EROS AWARD WINNER**

41 Tavistock Crescent, W11. Tel: 0171 727 9250

The third and probably not final venue from the team of Hibberd and O'Donnell opened in January 1997 in the farther-flung fields of Notting Hill. It's similar in design to the other Babushkas but is essentially a night-time venue. DJs perform every night of the week – house, hip-hop, jazz, soul. They even do flamenco dancing on Saturday at lunchtimes. There's a wide range of bottled beers, and the fridges can sometimes struggle to keep them chilled. The house wine should be avoided. Upstairs is a members' bar which is free to join but reflects the way of so many bars these days, where the owners dictate the type of clientele they want. Its first member was Melanie Sykes. She's the girl from the Boddington's advertisement who asks Tarquin if he's 'got his trollies on the wrong way round'. I was told I'd be their second member, and I often have my trollies on the wrong way round.

*Open: 17.00–23.00 (Mon–Fri), 12.00–23.00 (Sat)*
*Food: as opening hours*
*Credit cards: all major cards*
*Draught beers: Adnams, Kilkenny, Old Speckled Hen, Carlsberg, Lowenbrau, Guinness, Strongbow*
*Wheelchair access to venue*
*Private room seats 50*
*Nearest tube station: Westbourne Park*

# Back Bar

8–10 Brewer Street, W1. Tel: 0171 734 2626

Located in the colourful part of Brewer Street where it meets the alley of adventure leading into Berwick Street market, Back Bar is mostly gay and has a peculiar metal floor and blacked-out windows. When we went, there was a nightclub atmosphere even very early in the evening, and the barman danced constantly in such a fashion that it seemed like he must surely have several vertebrae missing. The clientele – young pseudo-trendy – didn't seem to be enjoying themselves very much but I hear that Friday and Saturday nights are lively affairs.

*Open: 12.00–15.00 (Mon–Sat), 18.00–22.30 (Sun)*
*Credit cards: none taken*
*Nearest tube station: Piccadilly Circus*

# The Backpacker

126 York Way, N1. Tel: 0171 278 8318

This is, quite possibly, the most famous Australasian hang-out in the world, known to every man, woman and beast with any Antipodean connection what-soever. It is so famous that they don't advertise and certainly don't encourage this Guide to write about it. As soon as Aussies and Kiwis arrive in London, this is where they head to party. And what a party! The action starts on Friday night with cheap drinks to oil the process. Until 10pm it's possible to get a pint for £1. The party goes on until the early hours and then they do it all over again on Saturday. Sunday is an even bigger day. This is when Aussies and Kiwis go to Church. The Church is a venue nearby which holds up to 1,000 people. Often, 1,000 people go there. If you have an English accent, keep it down a bit, as admission is to Aussies and Kiwis first, with the rest of the world some way down the list. From noon until 3.30pm you can down the tinnies or drink Squashed Frog and be entertained by comedians, singers, bands, male and female strippers, Australasian music and party games you wouldn't want your mother to know about. Then, if you can take the pace, it's back to the Back-packer, where the party goes on until midnight. Bonza!

*Open: 20.00–02.00 (Fri–Sat), 12.00–midnight (Sun)*
*Credit cards: none taken*
*Draught beers: John Smith's Extra Smooth, Budweiser, Foster's, Holsten Export, Miller, Guinness, Merrydown, Scrumpy Jack, Strongbow*
*Nearest tube stations: King's Cross, Kentish Town*

# Balls Brothers

Balls Brothers haven't ventured very far outside the City, where they seem to have got the formula for food and wines just right. All their branches are of a high standard, clean, comfortable and often air-conditioned. They have established a traditional style and City folk take to it very well. The staff are friendly and knowledgeable about the wines offered from the list and the selection of specials chalked up on the blackboard.

*Balls Brothers restaurants with wine bars:*

**City (EC2)**: 5–6 Carey Lane (off Gutter Lane), EC2. Tel: 0171 600 2720. Nearest tube station: St Paul's

**City (EC2)**: Gows Restaurant, 81–82 Old Broad Street, EC2. Tel: 0171 920 9645. Nearest tube station: Liverpool Street

**City (EC2)**: Moor House, London Wall, EC2. Tel: 0171 628 3944. Nearest tube station: Moorgate

**City (EC3)**: 52 Lime Street, EC3. Tel: 0171 283 0841. Nearest tube station: Bank

**City (EC3)**: St Mary at Hill, EC3. Tel: 0171 626 0321. Nearest tube station: Monument

**City (EC4)**: Bucklersbury House, Cannon Street, EC4. Tel: 0171 248 7557. Nearest tube station: Cannon Street

**Southwark**: Hay's Galleria, Tooley Street, SE1. Tel: 0171 407 4301. Nearest tube station: London Bridge

**Southwark**: The Hop Cellars, 24 Southwark Street, SE1. Tel: 0171 403 6851. Nearest tube station: London Bridge

**West End**: 20 St James's Street (entrance Ryder Street), SW1. Tel: 0171 321 0882. Nearest tube station: Green Park

*Balls Brothers wine bars:*

**City (EC2)**: 11 Bloomfield Street, EC2. Tel: 0171 588 4643. Nearest tube station: Liverpool Street

**City (EC2)**: 6–8 Cheapside, EC2. Tel: 0171 248 2708. Nearest tube station: St Paul's

**City (EC2)**: Kings Arms Yard, EC2. Tel: 0171 796 3049. Nearest tube station: Bank

**City (EC2)**: 42 Threadneedle Street, EC2. Tel: 0171 628 3850. Nearest tube station: Bank

**City (EC3)**: Mark Lane, EC3. Tel: 0171 623 2923. Nearest tube station: Tower Hill

# The Barley Mow

8 Dorset Street, W1. Tel: 0171 935 7318

A traditional, real-ale drinkers' pub from the Nicholson stable that quietly serves the locals of Dorset Street and Gloucester Place. You wouldn't imagine this, but when there's a big game being played at Wembley, the place is overrun with supporters. Why so? Because it's just around the corner from Baker Street station and the travelling fans tend to use it as a resting place. Martin McDonald, the manager of 11 years, tells me The Beatles played darts here in the early sixties and would order up sausage, beans and chips while they played. The dartboard has gone, alas, but they still serve up a mean plate of sausage, beans and chips. The Barley Mow is full of authentic reminders of days gone by. Brass price lists are countersunk in the bar but are almost illegible now, which is just as well as the prices are more than a hundred years out of date. The pub still has an old brass tap labelled Old Tom, which used to dispense gin. You brought your own jugs and they filled it up. The best seats in the house are the two pawnbroker booths. Each has a pair of facing benches, a door with a lock and its own stretch of counter. The deal was you slunk in with the family silver under your jacket, did the deal and slunk out again. These days, people lucky enough to find a free booth tend to stay there for the rest of the evening.

*Open: 11.00–23.00 (Mon–Fri); often closed on Sat for private parties*
*Food: 11.00–15.30 (Mon–Fri)*
*Credit cards: none taken*
*Draught beers: Adnams, Brakspear, Calders Cream Ale, Marston Pedigree, Tetley, Carlsberg Export, Castlemaine, Lowenbrau, Guinness, Addlestone's Cask*
*Wheelchair access to venue*
*Nearest tube station: Baker Street*

# The Barley Mow

Narrow Street, E14. Tel: 0171 265 8931

This listed building – 'red brick, domestic, early 18th-century style with rusticated stucco quoins' – was the Customs House to Limehouse Basin in the days when the Basin was the way in from the Thames to the whole Docklands system. It is now in the hands of Taylor Walker and the listing prevents them doing too much to it. The Barley Mow has an extra-large bar, sizeable restaurant, big function room upstairs and a huge riverside terrace.

*Open: 11.00–23.00 (Mon–Sat), 12.00–15.00 and 19.00–22.30 (Sun)*
*Food: bar 12.00–14.30 and 18.30–21.00 (Mon–Sat); restaurant 12.00–15.00 and 18.30–21.00 (Mon–Sat), 12.00–14.15 and 19.00–20.30 (Sun)*
*Credit cards: all major cards*
*Draught beers: Burton, Calder's Cream Ale, Tetley, Carlsberg, Castlemaine, Guinness, Dry Blackthorn*
*Wheelchair access to venue*
*Nearest railway station: Limehouse*

# Bar M at The Star and Garter

4 Lower Richmond Road, SW15. Tel: 0181 788 0345

What a magical transformation of the bars at Putney's Star and Garter. This famous Victorian pub was until recently looking quite the worse for wear. Now, thanks to Glendola Leisure (Waxy O'Connor's and Bootsy Brogan's, qv), Bar M has been thoroughly refurbished, offering something just a little different to the Putney toper. It has one very long room fronting on to the river, a bar on the opposite wall, a highly polished light oak floor and a carpeted raised level running underneath the windows. The seating looks as though it was designed by someone who always goes out with three friends. Most of the floor space is taken up with small tables, spaced far apart, all designed to seat four people. The same applies to the high pedestal tables, and the tables in the window (very few people get a river view, by the way). When we last called, every table was occupied by only two people, leaving nowhere to sit in a half-empty bar. The *pièce de résistance* comes at the bar, though. The five or six stools stand cluttered together at one end, in the service area. You can't order drinks here so you must leave your stool, slide down the bar, order your drinks, and then slide back again. It beggars belief! They've made the menus out of an un-nickable stainless steel. Is there a major problem with menus going missing? I thought I was the only saddo who stole menus from bars, but I have a tip for the anarchists – if you scratch the lettering on the menu, it disappears. They are making an admirable attempt at table service but to do this effectively in a large bar you need more than just the few girls we saw running around. The music is set at just a decibel too high.

*Open: 11.00–23.00 (Mon–Sat), 12.00–22.30 (Sun)*
*Food: 12.00–22.00 (Mon–Sat), 12.00–21.00 (Sun)*
*Credit cards: all major cards*
*Draught beers: Kilkenny, Tetley's, Foster's, Kronenbourg, Guinness, Dry Blackthorn*
*Private room seats 120*
*Nearest tube station: Putney Bridge*

## Bar Oz

51 Moscow Road, Bayswater, W2. Tel: 0171 229 0647

Oh dear, they're at it again! The Ministry of Nonsense has dreamt up another theme for their bars, this one linked somewhat tenuously to the Sydney Olympics in the year 2000. Apparently we're going to go all Oz-ified – eating tucker out of billycans, having barbies all day, using words without definitions and generally not doing any work. They have even created their own slogan: 'No worries mate!' Someone got paid for that!

*Open: 11.00–23.00 (Mon–Sat), 12.00–22.30 (Sun)*
*Food: 11.00–22.00 (Mon–Sat), 12.00–22.00 (Sun)*
*Credit cards: Visa*
*Draught beers: Beamish Red, John Smith's Extra Smooth, Becks, Foster's, Kronenbourg, Beamish, Strongbow*
*Wheelchair access to venue*
*Nearest tube stations: Queensway, Bayswater*

## The Barrow Boy and Banker

6–8 Borough Street, SE1. Tel: 0171 403 5415

I can't imagine what Fuller's might have been trying to suggest in the naming of this pub. Whatever the speculation, nothing sinister went on here. This was a bank until Fuller's got hold of it and converted it into a pub in 1996, and a very good job they made of it too. Immediately south of London Bridge, The Barrow Boy is handy for City workers and equally handy for the real-life barrow boys in Borough High Street. It has one large, almost circular room, spacious banquettes and plenty of tables to sit at. There can be a bit of a fight for a seat in the evenings and there's often a scrum at the bar. You can normally escape to an even bigger bar upstairs, although this is sometimes closed for private functions.

*Open: 11.00–23.00 (Mon–Fri)*
*Food: 12.00–20.00 (Mon–Fri)*
*Credit cards: AmEx, Mastercard, Visa, Switch*
*Draught beers: Chiswick Bitter, ESB, Fuller's seasonal ale, London Cream Ale, London Pride, plus a guest ale, Carling Black Label, Grolsch, Heineken, Stella Artois, Guinness, Scrumpy Jack*
*Three private rooms: 14, 20 and 40 seated; 20, 40 and 80 standing*
*Nearest tube station: London Bridge*

## Bar Zola

33 Wellington Street, WC2. Tel: 0171 836 0038

When you've had a long day at the office, want a bit of fun, a few drinks, fairly loud music in a post-modernist environment, and you might just be up for pulling someone, then this is a great place. It fills up quickly in the evenings with suited boys and skirted girls looking for a bit of action.

*Open: 16.00–23.00 (Mon–Fri), 12.00–23.00 (Sat)*
*Food: 16.00–22.30 (Mon–Thurs), 16.00–19.00 (Fri–Sat)*
*Credit cards: all major cards*
*Draught beers: Caffrey's, Staropramen, Stella Artois*
*Wheelchair access to venue*
*Private room: 80–100 seated, 120 standing*
*Nearest tube stations: Covent Garden, Charing Cross*

## B Bar

94 Northcote Road, SW11. Tel: 0171 738 9781

I'd heard so many decent things about the B Bar on Northcote Road that we popped down there one evening to check it out. It's a large corner building with a very welcoming bar styled in blue, orange and mustard, and a small but pleasant outside seating area. There's a gloomier room around the back, but on busy nights you won't notice that. The B Bar has an interesting menu, including ostrich fillet with carrot and swede (£10.90), salads, pasta and fish dishes. It attracts a mix of young and old, and at the weekends, I am reliably informed, it gets quite lively. Should you go on a Monday night at 10.20pm and be greeted by the manager, Adele Harrington, refusing to serve you food, you might want to point out that they state food times as listed below. If Adele says the kitchen is closed, then the kitchen is closed. If you say it's Monday and she says it's Thursday, then go along with her and bow out gracefully. You have been warned!

*Open: 12.00–23.00 (Mon–Fri), 12.00–midnight (Sat), 12.30–22.30 (Sun)*
*Food: 12.00–15.00 (Mon–Fri), 12.00–15.30 and 18.30–23.00 (Sat), 12.30–15.30 and 18.30–22.30 (Sun)*
*Credit cards: all major cards except AmEx*
*Wheelchair access to venue and loo*
*Nearest tube station: Clapham South*

## Beach Blanket Babylon

45 Ledbury Road, W11. Tel: 0171 229 2907

Striking, stylish, sexy and sophisticated, this bar quickly became a mecca for fashionable Notting Hill when it opened in 1991. It was then owned by Carmel Azzopardi (now of the Cross Keys in Chelsea, qv) and was designed by Tony Weller. It makes a decent job of the food it serves – you find the restaurant by winding your way behind the bar, along a gangplank and down the spiral stairway into the cosy cellar. BBB has been much copied but remains the original New Age bar, and is a very useful port-of-call in a Notting Hill crawl.

*Open: 12.00–23.00 (Mon–Sat), 12.00–22.30 (Sun)*
*Food: 12.00–23.00 (Mon–Sun)*
*Credit cards: all major cards*
*Wheelchair access to venue*
*Three private rooms: 40, 30 and 50 seated, 100 standing*
*Nearest tube station: Notting Hill Gate*

## The Beaufoy Arms

18 Lavender Hill, SW11. Tel: 0171 228 9246

This is London's leading reggae pub and the sound is up to blast off, although there's no live music. Strictly for reggae lovers only, with elements of dancehall, ragga and the safe side of jungle. Every night is reggae night but Thursday is Ragga Night with top DJs. Friday night has Daddy Ernie of Choice FM and other well-known reggae DJs, and Saturday is revival night with reggae from the sixties, seventies and eighties – Bob Marley time. There is traditional West Indian food all day – jerk chicken and pork, dumplings, curried goat and rice, salt fish, patties, breadfruit, fritters – and the strategically placed mirrors tell you that there are exotic dancers about. They are currently about to move the bar, allowing more space for dancing, and are preparing to replace all the furniture to give the pub a more modern edge.

*Open: 11.00–midnight (Mon–Sat), 11.00–23.00 (Sun)*
*Food: as opening hours*
*Credit cards: all major cards*
*Draught beers: Webster's, Budweiser, Carlsberg, Foster's, Holsten, Red Stripe, Guinness, Dry Blackthorn*
*Wheelchair access to venue*
*Nearest railway station: Clapham Junction*

## Bell and Crown

72 Strand on the Green, W4. Tel: 0181 994 4164

If you walk along this riverside path starting at Kew Bridge, you come to the Bell and Crown first, then The City Barge, then the Bull's Head (qv). The Bell and Crown is marginally the biggest, a well-appointed, comfortable old pub with an air of no expense spared. The polished central counter serves a number of separate drinking areas and a spacious conservatory, now a non-smoking area. There's no music ever, and no games of any sort.

The conservatory feels a bit cut off in winter, but in the summer the whole pub seems to turn towards the river and the conservatory becomes part of the outdoors. Beneath it is a terrace under a green awning, and beneath that a patio by the towpath filled with picnic tables under umbrellas. If you can't get a seat in any of these places, you can sit on the river wall. People do in great numbers.

*Open: 11.00–23.00 (Mon–Sat), 12.00–22.30 (Sun)*
*Food: 11.00–22.00 (Mon–Sat), 12.00–22.00 (Sun)*
*Credit cards: AmEx, Mastercard, Visa*
*Draught beers: Chiswick, ESB, Fuller's IPA, Carling Black Label, Grolsch, Stella Artois, Guinness, Murphy's, Scrumpy Jack, Strongbow*
*Wheelchair access to venue*
*Private room seats 40*
*Nearest railway station: Kew Bridge*

## La Belle Époque

151 Draycott Avenue, SW3. Tel: 0171 460 5000

I'm giving out a special award for the worst service in London. In fact, the service in the bar of this stylish London eating emporium was so slow that it's still in the running for next year's award. After 27 minutes of waiting to get served, we waited another 16 minutes for the drinks to arrive. The wine was corked (OK, not their fault, perhaps), and 12 minutes later the situation was rectified. Having polished off the wine we ordered our bill and waited a staggering 35 minutes (including three repeated requests) before I gave up and went to the till to demand to make my payment. The staff seemed genuinely surprised when I asked them to deduct the service charge from the bill, and made a note of it on their summary sheet. An hour and a half for quick drinks? Think several times about this one!

*Open: 08.00–midnight (Mon–Sat). 10.00–23.00 (Sun)*
*Food: as opening hours*
*Credit cards: all major cards*
*Wheelchair access to venue and loo*
*Nearest tube station: South Kensington*

## Belle Vue

1 Clapham Common Southside, SW4. Tel: 0171 498 9437

A large corner building with big windows houses this bar-cum-restaurant. The long bar at the back of the room is also the food servery and this is where you wait to find a seat if you can't get a table or one of the couches near the fire-place. The staff will quite happily drag the tables and chairs around and push them together to cater for larger gatherings. The food is constantly changing but is Modern British-based and reasonably priced. There's a notice on each table telling you that priority is given to diners, so if you're drinking only, you might well be asked give up your table – fair enough, you have been warned.

*Open: 12.00–23.00 (Mon–Sat), 12.00–22.30 (Sun)*
*Food: 12.00–16.00 and 18.30–22.30 (Mon–Sun)*
*Credit cards: none taken*
*Draught beers: John Smith's Extra Smooth, Foster's, Kronenbourg, Beamish*
*Nearest tube station: Clapham Common*

## Bellini's

Kensington Court, W8. Tel: 0171 937 5520

This Kensington wine bar is worth mentioning should you come across it. Let's forget the decor and the ambience and cut to the chase – here's what can, and often does, happen on a visit here. Enter on a quiet evening to find staff sitting around doing whatever they do when they have nobody to serve. Stand at the bar and smile, indicating you might want a drink. Beg, plead or manhandle the staff to their rightful place behind the bar only to be foiled when they immediately find something else to do. Order a drink, eventually. Hang around for a while until they find the warmest bottle of wine from the fridge. Go to your table. Clear the debris left by the previous occupant. Prepare to be ignored. When you want to settle the bill, do as you please.... Only La Belle Epoque is slower but at least they try!

*Open: 12.00–23.00 (Mon–Sat), 17.30–10.30 (Sun)*
*Food: as opening hours*
*Credit cards: all major cards*
*Wheelchair access to venue*
*Private room seats 35*
*Nearest tube station: High Street Kensington*

## Belushi's

9 Russell Street, WC2. Tel: 0171 240 3411

This rather rakish Covent Garden venue has the feel of a student-union bar, with pictures plastered over the walls and limited Blues Brothers memorabilia.

*Open: 11.00–midnight (Mon–Sat), 12.00–22.30 (Sun)*
*Food: as opening hours*
*Credit cards: all major cards except AmEx*
*Draught beers: Beamish Red, John Smith's, Coors, Foster's, Kronenbourg, Guinness, Dry Blackthorn*
*Private room: 30 seated, 40 standing*
*Nearest tube station: Covent Garden*

## Bier Klinik

74 Queen Victoria Street, EC4. Tel: 0171 489 9895

A downstairs bar at the end of Bow Lane that could potentially cause a lot of damage. There's a purple-painted stairway to damage the psyche, low-suspended air-conditioning units to damage the head, and plentiful beers to damage the parts other objects can't reach. Bier Klinik has a small island bar on a flagstone floor and attracts a curious combination of City folk and sub-urbanites. There's a rather handy cubbyhole at the back with its own table seating up to 12 people. The 12 people who had sat there before us had been gone for some time but the debris remained for several hours. Still, the bar staff smiled at the mess every time they walked past.

*Open: 11.00–23.00 (Mon–Fri)*
*Food: 12.00–23.00 (Mon–Fri)*
*Credit cards: all major cards*
*Private room seats 120*
*Nearest tube station: Mansion House*

## BierRex

22 Putney High Street, SW15. Tel: 0181 785 0266

Putney High Street is coming alive somewhat with yet another useful drinking venue opening near the river end of the street. BierRex has been operating for over a year now, offering a decent range of European bottled and draught quality beers and lagers. There is a short line of casual booths on the right as you enter. Pass the bar and you come to a larger room with sofas, armchairs, decent-sized dinner tables and a 40-foot-wide, glass-covered, rear-illuminated Chimay mural. French windows open up in the warm weather. The service is casual, student quality: when the waitress brought us our food, there was her thumb, reaching far into the plate and displacing the salad. It was one of the few occasions last year when I was able to control my restaurant rage tendencies. This may put you off the food, but they'll get the hang of it, and apart from that, it is really rather an attractive bar. One worrying point is that Pubmaster, the former owners, sold BierRex in their managed house portfolio recently and it is now a part of Century Inns.

*Open: 11.00–23.00 (Mon–Sat), 12.00–22.30 (Sun)*
*Food: 12.00–21.30 (Mon–Fri), 12.00–22.00 (Sat), 11.00–15.00 for breakfast and 15.00–22.00 normal menu (Sun)*
*Credit cards: all major cards except AmEx*
*Draught beers: De Koninck, Heineken Export, Hoegaarden, Le Trappe, Leffe Blonde, Liefman's Kriek, Stella Artois*
*Wheelchair access to venue and loo*
*Nearest tube station: Putney Bridge*
*Nearest railway station: Putney*

*Also at:*

2–3 Creed Lane, EC4. Tel: 0171 329 3118

# Bill Bentley's

18 Old Broad Street, EC2. Tel: 0171 588 2655

Bill Bentley set up Bill Bentley's some 27 years ago in the form of a wine bar in Beauchamp Place. Since then it has grown to a chain of six wine bars and restaurants, which was acquired by Finch's and subsequently by Young's. Bill Bentley has retired now and so has the bar in Beauchamp Place, but five bars still remain in the City, including this one. It is easy to stray past, and you'd be surprised to discover that it has an outside seating area beyond the modern, long and narrow bar. There's a short terrace overlooking a split-level patio – if you can manage the steps, you can sit and listen to the hum of the air-conditioning extractor fan. The walls surrounding the patio are so high that I doubt the sun ever peeps through. Food is served at lunchtimes – mostly fish and meat dishes – with main courses running in at £6.90 for fish cakes and £12.95 for a fresh crab salad. There are almost 70 wines on the list, starting at £8.80 for the house with a decent selection in the £10–£20 range. It's very business-like during the day, and a decent place to hang out on a summer's eve.

*Open: 11.00–21.30 (Mon–Fri)*
*Food: 11.45–15.00 (Mon–Fri)*
*Credit cards: all major cards*
*Nearest tube stations: Bank, LIverpool Street*

Branches at:

202 Bishopsgate, EC2. Tel: 0171 283 1763
5 The Minories, EC3. Tel: 0171 481 1779
1 St George's Lane, off Botolph Lane, EC3. Tel: 0171 929 2244
Willy's Wine Bar, 107 Fenchurch Street, EC3. Tel: 0171 480 7289

# The Blackbird

209 Earls Court Road, SW5. Tel: 0171 835 1855

This converted bank has made a useful addition to Fuller's ever-growing chain of Ale & Pie houses – thanks Nat West! To look at it now you would never guess that The Blackbird had ever been anything but a pub or that the builders had a terrible job converting it. The walls were several feet thick and highly rein-forced. It took one man eight days to cut a reasonable opening between two vaults to make one decent-sized beer cellar.

Upstairs in the banking hall (I beg your pardon, the saloon bar), the pillars are original and so is the mahogany panelling, but the rest is a 1990s version of the 1890s, the golden age of pub interiors. This, though, is the golden age of pub pies – steak and ale, chicken and bacon. No blackbird pies, I notice. A drinking house suitable for the area.

*Open: 11.00–23.00 (Mon–Sat), 12.00–22.30 (Sun)*
*Food: 12.00–21.00 (Mon–Sun)*
*Credit cards: Visa, Mastercard*
*Draught beers: Chiswick Bitter, ESB, Fuller's Cream Ale, London Pride, Carling Black Label, Grolsch, Stella Artois, Guinness, Scrumpy Jack*
*Nearest tube station: Earls Court*

# The Black Cap

171 Camden High Street, NW1. Tel: 0171 485 1742

Every day of the week stars of the gay pub circuit will be performing some-where. Elaborately wigged, extravagantly gowned, tottering on the highest heels, these starry ladies are in great demand. Some sing, belting out stan-dards like Ethel Merman but louder. Some mime to Shirley Bassey or kd lang, but the top stars are the stand-up comics, formidable dames not to be crossed. They have strong personalities and a large following. Wherever they play they get a welcome that would not disappoint Miss Bassey herself. The Black Cap in Camden Town is the London Palladium of late-night drag. It has a cabaret bar that opens at 9pm and closes at 2am, the music turned up to the threshold of pain. It is dimly lit and crowded. As I write, changes are taking place and the long bar is being replaced by a shorter one to allow more room on the dance floor. Shufflewick's Bar upstairs is now extremely smart and stretches the length of the building, opening onto Fong Terrace, a splendid new roof garden full of tables.

The bar is named after Mrs Shufflewick, a great drag artist who often appeared downstairs. The terrace is named after HIH Regina Fong, a star of the moment who reigns in the cabaret bar every Tuesday night. There is an endless programme of entertainment, and regular turns include Kelly, David Dale and Lipsink, The Dame Edna Experience, Oldies and Trash (seventies and eighties music), and Corruption with Sandra!

*Open: 12.00–02.00 (Mon–Thurs), 12.00–03.00 (Fri–Sat), 12.00–22.30 (Sun)*
*Food: 12.00–21.00 (Mon–Sun)*
*Credit cards: all major cards except AmEx*
*Draught beers: Caffrey's, Worthington, Carling Black Label, Carling Premier, Grolsch, Guinness, Red Rock*
*Wheelchair access to venue*
*Nearest tube station: Camden Town*

## The Blackfriar

174 Queen Victoria Street, EC4. Tel: 0171 236 5650

The Blackfriar is extraordinary in its beauty. This is the wedge-shaped building opposite Blackfriars station, a splendid example of Art Nouveau, with multi-coloured marble and spectacular friezes. You might think the interior was hundreds of years old but it was only built in 1875 on the site of the old Dominican monastery, now reflected in the friezes. It gets busy in the early evening, and on warm nights the crowds swell onto the large pavement area outside. Don't forget to explore the alcoves.

*Open: 11.30–22.00 (Mon–Tues), 11.30–23.00 (Wed–Fri)*
*Food: 12.00–14.30 (Mon–Fri)*
*Credit cards: Mastercard, Visa*
*Draught beers: Adnams, Brakspear, Calder's Cream Ale, Marston's Pedigree, Tetley, Carlsberg Export, Castlemaine, Lowenbrau, Guinness, Dry Blackthorn*
*Wheelchair access to venue*
*Nearest tube station: Blackfriars*

## Black Lion

2 South Black Lion Lane, W6. Tel: 0181 748 7056

Walk along the river from Hammersmith Bridge, first along the Lower Mall and then the Upper, and you pass five very different and interesting pubs. This is the fifth you come to. Like the others it has lovely views of the river and provides a pleasant place to eat and drink outside. In the Black Lion's case, it is a garden shaded by a massive chestnut tree even older, they say, than the pub. Local rumour suggests that the pub has a ghost, but the new manager Andrew Hoggart hasn't seen any unusual spirits in the bar – yet!

*Open: 11.00–23.00 (Mon–Sat), 12.00–22.30 (Sun)*
*Credit cards: Mastercard, Visa*
*Draught beers: Theakston Best, Courage Best, Foster's, Holsten Export, Kronenbourg, Guinness, Beamish, Strongbow*
*Wheelchair access to venue*
*Private room seats 44*
*Nearest tube stations: Ravenscourt Park, Stamford Brook*

# Blakes

Blakes Hotel, 33 Roland Gardens, SW7. Tel: 0171 370 6701

A very bijou bar next to the restaurant-of-the-hotel demands confidence in its clientele. That confidence may well come with the prices charged – this was one of the most expensive bars I visited when preparing this Guide. Black decor, a sofa to collapse in, and only a few stools at the bar also make it one of the smallest. But it has style. Where else would you use a Louis Vuitton trunk to rest your drinks, and take nibbles from black Japanese lacquered bowls? The nibbles were somewhat disappointing, by the way – rather than the Oriental delicacies promised, we were given greasy, barbecue-flavoured kettle chips. The bar oozes richness and sophistication and is definitely a place for a late-night rendezvous with someone who will pick up the bill. Service is formal and stilted. Did I say it was small? Ten people would pack the place.

*Open: 12.00–23.00 (Mon–Sat), 12.00–22.30 (Sun)*
*Food: bar as opening hours; restaurant 19.30–midnight (Mon–Sun)*
*Credit cards: all major cards*
*Nearest tube stations: South Kensington, Gloucester Road*

# The Blenheim

27 Cale Street, SW3. Tel: 0171 349 0056

The Blenheim is a handsome four-storied Georgian pub tucked away in an almost quiet back street in the heart of Chelsea. It has a peculiar history. In the gales of 1987 the chimney blew down and crashed through the roof into the back room, almost recreating the mortuary it once was. Luckily, no one was injured. Following a period of decline, it was completely refurbished with lanterns from a church in Halifax, oak floorboards from old French railway carriages, and radiators from the old County Hall. This revitalisation was short-lived and the pub closed again in the mid-nineties. Badger Inns came to the rescue and it is now leading a promising life once again. Decent pub food is offered most of the day, including beef and Guinness stew, fish pie, chilli con carne, 6oz rump steak (£3.95–£6.50), and snacks of jacket potatoes, burgers and sandwiches (£1.80–£3.95). In addition to the Badger ales, The Blenheim has more than 20 wines and a few champagnes. It's a delightful pub that can every so often be just a little bit rakish.

*Open: 11.00–23.00 (Mon–Sat), 12.00–22.30 (Sun)*
*Food: 12.00–14.30 and 18.00–22.00 (Mon–Sun)*
*Credit cards: all major cards*
*Draught beers: Badger, Dorset IPA, Hard Tackle, Tanglefoot, Wadworth 6X, Dempsey's, Hofbrau, Pilsner, Premium Export, Guinness, Dry Blackthorn*
*Wheelchair access to venue*
*Private room seats 35*
*Nearest tube stations: Sloane Square, South Kensington*

# The Blind Beggar

337 Whitechapel Road, E1. Tel: 0171 247 6195

On 8 March 1966 George Cornell of the Richardson gang was drinking in The Blind Beggar in Whitechapel Road when Ronald Kray walked into the bar and shot him dead. It is a scene that has passed into legend: the crowded bar, the Walker Brothers hit on the juke box, the shots in the air from Kray's minder, customers diving for the floor, the two gangsters facing each other for a long moment. 'Well, look who's here,' Cornell said, whereupon Kray raised his Mauser 9mm and shot him through the forehead. The Blind Beggar already had a more respectable place in the history of the East End. In 1865 the young evangelist William Booth had spoken at an open-air meeting on the pavement outside. This was the genesis of the Salvation Army. Parties of Salvationists regularly arrive on William Booth tours, but, alas, it is the other event that holds centre stage.

The Blind Beggar has been refurbished time and again. A big conservatory has been added and a beer garden tacked on at the side; people drinking in the comfortable modern bar with its button-backed sofas and red-shaded wall lights talk of other things. All the same, more than 30 years later, The Blind Beggar is still the pub where Ronnie Kray, hearing that George Cornell had called him a fat poof, sought him out and shot him down. It has been for sale for many years now. The latest asking price is £150,000 for a 13-year lease. Surely someone wants this important piece of English history?

*Open: 11.00–23.00 (Mon–Fri)*
*Food: 11.30–14.30 (Mon–Fri), 12.00–14.30 (Sun)*
*Credit cards: none taken*
*Draught beers: John Smith's Extra Smooth, Ruddles County, Ruddles Best, Webster's Yorkshire Bitter, Carlsberg, Foster's, Holsten, Kronenbourg, Guinness, Strongbow*
*Wheelchair access to venue*
*Private room: conservatory stands 30*
*Nearest tube station: Whitechapel*

## The Blue Anchor

13 Lower Mall, W6. Tel: 0181 748 5774

The Blue Anchor is the first of the pubs on Hammersmith's riverside, a handsome old building at least 300 years old. There have, of course, been changes along the way. The Victorians installed a host of partitions, our generation took them down, and so it goes. The old panelling survives, though, as does the beautiful pewter bar counter. The Blue Anchor is popular with the rowing club next door and goes in for old rowing photographs. There is a rather sombre collection of First World War artefacts – helmets, gasmasks and so on – and banknotes of many lands are pasted up over the bar counter. On a summer's day, it seems that almost half the world comes to The Blue Anchor. Its customers fill the picnic tables lining the river wall, and there are cool marble-topped tables for them inside.

*Open: 11.00–23.00 (Mon–Sat), 12.00–22.30 (Sun)*
*Food: 12.00–14.30 and 18.00–21.00 (Mon–Sun)*
*Credit cards: Eurocard, Delta, Mastercard, Visa*
*Draught beers: Courage Best Bitter, Courage Directors, Young's Special, Foster's, Holsten Export, Kronenbourg, Guinness, Scrumpy Jack*
*Wheelchair access to venue*
*Private room seats 38*
*Nearest tube station: Hammersmith*

## Bluebird

350 King's Road, SW3. Tel: 0171 559 1000

I was desperate to fall in love with the Bluebird gastrodome when it opened in a blaze of publicity in the summer of 1997. Although my job was to look at the bars, I couldn't resist doing a quick tour of all the other offerings on the way in. Some of the interior didn't quite look finished so I asked, and was politely informed that I had missed the point about Sir Terence's concept of exposed ceilings and pipework. I decided to leave this alone, figuring that Conran's success in the design field speaks for itself and should not be questioned by the likes of me, so off I went to the café bar on the ground floor. This is small, but I managed to squeeze in beside the PR girlies and tourists, and ordered the Bluebird wine – a rather poor quality vin de pays d'Oc, which needs serious consideration at most prices and not least at £11.75 plus service. I thought about ordering a glass of cider but quickly came to the conclusion that £3.50 for a half-pint of anything was outside any reasonable budget. Upstairs in the bar of the restaurant, things took a turn for the worse. I ordered a quality gin – Tanqueray (£3.25 for 50ml) – only to see it drowned by a spectacular amount of hosed-in tonic, for which I was charged an additional £1.50. My love affair with Bluebird was short-lived. I went back to the foodhall on the way home to pick up some fresh coriander, and do you know what? They didn't know what it was.

*Open: restaurant bar 12.00–23.00 (Mon–Fri), 11.00–23.00 (Sat), 12.00–22.00 (Sun); café 12.00–22.50 (Mon–Sat), 12.00–21.50 (Sun)*
*Food: restaurant 11.00–15.30 and 18.00–22.00 (Mon–Fri), 11.00–15.30 and 18.00–23.00 (Sat), 11.00–15.30 and 18.00–22.00 (Sun); café 09.00–22.00 (Mon–Sat), 11.00–20.30 (Sun)*
*Credit cards: all major cards*
*Draught beers: Beck's, Kronenbourg*
*Wheelchair access to venue and loo*
*Private room: 24 seated, 40 standing*
*Nearest tube station: Sloane Square*

## Blues Bar

20 Kingly Street, W1. Tel: 0171 287 0514

Ain't Nothin' But ... – The Blues Bar is its Sunday name – is a hang out for students of all ages. For a major venue which is a legend in Kingly Street, it's surprisingly small and dark, with a handkerchief-sized stage, three rows of tiny tables squashed together and an assortment of stray guitars, album covers and photographs adorning the walls. This ain't gonna win any awards for style, decor or service, but it is a fun, intimate bar with live music every night of the week.

*Open: 17.30–01.00 (Mon–Thur), 17.30–03.00 (Fri), 18.30–03.00 (Sat), 20.00–midnight (Sun)*
*Credit cards: None taken*
*Draught beers: Fosters, Kronenbourg*
*Nearest tube station: Oxford Circus*

## Bootsy Brogan's

1 Fulham Broadway, SW6. Tel: 0171 385 2003

There's nothing much Irish about this bar, which opened in the early part of 1997, replacing the very naughty Swan, which previously occupied this spot. The interior, designed by the people who did its sister pub, Waxy O'Connor's (qv), is a massive wooden structure of steps and platforms circumnavigating the central island bar. Wander around, up and down, and perplexingly you'll end up where you started but on a higher level.

Bootsy Brogan's is extremely popular at weekends so a couple of very polite doormen are employed to keep control of the numbers of young Fulham drinkers in what is a useful addition to an increasingly acceptable crawl of drinking venues around the Fulham Broadway. I spotted the management from the White Horse in Parson's Green supping there one evening and they confessed to weighing up the opposition. No greater compliment could have been paid.

*Open: 11.00–23.00 (Mon–Sat), 12.00–22.30 (Sun)*
*Food: bar 11.00–20.00 (Mon–Sat), 12.00–20.00 (Sun); carvery 12.30–14.30 (Mon–Sun)*
*Credit cards: all major cards except AmEx*
*Draught beers: Beamish Red, Kilkenny, Tetley, Foster's, Holsten, Guinness, Dry Blackthorn*
*Wheelchair access to venue*
*Nearest tube station: Fulham Broadway*

# La Bouffe

11–13 Battersea Rise, SW11. Tel: 0171 228 3384

In a row of up-graded shops and cafés on Battersea Rise, La Bouffe stands out as one of the most inviting. It has a small terrace by which you enter the bar, an enormous mural by the ex-manager Johnny Reid, and a soothing cream and green painted interior. It needs to be soothing as the atmosphere can get quite frenetic in the evenings. It's a friendly place, though, and the staff cope well with the seemingly insatiable palate of the Battersea toper. They have bottled Budwar, London Pride and Fischer, draught Hoegaarden and St. Omer, and get through lashings of Calvados. As there is a restaurant next door, the kitchen is able to proffer some good quality dishes: steak frites (£9.95), large salads (£5.95) and the ever-popular French onion soup (£3.95).

*Open: 11.00–23.00 (Mon–Sat), 11.00–22.30 (Sun)*
*Food: bar 11.00–22.30 (Mon–Sat), 11.00–22.00 (Sun); restaurant 12.00–15.00 and 19.00–23.00 (Mon–Sat), 11.00–22.30 (Sun)*
*Credit cards: all major cards*
*Draught beers: Hoegaarden, St Omer, Murphy's*
*Wheelchair access to venue and loo*
*Nearest tube station: Clapham Common*
*Nearest railway station: Clapham Junction*

# The Box

32–34 Monmouth Street, WC2. Tel: 0171 240 5828

This is an unobtrusive, mostly gay bar behind a fairly nondescript modern shop front close to Seven Dials. The ground floor is café-style during the day, but they whip off the menus in the evening and the place gets down to the more serious business of consuming alcohol. Frozen margaritas, jugs of beer, wines and cocktails oil the proceedings, and the downstairs lounge bar holds many charity and themed events. The last Friday of every month is Fab Friday – party, party, party! Sundays are Box Babes – ladies night.

*Open: 11.00–23.00 (Mon–Sat), 12.00–22.30 (Sun)*
*Food: bar 11.00–17.30 (Mon–Sat), 12.00–17.30 (Sun)*
*Credit cards: all major cards*
*Draught beers: Box Lager, Red Stripe*
*Wheelchair access to venue and loo*
*Private room: 60–80 standing*
*Nearest tube station: Leicester Square*

# Brasserie Rocque

Unit G, Broadgate Central Square, EC2. Tel: 0171 638 7919

A bar brasserie with concertina doors opening onto the lower level of Broadgate Circle, where the crowds spill out in the fine weather. At lunch the place is split into a bookable restaurant and an unbookable brasserie. Three courses in the restaurant will set you back £27.50; the brasserie offers a marginally cheaper similar menu but you can, of course, have just one course. In the evening the place is turned over to a drinking venue. The evening menu includes a choice of four dips (deep-fried mushrooms, vegetarian samosas and the like) for £5.75, and a char-grilled steak sandwich with fries for £7.95. Brasserie Rocque, they say, is named after John Rocque, a Huguenot whose finely detailed maps of London brought him great acclaim.

*Open: 11.30–22.00 (Mon–Fri)*
*Food: restaurant and brasserie 10.00–15.00 (Mon–Fri); snacks available after 15.00 (Mon–Fri)*
*Credit cards: all major cards*
*Wheelchair access to venue and loo*
*Nearest tube station: Liverpool Street*

# Bread & Roses

**EROS AWARD WINNER**

68 Clapham Manor Street, SW4. Tel: 0171 498 1779

New Labour? New philosophy on fund-raising. The party formerly known as the Opposition is capitalising on our marginal propensity to consume and dispose of our income in pubs and bars. Bread & Roses – a Workers' Beer Company free house owned by the Battersea & Wandsworth Trades Union Council – is proving to be a useful fund-raising tool. The name apparently comes from a movement song written during a strike of women textile workers in the USA in 1912: 'Our lives shall not be sweated from birth until life closes/Hearts starve as well as bodies/Give us bread but give us roses!' The Bread & Roses publicity material goes on: 'They won the right to a 54-hour working week; their struggle was not just for money but for a better quality of life, and that struggle continues.' The philosophy might be the same but the bar has been stylised and adapted for the modern campaigner: highly polished wooden floors, purple and green painted walls (colours of the Suffragettes) and a large conservatory at the back leading out to a small garden with barbecue facilities. The vittles include a variety of flavoured bangers supplied by Simply Sausages – simply delicious. Wine flows endlessly and the house beer (Worker Ale) has apparently been recently sampled by the Camra people – disguised as rotund pullover-wearers hiding behind bushy beards. We await their verdict. As you might expect, there are free coffee mornings on Tuesdays for mothers with toddlers and the same on Thursdays for pensioners. Whether or not this is to be a new range of theme bars with branches in Parliament Square and the head office in Downing Street remains to be seen. Meanwhile, the rest of us can eat with a conscience and drink to the cause. *Na zdorovye!*

*Open: 11.00–23.00 (Mon–Sat), 12.00–22.30 (Sun)*
*Food: 12.00–15.00 and 17.30–21.30 (Mon–Fri), 12.00–22.00 (Sat)*
*Credit cards: all major cards*
*Draught beers: Adnams, Calder's Cream Ale, Wadworth 6X, Worker Ale, Carlsberg,*
*Carlsberg Export, Lowenbrau, Guinness, Dry Blackthorn*
*Wheelchair access to venue and loo*
*Two private rooms: 20 and 50 seated, 40 and 100 standing*
*Nearest tube station: Clapham Common*

# Brendan O'Grady's

67–69 Kennington Road, SE1. Tel: 0171 928 5974

Kennington has an Irish pub now – this one, an old Victorian pub that used to be Charlie Chaplin's local. It was the last place he saw his father alive. It was called The Three Stags in those days – indeed, it was The Three Stags for about a hundred years, but in June 1995 Greene King, whose pub it is, decided it should have a new lease of life, and that is what it got. There's Irish food now and Irish music and a sea of Irish stout. The English like it a lot. When it was The Three Stags, charabancs would regularly bring parties of American tourists, who would be charmed by lovable Cockneys engaged by the manager to do lovable Cockney things. Everyone always ended up doing the Lambeth walk. Tourists still come. Well, the pub is opposite the Imperial War Museum and Captain Bligh's house is two doors away. Now, however, there's a lovable Irish carry-on at Brendan O'Grady's, and a new landlord, Michael O'Brien.

*Open: 11.00–23.00 (Mon–Wed), 11.00–01.00 (Thurs–Sat), 12.00–22.30 (Sun)*
*Food: 12.00–21.00 (Mon–Sun)*
*Credit cards: all major cards*
*Draught beers: Abbot Ale, Greene King IPA, Harp Irish, Kilkenny, Wexford Irish Ale,*
*Carling Premier, Kronenbourg, Stella Artois, Guinness, Scrumpy Jack*
*Wheelchair access to venue*
*Private room seats 30–40*
*Nearest tube station: Lambeth North*

# Brief Encounter

42 St Martin's Lane, WC2. Tel: 0171 240 2221

Brief encounters are what it's all about at Brief Encounter. This is a long-established gay venue which has just had £650,000 spent on it, making it ready for even more encounters. I'm not sure the people who frequent the bar are that bothered about the decor, but nevertheless it looks a whole sight prettier these days. The diminutive basement bar is where all the action is: loud music, DJs, close encounters of any particular kind. Upstairs, the unlit, even smaller bar is rather quieter, but packed with City-suited after-work drinkers and an eclectic mix of others looking to create a brief moment of time.

*Open: 11.00–23.00 (Mon–Sat), 12.00–22.30 (Sun)*
*Credit cards: all major cards*
*Nearest tube stations: Leicester Square, Charing Cross*

# Brompton's and the Warwick Bar

294 Old Brompton Road, SW5. Tel: 0171 370 1344

Brompton's is a long-established, extremely busy, late-night gay venue in Earls Court. The newly refurbished upstairs bar, with its own separate entrance, is now called the Warwick Bar, and is open all day until 2am. It serves food (S & N's Sizzler menu) until 9pm but then they get on with the business of social interaction. Men of all ages fill this place nightly.

*Open: Brompton's 22.00–02.00 (Mon–Sat), 22.00–midnight (Sun)*
*Warwick Bar 12.00–02.00 (Mon–Sat), closed Sun*
*Food: 12.00–21.00 (Mon–Sat)*
*Credit cards: none taken*
*Draught beers: Director's, John Smith's, Budweiser, Foster's, Kronenbourg, Beamish, Strongbow*
*Private room seats 25 seated, 50 standing*
*Nearest tube station: Earls Court*

# Browns

1 Hackney Road, E2. Tel: 0171 739 4653

Men in City suits line their briefcases up next to each other. They stand quietly and alone at the bar, holding their drinks close to their chests. On the other side of the room a group of young men from an office party are being loud and obnoxious, but the squat, thick-set bouncer (who appears to be missing his neck) is keeping a close eye on them. A bikini-clad girl in stilettos wanders towards me, thrusting a glass full of money in my face (mostly coins but it includes a few strategically placed fivers). 'I'm dancing next,' she declares, shaking the glass. I try all my excuses (no change, waiting for a friend ... ) but she won't budge. I put in 50p – she still doesn't budge. A pound later and she moves along to another customer. You tip before you see here, and with the cast of dancers changing with each record it cost me a small fortune. On to the stage they go, discarding all their clothes and stretching parts of the body you wouldn't normally see stretched in public. The office party cheer them on. The men on their own by the bar pretend not to be looking. There are curtained-off rooms so that you can watch a dancer in the privacy of your own cubicle. It's £10 to watch on your own, £15 to share with a friend or £20 for three in the audience. There are house rules to be followed. One, purchase your tokens at the bar. Two, inform the manager of your name, the number in your group, and the name of the dancer of your choice. Three, you will be given a token and a number, and the DJ will call you when your dancer is ready. Go to the table area (in the cubicle) and give your token to the dancer. Four, any person who touches the dancer will be ejected from the premises.

*Open: 12.00–midnight (Mon–Sat), 12.00–19.00 (Sun)*
*Credit cards: none*
*Draught beers: John Smith's Smooth, Webster's, Budweiser, Foster's, Holsten, Guinness, Dry Blackthorn, Scrumpy Jack*
*Wheelchair access to venue*
*Private rooms seats 1,2 or 3*
*Nearest tube stations: Old Street, Shoreditch*

## Browns

82–84 St Martin's Lane, WC2. Tel: 0171 497 5050

The old Westminster County Court has undergone a spectacular conversion to create one massive room, beautifully furnished, simply decorated and as sumptuous as a Victorian parlour. The proliferation of palms, hanging baskets and greenery blends rather well with the cream painted walls and highly polished woodwork. The high bar-back shows off an impressive display of spirits, cocktail ingredients, wines and bottled beers. There are plenty of staff, all smartly uniformed in white shirts with their ties tucked into them. On the visits I made, they were all remarkably efficient, expert cocktail-makers, very friendly and highly industrious. The bar appeals to an upmarket clientele, mostly in their twenties and thirties, but has resisted the temptation to rob us blind. Free-poured cocktails are £4.35–£4.55, the choice of more than 30 wines sit in the £9.95–£27.95 range, bottled beers are £2.65 and there is a small but quality choice of sparkling wines and champagnes (£18.50–£69.50 for a Perrier Jouet Belle Epoque). The food is firmly rooted in what is fast becoming the modern British tradition, and is well presented and reasonably priced. There are deals to be had on the food at lunch (under £5), and a pre-theatre menu offers two courses for £9.95 (until 6.30pm). This is the third Browns in London and certainly the most spectacular. Browns was started in 1973 by Jeremy Mogford when he opened his first bar in Brighton. He followed the student trail for a while before pitching to a more up-market clientele in London. It seems to have worked.

*Open: 12.00–midnight (Mon–Thurs), 12.00–00.30 (Fri–Sat), 12.00–23.30 (Sun)*
*Food: bar 12.00–midnight (Mon–Thurs), 12.00–00.30 (Fri–Sat), 12.00–23.30 (Sun); restaurant 12.00–midnight (Mon–Thurs), 12.00–00.30 (Fri–Sat), 12.00–23.30 (Sun)*
*Credit cards: all major cards*
*Wheelchair access to venue and loo*
*Private room: 200 seated, 300 standing*
*Nearest tube station: Leicester Square*

*Branches at:*

114 Draycott Avenue, SW3. Tel: 0171 584 5359
47 Maddox Street, W1. Tel: 0171 491 4565

## The Bull

Coppice Row, Theydon Bois, CM16. Tel: 01992 812145

This traditional village inn is recorded as a building in parish records dating back to 1656. It is thought that it became a pub in 1718, when the name Bull's Head appears on records, and it has been known as The Bull since 1801. It's very traditional – they don't bother with pool tables and juke boxes, and offer decent home-cooked fare in the bar and restaurant.

*Open: 11.00–23.00 (Mon–Sat), 12.00–22.30 (Sun)*
*Credit cards: all major cards*
*Draught beers: Abbot Ale, Burton, Tetley's, Becks, Carlsberg, Castlemaine, Guinness, Dry Blackthorn*
*Private room seats 40*
*Nearest tube station: Theydon Bois*

# Bull and Gate

389 Kentish Town Road, NW5. Tel: 0171 485 5358

A series of murals in the main bar shows the Bull and Gate standing proudly alone in an idyllic Kentish Town. Nowadays it is dwarfed by The Forum next door. Still, it has kept its cheerfully ornate exterior, which is echoed inside with two bars, one for customers who go for the beer, the other for the choosier ones who go for the music. The Bull and Gate specialises in breaking new bands, with at least three playing every night of the week in a music room beyond the little bar. The music room is basic but it does have tables and chairs along each side. Most of the indie acts that play here are entirely unknown, which means you can usually find somewhere to sit. Nirvana, Carter and Suede all played here in their early days, so you never know. Today's band at the Bull and Gate could be playing next door at The Forum tomorrow.

*Open: bar 11.00–23.00 (Mon–Sat), 12.00–22.30 (Sun); music bar 11.00–midnight (Mon–Sun)*
*Credit cards: none taken*
*Draught beers: Bass, Hand Pump, Speckled Hen, Toby, Carling Black Label, Carling Premier, Foster's, Kronenbourg, Staropramen, Tennent's Extra, Guinness, Scrumpy Jack, Strongbow*
*Wheelchair access to venue*
*Nearest tube station: Kentish Town*

# Bull's Head

Strand on the Green, W6. Tel: 0181 994 1204

Every month the Thames, which runs beneath this pub's windows, washes over the towpath, causing great concern to those inside. Four or five times a year it covers the benches against the pub walls. It has not got into the pub itself since New Year's Eve 1977, when it swamped the saloon bar. High tide, low tide, this is a lovely site for a pub. District Line trains rattle across the railway bridge almost overhead but it is surprising how quickly you get used to that. The swans on the foreshore take no notice, nor does the heron on the post in the river or the cormorants on Oliver Island, nor, indeed, do the customers of the Bull's Head. The pub has been there for almost 400 years now and has been expanding lately. It took over two of the pretty cottages on its right for the staff and the one on its left for extra room, but from the outside you could never tell. There's an old plan of the interior dated 1803 on the wall, and the pub looks much the same today. The main bar with its old beams and nicotined ceiling seems hardly to have changed, and neither do the outhouses and the entrance hall they call the games room because that's where the darts board is. There is a big flagged room next to it where people eat, and picnic tables just off the towpath for sunny days.

There is meant to be a secret tunnel from the pub to Oliver's Island, which is said to have saved Oliver Cromwell's bacon during the Civil War. No one lives on the little island now.

*Open: 11.00–23.00 (Mon–Sat), 12.00–22.30 (Sun)*
*Food: 12.00–22.00 (Mon–Sun)*
*Credit cards: all major cards*
*Draught beers: Wadworth 6X, Theakston Old Peculier, Greene King IPA, Courage Directors, Holsten, Foster's, Kronenbourg, Guinness, Strongbow*
*Nearest railway station: Kew Bridge*

# Bunch of Grapes

207 Brompton Road, SW3. Tel: 0171 589 4944

In its high Victorian days the Bunch of Grapes had six bars with a separate entrance to each. It still has four bars and three entrances and has kept a lot of

the old partitions and a set of snob screens in good working order. It is a protected building and looks it – granite piers, painted stucco, Corinthian columns,
a cast-iron balcony, spectacular painted mirrors, etched glass, and a splendid
mahogany set piece in the bar – a hand-carved vine with the ripest grapes. The
management regrets that customers in dirty clothing will not be served. The
people of Knightsbridge are duly warned.

*Open: 11.00–23.00 (Mon–Sat), 12.00–22.30 (Sun)*
*Food: as opening hours, not Sat*
*Credit cards: all major cards*
*Draught beers: Courage Best, Courage Directors, John Smith's Extra Smooth,*
*Theakston Best, Budweiser, Foster's, Holsten, Guinness, Strongbow*
*Wheelchair access to venue*
*Nearest tube stations: Knightsbridge, South Kensington*

## Cactus Blue

86 Fulham Road, SW3. Tel: 0171 823 7858

Fuller's, the people who seem to be making a theme out of opening bars in
banks, decided to sell this long-established theatre bar, known previously as
The Rose. Enter Brian Stein with one and a half million pounds, and the result
was the Cactus Blue. There has been a dramatic change, with much of the
ceiling in the bar gone, creating a galleried upper level with a massive chandelier. At the back there's a conservatory restaurant serving light dishes from
quesadillas and tamales to main courses of crawfish chalupas (£9.95), lobster
succotash (£12.95) and fried chicken salad (£7.95). There are dozens of different tequilas from all over the world, no draught beers but plenty of bottled
beers and cocktails. If you're sitting upstairs, a mechanical tray raises the
drinks from the main bar. Those who sit at the bar bounce up and down on the
spring-loaded bar stools – irritating to watch, irresistible to do.

*Open: 12.00–23.45 (Mon–Fri), 12.00–23.45 (Sat), 12.00–22.45 (Sun)*
*Food: bar 12.00–23.00 (Mon–Sat), 12.00–22.30 (Sun); restaurant 12.00–23.45*
*(Mon–Sat), 12.00–22.45 (Sun)*
*Credit cards: all major cards*
*Wheelchair access to venue*
*Nearest tube station: South Kensington*

## Café Bohème

13 Old Compton Street, W1. Tel: 0171 734 0623

Extraordinarily popular venue which could be a hundred times its current bijou
size and still be packed. People stand on the pavement so they can be a part
of the bohemian experience. There's live jazz on Wednesday afternoons and
acoustic funk on Sunday evenings. A great bar but just a tad too small for comfort, so you might want to consider booking a table in the restaurant.

*Open: 08.00–03.00 (Mon–Wed), 24 hours (Thurs–Sat)*
*Food: as opening hours*
*Credit cards: all major cards*
*Draught beers: White Beer, Stella Artois*
*Wheelchair access to venue*
*Nearest tube station: Leicester Square*

## Café Latino

25 Frith Street, W1. Tel: 0171 287 5676

Do you remember Diva – the bar with transvestite waiting staff? Café Latino has
taken its place. It is painted orange and blue – the only colours available to
designers last year – so the Latin flavour is not strong, although it manages to
capture a certain taste with its food and drinks. Tapas range between £2.50

and £3.95 and you can buy a platter of six different types for £9.50. There is a fuller menu of antojotos (starters, £3.25–£6.50), platillos fuertes (substantial dishes, £5.25–£7.95). Cocktails – Cuba libra and frozen margaritas – are £4.95. A large spiral staircase occupies much of the ground floor and takes you up to the larger, brighter room with glitter sprinkled over the seats and floor. The basement bar is the best: cosy, intimate and perfect for a drinks party of 15–20 people. It attracts a very mixed clientele – the management have clearly decided not to jump, overtly, on any particular bandwagon.

*Open: 12.00–midnight (Mon–Wed), 12.00–01.00 (Thurs–Sat), 15.00–22.30 (Sun)*
*Food: as opening hours*
*Credit cards: all major cards*
*Two private rooms seat 25 and 35*
*Nearest tube stations: Leicester Square, Tottenham Court Road*

## Café Sol Dos

56 Clapham High Street, SW4. Tel: 0171 498 9319

Stroll along Clapham Park Road and it's hard to miss the bright red and yellow painted front of this big, Mexican theme bar – sister of the original Café Sol in Streatham. The bar of the restaurant gets very busy at weekends, mainly due to its late opening. The bar staff seem to cope admirably with the crowds, serving bottled beers (£2.20), wines by the glass (£2) and shooters (£2.95). The cocktail list is long and they seem to shift rather a lot of them, but at £3.50 per cocktail that's hardly surprising. There is a catch for late-night topers – the prices rise later in the evening (10–15%).

*Open: 12.30–00.30 (Sun–Thurs), 12.30–02.00 (Fri–Sat)*
*Food: 12.30–midnight (Sun–Thurs), 12.30–01.00 (Fri–Sat)*
*Credit cards: all major cards*
*Wheelchair access to venue*
*Nearest tube station: Clapham Common*

## Cahoots

2 Elystan Street, SW3. Tel: 0171–584 0140

I've been in cahoots with Cahoots to keep quiet about the place, as to chance across this bar is a pleasure indeed. Scottish & Newcastle established Cahoots to try out a new theme for some of its bars but sadly didn't follow this up. It has a prime location overlooking the small area of land known locally as Chelsea Green and has a rather smart interior of exposed walls with green foliage. On a summer's day, the windows fold back to allow a gentle breeze to cool the bar and there are few better venues for a relaxing drink. The interesting menu of burgers, sandwiches, chilli and pasta dishes lets itself down a little in the presentation – they might try disguising the fact that they use a microwave to heat the food.

*Open:  11.00–23.00 (Mon–Sat), 12.00–22.30 (Sun)*
*Food:  11.00–22.00 (Mon–Sat), 12.00–21.00 (Sun)*
*Credit cards: all major cards*
*Draught beers: John Smith's Extra Smooth, Coors, Becks, Beamish*
*Wheelchair access to venue*
*Nearest tube station: Sloane Square*

## Cairo Jacks

10 Beak Street, W1. Tel: 0171 439 4258

This is possibly one of the worst attempts at an ersatz Egyptian bar, if not any genre, you will find in London. The design of stone walls and a thatched bar is so tacky it makes you want to giggle. I decided I couldn't stay long, so ordered a quick glass of the house wine, which seemed remarkable value at £1.25 (this was *their* happy hour, not mine). The last time I remember tasting anything so revolting was when I forgot to remove the siphon from my mouth when draining the car radiator and ended up with a mouthful of anti-freeze. I genuinely couldn't finish the glass, and as people who know me will testify, that is a very rare event indeed.

*Open: 12.00–03.00 (Mon–Thurs), 12.00–03.30 (Fri), 17.00–04.00 (Sat)*
*Food: 12.00–16.00 (Mon–Fri)*
*Credit cards: Mastercard, Visa*
*Draught beers: Tennent's, Worthington, Carling, Grolsch, Guinness, Caffrey's, K6*
*Wheelchair access to venue*
*Private room seats 220 (Mon–Thurs)*
*Nearest tube stations: Oxford Circus, Piccadilly Circus*

## The Camden Head

Camden Walk, N1. Tel: 0171 359 0851

Visitors to Camden Passage antique market need not look far for what they might consider to be a real find. The Camden Head will celebrate its centenary next year and is a wonderful example of high Victorian architecture: perfectly proportioned, richly appointed with lovely engraved glass and brilliant-cut mirrors. You can choose between a red plush banquette and one of the stools around the imposing island bar counter, or, on fine days, sit under the large parasols on the terrace. It may be quite a while before you feel inclined to return to the fray. The Comedy Brewhouse is still going strong on Friday and Saturday nights. You pay £4.50 to get in. It is very popular, and usually sells out.

*Open: 11.00–23.00 (Mon–Sat), 12.00–22.30 (Sun)*
*Food: as opening hours*
*Credit cards: all major cards except AmEx*
*Draught beers: Directors, John Smith's Extra Smooth, Theakston Best, Younger IPA, plus a guest ale, Becks, Foster's, Kronenbourg, Beamish, Strongbow*
*Wheelchair access to venue*
*Private room: 30 seated, 55 standing*
*Nearest tube station: Angel*

## The Cannon

95 Cannon Street, EC4. Tel: 0171 626 8480

The futures traders – curiously adorned in their brightly coloured floppy jackets – spend a large part of their day battling on the floor of the London International Futures Exchange in Cannon Bridge, and a smaller part of their day grabbing a sandwich and a pint over lunch in The Cannon. It's a loud, laddish, lager-drinking bar, serving hot meat sandwiches at lunch (£3), and fries, chicken dips and mozzarella melts (£2.50–£4.50) in the evening. The boys come back again in the evening, this time wearing their own clothes.

*Open: 11.00–23.00 (Mon–Fri)*
*Food: as opening hours*
*Credit cards: all major cards*
*Draught beers: Bass, Caffrey's, Greene King IPA, London Pride, Carling Black Label, Carling Premium, Grolsch, Guinness, Dry Blackthorn*
*Wheelchair access to venue*
*Nearest tube station: Cannon Street*

## Cantaloupe Bar and Grill

35 Charlotte Road, EC2. Tel: 0171 613 4411

'It's great,' everyone tells me. 'For the area,' they add quickly. This dimly lit warehouse conversion certainly draws in the crowds from local design agencies and media shops, who all gather round the large wooden tables. The bar is quite mellow in the afternoons but speeds up a bit in the evenings. However, the staff fail to keep up with the pace. A trip to the loo is a major commitment.

*Open: 11.00–midnight (Mon–Fri), 18.00–midnight (Sat)*
*Food: as opening hours*
*Credit cards: all major cards*
*Draught beers: Budwar, Heineken, Stella Artois*
*Wheelchair access to venue*
*Nearest tube stations: Old Street, Liverpool Street*

## Captain Kidd

108 Wapping High Street, E1. Tel: 0171 480 5759

The Captain Kidd is a large and exuberant theme pub built on the ground- and first-floor site of a magnificent warehouse conversion on the river at Wapping. The theme is, of course, Captain Kidd, the 17th-century privateer, who was hanged at nearby Execution Dock. His full story is graphically told on the walls of the bar. The pub, accessed by a cobbled path, has a big, cheerful ground-floor bar with a flagstone floor and genuinely brand-new 17th-century features. Above it is the Café Brasserie Bar, where children can have drinks and play video games. Food is served all day here but there is also a more formal restaurant. Each floor has fine river views, though the big river terrace at the side has the best, with Canary Wharf downstream. The Captain Kidd seems to have been here for ever – massive timbers support the ancient structure, and open-tread wooden stairs lead uncreaking from floor to floor, all bleached and split, you might suppose, by centuries of spray and sun. You would suppose wrong. The Captain Kidd is what you might call ship-shape and Sam-Smith fashion, and is a fine addition to tourist London. Wapping Police Station, home to the world's oldest uniformed police force, is nearby and you can visit its museum with prior arrangement.

*Open: 11.00–23.00 (Mon–Sat), 12.00–22.30 (Sun)*
*Food: restaurant 12.00–15.00 and 18.30–23.00 (Mon–Sat), 12.00–18.00 (Sun)*
*Credit cards: all major cards*
*Draught beers: Old Brewery, Sovereign Best, Ayingerbraü, Ayingerbraü Pils, Ayingerbraü Prinz, Samuel Smith's Stout, Samuel Smith's Special Reserve*
*Wheelchair access to venue and loo*
*Private room seats 70*
*Nearest tube station: Wapping*

## Caravaggio

107–112 Leadenhall Street, EC3. Tel: 0171 626 6206

A restaurant by day, a bar in the evening. The blue-lit exterior of this former banking hall draws you towards the place. The entrance hints quite strongly at a hotel foyer, with its display cabinets and very high-tech reception area. The conference-style seating area is on the ground floor with a gallery above. There were two or three people standing idly at the reception when we last called, with one person struggling in vain behind the bar. We gave up after the first drinks and went to a pub.

*Open: 11.30–23.00 (Mon–Fri)*
*Food: 11.30–15.00 and 18.00–22.00 (Mon–Fri)*
*Credit cards: all major cards*
*Draught beers: Bitburger*
*Nearest tube station: Bank*
*Nearest railway stations: Fenchurch Street, Liverpool Street*

# The Cardinal

23 Francis Street, SW1. Tel: 0171 834 7260

There's a conclave of cardinals in The Cardinal. Cardinals Pole, Mazarin, Richelieu, Manning, Bourne, Lavigerie, Newman and Beaton in their copes and birettas, and the St Louis Cardinals in their baseball gear occupy the walls of the bars and the stairs in this quiet, comfortable pub at the back of Westminster Cathedral. Cardinal Hume, Archbishop of Westminster, is often glimpsed walking by, but he does not call in. If he did he might find a future cardinal drinking at the bar. Young priests often look in after mass. The Bach Choir fills the place after its Monday-night rehearsal in Westminster Cathedral Hall, and signs direct you upstairs to the Bishop's Table Restaurant. Alas, it is a humble pool room now. You eat downstairs in the back bar. The Cardinal is a Sam Smith pub, which means a steady stream of good cask beer and draught lager from Yorkshire flowing into Westminster. The pub food is standard pub fare: Tex-Mex-inspired bar snacks (from £2.45) and pasta, fish, chicken and steak dishes (£4.45–£8.75).

*Open: 11.30–23.00 (Mon–Fri), 12.00–15.00 and 19.00–23.00 (Sat), 12.00–15.00 and 19.00–22.30 (Sun)*
*Food: 12.00–14.30 and 17.30–21.00 (Mon–Sat), 12.00–14.30 and 19.00–22.30 (Sun)*
*Credit cards: Mastercard, Visa*
*Draught beers: Old Brewery Bitter, Sovereign Bitter, Samuel Smith's Mild, Ayingerbraü, Ayingerbraü Pils, Ayingerbraü Prinz, Samuel Smith's Extra Stout, Special Reserve*
*Wheelchair access to venue*
*Private room: 40 seated, 60 standing*
*Nearest tube station: Victoria*

# The Cartoonist

276 Shoe Lane, EC4. Tel: 0171 353 2828

When the newspapers left Fleet Street, taking their cartoonists with them, The Cartoonist, a bright modern pub in Shoe Lane, took it hard. At a stroke it lost many of its most free-spending, which is to say booziest, customers. The pub struggled. Scottish & Newcastle called in Front Page Pubs, a small chain of quality pub operators, who spruced the place up and introduced their own range of meals and wines. They called it The Cartoon Page. A year later and Front Page Pubs were pulling out of the deal. They tell me that the big noises at S & N, who are hardly renowned for their food, insisted that they use their own official food suppliers. Front Page couldn't agree and withdrew, taking their name with them. It is The Cartoonist once again. Margaret Thatcher, Tony Benn, Ken Livingstone, Frank Bruno, Terry Venables and Terry Waite (twice, once before, once after) have all been here to receive the Cartoonist Club of Great Britain's annual award. What will become of the place now? Watch this space.

*Open: 11.00–23.00 (Mon–Fri)*
*Food: 12.00–21.00 (Mon–Fri)*
*Credit cards: all major cards*
*Draught beers: Courage Best, Courage Directors, John Smith's, Theakston XB, Foster's, Kronenbourg, Guinness, Strongbow*
*Wheelchair access to venue*
*Private room seats 40*
*Nearest tube station: Chancery Lane*

# The Cat and the Canary

1–24 Fisherman's Walk, E14. Tel: 0171 512 9187

For those who work in or around Canary Wharf, here is a refuge. You get off the DLR, go down the escalator, through the North Colonnade door, and there it is, a dark pub that has been there for ever. Well, since June 1992. That is for ever on Canary Wharf. Most of the woodwork is pretty old, as it happens. It came from redundant Victorian churches and includes some impressive pews and a telephone kiosk that used to be a pulpit. It has a sunny patio, good cask ales (including Fuller's), bar billiards and darts. The Oak Room is a secluded place to avoid the hoi polloi, and there's another cosy corner known as the cuddy.

*Open: 11.00–23.00 (Mon–Fri)*
*Food: 12.00–15.00 (Mon–Fri)*
*Credit cards: all major cards*
*Draught beers: Chiswick Bitter, ESB, London Cream Ale, London Pride, Carling Black Label, Tennent's Extra, Grolsch, Heineken, Guinness, Strongbow*
*Wheelchair access to venue and loo*
*Nearest railway station: Canary Wharf (DLR)*

# The Catcher in the Rye

317 Regents Park Road, N3. Tel: 0181 343 4369

The Catcher in the Rye looks rather as if three small buildings have been knocked together. This is what happened, actually. A shop, a solicitor's office and another shop gave its all to this nice modern pub with several little bars. People play chess and backgammon here, and they have recently installed air conditioning. The Catcher's best seller is a low-gravity bitter which it has specially brewed for it in Suffolk. The Catcher in the Rye is a novel by J. D. Salinger.

*Open: 11.00–23.00 (Mon–Sat), 12.00–22.30 (Sun)*
*Food: 12.00–15.00 and 18.00–22.00 (Mon–Sun)*
*Credit cards: Visa, Mastercard*
*Draught beers: Bass, Caffrey's, Catchers, Theakston XB, Kronenbourg, Foster's, Heineken, Guinness, Dry Blackthorn*
*Wheelchair access to venue*
*Nearest tube station: Finchley Central*

# Central Station

37 Wharfdale Road, N1. Tel: 0171 278 3294

The owners of Central Station, Duncan Irvine and Martin Mason, won the licensed industry's UK Entrepreneur of the Year award in 1997. *Pink Paper* gave it the UK Pub of the Year award, and readers of *Scene Update* voted it their 'favourite pub'. Duncan and Martin bought the place in 1991, and it seems to get a bigger following as each year passes. There's nightly entertainment on the ground floor, live music, drag cabaret, strippers, quiz nights. Dockyard Doris appears regularly, and Edwina Currie's daughter Debbie performed here with her band The Mojams. Famous punters are drawn to the happy-go-lucky nightlife, and I hear tell that they regularly include Jean-Paul Gaultier, Jimmy Somerville and Julian Clary. They must all be insomniacs – just look below for the hours that Central Station keeps.

*Open: 17.00–02.00 (Mon–Wed), 17.00–03.00 (Thurs), 17.00–05.00 (Fri), 12.00–05.00 (Sat), 12.00–midnight (Sun)*
*Food: as opening hours*
*Credit cards: all major cards*
*Draught beers: Courage Directors, Theakston XB, Foster's, Holsten, Kronenbourg, Guinness, Beamish, Scrumpy Jack*

*Meeting room for gay groups. Four rooms for hire: 12–60 seated, 20–140 standing*
*Nearest tube station: King's Cross*

*Also at:*

80 Brunner Road, Walthamstow E17

## The Champion

1 Wellington Terrace, Bayswater Road, W2. Tel: 0171 229 5056

As I write, big changes are in the offing for this long-established, uncamp, uncomplicated gay local. This will include removing the massive heptagonal bar and replacing it with a linear bar against one wall that will undoubtedly allow more room for manoeuvre. There will be a new light and sound system that will create a party atmosphere. Karaoke comes and karaoke goes. At the moment it's in, but budding Shirley Basseys should check first.

*Open: 12.00–23.00 (Mon–Sat), 12.00–22.30 (Sun)*
*Credit cards: all major cards*
*Draught beers: Caffrey's, Worthington, Carling Black Label, Carling Premier, Grolsch, Red Rock*
*Nearest tube station: Notting Hill Gate*

## The Champion

13 Wells Street, W1. Tel: 0171 323 1228

The most notable thing about The Champion is its quite remarkable windows. When Samuel Smith bought the pub in the eighties the company commissioned a series of big stained-glass windows from Anne Sotheran of York. They are now splendidly in situ, filling two whole walls. Each celebrates a different champion – Fred Archer, Captain Webb, W. G. Grace – and they fill the bar with an extraordinary light.

*Open: 11.30–23.00 (Mon–Fri), 12.00–23.00 (Sat), 12.00–15.00 and 17.00-22.30 (Sun)*
*Food: as opening hours (not Sun)*
*Credit cards: all major cards except AmEx*
*Draught beers: Samuel Smith's Mild, Ayingerbräu, Samuel Smith's Extra Stout, Special Reserve*
*Wheelchair access to venue*
*Private room: 110 standing*
*Nearest tube station: Oxford Circus*

## The Chandos

29 St Martin's Lane, WC2. Tel: 0171 836 1401

Samuel Smith, the Yorkshire brewer, took no chances on unknown, untried Southern builders when they bought this busy London pub. There was a lot to be done so they brought men down from Yorkshire to do it.

   People hardly recognised the old Chandos when it reopened. The building seemed to have been totally refaced. It had a gleaming black and gold fascia and immaculate new stucco, and it was quite different inside – new fittings, new panelling, new just about everything. Victorian mahogany drinking booths, handmade by the joiners from Tadcaster, lined the walls of the big downstairs bar. Pairs of button-back leather sofas faced each other across coffee tables in the grandly named Opera Room upstairs. The Yorkshiremen, well pleased, went home again. The Opera Room has its own staircase to the street, opens for breakfast at 9am, and subsequently offers coffee, lunch, tea and supper. It is a useful, well-turned-out pub in a great position. If you are passing, wave to the burly cooper working on the ledge three floors up. He has been doing something to a barrel up there all day and all night for years now.

*Open: 11.00–23.00 (Mon–Sat), 12.00–22.30 (Sun)*
*Food: 09.00–21.00 (Mon–Sun)*
*Credit cards: all major cards*
*Draught beers: Samuel Smith's Old Brewery Bitter, Ayingerbraü, Samuel Smith's Extra Stout, Samuel Smith's Cider Reserve*
*Wheelchair access to venue*
*Nearest tube stations: Charing Cross, Leicester Square*

## The Chelsea Potter

119 King's Road, SW3. Tel: 0171 352 9479

This Potter holds prime position on the King's Road for people-watchers to sit and watch the world go by. In the summer, the windows open up and the outside seating is always full to capacity. Shoppers and tourists keep it busy by day, when you can also enjoy some traditional pub fare. In the evenings, there isn't really room for food. The place fills up, the music pipes up, the lights go down and the performance of young people enjoying themselves begins. Vanda Stiglic runs the place. Old hands may remember her from The Shuckburgh (qv) in the eighties. She loves Chelsea pubs, so much so that she now has another one, The Resident (formerly The Phoenix), down the road in Smith Street.

*Open: 11.00–23.00 (Mon–Sat), 12.00–22.30 (Sun)*
*Food: 12.00–16.00 (Mon–Sun)*
*Credit cards: all major cards except AmEx*
*Draught beers: Courage Best, John Smith's Extra Smooth, Theakston Best, Theakston XB, Beck's, Gillespies, Kronenbourg, Strongbow*
*Wheelchair access to venue*
*Nearest tube station: Sloane Square*

## The Chelsea Ram

32 Burnaby Street, SW10. Tel: 0171 351 4008

This is a fine, handsome, bright and cheerful pub with big arched windows and a reputation for above-average quality food of a Modern British design (chicken breast marinated in honey and thyme; seared salmon with a salad of plum tomatoes, rocket, pumpkin seeds and Italian sauce; prices from £7.95). The decor, simple and understated with large tables and creaky wooden chairs, is fast becoming the rage of modern pub restaurants. It works well here, and the antique dealers, artisans and wealthy City types who frequent the place obviously delight in it. The Chelsea Ram serves Young's beers, 20 or so wines from the list (from £8.45), and a few champagnes (house £23.45). The pub was recently extended at the back, and a new skylight covers a very pleasant corner where the best seats are. You can't book tables but it's worth taking your chances, even though the ever-apologising staff seem to be employed for their looks rather than efficiency. Note that The Chelsea Ram can be quite difficult to find.

*Open: 11.00–15.00 and 17.30–23.00 (Mon–Sat), 12.00–15.30 and 19.00–22.30 (Sun)*
*Food: 12.00–14.30 and 19.00–21.45 (Mon–Fri and Sun)*
*Credit cards: Mastercard, Visa, Switch*
*Draught beers: Ramrod Smooth, Young's Bitter, Young's London, Young's Premium, Young's Special, Guinness, Strongbow*
*Wheelchair access to venue*
*Private room seats 12*
*Nearest tube station: Fulham Broadway*

# Chelsea Square

145 Dovehouse Street, SW3. Tel: 0171–351 1155

This was the Princess of Wales – a rather rundown public house almost in Chelsea Square. Nicky Kerman – he of Scotts, Drones, Sheekey's and Mirabelle fame – bought the place and changed it beyond recognition. It is seriously upmarket today and doesn't serve draught ales at all – cocktails, wines, champagnes, Pimms and sangria are the main offerings. The big, modern bar has a beautiful south facing terrace which can be covered and heated during inclement weather.

*Open: 12.00–00.30 (Mon-Sat), 12.00–16.00 (Sun)*
*Food: 12.00–23.00 (Mon-Sat), 12.00–16.00 (Sun)*
*Credit cards: all major*
*Wheelchair access to venue*
*Nearest tube station: South Kensington*

# Cheshire Cheese

5 Little Essex Street, WC2. Tel: 0171 836 2347

This is not to be confused with Ye Olde Cheshire Cheese, though it often is. American visitors sometimes photograph it inside and out before discovering that there is a rather better-known Cheshire Cheese ten minutes' walk away. This, though, is quite an old pub, too, and a certain amount of haunting goes on here. A ghost pushes the fruit machine around at night, and managers alone in the pub at weekends sometimes hear the dumb waiter inexplicably on its way up. Abraham Pera, the present manager, says that he has gone to the cellar on occasions to discover previously stacked beer barrels strewn across the floor. It doesn't seem to worry him, though – he has a customer who dresses up as a 17th-century ghost and takes his other customers on a ghost trail of the area. The pub closes at weekends but during the week the saloon bar stays open all day. The dive bar's customers are noticeably younger. This is where the pool table and the music are.

*Open: 11.00–23.00 (Mon–Fri)*
*Food: as opening hours*
*Credit cards: all major cards*
*Draught beers: Courage Best, Courage Director's, Theakston Best, John Smith's Extra Smooth, Foster's, Holsten, Kronenbourg, Beamish, Strongbow*
*Wheelchair access to venue and loo*
*Private room: 26 seated, 50 standing*
*Nearest tube stations: Temple, Charing Cross*

# Chicago Rock Café

Throwley Road, Sutton, SM1. Tel: 0181 643 2606

The formula for this big themed rock bar obviously works as it seems to be packed during the week and again at weekends. The decor is brash, with plenty of rock memorabilia on display, and the music, mostly seventies and eighties singalong and disco, is very loud. They have live music, too – mainly tribute bands, but these can be good for a flashback to a more carefree time. Beers are around £2 a pint with spirits in the £2–£2.50 range, and the service is brisk and efficient. There's an extensive Tex-Mex menu but my man in Balham describes the cooking as 'heavy handed', saying, 'It doesn't stack up very well on the price-quality ratio, and the dishes are clumsily put together.' Main courses average around £8. Cutting edge it's not, but it has a decent-enough atmosphere, and after a few beers you can noisily reveal near-perfect recall of Wham lyrics, safe in the knowledge that you won't be the only one. There are admission charges of £2 Monday to Thursday after 9pm and £3 Friday and Saturday.

*Open: 11.30–15.00 and 17.00–01.00 (Mon–Thurs), 11.30–01.00 (Fri–Sat), 12.00–22.30 (Sun)*
*Food: as opening hours*
*Credit cards: all major cards*
*Draught beers: John Smith's, Budweiser, Foster's, Strongbow*
*Wheelchair access to venue and loo*
*Private room: part of café can be used for buffets*
*Nearest railway station: Sutton*

## Christopher's Speakeasy

18 Wellington Street, WC2. Tel: 0171 240 4222

During Prohibition in the USA, a speakeasy was a place where alcoholic drink was sold illicitly. There's nothing illegal about this place, although there should be, as those of us who remember the rather charming upstairs bar are disappointed to find it newly relegated to a converted cellar to make more room for the restaurant. It was spookily empty when I last called – can you imagine a bar with four people in at 10pm on a Friday night in Covent Garden? I think it's wonderful, and I'm going to keep quiet about it, as it's handy to know there's such a haven of tranquillity in an otherwise riotous area. The famous illustrations have joined the bar in the cellar and they cover just about every inch of wallspace. I was so pleased with my loneliness that I almost ordered a sandwich to celebrate, but at £5 for a BLT, I thought that might be pushing the boat out just a bit too far.

*Open: bar 11.30–23.00 (Mon–Fri), 12.00–16.00 (Sun); restaurant 12.00–15.00 and 18.00–23.00 (Mon–Fri), 12.00–16.00 (Sun)*
*Credit cards: all major cards*
*Private room: 50 seated, 90 standing*
*Nearest tube station: Covent Garden*

## The Cittie of Yorke

22 High Holborn, WC1. Tel: 0171 242 7670

There is no pub in London quite like this one. The main bar resembles the great hall of a medieval manor, rising to a soaring trussed roof and high Gothic windows. Along one wall is the famous bar, shorter than it used to be but still one of the longest in Britain. Above it, huge iron-hooped wine butts sit on a stout timber gallery supported by fluted iron pillars. Each butt once held 1,000 gallons of wine. They were in active use right up to the outbreak of the last war, when they were carefully drained. A well-placed bomb might have carried off the customers on a tidal wave of amontillado.

Small cubicles line the facing wall, a table and four chairs in each. They were originally kept for lawyers and their clients, who now have to take their chances like everyone else. The cubicles are very popular, as is the massive stove on cold days. It was made in 1815 and still works perfectly. Each of its three sides has an open grate and there is no sign of a chimney. That is under the floorboards. The present owners, Samuel Smith, have made a second, smaller bar at the Holborn end and a long cellar bar downstairs. Food is of an average pub-fare standard with main meals of sausage and mash (£4.50) and steaks or salmon (£7.25). It remains a spectacular pub.

*Open: 11.30–23.00 (Mon–Sat)*
*Food: 12.00–14.30 and 17.30–22.00 (Mon–Fri)*
*Credit cards: AmEx, Mastercard, Visa*
*Draught beers: Ayingerbräu Wheat Beer, Old Brewery Bitter, Samuel Smith's Dark Mild, Ayingerbräu Pils, Samuel Smith's Extra Stout, Special Reserve*
*Wheelchair access to venue*
*Private room seats 260*
*Nearest tube station: Holborn*

# The City Barge

27 Strand on the Green, W4. Tel: 0181 994 2148

An elderly regular remembers arriving at The City Barge after it was bombed during the Second World War, finding the roof gone and rubble up to here. He got his drink as usual but, incredibly, someone had pinched Queen Elizabeth I's charter. It had been on the wall and it hasn't been seen since.

However, the ancient fireplace with its grate raised to stop floods putting the fire out did survive the Blitz, and so did the bar counter and the parliamentary clock made without glass to save tax. After the war the pub was rebuilt on the original 1484 foundations. It is slightly bigger now, with an old bar and a new bar. You go down a few steps to the old bar, which is much as it was before the bombing – small, homely, old fashioned. The new bar is up a few steps, and is substantially larger with a long counter and drinking booths. Part of The Beatles' film *Help* was shot here, and John, Paul, George and Ringo had a few days filming by the river. The bit where Ringo falls into the cellar was shot in the studio. The City Barge doesn't have a cellar. The river tries to get in from time to time without much success. The old pub has a watertight ship's door on the towpath now.

*Open: 11.00–23.00 (Mon–Sat), 12.00–22.30 (Sun)*
*Food: as opening hours*
*Credit cards: Mastercard, Visa*
*Draught beers: Courage Director's, Theakston Best, Theakston Old Peculier, Foster's, Holsten Export, Kronenbourg, Guinness, Strongbow*
*Wheelchair access to venue*
*Nearest railway station: Kew Bridge*

# City Page

2a Suffolk Lane, EC4. Tel: 0171 626 0996

Front Page Pubs are doing a marvellous job in lifting the standards of some of London's pubs and bars, and the City Page is the fifth in their slowly expanding yet highly efficient portfolio. Being underground, almost like a series of tunnels knocked together, it reminds you of those wine cellars from the early eighties, and they seem to have found a carpet from that era to complement the decor. It's too bad these wonderful cellars can't be air conditioned. You can't tell by looking that this is a part of the Page family.

*Open: 11.00–23.00 (Mon–Fri)*
*Food: 11.00–21.00 (Mon–Fri)*
*Credit cards: all major cards*
*Private room: 30 seated, 100 standing*
*Nearest tube stations: Cannon Street, Bank*

# The Clachan

34 Kingly Street, W1. Tel: 0171 734 2659

Clachan is the old Scots word for a meeting place. On occasions Scots do meet here – on Burns Night when the haggis is piped in. Haggis isn't usually on the menu, though; you're more likely to find moules or breaded brie wedges alongside the more traditional ploughman's lunches and pies. The Clachan is a large air-conditioned bar, with real ales on tap and a function room (The Highland Bar) upstairs bookable for parties and business meetings. It was originally owned by its neighbour Liberty, who wanted to close it down and create more warehouse space. It is a protected building, however, and as Liberty had little use for a pub, they sold it to Nicholson's. What a relief!

*Open: 11.00–23.00 (Mon–Sat)*
*Food: bar 11.00–20.30 (Mon–Sat)*
*Credit cards: all major cards*
*Draught beers: Tetley, IPA, Kilkenny and three guest ales, Carlsberg, Carlsberg*

Export, Castlemaine, Guinness, Olde English
Wheelchair access to venue
Private room seats 36
Nearest tube station: Oxford Circus

## The Clarence

53 Whitehall, SW1. Tel: 0171 930 4808

Ancient overhead timbers from a Thames pier, wonderful cellars under White-hall, leaded windows throwing delicate patterns on the pale wooden floor – this is a most romantic old pub with tremendous appeal for tourists. They are pleased to find old-fashioned settles and benches still in place, though sadly the gaslights went in the recent redecoration.

The Clarence is a real ale house and hosts Medieval nights for parties of 12 or more.

*Open: 11.00–23.00 (Mon–Sat), 12.00–22.30 (Sun)*
*Food: 11.00–23.00 (Mon–Sat), 12.00–17.00 (Sun)*
*Credit cards: all major cards*
*Draught beers: Abbot Ale, John Smith's Smooth Cask Ale, Theakston Best, Theakston Old Peculier, Becks, Foster's, Kronenbourg, Gillespies, Strongbow*
*Wheelchair access to venue*
*Private room seats 52*
*Nearest tube stations: Charing Cross, Embankment*

## The Clifton

96 Clifton Hill, NW8. Tel: 0171 624 5233

The Clifton is a substantial Georgian villa in a particularly pleasant street in St John's Wood. It has been a pub since 1834, and in recent years has been beautifully restored and refurbished in an Edwardian style, all pine panelling, polished floors with Persian rugs and ornate open fireplaces. It is also full of quiet corners for lovers to hold hands. In 1985 it was the *Evening Standard's* pub of the year, the unanimous choice of the judges, and in that year, too, an extremely nice conservatory was added, which is now the restaurant. There is a sunny terrace at the back and tables in the garden flanking the street; in the winter The Clifton is particularly inviting, with fires in each of the main rooms.

*Open: 11.00–23.00 (Mon–Sat), 12.00–22.30 (Sun)*
*Food: 12.00–14.30 and 18.30–21.30 (Mon–Sun)*
*Credit cards: all major cards*
*Draught beers: Adnams, Calders Cream Ale, Pedigree, Tetley and two guest ales, Carlsberg, Castlemaine, Lowenbrau, Guinness, Dry Blackthorn*
*Wheelchair access to venue*
*Nearest tube stations: St John's Wood, Maida Vale*

## The Coach and Horses

29 Greek Street, W1. Tel: 0171 437 5920

One of Soho's most celebrated pubs, The Coach and Horses stands proud on the corner of Romilly Street and Greek Street. Inside, its red plastic stool covers, black Formica table tops and Basic Food Hygiene Certificate announce that this is a pub for serious drinkers. For many years *Private Eye* had its offices opposite the pub, which became a haunt of Richard Ingrams, Peter Cook, William Rushton, Michael Heath and Jeffrey Bernard. *Private Eye* still has its fortnightly lunches in an upstairs room, although lunches in the pub itself have been stopped. A sandwich in the bar is quite enough.

The landlord, Norman Balon, is known to many as London's rudest landlord, a reputation borne out of much self-perpetuation, I suspect.

*Open: 11.00–23.00 (Mon–Sat), 12.00–22.30 (Sun)*
*Food: sandwiches at bar*

*Credit cards: all major cards*
*Draught beers: Burton Ale, Calder's Cream Ale, Marston's Pedigree, Tetley, Carls-*
*berg Export, Lowenbrau, Guinness, Dry Blackthorn*
*Wheelchair access to venue*
*Nearest tube station: Leicester Square*

## The Coal Hole

91 The Strand, WC1. Tel: 0171 836 7503

In the distant days of The Coal Hole's notoriety it was a coalheavers' hang out in old converted cellars off The Strand. It was very rough. The coalheavers drank and carried on, word got round and others started going, actors and the like. The coalheavers moved on to the Ship and Shovel, also still going strong, and The Coal Hole moved further along The Strand to proper premises in the Savoy buildings, where it is today. The main bar on The Strand is high and handsome with large windows, hanging banners and marble reliefs of frisking maidens, muses perhaps, or seasons. The cellar bar has been much smartened up lately. It has its own entrance and its own lively following. It is an interesting bar, wandering off downhill a bit, and at its far reaches is a locked gate, beyond which some steps lead down to a little windowless snug. This, they will tell you, is the coal hole. It certainly could be one. People drink in it sometimes. It is not for claustrophobics.

*Open: 11.00–23.00 (Mon–Sat)*
*Food: 11.30–14.30 (Mon–Sat)*
*Credit cards: Mastercard, Visa*
*Draught beers: Adnams, Brakspear, Tetley, Timothy Taylor Landlord, Carlsberg, Castlemaine, Lowenbrau, Guinness, Addlestone*
*Nearest tube stations: Charing Cross, Covent Garden*

## Coates

45 London Wall, EC2. Tel: 0171 256 5148

Corney and Barrow (qv), the rather up-market chain of City bars, goes down-market a little with its two Coates outlets. This one opened in 1991, and provides good value food in an up-beat atmosphere. The food is pizza – not a bad idea in a bar for City workers. In the evenings the atmosphere gets quite lively; there's karaoke on Wednesday and Friday, and a disco on Thursday. As one of the researchers of this Guide put it: 'Essex nymphos by night and an easy place to pull on Thursdays.'

*Open: 11.00–23.00 (Mon–Sat), 12.00–22.30 (Sun)*
*Food: 12.00–17.00 and 19.00–22.00 (Mon–Sat)*
*Credit cards: Mastercard, Visa*
*Draught beers: Young's Ordinary, Young's Special, London Lager, Premium Lager, Guinness, Young's Oatmeal, Scrumpy Jack*

*Also at:*

**City**: 46 Cowcross Street, EC1. Tel: 0171 251 3128. Nearest tube station: Farringdon

## Cocktail Bar at the Connaught

Connaught Hotel, 16 Carlos Place, W1: Tel 0171 499 7070

If the entire country gave up smoking, there would be one last remaining humidor circulating the Cocktail Bar at the Connaught Hotel. This is where you'll find gentlemen sitting in big leather chairs puffing away on large Havanas or the like, sipping brandies and probably speculating on government policy, economic trends and profit forecasts of the major internationals. The bar is extraordinarily handsome, elegant, exclusive and serene with service that is military prompt yet very discreet. When I went with my colleagues Andrew Jefford and Angus McGill they were quietly and politely asked if they'd care to repair to the cloak-room where they would be furnished with ties. They didn't mind in the slightest, and the cloakroom attendant told them they now looked like a million dollars. They gave him a pound. Back in the bar we tucked in to the wonderful free nib-bles, and suggested that this would be a great place for a clandestine meeting.

*Open: 11.00–15.00 and 17.30–23.00 (Mon–Sat), 12.00–14.00 and 19.00–22.30 (Sun)*
*Credit cards: all major cards*
*Wheelchair access to venue*
*Nearest tube station: Bond Street*

## The Coleherne

261 Old Brompton Road, SW5. Tel: 0171 373 9859

The Coleherne is a cavernous Victorian pub in Earl's Court and the most famous gay pub in the world. The atmosphere is macho and menacing, with lit-tle of the gaiety of the usual gay pub. The clientele – mostly 'tached, tattooed and pierced – wear elaborate leather gear as a rule: biker jackets, leather trousers, studs everywhere. The Coleherne has two sets of customers, the ones in leather and the rest. Some stand holding bottles and staring straight ahead. Less flamboyant customers gather in large numbers on the other side of the bar. There is not a lot of conversation even among this group. The Coleherne isn't strong on conversation. Serial killer Colin Ireland, now serving life, met his victims here. During his trial there were said to be more reporters in The Coleherne than regular customers. Armistead Maupin's character Mouse, from his *Tales of the City* books, came here when he first visited London.

*Open: 12.00–23.00 (Mon–Sat), 12.00-22.30 (Sun)*
*Draught beers: Worthington Best, Caffrey's Grolsch, Carling Premier, Guinness, Red Rock*
*Credit cards: all major cards*
*Wheelchair access to venue and loo*
*Nearest tube station: Earls Court*

## The Collection          EROS AWARD WINNER

264 Brompton Road, SW3. Tel: 0171 225 1212

Mogens Tholstrup's empire continues to grow, with the addition of The Collec-tion to his collection of fine eating and drinking emporia in London. Tholstrup was responsible for Est in Soho (qv) but recently sold his interest and appears to be concentrating his activities in the Brompton Cross area. Daphne's (around the corner from here) is a decidedly up-market restaurant, and in an attempt to appeal to a wider audience he opened this restaurant, café and bar on the Brompton Road. A 100-foot-long portal with an illuminated glazed floor leads you into a vast warehouse conversion, housing a mezzanine restaurant with bar and café area on the ground floor. The 60-foot bar sweeps wide and high into the distance, rising with the peculiar inclination of the floor, which allows those of us who are vertically challenged to survey the proceedings from a confident position. And survey we will. It attracts beautiful and well-heeled people, who compose themselves by resting in the café area or milling around the large, open floor space, tippling cocktails and tapping out the beat of the background acid jazz. The impressive display of drinks served up by the appropriately friendly, comely staff make you feel like experimenting with something expen-sive, which is rather handy, because you very probably will.

The Collection isn't really a daytime venue – if you sit there in the day, your only amusement is the District Line trains rattling by – but things liven up a lot in the evening. They don't have a dress code, but getting in can be quite tricky. What they're trying to do is resist the pattern of other, similar bars, which have gone the way of being pick-up joints. If they give a fairly weak reason for not letting you in, then that, I'm afraid, is that. The best thing to do is dress smart and don't turn up with a large gang.

*Open: 12.00–23.00 (Mon–Sat)*
*Food: bar and restaurant upstairs 12.00–15.00 and 19.00–23.30 (Mon–Sat); restaurant downstairs 12.00–23.00 (Mon–Sat)*
*Credit cards: all major cards*
*Wheelchair access to venue and loo*
*Nearest tube station: South Kensington*

## Come the Revolution
541 King's Road, SW6. Tel: 0171 610 9067

The title has nothing to do with any affiliation of a political kind, and the owners would be very happy if you'd stop asking that question. Come the Revolution opened up nearly five years ago and was an immediate hit with the younger element of Fulham, since it's very handy for a couple of neighbouring clubs, Crazy Larry's and Embargo. It's loud, sometimes impossibly fashionable and occasionally a little bit eccentric. Food and music being the love of Fulhamites, the Thai chef Toni serves some formidable Thai dishes at remarkably cheap prices (nothing over £5.50). There is no let-up to the music: R & B Mondays, Latin American acoustic guitars on Tuesdays, happy house Wednesdays, a very loud but fabulous Japanese funk band on Thursdays, DJs Fridays and Saturdays, jazz on Sunday at lunchtime with a traditional English roast lunch, and Caribbean and Creole in the evening. There's a minor escape from all this in the form of a wonderful walled garden at the back to while away the summer evenings. You can even while away the winter evenings now – they've installed a covering canopy and garden heaters. Did I mention the crushed velvet and velour furnishings? I wonder if they'll survive the next revolution.

*Open: 11.00–23.00 (Mon–Sat), 12.00–22.30 (Sun)*
*Food: bar 12.00–15.00 and 17.30–21.30 (Mon–Sun)*
*Credit cards: all major cards*
*Draught beers: Calder's Cream Ale, Kilkenny, Beck's, Kronenbourg, Warsteiner*
*Wheelchair access to venue*
*Nearest tube station: Fulham Broadway*

## Compton Arms
4 Compton Avenue, N1 Tel: 0171 359 2645

This is a quiet little pub hidden away off Canonbury Square. There's a small, cosy, low-ceilinged bar, and benches round cask tables under a friendly sycamore tree at the back. The 20th century encroaches, however. Crib and dominoes wait behind the bar but no one ever asks for them. There is still neither juke box nor gaming machine, but Sky TV has arrived. An extension is currently being built that will seat 30 people. The getting-bigger Compton is always busy when Arsenal is at home.

*Open: 11.00–23.00 (Mon–Sat), 12.00–22.30 (Sun)*
*Food: bar 12.00–15.00 and 18.00–21.00 (Mon–Fri), 12.00–21.00 (Sat–Sun)*
*Credit cards: all major cards*
*Draught beers: Abbot Ale, Greene King, Rayment's, Wexford Cream Ale, Harp, Kronenbourg, Stella Artois, Guinness, Bulmers*
*Wheelchair access to venue*
*Nearest tube station: Highbury & Islington*

## The Coopers' Arms
87 Flood Street, SW3. Tel: 0171 376 3120

A bright, warm and inviting pub holding on to its traditional values while preparing itself for the 21st-century market. The bartenders still wear aprons, and serve popular brasserie-style food (spinach and mushroom roulade on mixed leaves; chicken breast with tarragon and orange sauce).

A massive buffalo head, a gift from a customer, presides over the bar; a baker's dough table occupies an extravagant amount of floor space; a splendid long-case clock looks as though it was made for the end wall; and two massive air filters on the ceiling keep the air clear and smokers and non-smokers in harmony. Upstairs is a useful room for special occasions, with a magnificent 17-foot table, originally a draughtsman's table from a Jarrow shipyard. On Saturdays it is laden with food and drink for wedding receptions. Chelsea Register Office is round the corner.

*Open: 11.00–23.00 (Mon–Sat), 12.00–22.30 (Sun)*
*Food: 12.30–15.00 and 19.00–22.00 (Sun–Thurs)*
*Credit cards: all major cards*
*Draught beers: all Young's varieties, Beck's, Budweiser, Castlemaine, Holsten, Labatt's, Michelob, Red Stripe, Stella Artois, Scrumpy Jack*
*Wheelchair access to venue*
*Private room: 30 seated, 60 standing*
*Nearest tube station: Sloane Square*

## Cork and Bottle

44–46 Cranbourn Street, WC2. Tel: 0171 734 7807

I think that this was possibly the first wine bar I went to in London. It's almost impossible to find – entry is via a narrow doorway in bustling Cranbourn Street – and you descend a flight of steps into the basement, where a couple of air-conditioned bars extend warren-like underground. The place opened in August 1971 and was one of the first wine bars of its day. It was always packed, and offered a wide, mostly palatable range of wines. In 1984 it was voted the very first *Evening Standard* Wine Bar of the Year, and its success seemed to roll on even with the dawning of a new generation of wine bars. The Cork and Bottle is more than 27 years old now, and I have been back several times in the past year to check it out. It's wearing well, clearly dating from the seventies but still remarkably popular and unpretentious. Some of the customers look as though they have been frequenting the place since 1971, and many probably have. The bar staff I encountered were quite laid back in that Antipodean style which can appear off-hand, but were very knowledgeable about the wines and seemed willing to help when people were struggling with the extensive list. It usually took several goes to get a clean glass, but I'm a stickler for such things.

*Open: 11.00–midnight (Mon–Sat), 12.00–22.30 (Sun)*
*Food: 11.00–23.00 (Mon–Sat), 12.00–22.00 (Sun)*
*Credit cards: all major cards*
*Nearest tube station: Leicester Square*

## Corney and Barrow

Corney and Barrow have been established in the City since 1870, but their latest bars were introduced in 1988, with the opening of the branch at Broadgate. This is the glass structure in the gardens of Exchange Square, Broadgate, where they hold regular croquet tournaments during the summer. Exchange Square is the smallest Corney and Barrow in the entire world, although it benefits from an upstairs and a rather large expansion onto the pavement outside. The Cannon Street branch is about to be refurbished as I write, and will soon be introducing a new food concept that will be implemented in all subsequent Corney and Barrows (Masons Avenue, EC2, will be opening in early 1998). Cannon Street also opens at 8am for breakfast. The Eastcheap Corney and Barrow is in a basement close to Monument tube station, and is well frequented by local workers.

The branch at Broadgate Circle is the most spectacular. On the first level of the circle, a mostly glass structure houses the highly modern bar with TV monitors displaying financial data. Its outside terrace sweeps wide on both sides, all but encompassing the Circle, and has plenty of seating space and large parasols to shade customers from the midday heat. These tables are bookable, and when events are going on in the Circle, there is no better place from which to watch them. You might see dancing – even dancing horses – or ice skating in winter months. The food here is restricted to sandwiches and the like – they don't really have the facilities in such a confined space. The clientele is predominantly City males, but in the evenings the crowd becomes much more mixed, and groups gather on the terrace, sipping wines, champagnes and bottled beers. A perfect location.

*Open: 11.00–22.30 (Mon–Wed), 11.00–23.00 (Thurs–Fri); Cannon Street opens at 08.00, Leadenhall Place at 09.30, Exchange Square, Canary Wharf and Broadgate at 10.00.*
*Food: 11.00–22.30 (Mon–Fri); Cannon Street 08.00–22.30*
*Credit cards: all major cards*

*Branches at:*
**Canary Wharf**: 9 Cabot Square, Canary Wharf, E14. Tel: 0171 512 0397. Nearest railway station: Canary Wharf (DLR)

**City (EC2)**: 19 Broadgate Circle, EC2. Tel: 0171 628 1251. Nearest tube station: Liverpool Street

**City (EC2)**: 2b Eastcheap, EC2. Tel: 0171 929 3220. Nearest tube station: Monument

**City (EC2)**: 5 Exchange Square, Broadgate, EC2. Tel: 0171 628 4367. Nearest tube station: Liverpool Street

**City (EC3)**: 1 Leadenhall Place, EC3. Tel: 0171 621 9201. Nearest tube station: Bank, Monument

**City (EC3)**: 16 Royal Exchange, EC3. Tel: 0171 929 3131. Nearest tube station: Bank

**City (EC4)**: 44 Cannon Street, EC4. Tel: 0171 248 1700. Nearest tube station: Mansion House

**City (EC4)**: 3 Fleet Place, EC4. Tel: 0171 329 3141. Nearest tube station: St Paul's

# The Coronet

338–346 Holloway Road, N7. Tel: 0171 609 5014

Large cinemas up and down the country have proven to be useful venues for developers to transform into multiplexes, bingo halls and shopping centres. But a pub? In 1996 J. D. Wetherspoon spent £1.5 million transforming the old Coronet cinema into what might possibly be London's biggest pub. It can accommodate more than 1,000 customers at a time, and night after night it does. Its showbiz antecedents are plain for all to see. It is unmistakably a one-time cinema, and its neon sign, CORONET, splashed across the cream tiled frontage, can be seen at night all along Holloway Road from Islington to Archway.

So in you go, through the glass doors, across the foyer and down the flight of steps almost the width of the building. There, instead of the stalls, is this vast bar. The circle, now full of air-conditioning gear and such, still covers half of it, and the ceiling soars over the front stalls as ceilings did when cinemas were cinemas. On every side, images of the gods and goddesses of the silver screen look down, languorous and glamorous as ever: Fred Astaire, Ginger Rogers, Humphrey Bogart, Ingrid Bergman. It was once their job to fill The Coronet but now the attraction is the building itself, and the beer it sells at such amazing prices: Younger's Scotch Bitter 99p a pint, Theakston Best £1.10, Courage Directors £1.40, Foster's £1.50. The Coronet shifts vast quantities of Guinness and at £1.45 a pint who could wonder?

Wetherspoon's rules apply: a no-smoking area bigger than some pubs I know, and no TV, pool, pinball or music of any sort. You couldn't hear it anyway when the crowds pour in.

*Open: 11.00–23.00 (Mon–Sat), 12.00–22.30 (Sun)*
*Food: 11.00–22.00 (Mon–Sat), 12.00–21.30 (Sun)*
*Credit cards: AmEx, Delta, Mastercard, Switch, Visa*
*Draught beers: Caffrey's, Courage Directors, John Smith's Extra Smooth, Theakston Best, Younger's Scotch Bitter, Becks, Kronenbourg, McEwan's Export, Guinness, Dry Blackthorn*
*Wheelchair access to venue and loo*
*Nearest tube station: Seven Sisters*

## The Cow

89 Westbourne Park Road, W2. Tel: 0171 221 0021

Tom Conran's Cow is an Irish-style bar but not quite in the vein of those being churned out by the big brewers with monotonous regularity. 'Guinness and Oysters' boasts one sign. That's what they do in Ireland. This is a small pub with one long, narrow room that specialises in seafood. The upstairs restaurant is receiving much acclaim. It is in the hands of Francesca Melman (she of River Café and Alastair Little fame). The staff here are very knowledgeable and helpful with the menu. Tom himself will often be found in the bar, as will a gathering of other local celebrities. The Cow is unobtrusive, gentle and a calm place to spend an evening in this developing part of Westbourne Park.

*Open: 12.00–23.00 (Mon–Sat), 12.00–22.30 (Sun)*
*Food: bar 12.30–15.00 and 18.30–22.30 (Mon–Sat), 18.30–22.00 (Sun); restaurant 19.00–23.00 (Mon–Fri), 12.00–15.00 (Sat–Sun)*
*Credit cards: Eurocard, Mastercard, Visa*
*Draught beers: ESB, Fuller's, London Cream, London Porter, London Pride, Budwar, Hoegaarden, Red Stripe, Guinness*
*Nearest tube stations: Royal Oak, Westbourne Park*

## The Crescent

99 Fulham Road, SW3 Tel: 0171 225 2244

The rather bijou ground-floor bar fills up quickly and hides a much bigger basement area. It's clinically clean, modern and nicely air-conditioned. The food seems to be improving with each visit and although not especially cheap, provides a good quality alternative to the other rather more expensive restaurants in Brompton Cross. With a wine list in excess of 200 wines and useful descriptions to help you choose, this is surely a wine lover's fantasy.

*Open: 11.00–midnight (Mon–Fri), 10.00–midnight (Sat), 11.00–22.30 (Sun)*
*Food: as opening hours*
*Credit cards: all major cards*
*Nearest tube station: South Kensington*

## Cricketers

Maids of Honour Row, The Green, Richmond, TW9. Tel: 0181 940 4372

This is the pub that Rolling Stone Ronnie Wood tried to buy with his drinking pal Jimmy White. Ronnie lived just across the way and the Cricketers was his local, but £400,000 later, Greene King had beaten him to it. Over the last few years, standards at the Cricketers have risen stratospherically. It is now as clean and tidy a pub as you will find in Richmond, with a fully refitted bar, new kitchen and the sort of customers who don't go in for loud music. It has been noticed that cricketers who play cricket on the green on summer evenings usually end up in the Cricketers.

*Open: 11.00–23.00 (Mon–Sat), 12.00–22.30 (Sun)*
*Food: 12.00–15.30 and 17.30–20.30 (Mon–Sat)*
*Credit cards: all major cards*

*Draught beers: Abbot Ale, Greene King IPA, Wexford Cream Ale, Harp, Kronen-*
*bourg, Stella Artois, Guinness, Strongbow*
*Wheelchair access to venue*
*Nearest tube station: Richmond*

## Crocker's Folly

24 Aberdeen Place, NW8. Tel: 0171 286 6608

Frank Crocker was the man who built this hotel at the height of the Victorian railway boom. He'd been given a tip that Marylebone Station was to be built across the road and, being an entrepreneurial spirit, decided to buy the adjacent land which he hoped would result in his fame and fortune. The tip was not worth listening to. Marylebone Station was built where it is, and the desperate Mr Crocker jumped from one of the upper windows. The Crown Hotel – as he called it – faced difficult times. Today it is owned by Regent Inns, who spent a lot of money on making it look as marvellous as it does. There are marble columns, marble walls, marble counters, massive baronial fireplaces, rich mahogany fittings, plus a magnificent saloon bar and a noble public bar with nine cask ales on the hand pumps. The cellars are as roomy as everywhere else. There is also a pleasant restaurant room, which used to be the billiard room and has an enormous fireplace. They changed the name to commemorate Frank Crocker. Fame at last!

*Open: 11.00–23.00 (Mon–Sat), 12.00–22.30 (Sun)*
*Food: bar 12.00–14.30 and 18.00–21.30 (Mon–Sat), 12.00–21.00 (Sun); restaurant*
*12.00–14.30 and 18.00–21.00 (Mon–Sat), 12.00–21.00 (Sun)*
*Credit cards: all major cards*
*Draught beers: Adnams, Boddington's, Brakspear, Caffrey's, Crocker's, Greene*
*King, John Smith's Extra Smooth, Shepherd Neame, Theakston Best, Foster's,*
*Heineken, Kronenbourg, Stella Artois, Tennent's Extra, Murphy's, Guinness, Dry*
*Blackthorn, Stowfold Press*
*Wheelchair access to venue*
*Private room: 15 seated, 25 standing*
*Nearest tube station: Warwick Avenue*

## The Crooked Billet

14 Crooked Billet, SW19. Tel: 0181 946 4942

The Crooked Billet is in the tiny hamlet of that name hard by Wimbledon Common, and it has been slipping in and out of local records for nearly 500 years. The recently refurbished bar has proved popular, but in fine weather people do as they have done for centuries. They sit with their drinks on the green opposite the Crooked Billet, enjoying the sunshine.

*Open: 11.00–23.00 (Mon–Sat), 12.00–22.30 (Sun)*
*Food: 12.00–14.30 and 18.30–21.30 (Mon–Sat), 12.00–14.30 and 19.00–21.00 (Sun)*
*Credit cards: Mastercard, Visa*
*Draught beers: Young's Bitter, Young's Special, Young's Pilsner, Young's Export,*
*Grolsch, Guinness, Scrumpy Jack*
*Wheelchair access to venue*
*Nearest tube station: Wimbledon*

## Cross Keys

1 Lawrence Street, SW3. Tel: 0171 349 9111

The present-day Cross Keys is the result of a dramatic conversion from a small Victorian bar into a beautiful, modern, spacious bar, gallery and restaurant, designed by Tony and Rudy Weller (they of Beach Blanket Babylon fame, qv). It is owned by the rather romantically named Carmel Azzopardi, who is also a product of those Babylon days. The downstairs bar is unrecognisable from old: large tables, low chairs, comfortable seating around the fire-place, high stools at pedestal tables, York-stone-paved floor, modern bar counter against the far wall and a stone-moulded Friar Tuck above the fire-place, warming the parts of himself that need warming. A good section of the ceiling has gone, making way for a high gallery with a massive wrought-iron chandelier. The galleried balcony is often used as a gallery, with art exhibitions and a variety of other events. At other times it is home to office parties and wedding receptions. Back downstairs, a walk to the back of the bar brings you into a large glass conservatory which houses the always-busy restaurant, for which it is usually advisable to book. I regularly recommend this place to numerous people, and although I haven't personally experienced any problems on my many visits to the Cross Keys, I have received enough complaints not to ignore the claims of *occasional* bad attitude from the staff, particularly when trying to negotiate a booking over the telephone, and, an apparent reluctance to top-up drinks when researchers have suggested that a short measure of beer just *might* have been poured. But don't let this put you off. Whether you're going for drinks or for a sit-down meal, this place is a real find.

*Open: 11.00–23.00 (Mon–Sat), 12.00–22.30 (Sun)*
*Food: bar 12.00–15.00 and 18.00–21.00 (Mon–Sun); restaurant 12.00–15.00 and 19.00–midnight (Mon–Sat), 12.00–16.00 and 19.00–23.00 (Sun)*
*Credit cards: all major cards*
*Draught beers: Beamish Red, John Smith's Extra Smooth, Theakston Best, Foster's, Kronenbourg, Guinness, Dry Blackthorn*
*Wheelchair access to venue*
*Nearest tube station: Sloane Square*

## The Crown

116 Cloudesley Road, N1. Tel: 0171 837 7107

The Crown had been sitting happily tucked away behind Liverpool Road for the past hundred years when Fuller's decided to revamp it as one of their Bohemia pubs (or bulimia, as I thought the PR girl said). These concentrate on food (which is why I thought I'd heard her correctly). The renovation did not destroy any of the original features of the pub; it has simply had a lick of paint, a good polish and a general sprucing up all round. The old kitchen was gutted to make way for the new dining room. With so many pubs offering decent food these days, The Crown is probably not going to be a destination, but I would be very happy to have it in my neighbourhood.

*Open: 11.00–23.00 (Mon–Sat), 12.00–22.30 (Sun)*
*Food: 12.00–14.00 (Mon–Fri)*
*Credit cards: all major cards*
*Draught beers: Boddingtons, Brakspear, London Pride, seven real ales changed on a regular basis, Heineken, Stella Artois, Guinness, Scrumpy Jack*
*Wheelchair access to venue*
*Private room seats 30*
*Nearest tube station: Angel*

## The Crown

49 Tranquil Vale, SE3. Tel: 0181 852 0326

There are not many older buildings than this in Blackheath village. The Crown was built in 1740 and has been a village alehouse, a stout warehouse, a staging post for horse buses and a boozy local. Now it is a village alehouse again, doing its best to keep modern times at bay with old floorboards, stout wooden furniture, traditional English pies on the menu and plenty of English ale in the cellar. It is a handsome, old-fashioned pub.

*Open: 11.00–23.00 (Mon–Sat), 12.00–22.30 (Sun)*
*Food: 11.00–21.00 (Mon–Sat), 12.00–21.00 (Sun)*
*Credit cards: all major cards*
*Draught beers: Courage Best, Theakston Best, Theakston Old Peculier, Theakston XB, three guest ales, Becks, Foster's, Gillespies, Bulmer's Traditional*
*Wheelchair access to venue*
*Nearest railway station: Blackheath*

## The Crown and Greyhound

73 Dulwich Village, SE21. Tel: 0181 693 2466

This is a story of two pubs, The Crown and The Greyhound. The Greyhound was the grand one with the ballroom and the pleasure grounds. The London–Sevenoaks stage stopped there twice a day. Charles Dickens dined there with the Dulwich Club, so Dulwich was where Mr Pickwick retired. No one thought much of The Crown, the small pub on the other side of the road. In 1895 the manager of the humble Crown bought the fine Greyhound and pulled it down. Three years later The Crown was pulled down as well, and a splendid new pub built on the site, the imposing Crown and Greyhound, which has been a centre of village life ever since. It is one of the biggest and most successful pubs in south London, so busy you can hardly move in the evenings. It has four bars, one non-smoking, the others joined by the original mahogany counter, and a lot of the original furniture, including high-backed Victorian settees of unusual discomfort. There is a busy restaurant, and every Saturday a wedding reception in the suite of function rooms. Lunch specials can include penne pasta with mince and mushrooms, vegetable moussaka or steak and mushroom pie (£5.25), and there's a simpler menu of jacket potatoes, sandwiches, and gammon and chips. The evening menu covers rainbow trout, tarragon chicken and Dijon pork (from £6.75). The garden is huge and full of tables, with steps taking you up to the nicest, greenest bit, and yet more tables under a magnificent horse chestnut tree.

*Open: 11.00–23.00 (Mon–Sat), 12.00–22.30 (Sun)*
*Food: 12.00–14.30 and 18.00–22.00 (Mon–Sat), 12.00–15.00 (Sun)*
*Credit cards: all major cards*
*Draught beers: Burton Ale, Calder's Cream Ale, Kilkenny, John Bull, Tetley, Young's, Carlsberg, Carlsberg Export, Castlemaine, Guinness, Dry Blackthorn, Sweet Blackthorn*
*Wheelchair access to venue*
*Two private rooms: 25–90 seated, 30–110 standing*
*Nearest railway station: North Dulwich*

## The Crown and Shuttle

Shoreditch High Street, E1. Tel: 0171 247 7696

A respectable East End local noted for its entertainment. At lunchtime and in the early evening exotic dancers dance exotically round the pool table, taking off all their clothes except their shoes. City workers in suits watch without comment or expression, and applaud politely as the dance concludes. Pool players then resume their interrupted game.

*Open: 11.00–23.00 (Mon–Sat), 12.00–22.30 (Sun)*
*Credit cards: none taken*
*Draught beers: Courage Best, Websters, Becks, Carlsberg, Foster's, Holsten Export, Kronenbourg, Beamish, Guinness, Strongbow*
*Nearest tube station: Liverpool Street*

# The Crown and Two Chairmen

31 Dean Street, W1. Tel: 0171 437 8192

A few years back Allied Domecq spent a vast amount of money reorganising the interior of this pub, dramatically increasing the drinking space. They did a wise thing, as it happens, as the space has quickly filled up with new customers, who come to eat and enjoy the real ales. The crowd spill out onto the pavement in the warm weather, and seem to spend most of the day there. Best buys include the wonderful door-step sandwiches and real chips.

*Open: 11.00–23.00 (Mon–Sat), 12.00–22.30 (Sun)*
*Food: 12.00–17.00 and 18.00–22.30 (Mon–Sun)*
*Credit cards: all major except AmEx*
*Draught beers: Calder's Cream Ale, Marston's Pedigree, Old Speckled Hen, Tetley, Budwar, Carlsberg, Castlemaine, Lowenbrau, Guinness, Dry Blackthorn*
*Wheelchair access to venue*
*Private room: 50 seated, 120 standing*
*Nearest tube station: Piccadilly Circus*

# Crusting Pipe

27 The Market, Covent Garden, WC2. Tel: 0171 836 1415

On the lower level of the covered market hall, the tables and chairs in the courtyard belong to this wine bar, part of the Davys (qv) portfolio. Inside, it is a warren of old wine vaults with stone-flagged floors covered in sawdust. You would imagine that it would be full of tourists, and it often is. The cacophony of sound made by the nearby musicians and the applauding audiences lends a festive air to this and its neighbouring bars. Londoners seem to take over on weekday evenings. The wine list is the attraction, with a decent-sized range of quality wines which are constantly changing.

*Open: 11.30–23.00 (Mon–Sat), 11.30–18.00 (Sun)*
*Food: bar as opening hours; restaurant 12.00–15.00 and 17.30–22.00 (Mon–Sat), 12.00–15.00 (Sun)*
*Credit cards: all major cards*
*Nearest tube station: Covent Garden*

# Crutched Friar

Crutched Friars, EC3. Tel: 0171 488 9886

A Crutched Friar was a member of the mendicant (a less common word for begging) order of monks, who were suppressed in 1656. If you wander along Crutched Friar Street today, you will notice that many of the buildings recognise this link, with friars of all shapes and sizes integral to the architecture. The Crutched Friar we want to talk about is the new pub close to Farringdon station, and what a popular place it is. I've been several times now and still haven't managed to see the walls for the sheer enormity of the City crowds who go there after work. There are three long linear rooms, two of them on either side of what is really only a wide corridor, and they all get packed very quickly. There is also the tiniest of terraces – you probably have to arrive at opening time to have a chance there – and a very agreeable patio garden at the back, from where you could hear your train whistling its departure, if they still whistled, of course.

*Open: 11.00–23.00 (Mon–Fri)*
*Food: as opening hours*
*Credit cards: all major cards*
*Draught beers: Bass, Caffrey's, London Pride, Carling Black Label, Grolsch, Staropramen, Guinness, Cidermaster*
*Wheelchair access to venue and loo*
*Nearest tube station: Tower Hill*
*Nearest railway station: Fenchurch Street*

# The Cutty Sark Tavern

Ballast Quay, SE10. Tel: 0181 858 3146

Here's a period piece: The Union Tavern was built in 1804 and was a small working men's pub used by seafarers and riverboat men. It is now a listed building in the hands of licensee Sydney Haines. He changed the name in 1954 to welcome the last of the great tea clippers to her new home in Greenwich. The Cutty Sark Tavern is now a very amiable old dear, and the destination of many a riverbank walker. On warm days they'll sit on the river wall having a drink. If not they will be in the bar with its old beams and comfortable wooden furniture, or in the upstairs panelled room, where you can also eat.

*Open: 11.00–23.00 (Mon–Sat), 12.00–22.30 (Sun)*
*Food: 12.00–21.00 (Sun–Fri), 12.00–19.00 (Sat)*
*Credit cards: all major cards except AmEx*
*Draught beers: Bass, Caffrey's, five traditional cask ales changed on a regular basis, Carling Black Label, Carling Premier, Tennent's Extra, Staropramen, Guinness, Dry Blackthorn*
*Wheelchair access to venue*
*Nearest railway station: Maze Hill*

# Daly's Wine Bar

210 Strand, WC2. Tel: 0171 583 4476

The Royal Courts of Justice, where those learned judges have to decide on the most important legal issues in the land, is an extraordinarily austere experience for anyone involved. Television pictures are broadcast from the steps of the Courts so that the nation can share in the jubilation and disappointment of both sides. We've witnessed some remarkable scenes on these steps, and no doubt, off-camera, they repair to Daly's Wine Bar across the road to open a bottle or two. We're not talking draught beer, you understand; the fridge is stocked with a variety of fine wines and champagnes – Laurent Perrier (£34.50), Perrier Jouet (£32.50), Bollinger (£39.50) and Krug Grande Cuvée (£85). In the evenings it's still a legal hang out, being so close to all the chambers. This is presumably when the briefs try to lose their briefs to another brief. Considering this is a lawyers' den, there's an alarming number of anti-crime posters scattered around the place (Watch Out There Are Thieves About). But then again, if you consider what they charge, it almost makes you wonder!

*Open: 10.00–23.00 (Mon–Fri)*
*Food: coffee and Danish pastries 10.00–12.00 and 15.00–17.00; buffet and à la carte 12.00–14.30 (Mon–Fri)*
*Credit cards: all major cards*
*Wheelchair access to venue*
*Private room: 80 seated, 100–200 standing*
*Nearest tube station: Temple*

# Davys

Davys is a long-established shipper of wines but is probably better known today as a company operating a large chain of wine bars. The theme for the bars, if we have to specify one, is a modern version of Medieval England, and they've done a cracking job recreating the feel of an Olde English inn. Many of these places look as if they're hundreds of years old. They're not, of course, but you'll often find stone-flagged floors, old wooden-panelled walls, partitions, private booths, and nearly always, sawdust on the floor. They're not all fully licensed, but you can always get wines, and many serve bottled and draught lagers, and in some cases draught ales. (Beware the Old Wallop ale, it can hit quite hard!) The limited food includes curious plates of ham off the bone, half-chickens, fish and beef dishes. The hours vary slightly at each location so it's worth checking before you go, but Davys in EC postcodes open Monday–Friday only and close at either 8.30 or 9pm.

*Branches at:*

**Barbican**: Davys, 15–17 Long Lane, EC1. Tel: 0171 726 8858. Nearest tube station: Barbican

**Barking**: Spotted Dog/Colonel Jaspers, 15 Longbridge Road, IG11. Tel: 0181 507 7155. Nearest tube station: Barking

**Bayswater**: Gyngleboy, 27 Spring Street, W2. Tel: 0171 723 3351. Nearest tube station: Lancaster Gate

**Canary Wharf**: Davys, 31–35 Canary Wharf, E14. Tel: 0171 363 6633. Nearest railway station: Canary Wharf (DLR)

**City (E1)**: Grapeshots, 2–3 Artillery Passage, E1. Tel: 0171 247 8215. Nearest tube station: Liverpool Street

**City (E1)**: Vineyard, International House, 1 St Katharine's Way, E1. Tel: 0171 480 6680 and 0171 480 5088 (Coffee House). Nearest tube station: Tower Hill

**City (EC1)**: Bottlescrue, Bath House, 53–60 Holborn Viaduct, EC1. Tel: 0171 248 2157. Nearest tube station: Chancery Lane

**City (EC1)**: City Pipe, Foster Lane, off Cheapside, EC1. Tel: 0171 606 2110. Nearest tube station: St Paul's

**City (EC1)**: City Vaults, 2 St Martin's le Grand, EC1. Tel: 0171 606 8721. Nearest tube station: St Paul's

**City (EC1)**: Colonel Jaspers, 190 City Road, EC1. Tel: 0171 608 0925. Nearest tube station: Old Street

**City (EC2)**: Bangers, 12 Wilson Street, EC2. Tel: 0171 377 6326. Nearest tube station: Liverpool Street

**City (EC2)**: Bishop of Norwich, 91–93 Moorgate, EC2. Tel: 0171 920 0857 and 0171 588 2581 (Bishops Parlour). Nearest tube station: Moorgate

**City (EC2)**: City Boot, 7 Moorfields High Walk, EC2. Tel: 0171 588 4766. Nearest tube station: Moorgate

**City (EC2)**: Davys at Russia Row, Russia Court, Russia Row, EC2. Tel: 0171 600 2165 (Ale & Port House) and 0171 606 7252 (Wine Rooms). Nearest tube station: St Paul's

**City (EC2)**: Pulpit, 63 Worship Street, EC2. Tel: 0171 377 1574. Nearest tube station: Moorgate

**City (EC3)**: Bangers Too, 1 St Mary at Hill, EC3. Tel: 0171 283 4443. Nearest tube station: Monument

**City (EC3)**: City Flogger, Fenn Court, 120 Fenchurch Street, EC3. Tel: 0171 623 3251. Nearest tube station: Bank

**City (EC3)**: City FOB, below London Bridge, Lower Thames Street, EC3. Tel: 0171 621 0619. Nearest tube station: Monument

**City (EC3)**: Habit, 65 Crutched Friars, Friary Court, EC3. Tel: 0171 481 1131. Nearest tube station: Tower Hill

**City (EC4)**: Davys, 10 Creed Lane, EC4. Tel: 0171 236 5317. Nearest tube station: St Paul's

**City (EC4)**: Shotberries, 167 Queen Victoria Street, EC4. Tel: 0171 329 4759. Nearest tube station: Blackfriars

**City (SE1)**: Cooperage, 48–50 Tooley Street, SE1. Tel: 0171 403 5775. Nearest tube station: London Bridge

**City (SE1)**: Mug House, 1–3 Tooley Street, SE1. Tel: 0171 403 8343. Nearest tube station: London Bridge

**City (SE1)**: Skinkers, 42 Tooley Street, SE1. Tel: 0171 407 9189. Nearest tube station: London Bridge

**Covent Garden**: Champagne Charlies, 17 The Arches, Villiers Street, WC2. Tel: 0171 930 7737. Nearest tube station: Charing Cross

**Covent Garden**: Crusting Pipe (qv), 27 The Market, Covent Garden, WC2. Tel: 0171 836 1415. Nearest tube station: Covent Garden

**Covent Garden**: Tappit Hen, 5 William IV Street, WC2. Tel: 0171 836 9839. Nearest tube station: Charing Cross

**Croydon**: Wine Vaults, 122 North End, Croydon. Tel: 0181 680 2419. Nearest railway station: West Croydon

**Farringdon**: Burgundy Ben's, 102–108 Clerkenwell Road, EC1. Tel: 0171 251 3783. Nearest tube station: Farringdon

**Greenwich**: Davys Wine Vaults, 65 Greenwich High Road, SE10. Tel: 0181 858 7204. Nearest railway station: Greenwich

**Greenwich**: Davys Wine Vaults/Colonel Jaspers, 161 Greenwich High Road, SE10. Tel: 0181 853 0585. Nearest railway station: Greenwich

**Holborn**: Bung Hole, Hand Court, 57 High Holborn, WC1. Tel: 0171 831 8365 and 0171 242 4318 (Bung Hole Cellars). Nearest tube station: Holborn

**Holborn**: Truckles of Pied Bull Yard, Off Bury Place, WC1. Tel: 0171 404 5338. Nearest tube station: Holborn

**St James's**: Crown Passage Vaults, 20 King Street, St James, SW1. Tel: 0171 839 8831. Nearest tube station: Green Park

**St James's**: Tapster, 3 Brewers Court, Buckingham Gate, SW1. Tel: 0171 222 0561. Nearest tube station: St James's Park

**Southwark**: Boot and Flogger, 10–20 Redcross Way, SE1. Tel: 0171 407 1184. Nearest tube station: London Bridge

**West End**: Chiv, 90–92 Wigmore Street, W1. Tel: 0171 224 0170. Nearest tube station: Bond Street

**West End**: Chopper Lump, 10c Hanover Square, W1. Tel: 0171 499 7569. Nearest tube station: Oxford Circus

**West End**: Dock Blida, 50–54 Blandford Street, W1. Tel: 0171 486 3590. Nearest tube station: Baker Street

**West End**: Lees Bag, 4 Great Portland Street, W1. Tel: 0171 636 5287. Nearest tube station: Oxford Circus

## DCO

84–86 Rosebery Avenue, EC1. Tel: 0171 833 9144

The modern phenomenon of converting banks into eating and drinking emporia continues at DCO, which is located in a part of town that seems to have been described as up-and-coming for the past twenty or so years. The initials, I am told, stand for Dominion, Colonial and Overseas, but they could easily stand for Dreary, Cathartic and Overpriced. That may sound a little harsh, but paying a visit to DCO – which is half bar, half restaurant – is rather like going to see your bank manager. Save for a couple of partitions thrown up here and there, and the obvious inclusion of a bar, they have done little with the building since its banking days, and it strikes me that it wasn't that nice to start with. My heart always sinks when I find La Croix on the wine list, and here this is the only wine below £10. There is a good range of draught lagers but with cellars like DCO must have I would have expected a better range of real ales. They have other plans for the cellars, as I discovered chatting to the manager one evening. He told me they intend to convert the basement vaults into a private members' bar where they get to choose the members. Yawn!

*Open: 12.00–23.00 (Mon–Fri), 17.30–23.00 (Sat), 17.30–22.30 (Sun)*
*Food: 12.00–22.45 (Mon–Fri), as opening hours (Sat–Sun)*
*Credit cards: all major cards except AmEx*
*Draught beers: Boddingtons, Caffrey's, Carling Black Label, Grolsch, Hoegaarden, Staropramen, Stella Artois, Guinness*
*Wheelchair access to venue*
*Private room: 12 seated, 25 standing*
*Nearest tube stations: Angel, Farringdon*

## Deacons

Walbrook, EC4. Tel: 0171 248 1070

Obliquely opposite St Stephen Walbrook church is this modern bar neatly sandwiched between a car park and a Japanese restaurant. This is a good example of how City pubs cater for the young and those crazy for bar games. Loud music, computer games, gambling machines, more loud music and five pool tables attract large crowds in the evenings. If you stand outside – and many do – you can watch the commuters galloping down Walbrook towards Cannon Street at the end of the day. Don't stray to the other side of the wall, though – they don't like it if you do that.

*Open: upstairs 11.00–22.00 (Mon–Wed), 11.00–23.00 (Thurs–Fri); downstairs sports bar 11.00–22.00 (Mon–Wed), 11.00–23.00 (Thurs), 11.00–midnight (Fri)*
*Food: 11.00–21.00 (Mon–Fri)*
*Credit cards: all major cards*
*Draught beers: Caffrey's, London Ale, Carling Black Label, Grolsch, Staropramen, Guinness, Red Rock*
*Wheelchair access to venue*
*Two private rooms: 20 seated, 200 standing; no seating, 150 standing*
*Nearest tube stations: Cannon Street, Bank*

## De Hems

11 Macclesfield Street, W1. Tel: 0171 437 2494

De Hems claims to be London's only Dutch pub, and very few people doubt that. It looks Dutch. See its gable. It behaves Dutch. *Proost.* It's Dutch, all right – they even serve mayonnaise with the chips. De Hems used to be called The Macclesfield – you find it in Macclesfield Street adjacent to the arched entrance to Chinatown. It is named after a Dutch sailor called de Hems, who took it over in the 1920s, so it's Dutch plates, Dutch photographs and Dutch old masters. *'Oranjeboom Gezondheid'* declares the mirror behind the bar, a friendly greeting apparently. It is a very friendly pub, this one. The noise level rises as the evening goes on, and the evening goes on until midnight, courtesy of a music licence. The ceiling is a subtle shade of nicotine, though the ceiling fans do their best, and in the summer the doors fold right back, opening the whole bar to the air and other delights of Macclesfield Street. They call the upstairs bar 't'Oude Trefpunt', or the old meeting place, and on the first Thursday of every month many Dutch people living in London meet there. Wednesdays is the comedy club.

*Open: 11.00–midnight (Mon–Sat), 12.00–22.30 (Sun)*
*Food: 12.00–22.30 (Daily)*
*Credit cards: all major cards*
*Draught beers: Calder's Cream Ale, Leffe, Pedigree, Tetley, Dry Blackthorn*
*Wheelchair access to venue*
*Private room: 100 standing*
*Nearest tube stations: Piccadilly Circus, Leicester Square*

## Desperados Bourbon Bar

127 Clapham High Street, SW4. Tel: 0171 622 3636

With a name like this, it would be almost criminal not to include this establishment in the Guide. The style is unashamedly American kitsch, with various Hollywood mementos on the wall, and, as if one wasn't enough, five star-spangled banners hanging around. It's new, it's early days, and the owners Colin Cole and John Gardner are making a go of it. They've resisted Tex-Mex predictability in their choice of menu and opted for gumbo, snapper and New York Sub sandwiches. Bottled beers are very reasonably priced at £2, and cocktails between £3 and £4.50. The cocktails man is Mario, freshly imported from Portugal to do his shaking and stirring, and he's wasted no time in putting together a rather long list.

*Open: 11.00–23.00 (Mon–Sat), 12.00–22.30 (Sun)*
*Food: 12.00–22.00 (Mon–Sun)*
*Credit cards: none taken*
*Draught beers: Heineken*
*Wheelchair access to venue*
*Nearest tube station: Clapham Common*

# The Devereux

Devereux Mews, WC2. Tel: 0171 583 4562

In between The Strand and Middle Temple is this elegant public house where lawyers gather to tipple over their briefs. There is a rather smart restaurant upstairs serving fish and chips (£6.95), rump steak (£9.95), and a range of chicken, pasta and vegetarian dishes. The pub was built in 1844 and is looking smarter than ever after its recent refit.

*Open: 11.00–23.00 (Mon–Fri)*
*Food: 12.00–15.00 (Mon–Fri)*
*Credit cards: all major cards*
*Draught beers: Courage Directors, John Smith's Extra Smooth, Theakston Best, Theakston Old Peculier, Theakston XB, Foster's, Holsten, Kronenbourg, Guinness, Beamish, Strongbow*
*Wheelchair access to venue*
*Two private rooms: 25–55 seated, 100 standing*
*Nearest tube station: Temple*

# The Dickens Inn

St Katharine's Way, E1. Tel: 0171 488 1226

St Katharine's Dock is a bustling part of London which draws the tourists to its pleasant yacht-occupied waters, shopping areas and bars. The old warehouse that is now The Dickens Inn has five separate bars and restaurants and a staff of 55, and it won a major battle to let its customers drink outside. Here is a rare victory for the good guys, so a hat or two in the air please for two terraces full of tables and the tables full of people whenever the sun shines.

*Open: 11.00–23.00 (Mon–Sat), 12.00–22.30 (Sun)*
*Food: bar 11.30–17.00 (Mon–Fri), 11.30–16.00 (Sat), 12.00–17.00 (Sun); restaurant 11.30–17.00 (Mon–Fri), 11.30–16.00 (Sat), 12.00–17.00 (Sun)*
*Credit cards: all major cards*
*Draught beers: Courage Best, Courage Directors, Websters, Wadworth 6X, John Smith's Extra Smooth, Carlsberg, Foster's, Kronenbourg, Budweiser, Guinness, Beamish, Dry Blackthorn*
*Wheelchair access to venue*
*Private room seats 110*
*Nearest tube station: Tower Hill*

# T. E. Dingwalls

11 Camden Lock Place, NW1. Tel: 0171 267 0545

Camden Lock is one of the biggest markets in Europe. On a summer's day it can get a quarter of a million visitors, and it sometimes seems that they are all trying to get a drink in T. E. Dingwalls. It is a light, high, roomy pub, with bare boards, bare brick, open rafters and stairs from the bar to a mezzanine. There are seven real ales on the hand pumps, plus Tex-Mex food and a sensational terrace with wooden decking and parades of tables and benches. When the sun comes out the new T. E. Dingwalls is a magnet, with customers packing the terrace, the bank of the canal and the pub itself. One day in May 1994, it made history. It became the first pub in Britain to get an all-day Sunday licence. It can hardly wait to get the extra hour on Fridays and Saturdays.

*Open: 11.00–23.00 (Mon–Sat), 12.00–22.30 (Sun)*
*Food: 12.00–15.00 (Mon–Fri), 12.00–16.00 (Sat–Sun)*
*Credit cards: Mastercard, Visa*
*Draught beers: Abbot Ale, Boddingtons, Brakspear, Caffrey's, Ted's Tipple, Carling Premier, Foster's, Kronenbourg, Stella Artois, Guinness, Dry Blackthorn*
*Wheelchair access to venue*
*Private room seats 500*
*Nearest tube station: Camden Town*

# Dirty Dick's

202 Bishopsgate, EC2. Tel: 0171 283 5888

The story goes that the bride-to-be of an 18th-century merchant, Nathaniel Bentley, died on their wedding day and, rather put out, Bentley locked the room in which the wedding breakfast was set, swearing it would never be re-opened. After that he neither changed his clothes nor washed. 'If you wash today,' he would say reasonably, 'you just have to wash again tomorrow.' He became quite a celebrity. People flocked to his hardware shop in Leadenhall Street, which daily grew dirtier, and when his landlord eventually got him out, Ye Olde Port Wine House in Bishopsgate bought the entire contents, rotting wedding breakfast, dead cats and all, and displayed them in its cellar bar. Ye Olde Port Wine House became Dirty Dick's. The artefacts stayed until the mid-1980s when they simply had to get rid of them. Dirty Dick's is owned by Young's now but it remains a very successful pub. The main bar with its wooden floor, old beams and copper counter is crowded and notably cheerful; the first floor restaurant, now called Hobson's, has been enlarged and done over, and the candle-lit Dive bar seems roomier since the clean-up and frankly a great deal more congenial. There's a photograph of it as it was. You will recognise the beams, the settles and the old wooden benches. If you miss the dead cats, look in the glass case at the bottom of the stairs.

*Open: main bar: 11.00–23.00 (Mon–Fri), 12.00–15.00 (Sat)*
*Hobsons Bar/Dive Bar 12.00–21.00 (Mon–Fri)*
*Food: 12.00–14.30 (Mon–Fri)*
*Credit cards: all major cards*
*Draught beers: Young's Bitter, Young's London, Young's Premium, Young's Special, Castlemaine, Grolsch, Guinness, Scrumpy Jack*
*Wheelchair access to venue*
*Private rooms: 90–150 seated, 40–100 standing*
*Nearest tube station: Liverpool Street*

# Dixie's

25 Battersea Rise, SW11. Tel: 0171 228 7984

American style Tex-Mex diner with an extraordinarily relaxed attitude. This is a casual drinking and dining experience with bottled beers from £1.85 and house wines from £6.95.

*Open: 12.00–23.00 (Mon–Fri), 10.00–23.00 (Sat), 10.00–22.30 (Sun)*
*Food: as opening hours*
*Credit cards: all major cards*
*Wheelchair access to venue and loo*
*Private room: 150 seated, 200 standing*
*Nearest tube station: Clapham South*
*Nearest railway station: Clapham Junction*

# Dog & Duck

18 Bateman Street, W1. Tel: 0171 437 4447

Tiny bar on the corner of Bateman Street and Frith Street that was Soho's Pub of the Year in 1991 and 1992. The Dog & Duck is still going strong and has a fine reputation for real ales. It is very friendly, principally because it's so small you get to know people intimately just by squeezing past.

*Open: 11.00–23.00 (Mon–Fri), 18.00–23.00 (Sat), 19.00–22.30 (Sun)*
*Credit cards: None taken*
*Draught beers: Landlord, Tetley's, two guest ales, Carlsberg Export, Castlemaine, Lowenbrau*
*Wheelchair access to venue*
*Private room seats 35*
*Nearest tube stations: Piccadilly Circus, Tottenham Court Road*

# The Dog and Fox

224 Wimbledon High Street, SW19. Tel: 0181 946 6565

The Dog and Fox occupies an enormous site, dominating its bit of the High Street with an impressive display of turrets, decorated gables and pillared porticoes. It is a very youthful pub these days, totally refurbished in the modern Victorian style that Young's and its customers like so much.

*Open: 11.00–23.00 (Mon–Sat), 12.00–22.30 (Sun)*
*Food: 12.00–15.00 and 19.00–22.00 (Mon–Thurs), 12.00–15.00 (Fri–Sat), 12.00–15.00 and 19.00–22.00 (Sun)*
*Credit cards: all major cards*
*Draught beers: Young's Bitter, Young's London Lager, Young's Premium Lager, Young's Ramrod Smooth, Young's Special, Castlemaine, Guinness, Scrumpy Jack*
*Wheelchair access to venue*
*Private room seats 160*
*Nearest tube station: Wimbledon*

# Dog House

187 Wardour Street, W1. Tel: 0171 434 2116

The tendency to party is somewhat at odds with the atmosphere of this cramped, air-conditioned, exuberantly colourful basement bar on the upper reaches of Wardour Street. The service is rugby-club style, so don't expect a lot. The staff profess to make decent cocktails while serving up an average range of bottled beers – no draught. The Dog House is independently owned and operated by Noel Cardew, who enforces a strict policy requiring men to remove their ties. I am told that ties intimidate people wearing skateboarding gear and the like. Get the picture?

*Open: 17.30–23.00 (Mon–Fri), 18.00–23.00 (Sat)*
*Credit cards: all major cards except AmEx*
*Nearest tube station: Tottenham Court Road*

# The Dog Star

389 Coldharbour Lane, SW9. Tel: 0171 733 7515

The Dog Star has a much-reported history under its former name, The Atlantic, when it was the scene of riots, and known as a drug venue. Once upon a time it was notorious for refusing to serve West Indian customers. The name was changed, and its past was almost behind it, when another riot disturbed the renaissance. Undeterred, The Dog Star battled on. It is now packed with musically hip youngsters, who adore the scrum of the crowds, the loud music from the serious sound system, and the pre-clubbing atmosphere. There are also plans for a conservatory, a covered beer garden and a gallery and new bar in the upper levels of the pub. Some say The Dog Star is a bit rough, but it still manages to attract a mean following.

*Open: 12.00–01.00 (Mon–Thurs), 12.00–03.00 (Fri–Sat), 12.00–midnight (Sun)*
*Food: 12.00–15.00 and 19.00–22.00 (Mon–Thurs), 12.00–15.00 and 18.00–22.00 (Fri–Sat), 12.00–18.00 (Sun)*
*Credit cards: all major cards*
*Draught beers: Kilkenny, Tetley, Carlsberg Export, Carlsberg Pilsner, Lowenbrau, Guinness, Scrumpy Jack*
*Wheelchair access to venue and loo*
*Private room seats 200*
*Nearest tube station: Brixton*

# Dome

354 King's Road, SW3. Tel: 0171 352 2828

Domes first appeared on our streets in 1983 when the theme team of Roger Myers and Karen Jones formed a joint venture with brewers Courage to transform old pub sites into something a little more innovative, mimicking the traditional Paris café society. So the Bird in Hand in Hampstead became the very first Dome, to be followed by this branch in Chelsea at the junction of the King's Road and Beaufort Street. Domes make up a part of the Pelican Group (with Café Rouge and Oriel), which was sold to Whitbread in 1996 but is still run autonomously with Ms Jones at the helm. They've tinkered with the brand over the years, improving the style, image, decor, food and drink. The Chelsea Dome is as popular as ever, and I've made many visits in the course of the past year. The important thing is you can just go for drinks, and in Chelsea many people do. The atmosphere is quite relaxed during the day (this is a good place for celebrity spotting); in the evenings the Dome goes into overdrive as the crowds pack in, filling the tables and the small conservatory at the back. During the summer months the wood and glass walls fold away in traditional Paris fashion, so the buzz from inside makes it quite difficult to walk past. The Prix Fix three-course menu of £4.99 is extraordinarily good value, and the salads, snacks and sandwiches from the main menu are also reasonably priced. The relaxed atmosphere tends to be taken a bit too seriously by the waiting staff, who are excruciatingly slow, so it's probably not a place to visit for a quick fix.

*Branches at:*

**Camden**: 18 Chalk Farm Road, NW1. Tel: 0171 428 0998. Nearest tube station: Camden Town

**City**: 57–59 Charterhouse Street, EC1. Tel: 0171 336 6484. Nearest tube station: Farringdon

**Covent Garden**: 32 Long Acre, WC2. Tel: 0171 379 8650. Nearest tube station: Covent Garden

**Earls Court**: 194–196 Earls Court Road, SW5. Tel: 0171 835 2200. Nearest tube station: Earls Court

**Hampstead**: 58–62 Heath Street, NW3. Tel: 0171 431 0399. Nearest tube station: Hampstead

**Islington**: 341 Upper Street, N1. Tel: 0171 226 3414. Nearest tube station: Angel

**Kensington**: Kensington Court, 35a Kensington High Street, W8. Tel: 0171 937 6655. Nearest tube station: High Street Kensington

**Oxford Street**: Selfridges, 400 Oxford Street, W1. Tel: 0171 318 3937. Nearest tube station: Bond Street

**Richmond**: 26 Hill Street, Richmond, TW9. Tel: 0181 332 2525. Nearest tube station: Richmond

**Soho**: 57–59 Old Compton Street, W1. Tel: 0171 287 0770. Nearest tube station: Tottenham Court Road

**West End**: 8–10 Charing Cross Road, WC2. Tel: 0171 240 5556. Nearest tube station: Leicester Square

**Wimbledon**: 91 High Street, Wimbledon Village, SW19. Tel: 0181 947 9559. Nearest tube station: Wimbledon

# The Dove

19 Upper Mall, W6. Tel: 0181 748 5405

The Dove comes to life on those lazy, sunny summer afternoons when people seem to gather from all over London to sit on the verandah and watch the Thames flow by. As you step inside from the narrow alleyway, look quickly to the right, or you could miss what is in the *Guinness Book of Records* as the smallest bar in the UK (it accommodates about four medium-sized drinkers). Next is a low-ceilinged, oak-beamed saloon bar with cushioned wall settles and copper-topped tables. This is popular in the winter when the fire is on. Up a few more steps are rooms serving food, where the microwave oven labours to keep up with the demand. Past these rooms is the terrace overlooking the river. This is a pub for the summertime.

*Open: 11.00–23.00 (Mon–Sat), 12.00–22.30 (Sun)*
*Food: 12.00–15.00 and 18.00–22.30 (Mon–Sat), 12.00–22.30 (Sun).*
*Credit cards: Visa, Mastercard, Switch*
*Draught beers: ESB, London Pride, Grolsch, Heineken, Guinness, Murphy's, Strongbow*
*Nearest tube station: Hammersmith*

## Dover Street Wine Bar

8–9 Dover Street, W1. Tel: 0171 405 1466

A long-established jazz venue renowned for attracting some of the biggest names in jazz, the Dover Street Wine Bar is still enormously busy and seems to be popular with office parties, who dine in the evenings. Essentially you can go for drinks, although you have to be pretty insistent: doormen make phone calls to the girls at the bottom of the stairs, and after much discussion you might be allowed in. When you get downstairs you get much the same interrogation before being escorted all of the three-foot journey to the tiny bar area. Admission, you will have gathered, is at the discretion of the door (and includes no denims). It's worth the effort. The bar really comes to life later in the evening, and remains one of the best jazz venues in London.

*Cover charges: Monday free before 22.00 then £4, Tuesday free before 22.00 then £5, Wednesday free before 22.00 then £6, Thursday free before 22.00 then £7, Fri–Sat £3 before 22.00 then £10.*

*Open: 12.00–15.00 and 17.30–03.00 (Mon–Thurs), 10.00–15.00 and 20.00–03.00 (Fri–Sat)*
*Food: as opening hours*
*Credit cards: all major cards*
*Nearest tube station: Green Park*

## Drayton Arms

153 Old Brompton Road, SW5. Tel: 0171 373 0385

A grand example of high Victoriana, all buff terracotta and purple brick. The interior is almost as grand as the exterior, with beautiful Art Nouveau lanterns and a wonderful mahogany bar with wrought-iron flourishes and marble columns. The Drayton Arms is a listed building now but it still likes to let its hair down, and at 9pm every Friday and Saturday it becomes a lively venue for folk, jazz and assorted entertainers.

*Open: 11.00–23.00 (Mon–Sat), 12.00–22.30 (Sun)*
*Food: bar 11.00–15.00 and 18.00–20.30 (Mon–Sat), 12.00–17.00 (Sun)*
*Credit cards: all major cards except AmEx*
*Draught beers: Bass, Hancock's Welsh Bitter, Carling Black Label, Staropramen, Guinness, Dry Blackthorn*
*Wheelchair access to venue*
*Nearest tube stations: Gloucester Road, South Kensington*

## The Dublin Castle

94 Parkway, NW1. Tel: 0171 485 1773

This little Victorian local in Camden Town has long been established as an influential venue on the pub circuit. The front bar is invariably packed, though when you reach the small music room at the back you may well find a young band playing to just a handful of friends. It is not always the case, however. This was, after all, where Madness got their first break, and there have been some very special times recently. The night Blur played here is fully documented in a framed tabloid story behind the bar. It is rap, ska, R & B and every customer a critic at The Dublin Castle nowadays.

*Open: 11.30–midnight (Mon–Sun)*
*Credit cards: none taken*
*Draught beers: John Smith's Extra Smooth, Websters, Budweiser, Carlsberg, Foster's, Holsten, Guinness, Strongbow*
*Wheelchair access to venue*
*Nearest tube station: Camden Town*

## Duke of Cambridge   EROS AWARD WINNER

228 Battersea Bridge Road, SW11. Tel: 0171 223 5662

Something rather special has been happening down Battersea way. The Duke of Cambridge has been taken over by those smart pub operators who also have The Chelsea Ram and The Queens on Regent's Park Road (qqv). Nick Elliot and Joanna Clevely took on this Young's pub and managed to carry out a full refurbishment while hardly closing at all. The new Duke of Cambridge opened in August 1997, and I managed to make only a few sneak visits before this Guide went to press, but what I found was a delightful pub. Two giant parasols cover the terrace at the front, from where you walk into a splendid room with plenty of space, newly varnished woodwork, large old tables, antique mirrors and cream painted walls. It's Young's beers, of course, which is no bad thing, and they've put together a carefully selected range of 26 bottled wines with four reds and whites by the glass. The good news on the food front is that they've brought with them the excellent chef Dan Brinklow from The Chelsea Ram. His tried-and-tested formula for producing simple and imaginative dishes means you should get restaurant-quality food at pub prices. Blinis, Welsh rarebit and club sandwiches are on the light-meals menu at £3.95. Main courses change fairly regularly but might include a char-grilled Angus rib-eye (£8.95), blackened chicken leg with rösti and rocket salad (£5.95), or pork, apple and sage cake with garlic mash and charred leeks (£5.95).

*Open: 11.00–23.00 (Mon–Sat), 12.00–22.30 (Sun)*
*Food: 12.00–14.30 and 19.00–21.45 (Mon–Sat), 12.00–14.45 and 19.00–21.30 (Sun)*
*Credit cards: all major cards except AmEx*
*Draught beers: Young's, Pilsner Export, Stella Artois, Castlemaine, Guinness, Strongbow*
*Wheelchair access to venue*
*Private room: 40 seated, 60 standing (from February 1998)*
*Nearest railway station: Clapham Junction*

## Duke of Cumberland

235 New King's Road, SW6. Tel: 0171 736 2777

This is a big, swanky, four-storey pub looking across New King's Road to Parson's Green. It has balusters, arched windows and soaring chimneys, and is superbly fitted inside. The cost of such a display of mahogany, engraved glass and so on was well spent. The pub was The Duke's Head until a thorough renovation in 1971 when it became The Duke of Cumberland and won the *Evening Standard* Pub of the Year competition. The public bar at the back has now been merged with the great saloon bar at the front, leaving the entire pub as one huge open-plan room. There is a substantial television in a cupboard over the front entrance, but a sporting event has to be very important for the cupboard doors to open. The Duke of Cumberland is a fine upstanding public house, proud of the character and achievements of the man whose name it now bears. A large board, prominently displayed in the saloon bar, recalls that he murdered his valet, committed adultery, sodomy and incest, blackmailed his brother, indecently assaulted the wife of the Lord Chamberlain and plotted the assassination of his niece, the future Queen Victoria. A man, in short, of broad and varied interests, most suited to the role of King of Hanover, which is what he became.

*Open: 11.00–23.00 (Mon–Sat), 12.00–22.30 (Sun)*
*Food: 12.00–15.00 and 19.00–22.30 (Mon–Sun)*
*Credit cards: none taken*
*Draught beers: All Young's bitters, Castlemaine, Grolsch, London Lager, Premium Lager, Beamish, Guinness, Oatmeal Stout, Dry Blackthorn*
*Wheelchair access to venue*
*Nearest tube station: Parsons Green*

## The Duke of Devonshire

39 Balham High Road, SW12. Tel: 0181 673 1363

This is a Victorian pub of gigantic proportions, complete with gilded mirrors, wooden panelling and high ceilings. The refurbishment teams have done a good job in maintaining the place without diminishing its sense of grandeur. Pizza, curiously, seems to be the favoured food, and is available until late in the evening. A room at the back was turned into a jazz bar last year, and they have live music every night of the week. Membership is not required, but as access is from the pub, you'll need to be in before 11pm when the main pub closes down.

*Open: 11.00–midnight (Sun–Thurs), 11.00–02.00 (Fri–Sat)*
*Food: bar 11.00–22.30 (Mon–Sat), 11.00–22.00 (Sun); jazz bar 11.00–23.30 (Sun–Thurs), 11.00–01.00 (Fri–Sat)*
*Credit cards: Delta, Mastercard, Switch, Visa*
*Draught beers: London Lager, Young's Bitter, Young's Oatmeal, Young's Premium Lager, Young's Special, Dry Blackthorn*
*Wheelchair access to venue*
*Nearest tube stations: Balham, Clapham South*

## The Duke of Edinburgh

299 Green Street, E13. Tel: 0181 472 2546

When West Ham are playing at home, this is where the action is. The Hammers Bar with its football memorabilia and pool tables pulls them in. They fill the main bar, too, and the yard at the back. Then they all go off to the match and come back again afterwards. They have a big screen for the away games. The fans like that.

*Open: 11.00–23.00 (Mon–Sat), 12.00–22.30 (Sun)*
*Food: 12.00–15.00 and 18.00–20.00 (Mon–Sun)*
*Credit cards: none taken*
*Draught beers: Caffrey's, Toby, Worthington Best, Carling Black Label, Carling Premier, Tennent's Pilsner, Guinness, Dry Blackthorn*
*Wheelchair access to venue and loo*
*Nearest tube station: Upton Park*

## The Eagle

159 Farringdon Road, EC1. Tel: 0171 837 1353

The Eagle is basically a robust local boozer. When Michael Belben and David Eyre took it over, they made half the bar counter an open kitchen and started cooking the kind of things people have on their hols. Fay Maschler put it in her *Evening Standard* London Restaurant Guide, Egon Ronay gave it a star, and Carlton Television voted it the Best Pub Restaurant of 1997. They must be doing something right. You see and smell what is being cooked, order your food from the bar and have a drink at your table. There are Italian sausages sizzling on the grill, crostini, fresh tuna, grilled squid and delicious pasta dishes. Nothing takes more than ten minutes. They also do good cask beers and get through a lot of wine. In the afternoon, when The Eagle empties, you can see what a nice old pub it is.

*Open: 12.00–23.00 (Mon–Sat)*
*Food: 12.30–14.30 and 18.30–22.30 (Mon–Fri), 12.30–15.30 and 18.30–22.30 (Sat)*
*Credit cards: none taken*
*Draught beers: Boddingtons Bitter, Marston's Pedigree, Wadworth 6X, Heineken, Hoegaarden, Stella Artois, Gambrinus, Guinness*
*Wheelchair access to venue*
*Nearest tube station: Farringdon*

## The Eagle Tavern

2 Shepherdess Walk, N1. Tel: 0171 253 4715

The words of the song that still makes this pub a household name are high on the side wall so that all who turn into Shepherdess Walk from the City Road can read them:

> *Up and down the City Road*
> *In and out the Eagle*
> *That's the way the money goes*
> *Pop goes the weasel!*

The Eagle of the song was actually the Royal Eagle Music Hall, which stood on this site. It had pleasure grounds with fountains, gas devices, illuminations, cosmoramas, magic mirrors and the famous Grecian Saloon, and became so notorious that General Booth of the Salvation Army took it over to close it down. The whole lot was demolished in 1901, and this pub went up instead. It is looking very well just now, with its confident Edwardian frontage all spruced up, and the handsome eagle on the cupola brightly gilded. There is also a big saloon bar with a new horseshoe-shaped bar and pictures of music-hall stars, plus a public bar with bar billiards and TV sport, and a big beer garden at the back. You have to get there early at lunchtimes in the summer or you don't get a table. The Eagle is part of local life, of course, but there is always the Pop Goes the Weasel bonus. It brings in the most unexpected people. The Brits know all the words. We learnt this song about pawning our tailor's iron or whatever at our mother's knee. Weird, really. It doesn't even rhyme.

> *Half a pound of twopenny rice*
> *Half a pound of treacle*
> *That's the way the money goes*
> *Pop goes the weasel!*

*Open: 11.00–23.00 (Mon–Fri), 12.00–17.00 (Sat)*
*Food: 12.00–15.00 and 18.00–21.00 (Mon–Fri), 12.00–16.00 (Sun)*
*Credit cards: Mastercard, Switch, Visa*
*Draught beers: Bass, Caffrey's, nine guest ales, Carling Black Label, Carling Premier, Grolsch, Guinness, Red Rock*
*Nearest tube station: Old Street*

## Eclipse

157 Balham High Road, SW17. Tel: 0181 772 0082

Eclipse is a large venue split on three levels, each with its own bar and atmosphere. For an artistic ambience, head straight for the pink-upholstered upstairs bar, where the music is also louder but not to the point where miming is necessary in order to communicate. The venue is clean and comfortable throughout, with room for around 300 people. The clientele is mostly young locals.

*Open: 11.00–23.00 (Mon–Sat), 12.00–22.30 (Sun)*
*Food: 11.00–21.00 (Mon–Fri), 11.00–20.00 (Sat–Sun)*
*Credit cards: all major cards*
*Draught beers: Bass, Hancocks HB, IPA, one guest ale, five traditional ales, Carling Premier, Foster's, Stella Artois, Guinness, Blackthorn*
*Wheelchair access to venue and loo*
*Private room: 100 standing*
*Nearest tube station: Balham*

## The Edgar Wallace

40 Essex Street, WC2. Tel: 0171 353 3120

In 1975 The Essex Arms, a small pub in a little street off Fleet Street, was renovated and given a new name. Whitbread decreed that to mark the 100th anniversary of the birth of the writer Edgar Wallace it would henceforth be called The Edgar Wallace. The great man's daughter Penny Wallace loaned the pub a collection of photographs, letters, newspaper cuttings, playbills and other memorabilia. The Edgar Wallace Society, whose members include Miss Wallace, meet in the first-floor restaurant every year.

*Open: 11.00–23.00 (Mon–Fri)*
*Food: 12.00–15.00 (Mon–Fri)*
*Credit cards: all major cards*
*Draught beers: Boddingtons, Flower's, up to 12 cask ales which change on a regular basis, Heineken, Hoegaarden, Stella Artois, Murphy's, Scrumpy Jack*
*Wheelchair access to venue*
*Private room: 28 seated, 50 standing*
*Nearest tube station: Temple*

## The Edge

11 Soho Square, W1. Tel: 0171 439 1313

On the north side of Soho Square you will find this four-storey former office building, three of the floors now used as one of Soho's many gay bars. Every floor has its own bar – the ground floor is geared towards coffees and the like during the day, the first floor has a bigger seating area, and the top floor has its own dance floor. The prices aren't cheap, and bottled beers were warm when I was last there.

*Open: 12.00–01.00 (Mon–Sat), 14.00–22.30 (Sun)*
*Credit cards: all major cards except AmEx*
*Private room: 50 standing*
*Nearest tube station: Tottenham Court Road*

## Edward's

40 Hammersmith Broadway, W6. Tel: 0181 748 1043

Arriving by public transport at Hammersmith these days will bring you into the all-new, 700-years-in-the-construction Broadway Centre. If you take the King Street exit, the first sight to greet you is Edward's, one of Bass's latest generation of quality bars with something going on all day. Edward's opens for breakfast at 8am, moves into morning coffees at 10am and on to lunch at 12pm. Then there's afternoon tea and a loud bang in the evening when the disco gets going. The beautiful function room upstairs with its cream walls and lovely windows has a new role, too, and its own name. It is now Upstairs at Edward's, hosting themed evenings with jazz, comedy and blues. Edward's occupies a splendid Victorian building, and Bass have taken good care of it in the £500,000 restoration. It used to be called The Swan, and the swan still sways gently in the breeze on the inn sign outside.

*Open: 08.00–23.00 (Mon–Fri), 10.00–23.00 (Sat), 11.00–22.30 (Sun)*
*Food: 08.00–20.00 (Mon–Fri), 10.00–20.00 (Sat), 11.00–20.00 (Sun)*

*Credit cards: all major cards*
*Draught beers: Bass, Caffrey's, London Pride, Carling Black Label, Carling Premier, Grolsch, Staropramen, Guinness, Cidermaster*
*Wheelchair access to venue*
*Private room seats 60*
*Nearest tube station: Hammersmith*

Branches at:

**Camden**: 1 Camden High Street, NW1. Tel: 0171 387 2749. Nearest tube station: Camden Town

**Ealing**: 28–30 New Broadway, W5. Tel: 0181 567 9438. Nearest tube station: Ealing Broadway

**Shepherd's Bush**: 170 Uxbridge Road, W12. Tel: 0181 743 3010. Nearest tube station: Shepherd's Bush

## Elbow Room

103 Westbourne Grove, W2. Tel: 0171 221 5211

Fancy a game of pool? There's plenty of elbow room in here, with seven pool tables to play on. It's well designed, decently laid out and serves brilliant burgers from an open kitchen. You hire the pool table by the hour. It's £6 before 7pm on weekdays then £9 per hour later on. At weekends it's £6 before 5pm, then £9. You turn up, they write your name on a board and call you when it's your turn. Waiting around is a pleasurable experience – there's a restaurant/bar area at the front and away from the tables. Draught beers are £2 a pint and bottles are £2.30. There's no better way to while away an afternoon or evening. Perfect!

*Open: 12.00–23.00 (Mon–Sat) 12.00–22.30 (Sun)*
*Food: 12.00–22.30 (Mon–Sat), 12.00–22.00 (Sun)*
*Credit cards: all major cards*
*Draught beers: Boddingtons, Heineken, Hoegaarden, Stella Artois, Guinness*
*Wheelchair access to venue*
*Nearest tube station: Bayswater*

## Elephant & Castle

40 Holland Street, W8. Tel: 0171 937 0316

There is an Elephant and Castle in the Elephant and Castle, and an Elephant and Castle in Kensington. Quiz masters like to ask where this name came from, and the common answer is it had something to do with the Infanta of Castile, but the Brits of the day got it wrong. There is another theory that it comes from the sign of the Cutlers' Company, and this is probably the true origin. But who cares? This is a perfectly agreeable pub, which has been run by Greg and Yvonne Porter for the past five years. Since their arrival the pub has won a clutch of awards for its floral displays, including the London in Bloom award for the best public house in 1994. It will doubtless win again, as Greg continues to apply the daily TLC to his pride and joy. While he's pottering away outside, Yvonne takes control of the kitchen and serves above-average pub grub most of the day. The Elephant and Castle is a quiet little pub, with conversation being the music to listen to. You might have to squeeze past people standing at the side of the bar, but that can be fun in an intimate way.

*Open: 11.00–23.00 (Mon–Sat), 12.00–22.30 (Sun)*
*Food: 11.00–21.00 (Mon–Fri), 12.00–19.30 (Sat), 12.00–18.00 (Sun)*
*Credit cards: all major cards except AmEx*
*Draught beers: Bass, Caffrey's, London Pride, Carling Black Label, Grolsch, Staropramen, Guinness, Dry Blackthorn*
*Nearest tube station: High Street Kensington*

# The Elephant and Castle

Newington Causeway, SE1. Tel: 0171 357 9134

The original Elephant and Castle was an 18th-century tavern which had the sense to pick a site where five major roads met. Then it became a stop on the Northern Line and the south London terminus of the Bakerloo, *and* got a place on the Monopoly board – and you can't get more famous than that. The planners promised to replace the old pub when they redeveloped the area after the war, and in the early sixties the work began – a vast new traffic system, a gargantuan shopping centre, and Alexander Fleming House, a huge office complex designed by the internationally famous architect Erno Goldfinger. The new pub had not been forgotten. When the redevelopment was completed, Alexander Fleming House appeared to have pupped. A smaller version stood in the lee of the big one, and a peculiarly uninteresting public house occupied the ground floor. It was called, of course, The Elephant and Castle. These days, Goldfinger's building stands empty, its unhappy occupant, the Department of the Environment, having fled. Is this, then, the end for Erno Goldfinger's only pub? Well, no. The Goldfinger camp seems to have carried the day. The building has been sold to developers, who are about to turn it into 420 flats. This means that the pub will survive, and more than survive. It will surely get a thorough facelift. It may even find some admirers. Meanwhile it soldiers on. The pool table is in daily use, and so too is the juke box.

Something very unexpected has happened to the view from The Elephant and Castle. The children's television programme *Blue Peter* invited its viewers to suggest improvements to their local environment. As a result, the nearby electricity substation is now floodlit, the colours changing as they wash over it. You can see it all from the pub.

*Open: 11.00–23.00 (Mon–Sat), 12.00–22.30 (Sun)*
*Food: 12.00–15.00 (Sun)*
*Credit cards: none taken*
*Draught beers: John Smith's Extra Smooth, Ruddle's Best, Ruddle's County, Carlsberg, Foster's, Holsten, Kronenbourg, Guinness, Scrumpy Jack, Strongbow*
*Wheelchair access to venue*
*Nearest tube station: Elephant and Castle*

# The Engineer

65 Gloucester Avenue, NW1. Tel: 0171 722 0950

An unexpected chapter in the life of actress Tamsin Olivier started in the summer of 1994. Tamsin – daughter of Lord Olivier and Joan Plowright – and the artist Abigail Osborne were thinking of opening a restaurant. They looked at Primrose Hill and came across the rather run-down Engineer.

Tamsin and Abigail loved the building, bought the lease and set about doing it up. They didn't hang about, and in five and a half weeks it was looking splendid. The saloon bar gleamed, restaurant tables lined the old public bar and filled the one-time snug, and there was an entirely new kitchen. Tamsin postponed her wedding, and people were beating a popular path to the door. The food, distinctly classy and not cheap, is a big draw at The Engineer. If you want a table in the restaurant, it is best to book, particularly in the evening. You can eat in the bar if you like, though it does get very crowded, and in the summer there's a big garden. Tamsin and Abigail are both in the thick of it, taking orders, serving, doing their stuff. The locals love it, and hope that the only boards Miss Olivier will tread in future are those on the floor of The Engineer.

*Open: 11.00–23.00 (Mon–Sat), 12.00–22.30 (Sun)*
*Food: bar 12.00–15.00 and 18.30–22.30 (Mon–Sat), 12.30–15.30 (Sun); restaurant 12.00–15.00 and 18.30–22.30 (Mon–Sat), 12.30–15.30 (Sun)*
*Credit cards: Mastercard, Switch, Visa*

*Draught beers: Caffrey's, London Pride, one guest ale, Grolsch, Tennent's Extra,*
*Guinness, Red Rock*
*Wheelchair access to venue and loo*
*Two private rooms: 12 and 32 seated, 20 and 50 standing*
*Nearest tube stations: Chalk Farm, Camden Town*

## Ennismore Arms

2 Ennismore Mews, SW7. Tel: 0171–584 0440

Charles Gray, narrator of the Rocky Horror Picture Show and a many time upper-crust villain in films, once said 'I prefer a pint at the local to drinking champagne in a dress suit'. True to his word he has been a regular at the Ennismore Arms for many a year and with such a handsome local, why wouldn't he? The Ennismore is what they call a decent pub in SW7 and it's so hidden away you're unlikely to stray past. The locals seem to like it that way.

*Open: 11.00–23.00 (Mon-Sat), 12.00–22.30 (Sun)*
*Food: 12.00–22.30 (Daily)*
*Credit cards: all major*
*Draught beers: Courage Best, Director's, Theakston's Best, Foster's, Kronenbourg,*
*Guinness, Strongbow*
*Wheelchair access to venue*
*Nearest tube station: Knightsbridge, South Kensington*

## Enterprise
**EROS AWARD WINNER**

2 Haverstock Hill, NW3. Tel: 0171 485 2659

Directly opposite Chalk Farm tube is this three-storey, multi-coloured building, home to a very individual interpretation of an Irish-influenced bar. I say Irish-influenced rather than thematic, as in the case of the poorer examples seen at Scruffy Murphy's (qv) and Finnegan's Wakes (qv). The Enterprise is really rather a pleasant place to walk into, decorated with prints of the great literati, Behan, Wilde and the like. The big, almost square bar extends into the well-furnished room, with tables big enough to seat a large crowd. One wall is completely filled with books, adding to the scholarly feel. The erudite, unpretentious clientele can get quite lively in the evenings, but this is also a good daytime pub, and there are too few of them around these parts.

*Open: 11.00–23.00 (Mon-Sat), 12.00–22.30 (Sun)*
*Food: sandwiches available as opening hours*
*Credit cards: none taken*
*Draught beers: Caffrey's, Courage Best, Courage Directors, Old Speckled Hen,*
*Budweiser, Foster's, Holsten Pils, Kronenbourg, Strongbow, Dry Blackthorn*
*Wheelchair access to venue and loo*
*Private room: 60 standing*
*Nearest tube station: Chalk Farm*

## The Enterprise

35 Walton Street, SW3. Tel: 0171 584 3148

For many years The Enterprise has been one of London's most unpublike pubs, a celebration of upward mobility. It is a pub, it has a pub licence, but with Stella Artois being the only beer – and only available in half-pints – and the seats allocated to those who are eating, it feels and behaves like a restaurant. Ever since Diana, Princess of Wales, was seen having lunch here with her chums, it has been hard to get a table. You can't book – you turn up and take your chances. The Enterprise is handsome, stylish and reasonably expensive: half a roast duck with prunes and pears (£10.95), Dover sole (£14.35), and artichoke heart with a spinach gratin and warm vinaigrette (£8.75). The tables are very close together, and the management has a rather irritating habit of levying a £1 cover charge. 'For napery,' they tell me. I was tempted to say I would do without. If you are invited to dinner at The Enterprise you know you can leave your cheque book at home – credit cards only, please.

*Open: 12.00–15.30 and 17.30–23.00 (Mon–Sat), 12.00–22.30 (Sun)*
*Food: 12.30–14.30 and 19.00–22.30 (Mon–Sun)*
*Credit cards: all major cards*
*Draught beers: Stella Artois (half-pints only)*
*Wheelchair access to venue*
*Nearest tube stations: South Kensington, Knightsbridge*

## Essex Yeoman

70 Station Road, Upminster, RM14. Tel: 01708 229289

Can you name the tube station that lies at the very eastern end of the District Line? Do you know how many teams entered the *Evening Standard* Pub Quiz Challenge? And who won it? There were big celebrations in Upminster the night that The Essex Yeoman beat off the final 20 teams from an original entry of 256. Trials are held in the pub every Sunday evening during winter.

*Open: 11.00–23.00 (Mon–Sat), 12.00–22.30 (Sun)*
*Food: as opening hours*
*Credit cards: all major cards*
*Draught beers: Director's, Theakston Best, Becks, Foster's, Holsten Export, Guinness, Strongbow*
*Nearest tube station: Upminster*

## Est

54 Frith Street, W1. Tel: 0171 437 0666

Once owned by Mogens Tholstrup, Est made a welcome arrival in Greek Street a few years ago. It concentrates on up-market drinking and eating in a clean, small, minimalist bar with oak and metal fittings and floor-to-ceiling windows. Most of the drinking is done at the bar, where you can eat as well. The tables, however, are reserved for diners. On a recent visit the bar was packed and, with all the tables empty, we asked if we could take a seat until the diners arrived. 'No,' the girl behind the bar told us flatly.

'But we'll happily give up the table when someone needs it,' I protested. 'We'll even clean it!' The girl was obdurate. We remained standing, finished our bottle of Pouilly Fumé (£17.50), and left. The tables were still empty when we passed by again an hour later.

*Open: 12.00–midnight (Mon–Sat)*
*Food: as opening hours*
*Credit cards: all major cards*
*Nearest tube stations: Leicester Square, Tottenham Court Road*

## The Falcon

33 Bedford Road, SW4. Tel: 0171 274 2428

They've painted this pub a very bright and cheery egg-yolk yellow, which actually looks much better than it sounds. There's a terrace of picnic tables at the front before you go into the big single-roomed bar with its rickety old furniture, pool table and student atmosphere. At the back of the building there is an enormous beer garden with its own bar, which can seat upwards of 100 people, and very often does.

*Open: 12.00–23.00 (Mon–Sat), 12.00–22.30 (Sun)*
*Food: 12.00–19.00 (Mon–Wed), 12.00–23.00 (Thurs–Fri), 12.00–22.30 (Sun)*
*Credit cards: all major cards*
*Draught beers: Bass, Caffrey's, Fuller's, London Pride, Newcastle Brown, Grolsch, Staropramen, Tennent's Extra, Guinness, Blackthorn*
*Nearest tube station: Clapham North*

# The Falcon

2 St John's Hill, SW11. Tel: 0171 924 8041

This is a handsome Victorian pub with large windows, flower baskets and copper lanterns. 'The longest bar in the UK' boasts their poster. It is in fact the longest *continuous* bar in the UK – there's a subtle difference. The Falcon's bar is circular, and at 125 feet it takes up to 12 bartenders to man it effectively. If you put a pint glass next to another one and so on all the way around the bar, you would need to drink 428 pints before you got back to where you started from. How's that for a challenge?

*Open: 11.00–23.00 (Mon–Sat), 12.00–22.30 (Sun)*
*Food: 12.00–19.00 (Mon–Sat)*
*Credit cards: none taken*
*Draught beers: Bass, Bombardier, Caffrey's, London Pride, Worthington, Carling Premier, Grolsch, Tennent's Extra, Guinness, Cider Master*
*Wheelchair access to venue and loo*
*Nearest tube station: Clapham South*

# Fashion Café

3–4 Coventry Street, W1. Tel: 0171 287 5888

Strictly speaking you can go for drinks here, although the bar is quite small and they would really rather prefer it if you ate. Your first task is to get over the wall of derisory attitude and sneers that inevitably greets you on arrival. Being a well-practised gatecrasher, I was over the wall, past the tacky merchandise shop, through the glitzy foyer and halfway up the stairs before the skeletal young lady – clearly just a French-fry away from malnutrition – caught me up. 'Can I help you?' she probed, horrified that I had managed to by-pass her clipboard. 'Maybe later,' I replied with a pleasant smile, and proceeded to mount the stairs. To give her credit, she didn't give up there, and like so many aggressive door-people at supposedly smart venues, what she really seemed to be asking was, 'What on earth do you think you're doing trying to get into a place like this?'

I impressed even myself with the lies and excuses I used for not waiting in the queue, and in as much time as it takes to fall off a high-heeled shoe, I was perched happily at the bar, leaving my poor, bemused inquisitor at her rightful place outside in the street. The bar is not the best place to sit. You see little other than waiting-staff scurrying back and forth carrying platefuls of burgers and salads. On the odd occasion, you might spot queue-weary tourists being helped to their tables. On an earlier visit, we couldn't resist asking our waitress what Misses Campbell, Schiffer, McPherson and Turlington were really like. 'Never seen them,' said she sullenly as she deposited the bottles of ketchup and sauce on our table (and we all know what sort of houses put sauce bottles on the tables).

So what of the fashion element of the café? A few frocks strewn around the walls do not a Fashion Café make. It is rather a dreary place and a very poor relation to its New York sister bar. When canvassing views, it seems there are two opinions of the Fashion Café. The first is held by those who wish to go once so that they can say they have been. Second, and a much more sensible view in my opinion, is held by those who make their own fashion statement by proudly declaring they have never been at all. There are enough tourists in London willing to give this place the once-over, thus safeguarding its existence for a long time hence. As for me? To err once is forgivable, twice is inexcusable.

*Open: 12.00–midnight (Mon–Sun)*
*Food: as opening hours*
*Credit cards: all major cards but not cheques*
*Wheelchair access to venue and loo*
*Nearest tube station: Piccadilly Circus*

# Ferret & Firkin

114 Lots Road, SW10. Tel: 0171 352 6645

The Ferret and Firkin in the Balloon up the Creek is actually its full title, making it the longest pub name in London. The ferret and the balloon appear on the pub sign, a rather cliquey set of regulars call themselves the Balloonatics, and the brewhouse in the cellar produces copious quantities of a bitter called Balloonastic. The best bitter is Ferret Ale (3.5%), and they make Dogbolter (5.6%) and Full Mash Mild (3.4%) too. The Ferret shows how well the classic Firkin style wears. The brass chandeliers, the ceiling fans, the wooden floor, the church pews – they will all last, you feel, for ever. The pews are unexpectedly roomy and comfortable. They come from a firm in the Midlands called Pew Corner. The Ferret serves food, substantial portions of an average quality (which actually is a compliment), which does the job for healthy appetites (those who want to put a lining on their stomach before hammering back the beer). There is live music, too, usually fun rather than talented, but the sporty clientele may well be amused when the Chelsea Operatic Society do their jamming sessions.

*Open: 12.00–23.00 (Mon–Sat), 12.00–22.30 (Sun)*
*Food: hot food 12.00–19.00 (Mon–Sun); sandwiches available up to closing time*
*Credit cards: all major cards except AmEx*
*Draught beers: Balloonastic, Dogbolter, Ferret Ale, Full Mash Mild, one guest ale, Carlsberg, Castlemaine, Guinness, Western Scrumpy*
*Wheelchair access to venue*
*Nearest tube station: Fulham Broadway*

# Fifth Floor Bar

Harvey Nichols, Knightsbridge, SW1. Tel: 0171 235 5250

The days when it was deemed trendy to be seen quaffing champers on the fifth floor of Harvey Nicks seem like a lifetime ago. Today you might question why anybody would want to pay hotel prices for a couple of drinks in a department store but I suspect the parvenus who drink there know the answer: 'It's a knocking shop,' boasted one regular, who declared a modicum of success. Ladies who lunch need not worry about the pulling power of the bar, as the action is usually confined to the evenings. In the daytime it is a pleasant little bar in which you can take the strain out of shopping and contemplate your next credit-card bill with a glass of the short-sharp-strong stuff. The massive island bar takes up much of the room, leaving space only for a small cluster of low tables fitted with dreary lamps – some held together with Sellotape – making it difficult to see the person sitting opposite. There is a rather sinister art collection: the theme being spooky eyes staring out from every wall. But let that be a source of reassurance – it's good to be looked at in a place like this, and you can bet your next cocktail it's not the waiters looking to see if you need a refill.

*Open: 12.00–23.00 (Mon–Sat)*
*Food: sandwiches 12.00–15.00 (Mon–Fri); sushi after 18.00 (Mon–Sat)*
*Credit cards: all major cards*
*Wheelchair access to venue and loo*
*Nearest tube station: Knightsbridge*

# Filthy McNasty and the Whiskey Café

68 Amwell Street, EC1. Tel: 0171–837 6067

Coming up with creative names for Irish theme pubs is clearly a tricky business. Filthy McNasty and the Whiskey Café is clearly poking fun at itself, and why not? This two-roomed pub is rather fun and has resisted temptations to go overboard on the Irish memorabilia front. It's a decent local and I'd be rather pleased to have one near me.

*Open: 12.00–23.00 (Mon–Sat), 12.00–22.30 (Sun)*
*Food: 12.00–15.00 and 18.00–22.30 (Mon–Sat), 12.00–16.00 (Sun)*
*Credit cards: none taken*
*Draught beers: Tetley, Kilkenny, Castlemaine, Lowenbrau, Carlsberg, Carlsberg
Export, Guinness, Olde English*
*Wheelchair access to venue includes loo*
*Nearest tube station: Angel*

## Finch's

### 190 Fulham Road, SW10. Tel: 0171 351 5043

Finch's tell me proudly that this is the last traditional public house in Chelsea. It
isn't, of course, but in this particular stretch of the Fulham Road, with its lively
bars, nightclubs and restaurants, Finch's does provide something a little less
frenetic. That's not to say that this is a haven of tranquillity far from the madding
crowd. On the contrary, it has quite a bit of life of its own, and is clearly not
geared to attracting just one specific age group. It is a handsome Victorian pub
retaining much of its mahogany and brass fittings, etched glass screens and
decorated mirrors.

*Open: 11.00–23.00 (Mon–Sat), 12.00–22.30 (Sun)*
*Food: 12.00–14.30 (Mon–Sun)*
*Credit cards: all major cards except AmEx*
*Draught beers: Ramrod Smooth, Young's Bitter, Young's Premium, Young's Spe-
cial, Castlemaine, Grolsch, London Lager, Guinness, Scrumpy Jack*
*Wheelchair access to venue*
*Nearest tube station: South Kensington*

## Finnegan's Wake

This is Scottish & Newcastle's vision of the Irish theme pub, and the poor relation of the genre. S & N seem to have stopped rolling them out now, and in fact
have one less than they had last year (see Shuckburgh Arms). The style of
these pubs is rather basic, the Irishness coming from old posters from the Irish
Tourist Board plastered over the walls and ceilings. They have Irish music, all
right, and Irish-ish food which is served almost all day. The Finnegan in question is apparently borrowed from the James Joyce novel *Finnegans Wake*,
except that James Joyce didn't bother with an apostrophe.

*Branches at:*

**Ealing**: The Green, W5. Tel: 0181 567 2439. Nearest tube station: Ealing Broadway
**Fulham**: 48 Fulham Palace Road, W6. Tel: 0181 748 3948. Nearest tube station:
Hammersmith
**Holborn**: 63 Lamb's Conduit Street, WC1. Tel: 0171 405 8278. Nearest tube sta-
tion: Russell Square
**Islington**: 2 Essex Road, N1. Tel: 0171 226 1483. Nearest tube station: Angel
**Kensington**: 34 Gloucester Road, SW7. Tel: 0171 584 0020. Nearest tube sta-
tion: Gloucester Road
**West Hampstead**: 37 Fortune Green Road, NW6. Tel: 0171 435 0653. Nearest
tube station: West Hampstead
**Westminster**: 2 Strutton Ground, SW1. Tel: 0171 222 7310. Nearest tube station:
St James's Park

## Finnegan's Wake

### 2 Strutton Ground, SW1. Tel: 0171 222 7310

A funny thing happened to Graftons in Victoria. It woke up one morning and
found it had become a Finnegan's Wake. It could happen to anyone. Graftons
was famous for the Goons. They started there upstairs in the front room –
Harry Secombe, Spike Milligan, Peter Sellers and Michael Bentine, young
comic hopefuls brought together by aspiring scriptwriter Jimmy Grafton, son of

the house. That was getting on for 50 years ago and, sadly, there's not much left of them in the old pub today, just three photographs in one of the alcoves. Well, it's the Irish pub now, so it is, and it's mostly Irish faces in the alcoves – Oscar Wilde, W. B. Yeats and, of course, James Joyce, the one who wrote *Finnegans Wake*. It is a literary masterpiece – but what is it about?

Scottish & Newcastle spent five weeks on the conversion, painting the front bright blue, putting in a second door, reducing the counter, making more room. Recorded Irish music has been playing more or less non-stop ever since, with Irish musicians and singers performing five nights a week, and Irish food served all day. At Graftons it was sausage, beans and chips. At Finnegan's Wake it is Dublin fry – bacon, sausage, egg, tomatoes, mushrooms, fried soda bread and potato cake, a light repast: £3.75.

*Open: 11.00–23.00 (Mon–Sat), 12.00–16.00 (Sun)*
*Food: 11.00–21.00 (Mon–Sat), 12.00–15.00 (Sun)*
*Credit cards: all major cards*
*Draught beers: Courage Best, Courage Directors, John Smith's, Theakston Best, Coors, Foster's, Kronenbourg, Beamish, Guinness, Strongbow*
*Nearest tube station: St James's Park*

## Fino's Wine Cellar

123 Mount Street, W1. Tel: 0171 491 1640

We spend a large amount of our social life underground, hiding away from predators, the elements and our bosses. In this underground wine bar you can hide away from the entire world, and it wouldn't surprise me if people were mistakenly locked in and left to contend with themselves for days on end. Can you imagine that? This is an old bar dating back some 25 years or so, and owned and operated by the Fiori family, who are still highly visible in the running of the place. It has one long bar with a function room, The Boardroom, at the back. Then it has some of the cosiest caves to be found in a London bar. Wandering around one evening I lost count of the number of little hideaways. I kept disturbing young, and not so young, couples who were trying to be hidden away before they went home, separately, to their loved ones. What are they all doing so deep underground – potholing? But back to the bar. It's efficiently run by a team of men, some wearing jackets and dickie bows, some wearing cellar aprons. They make fresh crisps on the premises which are given away free, as well as wonderful juicy beefburgers (£5.90).

*Open: 11.30–23.00 (Mon–Fri), 17.30–23.00 (Sat)*
*Food: 12.00–15.00 and 18.00–23.00 (Mon–Sat)*
*Credit cards: all major cards*
*Private room seats 30*
*Nearest tube station: Green Park*

## Firkin Pubs

David Bruce and his wife started the Firkin chain with an old Southwark pub, the one-time Duke of York, in 1979. Bruce opened the renamed Goose & Firkin after raising a loan against his home, and what he did here set the pattern for all the Firkins to come – plain wooden furniture, bare floorboards, one bar, a little stage with a piano, home-made food and, above all, a brewhouse in the cellar. This bold revival of an ancient tradition is still the heart of the Firkin philosophy, although it is not always economical or practical for all the pubs to have their own brewhouses. In the early eighties Firkins were a novel addition to the London drinking circuit, combining facilities for young drinkers with a decent range of real ales and modern lagers. The people at Camra were quite pleased, as were the millions of customers who used them. By 1988 there were 187 pubs nationwide in the Firkin portfolio, which David Bruce then sold for £6.6 million, intending to retire on his £2 million profit. He later tried to get them back again, but failed, and in 1991 the Firkins arrived in the hands of Allied Domecq, who now operate this idiosyncratic chain. New ones – being added all the time – are staying true to the old philosophy, while the older ones are demonstrating how well they stand the test of time.

To date there are 46 Firkins in and around London. They all love their pub games – some have so many they wouldn't be out of place on a pleasure beach. I'm told Firkins attract all ages, but generally you'll find a relatively young clientele. They can get quite loud at times with their bands, discos and school common-room mentality. While the pubs clearly stand the test of time, the Firkin joke wears a little thin after a while – the Firkin food, the Firkin toilets and the Firkin beers. As the beers are brewed in house, Firkins are always ready to rename a beer to recognise an event or occasion. In the summer of 1997 they introduced an Ice Cream Beer, flavoured with vanilla pods, to recognise National Ice Cream Week. Food is served all day, with a selection of burgers, pizzas, sandwiches and main meals of beef and Dogbolter Ale pie (£4.50), chilli (£3.95) and lasagne (£3.95). A firkin, by the way, is a small wooden barrel with a capacity of nine gallons.

*Branches at:*

**Battersea**: Faraday & Firkin, 66a Battersea Rise, SW11. Tel: 0171 801 9473. Nearest tube station: Clapham South

**Bayswater**: Fettler & Firkin, 15 Chilworth Street, W2. Tel: 0171 723 5918. Nearest tube station: Paddington

**Blackheath**: Fairway & Firkin, 16 Blackheath Village, SE3. Tel: 0181 318 6637. Nearest railway station: Blackheath

**Bow**: Flautist & Firkin, 588 Mile End Road, E3. Tel: 0181 981 0620. Nearest tube station: Mile End

**Bromley**: Philatelist & Firkin, 27–28 East Street, BR1. Tel: 0181 464 2361. Nearest railway station: Bromley

**Camden**: Fusilier & Firkin, 7–8 Chalk Farm Road, NW1. Tel: 0171 485 7858. Nearest tube station: Camden Town

**Chelsea**: Ferret & Firkin, 114 Lots Road, SW10. Tel: 0171 352 6645. Nearest tube station: Fulham Broadway

**City**: Pheasant & Firkin, 166 Goswell Road, EC1. Tel: 0171 253 7429. Nearest tube stations: Barbican, Angel

**Clapham**: Friesian & Firkin, 87 Rectory Grove, SW4. Tel: 0171 622 4666. Nearest tube station: Clapham Common

**Clapham**: Fringella & Firkin, 762–764 High Road, SW4. Tel: 0181 289 6473. Nearest tube station: Clapham Common

**Covent Garden**: Faun & Firkin, 18 Bear Street, WC2. Tel: 0171 839 3252. Nearest tube station: Leicester Square

**Covent Garden**: Flyman & Firkin, 166–170 Shaftesbury Avenue, WC2. Tel: 0171 240 7109. Nearest tube station: Leicester Square

**Covent Garden**: Fulmar & Firkin, 51 Parker Street, WC2. Tel: 0171 405 0590. Nearest tube station: Holborn

**Croydon**: Fiddler & Firkin, 14 South End, CR0. Tel: 0181 680 9728. Nearest railway station: East Croydon

**Ealing**: Photographer & Firkin, 23–25 High Street, W5. Tel: 0181 567 1140. Nearest tube station: Ealing Broadway

**Epping**: Forest & Firkin, High Street, CM16. Tel: 0181 680 9728. Nearest tube station: Epping

**Epsom**: Favel & Firkin, 4 East Street, KT18. Tel: 01372 723676. Nearest railway station: Epsom

**Euston**: Friar & Firkin, 120 Euston Road, NW1. Tel: 0171 387 2419. Nearest tube stations: Euston, King's Cross

**Ewell**: Friend & Firkin, High Street, KT17. Tel: 0181 393 1294. Nearest railway stations: Ewell East, Ewell West

**Fulham**: Pharaoh & Firkin, 90 Fulham High Street, SW6. Tel: 0171 731 0732. Nearest tube station: Putney Bridge

**Great Portland Street**: Fitz & Firkin, 240 Great Portland Street, W1. Tel: 0171 388 0588. Nearest tube station: Great Portland Street

**Greenwich**: Funnel & Firkin, Greenwich High Road, SE10. Tel: 0181 305 2088. Nearest railway station: Greenwich

**Harrow**: Fornax & Firkin, Northolt Road, HA2. Tel: 0181 422 0505. Nearest tube station: South Harrow

**Holloway**: Flounder & Firkin, 54 Holloway Road, N7. Tel: 0171 609 9574. Nearest tube station: Highbury & Islington

**Homerton**: Falcon & Firkin, 360 Victoria Park Road, E9. Tel: 0181 985 0693. Nearest railway station: Homerton

**Islington**: Finnock & Firkin, 100 Upper Street, N1. Tel: 0171 226 3467. Nearest tube station: Angel

**Kew**: Flower & Firkin, Kew Gardens Station, TW9. Tel: 0181 332 1162. Nearest tube station: Kew Gardens

**Kingston-upon-Thames**: Financier & Firkin, 43 Market Place, KT1. Tel: 0181 974 8223. Nearest railway station: Kingston-upon-Thames

**Lewisham**: Fox & Firkin, 316 Lewisham High Street, SE13. Tel: 0181 690 8925. Nearest railway station: Ladywell

**Marylebone**: Farrier & Firkin, 74–76 York Street, W1. Tel: 0171 262 1513. Nearest tube station: Marylebone

**Notting Hill**: Frog & Firkin, 96 Ladbroke Grove, W11. Tel: 0171 229 5663. Nearest tube station: Ladbroke Grove

**Peckham**: Phoenix & Firkin, Windsor Walk, SE15. Tel: 0171 701 8282. Nearest railway station: Denmark Hill

**Pinner**: Frothfinders & Firkin, Marsh Road, HA5. Tel: 0181 866 0766. Nearest railway station: Pinner

**Richmond**: Flicker & Firkin, Duke's Yard, 1 Duke's Street, TW9. Tel: 0181 332 7807. Nearest tube station: Richmond

**Shepherd's Bush**: Fringe & Firkin, 2 Goldhawk Road, W12. Tel: 0181 749 9861. Nearest tube station: Goldhawk Road

**Southwark**: Goose & Firkin, 47–48 Borough Road, SE1. Tel: 0171 403 3590. Nearest tube stations: Elephant & Castle, Borough

**Sydenham**: Fewterer & Firkin, 313 Kirkdale, SE26. Tel: 0181 778 8521. Nearest railway station: Sydenham

**Tooting**: Faith & Firkin, 1 Bellevue Road, SW17. Tel: 0181 672 8717. Nearest tube station: Tooting Bec

**Tooting**: Freedom & Firkin, 196 Tooting High Street, SW17. Tel: 0181 672 5794. Nearest tube station: Tooting Broadway

**West End**: Flintlock & Firkin, 108a Tottenham Court Road, W1. Tel: 0171 387 6199. Nearest tube station: Warren Street

**West Kensington**: Frigate & Firkin, Blythe Road, W14. Tel: 0171 602 1412. Nearest tube station: Olympia

**West Soho**: Fanfare & Firkin, 38 Great Marlborough Street, W1. Tel: 0171 437 5559. Nearest tube station: Oxford Circus

**Weybridge**: Formula & Firkin, Heath Road, KT13. Tel: 01932 845035. Nearest railway station: Weybridge

## The Flask

14 Flask Walk, NW3. Tel: 0171 435 4580

The Flask, made of Hampstead's nice yellow brick with big gas lanterns to guide you to the door, has always been a popular local. It has kept its separate public and saloon bars, which are divided by a fine listed Victorian screen. A big conservatory was recently added at the back; it is used for food, music-hall nights, live jazz and whatever else comes to mind.

*Open: 11.00–23.00 (Mon–Sat), 12.00–22.30 (Sun)*
*Food: 12.00–15.00 (Mon), 12.00–15.00 and 18.00–21.00 (Tues–Fri), 12.00–16.00 and 18.00–21.00 (Sat), 12.00–16.00 (Sun)*
*Credit cards: Mastercard, Visa*
*Draught beers: Young's Bitter, Young's Special, Castlemaine, London Lager,*

*Premium Lager, Red Stripe, Tennent's Extra, Oatmeal Stout, Scrumpy Jack*
*Wheelchair access to venue and loo*
*Private room: 25 seated, 50 standing*
*Nearest tube station: Hampstead*

## The Flask

77 Highgate West Hill, N6. Tel: 0181 340 7260

The Flask in Highgate is one of London's best-loved pubs. People like it for its age, for its character, for where it is. This is a lovely bit of London, with an old church, trees and comely houses. The Flask was built in 1663, rebuilt in 1767, done over in 1910 and again five years ago – a thorough renovation that closed the old pub for three months. People who had feared the worst were relieved by what they found when it reopened. It wandered along as always, up steps here, down steps there, ceilings still low, oak panelling and floorboards as they were.

There are several rather quaint customs maintained by The Flask, for instance, the annual Swearing on the Horns. This is one of those Merrie Olde England things and involves a set of antlers and strange oaths. You then get the freedom of Highgate and a chance to kiss the prettiest girl in the room. There is food all day at The Flask. They serve up to 1,500 meals a week, and in high summer half of Highgate seems to want to eat there. The forecourt has beautiful white wisteria and lots of picnic tables, which fill with people at the first glimpse of the sun. These tables are still occupied in the depths of winter, actually. The British, a hardy island race, sit snugly in their overcoats, warmed by ingenious outdoor heaters.

*Open: 11.00–23.00 (Mon–Sat), 12.00–22.30 (Sun)*
*Food: 12.00–21.15 (Mon–Sat), 12.00–22.30 (Sun)*
*Credit cards: all major cards*
*Draught beers: Adnams, Burton, Calder's Cream Ale, Kilkenny, Tetley's, Young's Special, plus guest ale, Carlsberg, Castlemaine, Lowenbrau, Guinness, Dry Blackthorn*
*Private room: 16 seated, 25 standing*
*Nearest tube stations: Archway, Highgate*

## Flicker & Firkin

Duke's Yard, 1 Duke Street, Richmond, TW9. Tel: 0181 332 7807

Strictly for the young and the party-animals, The Flicker is a large windowless room with a bar stretching the full length of one wall. In the remainder of the space you dance, yell at each other, or do seemingly anything else you want while drinking from plastic glasses. The loos are miles away and you need to climb one of the narrowest staircases I've come across to get there. Still, that all adds to the intimacy when you have to clamber past someone. You don't come here with a date, you come here to get one.

*Open: 12.00–23.00 (Mon–Sat), 12.00–22.30 (Sun)*
*Food: 12.00–15.30 and 17.00–23.00 (Mon–Sat), 12.00–16.00 (Sun)*
*Credit cards: all major cards*
*Draught beers: Dogbolter, Flicker, Golden Glory, Pecker, one guest ale, Carlsberg Export, Castlemaine, Lowenbrau, Guinness, Dry Blackthorn, Weston's Old Rosie*
*Wheelchair access to venue and loo*
*Nearest tube station: Richmond*

## Flower & Firkin

Kew Gardens Station, Kew, TW? Tel: 0181 332 1162

Temptation awaits the residents of Kew, alighting from the train or tube after a hard day at work. On the platform of their station, on the site of an old British

Rail buffet, is the Flower & Firkin – and it must be hard for them to resist popping in for a quickie from time to time. The Flower & Firkin serves food, provides entertainment, and is rather proud of its conservatory. I think Kew Gardens has the edge, though.

*Open: 12.00–23.00 (Mon–Sat), 12.00–22.30 (Sun)*
*Food: bar 12.00–17.00 (Mon–Sun); snacks 17.00–closing time (Mon–Sun)*
*Credit cards: Mastercard, Switch, Visa*
*Draught beers: Cactus Ale, Calder's Cream Ale, Dogbolter, Rail Ale, Carlsberg Export, Castlemaine, Lowenbrau, Guinness, Western Scrumpy*
*Wheelchair access to venue*
*Nearest tube station: Kew Gardens*

## Flyman & Firkin

166–170 Shaftesbury Avenue, WC2. Tel: 0171 240 7109

The location is not the most obvious one for a new pub, but the Flyman & Firkin opened here at the end of 1994 to almost instant success. It is now one of the three most profitable pubs in the Firkin chain. With its wooden floors, its settles and tables, and old yellow brick walls, it looks as if it has been a pub for ever. It was, however, a hair-care clinic and warehouse when the Firkin people took it over. This being Shaftesbury Avenue, albeit the wrong end, the flyman in the title is the chap who swings scenery about in the space above the stage. That wooden thing next to the Firkin piano is a rain machine in good working order. The main thing, though, is the Firkin food, baps and butties, pies and vegetable pot, and the Firkin ales brewed on site – Flyman Bitter (the best seller), Critic Ale (a bit lighter) and, of course, the strong dark Dogbolter.

*Open: 12.00–23.00 (Mon–Sat), 12.00–22.30 (Sun)*
*Food: hot food 12.00–21.00 (Mon–Sun); sandwiches 21.00–23.00 (Mon–Sun)*
*Credit cards: all major cards*
*Draught beers: Critic Ale, Dogbolter, Flyman Bitter, plus cask-conditioned ales from other Firkin pubs, Carlsberg Export, Castlemaine, Lowenbrau, Guinness, Dry Blackthorn, Old Rosie Scrumpy*
*Wheelchair access to venue and loo*
*Private room: 20 seated, 100 standing*
*Nearest tube stations: Covent Garden, Piccadilly Circus, Leicester Square*

## Football Football

57–60 Haymarket, SW1. Tel: 0171 930 9970

The strapline that appears throughout this place is 'the beautiful game'. I have a theory that the beautiful game in question is making pots of money on a well-marketed, well-publicised, celebrity-backed gimmick with nothing of any substance, interest or visual appeal. It's clear to me that some people could market a vacuum, and so long as there are enough of us prepared to go along with the idea (i.e., pay for it), places like this will continue to prosper. The bar is in the foyer of the building, across from the much more important merchandise shop and adjacent to the tunnel entrance to the restaurant. You don't sit down – there's just a lot of hanging-around space. The bar staff wear football strips, and football shirts are framed (how creative!) on the walls. There are three electronic games, or Playstations, which the kids adore. A rope hangs across the entrance to the restaurant to stop people going in. The reason for this? 'People want to come in and look at the memorabilia,' says the manager. 'We reserve that as a privilege for our dining customers.' A privilege? I don't think so.

*Open: 12.00–midnight (Mon–Sat), 12.00–22.30 (Sun)*
*Food: 12.00–23.00 (Mon–Sat), 12.00–22.30 (Sun)*
*Credit cards: all major cards*
*Draught beers: Tetley's, Carlsberg, Guinness (all half-pints only)*

*Wheelchair access to venue and loo*
*Private room: 50–60 seated, 100 standing*
*Nearest tube station: Piccadilly Circus*

## Foundation

Harvey Nichols, Knightsbridge, SW1. Tel: 0171 201 8000

Whatever your thoughts on this bar, you can't quite forget that you are in the basement of a department store. Sitting here in the evenings is rather like being in a shop that someone has forgotten to lock up. It has everything going for it except the quantity of people necessary to bring the place alive. It is good looking, has a fun 30-foot water-wall behind the bar, table service for drinks, excellent Oriental nibbles, and a good location. Drinks are not cheap but we would have stayed longer had we not been so lonely. The waiting staff were fun despite their starched uniforms. Lunchtime is a much livelier affair, when the shoppers pile in for refreshments. That's exactly what it should be used for.

*Open: 11.00–23.00 (Mon–Sat), 12.00–18.00 (Sun)*
*Food: 12.00–23.00 (Mon–Sat), 12.00–18.00 (Sun)*
*Credit cards: all major cards*
*Wheelchair access to venue*
*Nearest tube station: Knightsbridge*

## The Founders Arms

52 Hopton Street, Bankside (off Southwark Street), SE1.
Tel: 0171 928 1899

This fine modern pub stands boldly on the riverbank on the south side of Blackfriars Bridge. It is hard to find the first time but is worth the effort. The Dean of St Pauls managed all right. He formally opened it in 1979.

When you get there you have Young's beer, a glass-walled bar, a pleasant restaurant and a big riverside terrace, wonderful on a sunny day. Bar and terrace give you a fine view of the river and one of the great views of St Pauls.

*Open: 11.00–23.00 (Mon–Sat), 12.00–22.30 (Sun)*
*Food: bar 11.00–21.30 (Mon–Sun); restaurant 12.00–14.15 (Mon and Sun), 12.00–14.15 and 19.30–21.15 (Tues–Fri), 19.30–21.15 (Sat)*
*Credit cards: AmEx, Mastercard*
*Draught beers: All Young's variants, Castlemaine, Grolsch, Guinness, Dry Blackthorn*
*Wheelchair access to venue*
*Nearest tube station: Blackfriars*

## The Fox and Anchor

115 Charterhouse Street, EC1. Tel: 0171 253 4838

A wonderful Victorian boozer with many original features, such as the small cubbies, rather like confessional booths, which are bookable so you can reveal all to your companion in the knowledge that you won't be overheard. The Fox and Anchor has an all-day licence, a hangover from the days when the workers of Smithfield market clocked off after a long night of carcass chopping and popped in for refreshments. It's busier than ever now, although the early-morning clientele are more likely to be office workers having a pre-work breakfast meeting. And what a breakfast – sausages, bacon, black pudding, fried egg, fried bread, baked beans, tomatoes, toast – you can't see the plate. It is known as the English breakfast, costs £7 and is served until 3pm. I've never managed to finish one yet, they are so hearty. It is nothing for The Fox and Anchor to have 90 for breakfast and to turn another 20 away. There is a vegetarian alternative but this is, after all, Smithfield.

*Open: 07.00–21.00 (Mon–Fri)*
*Food: 07.00–15.00 (Mon–Fri)*
*Credit cards: all major cards*
*Draught beers: Burton Ale, Calder's Cream Ale, Eldridge Pope, Tetley's, Carlsberg,*
*Castlemaine, Guinness, Dry Blackthorn*
*Private room seats 20*
*Nearest tube stations: Farringdon, Barbican*

## The Fox and Grapes

Camp Road, SW19. Tel: 0181 946 5599

Camp Road potters along on the west side of Wimbledon Common, where the golf courses are, and an attractive low black and white pub overflows onto the narrow pavement. This is The Fox and Grapes, which has been there, part of it anyway, since 1787. It has a cosy, comfortable bar with a low wooden ceiling supported by huge oak pillars. They call it Caesar's Bar after a certain J. Caesar who built the Roman fort up the road. The stables now form the lounge bar, a large, high room with a gas log fire, wood panelling and a beamed and raftered roof. The Fox and Grapes serves home-cooked food all day. Special occasions like Burns Night and St Patrick's Day are huge thrashes, when all the tables and chairs are cleared out of the lounge. The Fox and Grapes is popular with most ages, shapes and sizes. Plastic glasses are provided for younger drinkers heading for the Common; golfers stock up here after their morning rounds, and dog-walkers particularly like to pop in. Dogs, unusually, are welcome. Children too.

*Open: 11.00–23.00 (Mon–Sat), 12.00–22.30 (Sun)*
*Food: 12.00–22.00 (Mon–Sat), 12.00–21.30 (Sun)*
*Credit cards: AmEx, Mastercard, Visa*
*Draught beers: Courage Best, Courage Directors, John Smith's Extra Smooth,*
*Theakston XB, Wadworth 6X, Foster's, Holsten Export, Kronenbourg, Guinness,*
*Scrumpy Jack, Strongbow*
*Wheelchair access to venue*
*Private room: 30 seated, 50 standing*
*Nearest tube station: Wimbledon*

## The Fox and Hounds

41 High Street, Carshalton, SM5. Tel: 0181 715 1612

The Fox and Hounds has had a somewhat troubled past, but let's not dwell on that. Plans were made to relaunch the pub as a music venue, and relaunch it they did. It opened to a chorus of trumpets and trombones, with live jazz playing most nights of the week, attracting a different clientele and ridding the pub of its image as a rough old pool emporium. It was by this time a better-than-average local pub. There's not so much music now but you'll still find jazz on Wednesdays and pop, rock or blues on Sundays. They have pop quizzes every other Thursday, and do a roaring trade when these are on. They're ale drinkers rather than lager swillers down here in Carshalton, and at under £2 a pint, who wouldn't be?

*Open: 12.00–23.00 (Mon–Sat), 12.00–16.00 and 19.00–22.30 (Sun)*
*Food: 12.00–14.30 and 18.00–20.30 (Mon–Fri), 12.00–18.00 (Sat), 14.00–14.30 (Sun)*
*Credit cards: Visa*
*Draught beers: Benskins, Burton, Tetley's, seven guest ales, Carlsberg, Carlsberg*
*Export, Castlemaine, Guinness, Calders, Dry Blackthorn*
*Wheelchair access to venue*
*Private room seats 30*
*Nearest railway station: Carshalton*

# Fox and Hounds

29 Passmore Street, SW1. Tel: 0171 730 6367

When the Hound stops chasing the Fox in a hunting pack, as may well happen, this pub's name will become all the more important a piece of social history. We will be able to take our grandchildren in and show them the prints on the wall, depicting country life until *circa* 1998. The Fox and Hounds is only licensed to sell beer or wine, so it's a no-go for gin or any other spirits, come to that. There used to be lots of pubs like this – known as beer houses, a Victorian notion. Beer, thought the licensing authorities of the time, was safer than gin for the working man. The Fox and Hounds may be the only such establishment left, and Diane Harvey, the licensee, doesn't mind at all.

The Fox and Hounds started out in the 1860s. The street door opened onto a small room with a wooden floor, settles round the walls and a couple of tables. The landlady would hand you your beer through a flap in her living-room door. Things hardly changed for a hundred years. One room for the pub, three for the licensees and their children. Family and customers shared one outside loo.

The outside lav stayed right up to 1980, by which time the whole character of the district had changed. What had been terraces of working men's cottages had become fashionable and expensive. In Passmore Street today the modish new shop on the corner is Lord Linley's, and if one of the small houses comes up for sale nowadays, the asking price is around £500,000.

The pub has changed too, of course, but thankfully it has not been spoiled. It is actually quite nice to have inside loos, a bar counter and more room. The Fox and Hounds remains a period piece, with Mrs Harvey still running the show in the old way. She has been at the pub for 29 years, has survived successive attempts to pull it down, and endured building work that closed the pub altogether for five months. People love this very agreeable old pub and long may it stay that way.

*Open: 11.00–15.00 and 17.30–23.00 (Mon–Fri), 11.00–15.30 and 18.00–23.00 (Sat), 12.00–14.00 and 19.00–22.30 (Sun)*
*Food: toasted sandwiches available all day*
*Credit cards: none taken*
*Draught beers: Adnams Bitter, Bass, Greene King IPA, Harvey's Sussex, Tennent's Extra, Carling Black Label, Guinness, Weston Stowfold Press*
*Wheelchair access to venue*
*Nearest tube station: Sloane Square*

# The Fox and Pheasant

1 Billing Road, SW10. Tel: 0171 352 2943

Situated in a smart enclave off the Fulham Road known to estate agents as The Billings, this pub is worth seeking out. It is a little country pub created 200 years ago by knocking two small houses into one, and it cheers you up just to look at it. It is extraordinarily pretty now, with its hanging baskets and antique lanterns. Inside it is quite unmodernised and has exposed beams, leaded windows, basic hardwood tables and chairs, and a big log fireplace. The two rooms are separated by a central bar, and both have lots of sporting prints. There is an excellent walled beer garden at the back, very popular in the summer. They have taken to doing basket meals at lunch and in the evenings for £2–£3.

A minor drawback, you may think, is the nearness of the Fox and Pheasant to Chelsea football ground. You can hear them score. Opening hours go a little peculiar when Chelsea play at home, as they try not to be the first port of call for the departing fans.

*Open: 12.00–15.00 and 17.30–23.00 (Mon–Sat), 12.00–15.00 and 19.00–22.30 (Sun)*
*Food: 12.00–15.00 and 19.00–21.30 (Mon–Sat), 12.00–15.00 and 19.00–22.30 (Sun)*
*Credit cards: all major cards*
*Draught beers: Abbot Ale, Brewer's Bitter, Greene King IPA, Budweiser, Carling Black Label, Harp, Kronenbourg, Stella Artois, Guinness, Red Rock*
*Nearest tube station: Fulham Broadway*

## Freedom

60–66 Wardour Street, W1. Tel: 0171 734 0071

Although this bar is mostly gay, you really don't need to be to drink here. In fact, on my first trip, if it hadn't been for the fact that I saw a couple of men necking and a couple of women looking longingly into each other's eyes, I would hardly have known. Freedom has a plain glass frontage and minimalist decor with a few patches of colour in the banquettes, tables and chairs. Lots of people come to eat the pasta dishes, sandwiches and salads (main courses around £5, two courses £8.50), and there is an extensive cocktail list starting at £5. Bottled lagers are too expensive at £2.80 and £2.90, and the house wine is £12. The place has changed its image over the years and may well be changing again in the near future.

*Open: 11.00–03.00 (Mon–Sat), 12.00–midnight (Sun)*
*Food: as opening hours*
*Credit cards: all major cards*
*Private room seats 100*
*Nearest tube station: Piccadilly Circus*

## The Freemasons Arms

32 Downshire Hill, NW3. Tel: 0171 435 4498

This is a big, modern pub near Hampstead Heath, built in 1932 to replace an earlier Freemasons Arms that was having trouble standing up. It has a splendidly prosperous and expansive air, with ample bars and spacious sitting and dining rooms. There can be few bigger pubs in north London. The Freemasons has just undergone a bit of a refurbishment and is now becoming more food focused. The garden is vast, full of roses and picnic tables. It also has a sunken courtyard with a fountain and more tables, and a flagged terrace overlooking the fountain. Downstairs in the basement is a true rarity – a skittle alley in fine fettle with a 21-foot pitch and big hornbeam skittles set in a diamond formation. Every Tuesday, Thursday and Saturday skittlers try to knock them over with massive lignum vitae cheeses. This game, London skittles, was once played in pubs all over the south of England. It is an endangered species now. How nice to find it alive and well in the Freemasons Arms.

*Open: 11.00–23.00 (Mon–Sat), 12.00–22.30 (Sun)*
*Food: bar 12.00–22.00 (Mon–Sun); restaurant 12.00–22.00 (Mon–Sun)*
*Credit cards: Mastercard, Switch, Visa*
*Draught beers: Bass, Caffrey's Cream Ale, London Pride, Carling Black Label, Staropramen, Guinness, Cidermaster*
*Wheelchair access to venue and loo*
*Nearest tube station: Hampstead*

## The French House

49 Dean Street, W1. Tel: 0171 437 2799

There's some serious drinking goes on in The French. This small, single-roomed pub is enduringly popular, and people still spill out into the streets to escape the smoke-filled room, the actress who never quite made it, or the television stars of yesteryear proffering their autographs to anyone who will have them. It is, perhaps, one of the friendliest pubs in London, and going alone is recommended: it'll take seconds before someone draws you into a conversation. The French is quite good for celebrity spotting, but booze is a great leveller of egos, and most of the names here will have left their star status behind them at the Groucho Club – the natural pre-French House drinking venue. The walls are filled with pictures of famous people who have frequented The French over the years, including Dylan Thomas, who once left the only manuscript of *Under Milk Wood* there. It sells Gauloise, Gitanes and an awful lot of Ricard. Its restaurant is much acclaimed and has a rather adventurous menu. After The French? You'll probably go off with your new-found friends to Blacks, further up the street, or to Jerry's, which is almost next door. Vive la French pub!

*Open: 12.00–23.00 (Mon–Sat), 12.00–22.30 (Sun)*
*Food: bar 12.30–15.00 and 18.30–22.00 (Mon–Sun); restaurant 12.30–15.00 and 18.30–23.00 (Mon–Sat)*
*Credit cards: all major cards*
*Draught beers: John Smith's Extra Smooth, Carlsberg, Guinness*
*Wheelchair access to venue*
*Private room seats 35*
*Nearest tube station: Leicester Square*

## Freud

198 Shaftesbury Avenue, WC2. Tel: 0171 240 9933

This small, somewhat sinister basement bar tries to be relaxed but the jazz music dictates the pace. It's the sort of place where Brylcreemed girls and boys stop by for coffee and cake and spend hours reading newspapers.

*Open: 11.00–23.00 (Mon–Sat), 12.00–22.30 (Sun)*
*Food: 11.00–16.30 (Mon–Sat), 12.00–16.30 (Sun)*
*Credit cards: none taken*
*Nearest tube stations: Tottenham Court Road, Covent Garden*

## Friar & Firkin

120 Euston Road, NW1. Tel: 0171 387 2419

Formerly The Rising Sun, this was the first of the new breed of Firkins, which emerged after the sale of the chain by the founding father, David Bruce. It closed for a month and opened its doors as the Friar and Firkin, with all the well-tested Firkin features: bare floorboards, pews, barrel tables, Firkin food and Firkin notices – 'The Firkin Loos', 'Mind the Firkin Step'. It was soon so popular you could hardly move, and the shop next door became part of it, almost doubling the floor space. It has a late licence on Thursday, Friday and Saturday nights, when the music is soul, R & B and traditional English blues. The five-barrel brewhouse in the cellar works to capacity to keep up with the demand for the four house ales. A carefully placed mirror gives you a glimpse of it working, while outside a friar sits astride a barrel on the new pub sign, beaming sunnily down on the impassable traffic of the Euston Road.

*Open: 11.00–23.00 (Mon–Wed), 11.00–midnight (Thurs–Sat), 12.00–22.30 (Sun)*
*Food: 12.00–15.00 and 19.00–22.30 (Mon–Sat)*
*Credit cards: all major cards except AmEx*
*Draught beers: Confession Ale, Dogbolter, Firkin Golden Glory, Friar Ale, Friar Full Mash Mild, Carlsberg, Castlemaine, Lowenbrau, Guinness, Murphy's, Weston's Scrumpy*
*Wheelchair access to venue*
*Nearest tube stations: Euston, King's Cross*

# The Fridge Bar

1 Town Hall Parade, Brixton Hill, SW2. Tel: 0171 326 5100

Next door to the world-famous nightclub of the same name (to which you can gain entry for a small charge), this small, mostly gay bar has free admission – but get there early.

*Open: 11.00–02.00 (Mon–Sat), 12.00–22.30 (Sun)*
*Food: 12.00–18.00 (Mon–Sun)*
*Credit cards: none taken*
*Draught beers: Red Stripe*
*Nearest tube station: Brixton*

# The Front Page

35 Old Church Street, SW3. Tel: 0171 352 2908

All sorts of people like this pleasant, comfortable, easy-going Chelsea pub, with its well-stocked cellars and good food. There is no music, and no fruit machines or fitted carpets. The big windows fill it with light, and the social mix is Chelsea as it used to be and still, sometimes, is. The locals go for lunch, actors rehearsing at the parish hall down the street look in for a drink, audiences from the Cannon cinema up the street go for pre-movie supper, and after 9pm crowds of young Chelsea denizens arrive. There is a private dining room upstairs, the staff are young and cheerful, the regulars are all ages and cheerful, and everyone gets on well.

*Open: 11.00–23.00 (Mon–Sat), 12.00–22.30 (Sun)*
*Food: 12.00–14.30 and 19.00–22.00 (Mon–Sat), 12.00–14.30 and 19.00–21.30 (Sun)*
*Credit cards: all major cards except AmEx*
*Draught beers: Brakspear, John Smith's Extra Smooth, Theakston XB, Foster's, Holsten Export, Kronenbourg, Beamish, Strongbow*
*Private room: 25 seated, 60 standing*
*Nearest tube station: Sloane Square*

# Las Fuentes Tapas Bar

36–40 High Street, Purley, CR8. Tel: 0181 763 1983

Tapas bars are springing up all over London, and in an area distinctly short of any drinking venues it comes as something of a pleasant surprise to stray across this busy, energetic example of the genre. Service is smart and efficient, and the generous portions of all things tapas are reasonably priced between £2 and £4. Bottled beers start at £1.30, spirits at £1.50 and wines at under £2. The room off the restaurant has a seating area with plenty of space at the bar to grab a stool. The pleasant atmosphere of Las Fuentes is due to the combined experience of eating and drinking in an attractive space with an open kitchen. No surprises in the decor, though – tiled walls, pictures of Spain, and the hackneyed use of wine bottles around the walls. Nevertheless, the place has an exuberant kick to it, and if you walk in on a busy night, you will be greeted with the rich aroma of Hispanic delicacies wafting gently through the air.

*Open: 12.00–15.00 and 18.00–23.00 (Mon–Fri), 18.00–midnight*
*Credit cards: all major cards*
*Nearest railway station: Purley*

# Fulham Tup

268 Fulham Road, SW10. Tel: 0171 352 1859

The Fulham Tup is actually in Chelsea, although as it's on the Fulham Road it chooses to use that name. The pub is owned and operated by Hugh Corbett, the man who created and sold the Slug and Lettuce chain, and this latest venture is not a million miles away from that concept.

The Fulham Tup is a large, airy and bright one-roomed bar with stripped pine flooring and half-panelled walls. The sizeable, well-spaced tables leave plenty of standing room for the crowds who flock here in the evenings. For the agriculturally challenged, a tup describes the process of a ram impregnating a ewe. Tupping is not particularly new on the Fulham Road, but if impregnating a ewe doesn't directly interest, then you could always eat one – whole legs of lamb are on offer at weekends, although you have to book in advance. The Tup is considering its own ale, Raddles (actually wax-covered harnesses worn by rams when copulating, which leave a deposit in the ewes' nether regions so the farmer can identify which ram did it with which ewe), and its own lager, Shear Delight. Should you spot a blue-bottomed ewe wandering raddled down the Fulham Road, you'll guess that she's been to the Tup for some Shear Delight and is no doubt on her way to bleat about it in the nearby Goat in Boots (qv).

*Open: 12.00–23.00 (Mon–Sat), 12.00–22.30 (Sun)*
*Food: 12.00–15.00 and 18.00–22.00 (Mon–Thurs), 12.00–15.00 and 18.00–21.00 (Fri–Sat), 12.00–21.00 (Sun)*
*Credit cards: all major cards*
*Draught beers: Brakspear, Courage Best, John Smith's Extra Smooth, Marston's Pedigree, Theakston XB, Foster's, Kronenbourg, Miller, Beamish, Scrumpy Jack*
*Wheelchair access to venue*
*Nearest tube stations: Earls Court, Fulham Broadway*

*Branches at:*

**City**: City Tup, 66 Gresham Street, EC2. Tel: 0171 606 8176. Nearest tube station: Bank
**West End**: Marylebone Tup, 93 Marylebone High Street, W1. Tel: 0171 935 4373. Nearest tube stations: Bond Street, Baker Street

## Fulmar & Firkin
51 Parker Street, WC2. Tel: 0171 405 0590

High jinks, three stuffed fulmars, and students and tutors from the LSE and St Martin's School of Art are the ingredients of this pub, formerly the Kingsway Tavern. Every Saturday it has free alternative comedy – four, five, even six alternative comedians one after the other – and it is packed. It has recently added a new-acts evening on Tuesdays, young stand-up comics facing their first audiences. They should all get a medal for heroism. On the alternative comedy circuit the Fulmar is considered a good audience. This means it does not actually throw things.

*Open: 12.00–23.00 (Mon–Sat)*
*Food: main meals 12.00–15.00; snacks 15.00–23.00 (Mon–Sat)*
*Credit cards: all major cards*
*Draught beers: Dogbolter, Firkin Mild, Fulmar Bitter, Golden Glory, Wingspan, one guest ale, Carlsberg Export, Castlemaine, Lowenbrau, Guinness, Olde English, Weston's Scrumpy*
*Nearest tube station: Holborn*

## Fusilier & Firkin
7–8 Chalk Farm Road, NW1. Tel: 0171 485 7858

This cavernous old pub stands directly opposite Camden Market, which is thick with people every week from Thursday onwards. Big as it is, the pub also gets packed. Stallholders, bargain-hunters, tourists, they all crowd in. Visiting bands occupy its little platform every Friday, Saturday and Sunday night. Every year, the pub celebrates National Naturist Day (26 May) with an afternoon of naked drinking. Customers who leave their clothes at the door are treated to a free pint of Bottoms Up, specially brewed for the occasion. I decided to give it a miss; all this sampling plays havoc with your waistline.

*Open: 12.00–23.00 (Mon–Wed), 12.00–midnight (Thurs–Sat), 12.00–22.30 (Sun)*
*Food: main meals 12.00–17.30 (Mon–Sun); sandwiches and snacks 12.00–closing time (Mon–Sun)*
*Credit cards: none taken*
*Draught beers: Calder's Cream Ale, Dogbolter, Fusilier Ale, Golden Glory, Musket Ale, Carlsberg Export, Castlemaine, Lowenbrau, Guinness, Olde English, Scrumpy*
*Wheelchair access to venue*
*Nearest tube station: Camden Town*

## The Gatehouse

North Road, N6. Tel: 0181 340 8054

J. D. Wetherspoon recently bought this pub. It was so named after the toll house on the top of the hill, a high gate spanning the road, which also gave its name to the area, Highgate. The Gatehouse has no music, gives non-smokers a big non-smoking bit, and serves good quick food all day (eight varieties of burger from £2.45). Its cask ales include the great Wetherspoon's bargain, a pint of Youngers Scotch Bitter for only 99p.

*Open: 11.00–23.00 (Mon–Sat), 12.00–22.30 (Sun)*
*Food: 11.00–22.00 (Mon–Sat), 12.00–21.30 (Sun)*
*Credit cards: all major cards*
*Draught beers: Courage Directors, Theakston Best, Youngers Scotch Bitter, Fuller's London Pride, plus guest ale, Becks, Foster's, Kronenbourg, McEwan's, Guinness, Dry Blackthorn*
*Wheelchair access to venue and loo*
*Nearest tube stations: Highgate, Archway*

## The Gazebo

Kings Passage, Kingston, KT1. Tel: 0181 546 4495

There are two gazebos at The Gazebo, one on either side of it, and very nice they look too. This is an attractive modern pub, built in the eighties in a lovely spot on the Thames, right next door to Young's Bishop out of Residence. Downstairs is the public bar, with wooden floors, a pinball machine and a pool table, and upstairs there's the saloon bar, with a big verandah overlooking the river and the green vistas beyond. There are steps down to moorings for customers who have come by boat, and picnic benches on the riverbank. The food is all right, too – good salads, a carvery on Sundays, a children's menu and good old-fashioned puds. And, of course, being a Sam Smith pub it's Sam Smith's beer, so that's reassuring.

*Open: 11.00–23.00 (Mon–Sat), 12.00–22.30 (Sun)*
*Food: as opening hours*
*Credit cards: Mastercard, Visa*
*Draught beers: Old Brewery Bitter, Sovereign Bitter, Ayingerbraü, Ayingerbraü Pils, Ayingerbraü Prinz, Samuel Smith's Stout, Special Reserve*
*Wheelchair access to venue and loo*
*Private room seats 150*
*Nearest railway station: Kingston*

## George IV

185 High Road, W4. Tel: 0181 994 4624

Fuller, Smith & Turner has more than 200 pubs, and this is one of the eight in Chiswick, encircling the brewery. There's also The Mawson Arms on the corner of the brewery itself, The Bell and Crown (qv) and The Dove (qv) on the river,

The Cross Keys, The Duke of York, The George and Devonshire, and two in the High Street, The Old Packhorse and the George IV. They are all historic old pubs. Fuller's spent more than £460,000 recently bringing the George IV slap-bang up to date. Some of the changes belong entirely to this end of the 20th century – the new lavatories and kitchens, the air conditioning, the compu-terised tills operated by a touch on the screen and recording every aspect of every sale, and a big television screen for major sporting events. There is also a single, open bar, low timber ceilings, bare floorboards, tongue-and-groove pan-elling, mahogany stairs leading to a gallery, drinking booths with old church pews, and a cobbled yard with a fountain. It is, in short, an old English Ale and Pie house, Fuller's seventh. Within a matter of weeks of its reopening, trade had doubled. The house speciality is Georgie Porgie Pie – pork and apple in a creamy cider sauce (£4.75).

*Open: 11.30–23.00 (Mon–Sat), 12.00–22.30 (Sun)*
*Food: 12.00–22.00 (Mon–Sat), 12.30–15.00 (Sun)*
*Credit cards: all major cards except AmEx*
*Draught beers: Chiswick Bitter, ESB, London Cream, London Pride, Carling Black Label, Grolsch, Heineken, Stella Artois, Guinness, Murphy's, Scrumpy Jack, Strongbow*
*Wheelchair access to venue and loo*
*Nearest tube station: Turnham Green*

## The George Inn

77 Borough High Street, SE1. Tel: 0171 407 2056

To come across The George Inn for the first time is to meet an old friend. You feel you know it already from Christmas cards, Dickens and old movies. It is the archetypal coaching inn. You should really arrive in a stagecoach, but instead you park where you can, walk through the wrought-iron gateway on Borough High Street, and there it is – the cobbled yard, the overhanging galleries, the south front, all still in daily use. It is a moving sight. We know a lot about The George. We know it was going strong in 1542, the year Henry VIII executed his fifth wife; we know it was rebuilt three times, emerging splendidly intact into the railway age, the same three-sided galleried building as before, with one big courtyard and a smaller one beyond it surrounded by stables. Then, humiliatingly, The George became a depot of the Great Northern Railway, which pulled down two of the fronts and built warehouses in their place. Luckily the south front sur-vived and the warehouses did not – they were bombed in the war. What replaced them is pretty awful – two dreadful modern blocks – but you can keep your back to these as you sit at one of the picnic tables in the courtyard. With only The George in view, you are in another age.

   The floorboards creak loudly as you pass from bar to bar in the old inn, twice as loudly as you go upstairs to the dark panelled restaurant and various function rooms. These upper storeys were, of course, bedchambers in The George's great days. You can't find a bed there now, but the food is good, the ale is bet-ter, old settles and chimney corners beckon, and in the summer there's the courtyard where Shakespeare, they say, once performed. It is a romantic place, safely in the hands of the National Trust, and never disappoints. It is, of course, an *Evening Standard* pub of the year.

*Open: 11.00–23.00 (Mon–Sat), 12.00–22.30 (Sun)*
*Food: bar 11.00–23.00 (Mon–Sat); restaurant 18.00–21.30 (Wed–Fri)*
*Credit cards: all major cards*
*Draught beers: Bishop's Restoration, Boddingtons, Brakspear, Castle Eden, Lon-don Pride, Heineken, Stella Artois, Guinness, Murphy's, Strongbow*
*Five private rooms: 20–60 seated, 30–80 standing*
*Nearest tube station: London Bridge*

# The Gipsy Moth

60 Greenwich Church Street, SE10. Tel: 0181 858 0786

The magnificent *Cutty Sark* and the gallant little *Gipsy Moth*, both enjoying new careers as tourist attractions at Greenwich, get perhaps 300,000 visitors every year. It is thirsty work, looking at famous ships, and after seeing two of them, the whole family needs a drink and a snack and a loo. This large, efficient pub is right on the spot. A bit of luck all round, really. It used to be, unmemorably, The Wheatsheaf, but changed its name to The Gipsy Moth when Sir Francis Chichester's little boat, having gone round the world with only him on board, settled on its doorstep. So now, every summer, tourists arrive in a never-ending stream, have a meal and a drink, go to the loo and move on, letting someone else have the table. There are seats in the garden for 150 at a time.

*Open: 11.00–23.00 (Mon–Sat), 12.00–22.30 (Sun)*
*Food: bar: 12.00–15.00 (Mon–Sat), 12.00–16.00 (Sun)*
*Credit cards: all major cards*
*Draught beers: Adnams, Burton Ale, Kilkenny, Tetley's, Carlsberg Export, Carlsberg Pilsner, Guinness, Dry Blackthorn*
*Wheelchair access to venue and loo*
*Nearest railway station: Greenwich*

# The Globe Tavern

83 Moorgate, EC2. Tel: 0171 606 4731

For more than 250 years two pubs stood side by side in Moorgate, a big one and a small one. The big one was The Globe Tavern. Next door was the more modest Swan and Hoop, later known as The Moorgate, and later still as the John Keats at Moorgate (qv). The Globe's great strength has always been its site. It occupies the strategic corner of Moorgate and London Wall, a great place for a pub. It has had lots of owners, hundreds of landlords, countless customers. Waves of builders have come and gone, the latest of these has recently completed a renovation costing the best part of £500,000 and involving radical alterations. They have left it a big, boisterous pub with its upstairs restaurant twice the size it was. In the wide-open L-shaped bar the music is so loud that if it's your shout, you have to shout. There are driving machines, gaming machines, a tireless juke box, two television screens, all that sort of thing. It gets packed. All around brood the great City institutions. You think, perhaps, that the City is peopled by serious persons with tastes running to string quartets? Go to The Globe. 'It's a bit of a madhouse,' says the manager fondly, in the comparative hush of the pub next door. He manages that as well. Bass has ended up owning them both.

*Open: 11.00–23.00 (Mon–Fri)*
*Food: 12.00–15.00 (Mon–Fri)*
*Credit cards: all major cards*
*Draught beers: Bass, Caffrey's, London Pride, Carling Black Label, Carling Premier, Grolsch, Guinness, Red Rock*
*Wheelchair access to venue*
*Two private rooms: 40–80 seated, 80–150 standing*
*Nearest tube station: Moorgate*

# The Gloucester

187 Sloane Street, SW1. Tel: 0171 235 0298

This is a small, comfortable pub in the heart of Knightsbridge, five minutes from Harrods and Harvey Nichols. It opens, remarkably enough, at 9am for breakfast – the full fandango for £5.60 – but, sorry, you'll have to wait until 11am to get a drink.

*Open: 09.00–23.00 (Mon–Sat), 12.00–22.30 (Sun)*
*Food: as opening hours*
*Credit cards: all major cards*
*Draught beers: Courage Best, Courage Directors, Theakston Best, plus a guest ale, Foster's, Holsten Pils, Kronenbourg, Guinness, Strongbow*
*Wheelchair access to venue*
*Private room: 20 seated, 35 standing*
*Nearest tube station: Knightsbridge*

## Goat in Boots

333 Fulham Road, SW10. Tel: 0171 352 1384

There is a small stretch of the Fulham Road that people refer to as The Beach. It is the Mediterranean atmosphere on summer evenings, the music, the drinks, the clothes. There has been a pub here for more than 400 years, and the original one enjoyed common rights for two cows and a heifer. The current building dates back to 1909 and has been at the epicentre of Chelsea nightlife for as long as anyone can remember. In 1994 Joel Cadbury, the son of Peter Cadbury, then an aspiring young 23 year old, wanted to buy the private drinking club upstairs, the King's Club. Courage didn't want to sell in piecemeal fashion, so Cadbury thought what the hell, and bought the whole lot. The price he paid was a mere £140,000, and last year he sold it for a package worth £1.5 million while retaining the management contract.

The Goat in Boots is a decent-enough pub – stripped floors, wooden beams, not much furniture but plenty of places to lean. There's a downstairs cocktail bar, also loud and packed with people, and doormen on the door at weekends with the universal preference for the young and scantily dressed. The juke box gets turned up high and the crowd hops to the music. In somewhere like Pontefract, this would be a workaday pub, but on The Beach, the up-market clientele use it as a rights-of-passage affair in a bid to get laid. The King's Club upstairs is a more sedate affair. The music is quieter and there's a pool table. Membership is £100 a year. There is a bridge club here, where daily, afternoon and early-evening sessions are very well attended. On Mondays £20 buys you supper, half a bottle of wine and all the bridge companions you need. Cadbury also owns the nearby Vingt-Quatre, a 24-hour café, and recently purchased SWXI in Battersea.

*Open: 11.00–23.00 (Mon–Sat), 12.00–22.30 (Sun), 19.00–01.00 (Tues–Sat)*
*Food: 12.00–15.00 (Mon–Sat)*
*Credit cards: all major cards*
*Draught beers: Courage Best, Courage Directors, John Smith's Extra Smooth, Ruddles, Beck's, Foster's, Kronenbourg, Miller, Guinness, Scrumpy Jack*
*Wheelchair access to venue*
*Nearest tube stations: South Kensington, Gloucester Road*

## Golden Lion

51 Dean Street, W1. Tel: 0171 434 0661

For years the Golden Lion in Dean Street was one of London's best-known gay pubs, packed with solitary and, if they were wise, watchful drinkers. It was one of the haunts of Dennis Nilsen, the serial killer. That, I'm afraid, is the most interesting thing about the place. Nilsen would find it harder to find victims there now. New managers and a new bar policy have wrought radical change. There are two bars, gaming machines, satellite television and a juke box, and traditional bar food upstairs (sausage, beans and chips, and pies).

*Open: 11.00–23.00 (Mon–Sat), 12.00–22.30 (Sun)*
*Food: 12.00–15.00 and 18.00–22.00 (Mon–Sat)*
*Credit cards: none taken*

*Draught beers: Courage Directors, John Smith's Extra Smooth, Theakston Best,*
*Beck's, Foster's, Kronenbourg, Guinness, Strongbow*
*Wheelchair access to venue*
*Private room: 25 seated, 50 standing*
*Nearest tube station: Piccadilly Circus*

## The Golden Lion

25 King Street, W1. Tel: 0171 930 7227

The Golden Lion, or Golden Lyon Tavern as it was in 1732, is a striking sight in
this rather uneventful street. It is five storeys high and has a mock-Jacobean
garret, black marble columns, projecting windows and a stucco balustrade. It's
also hemmed in by flat, modern office buildings, so you certainly can't miss it.
Something *is* missing, though. The lovely St James's Theatre, The Golden
Lion's old friend, which stood next to it for more than a hundred years, was
pulled down by developers in 1959. There were furious objections. Laurence
Olivier and Vivien Leigh led demonstrations but the demolition men went in
anyway. One of those office blocks replaced it – the one on the right....
theatre and pub were unusually close. A door led directly from the circle to The
Golden Lion's upstairs bar, which became the official theatre bar, with warning
bells for the start of performances and pre-ordered drinks waiting at the inter-
val. Playgoers flocked there, as did generations of actors, so it was a body
blow for The Golden Lion when the theatre was demolished. It went into rather
a depression for a while, actually, but it has now had a much-needed face-lift
and seems to be feeling a lot better. Most of its customers work in neighbouring offices. The offices close on Sunday. So does The Golden Lion.

*Open: 11.00–23.00 (Mon–Fri), 12.00–17.00 (Sat)*
*Food: bar: 12.00–15.00 (Mon–Fri)*
*Credit cards: all major cards*
*Draught beers: Adnams, Tetley's, plus three guest ales, Carlsberg Export, Carls-*
*berg Pils, Castlemaine, Guinness, Addlestone*
*Wheelchair access to venue*
*Private room seats 50*
*Nearest tube station: Green Park*

## Goose & Firkin

47–48 Borough Road, SE1. Tel: 0171 403 3590

The Goose & Firkin has come of age. It was eighteen in 1997 and is the elder
member of the Firkin (qv) family. Curiously, this remains the only pub in the
chain not to employ alliteration in its name – they probably didn't Firkin realise
they were onto a Firkin good gimmick. However, the old Duke of York set the
blueprint for more than 150 little Firkins born since 1979. Sadly it no longer has
its own brewhouse, but it takes its stocks from the Falcon & Firkin in Hackney.
Its old, battered bar was replaced in rather dramatic fashion. When the *East-
Enders'* Queen Vic burnt down a few years ago, it was the Goose & Firkin's bar
you saw ablaze. The Firkin music can be heard on Fridays.

*Open: 11.00–23.00 (Mon–Fri), 20.00–23.00 (Sat)*
*Food: 12.00–21.00 (Mon–Fri)*
*Credit cards: all major cards*
*Draught beers: Borough Bitter, Dogbolter, Firkin's Golden Glory, Goose, one guest*
*ale, Carlsberg Export, Castlemaine, Lowenbrau, Guinness, Dry Blackthorn*
*Nearest tube stations: Elephant & Castle, Borough*

## The Goose and Granite

196 Clapham High Street, SW4. Tel: 0171 622 1543

A massive, cavernous pub owned by the Just So Pub Co., which cost Bass
£250,000 to transform in 1996. Is there a bigger pub in London? Yes, there are

several, actually, but you can't help asking yourself that question when you've turned up to meet a blind date on a Saturday evening just as a major event is throwing out from Clapham Common. The Goose and Granite is so big you might well get lost on the way back from the bar to your seat – it really wouldn't be out of place in a major railway terminus or an airport.

*Open: 11.00–23.00 (Mon–Sat), 12.00–22.30 (Sun)*
*Food: 12.00–22.00 (Mon–Sun)*
*Credit cards: all major cards except AmEx*
*Draught beers: Caffrey's, Just So Bitter, London Pride, Worthington Best, Carling Black Label, Carling Premier, Grolsch, Guinness, Cidermaster*
*Wheelchair access to venue and loo*
*Nearest tube station: Clapham Common*

## The Goose and Granite

264 Hoe Street, E17. Tel: 0181 520 8341

Take the Victoria Line to Walthamstow Central and you can't miss it. It is the big, good-looking pub on the corner with luxuriant baskets of flowers all the way round. It is a huge improvement on what went before.

The Goose and Granite started life as the Tower Hotel in the 1870s, when rural Walthamstow was expanding as you looked, factories going up, houses following. It had its ups and downs, mostly downs, with the usual name changes. By the seventies it was Flanagan's Tower and was doing quite well, a busy pub downstairs, bed and breakfast on the floors above, but this didn't last. By the nineties it was a sad sight, a broken-down old boozer, clearly on its last legs. There was then a spectacular dash to the rescue. Backed by Bass, a new young group called the Just So Pub Co. took it over and just about rebuilt it. The job took three months and cost well over £500,000 but the old pub has been transformed. It is now handsome, comfortable and popular, with lovely arched windows flooding the place with light. People who had lived in Walthamstow for years found themselves going in for the very first time.

*Open: 11.00–23.00 (Mon-Sat), 12.00–22.30 (Sun)*
*Food: 12.00–21.00 (Mon-Sat), 12.00–17.00 (Sun)*
*Credit cards: all major cards except AmEx*
*Draught beers: Bass, Caffrey's, London Pride, Ruddles County, Carling Black Label, Carling Premier, Grolsch, Guinness, Cidermaster*
*Wheelchair access to venue and loo*
*Private room: 60 seated, 100 standing*
*Nearest tube station: Walthamstow Central*

## The Goose and Granite

381 Lordship Lane, SE22. Tel: 0181 290 9401

For more than a hundred years London's horse-drawn buses and subsequent motor buses carried the destination blind 'Dulwich Plough' as the terminus of the number 12 bus route. Unbeknown to the buses, Bass had plans to convert this historic coaching inn to a Goose and Granite, part of their Just So Pub Co., and early one morning in 1997, Dulwich awoke to find the name suddenly changed. Bus drivers and little old ladies got into a panic – no one knew where they were going. The London Central Bus Company acted promptly, and new blinds were hastily ordered, this time, quite wisely, displaying Dulwich Library (across the road from the pub) as their destination. If Bass have plans to change the name of the pub again in the future, can I suggest they call it The Dulwich Library and keep everybody happy?

*Open: 11.00–23.00 (Mon-Sat), 12.00–22.30 (Sun)*
*Food: 12.00–21.00 (Mon-Sat), 12.00–17.00 (Sun)*
*Credit cards: all major cards except AmEx*

*Draught beers: Bass, Caffrey's, London Pride, Ruddles County, Carling Black Label, Carling Premier, Grolsch, Guinness, Cidermaster*
*Wheelchair access to venue and loo*
*Private room: 60 seated, 100 standing*
*Nearest railway station: East Dulwich*

## Gordon's

47 Villiers Street, WC2. Tel: 0171 930 1408

Gordon's is something of an institution in London's drinking circles. It is located in a tatty but enchanting basement near Charing Cross, and its charm lies in its unpretentious, no-nonsense approach to drinking. It feels like you've walked onto the set of a period drama. You sit in former wine cellars, with exposed brickwork and old wooden furniture – you'd half expect water to be dripping down the walls. Gordon's specialises in wines (it has a good range at modest prices) and a range of snack foods, including excellent cheese plates. The real boon, though, is the outside seating on Watergate Walk, which runs along the edge of Embankment Gardens. On summer evenings, there are few places in this area that can provide a better resting spot. It remains a wonderful wine bar.

*Open: 11.00–23.00 (Mon–Fri), 17.00–23.00 (Sat)*
*Food: 12.00–21.00 (Mon–Sat)*
*Credit cards: all major cards except AmEx*
*Nearest tube stations: Embankment, Charing Cross*

## La Grande Marque

47 Ludgate Hill, EC4. Tel: 0171 329 6709

This excellent bank conversion on Ludgate Hill is notable for its gentlemanly and understated atmosphere and its elegant, sophisticated decor – strictly for lovers of wine and champagne. The list, as supplied by Lay & Wheeler of Colchester, totals more than a hundred varieties, and covers the range of prices, although those on a very tight budget shouldn't plan a long evening. There are 22 different champagnes from £19.95 rising to £85.00. Service can be a bit lacklustre, but all-in-all, this is an excellent bar.

*Open: 11.30–21.30 (Mon–Fri)*
*Food: 11.30–14.30 (Mon–Fri)*
*Credit cards: none taken*
*Draught beers: Bittberger*
*Wheelchair access to venue*
*Nearest tube stations: Blackfriars, St Paul's*

## The Grapes

76 Narrow Street, E14. Tel: 0171 987 4396

'The Six Jolly Fellowship-Porters, a tavern of a dropsical appearance, had long settled down into a state of hale infirmity', wrote Charles Dickens in *Our Mutual Friend*. 'In its whole constitution it had not a straight floor and hardly a straight line … it was a bar to soften the human breast.'

The real name of the Six Jolly Fellowship-Porters was, and is, The Grapes. Dickens knew it well, describing it perfectly, and it is still there on the river at Limehouse. It hasn't changed all that much. It was old when Dickens knew it, with a history of press-gangs and dark doings. It is more than a hundred years older now and, not surprisingly, there is still not a straight floor and hardly a straight line. Happily, a recent renovation doesn't show too much, but the ancient deck, which until recently hung dropsically over the river, has been replaced with a robust new one, and a flight of new teak steps leads to a smaller deck outside the little first-floor dining room where fresh fish is served every day. The Grapes has a lively and charismatic licensee in Barbara Haig, a one-time Playboy bunny who has set her heart on becoming a Master Cellarman. Her Dickensian cellar may be just 4ft 3in high, but the beer, she says, is superb.

*Open: 12.00–15.00 and 17.30–23.00 (Mon–Fri), 19.00–23.00 (Sat), 12.00–15.00 and 19.00–22.30 (Sun)*
*Food: bar 12.00–14.00 and 19.00–21.00 (Mon–Fri), 19.00–21.00 (Sat); restaurant 12.00–14.15 and 19.30–21.15 (Mon–Fri), 19.30–21.15 (Sat)*
*Credit cards: all major cards*
*Draught beers: Burton, Friary Meux, Tetley's, plus a guest ale, Carlsberg Export, Castlemaine, Guinness*
*Wheelchair access to venue*
*Two private rooms: 28 seated, no standing; 25 seated, 35 standing*
*Nearest tube station: Mile End*
*Nearest railway station: Westferry (DLR)*

## Ye Grapes

16 Shepherd Market, W1. Tel: 0171 499 1563

When you're beating a merry path to the West End it's easy to forget that there are decent drinking venues in this part of Mayfair. It's worth stopping for a while at this popular pub, which is privately owned, a true free house. It is hard to see the walls for the objects in Ye Grapes. You might suppose that the contents of the attic of a grand country house had been generously scattered around – the heads of horned beasts, a pair of oars, a pair of guns, fish in glass cases, birds in glass cases. There is a restaurant upstairs, the Vinery, which also does cream teas in the afternoon. The pub has an impressive display of real ales, and you should really sample them all before you leave. I did, I think!

*Open: 11.00–23.00 (Mon–Sat), 12.00–22.30 (Sun)*
*Food: 12.00–14.30 (Mon–Sun)*
*Credit cards: none taken*
*Draught beers: Boddingtons, Boston, Flower's Original, Greene King IPA, London Pride, Manchester Gold, Marston's Pedigree, Wadworth, Wexford Irish Ale, Heineken, Hoegaarden, Stella Artois, Guinness, Murphy's, Strongbow*
*Wheelchair access to venue*
*Nearest tube station: Green Park*

## The Green Man

Putney Heath, SW15. Tel: 0181 788 8096

Take the number 14 bus out of town and your destination is assured. The destination blind reads 'Green Man, Putney Heath'. The pub is really two cottages back to back. There are two bars – the public bar on the right, the saloon bar on the left, linked by the counter. They are light and cheerful on summer days, snug and cosy after dark. Outside the old pub is flanked by two pretty courtyards with tables and benches and a big garden at the back, finely landscaped. Has anyone heard of Ringing the Bull? Of all old English pub games this one is thought to have the longest history of continuous play, and here it is in the bar of The Green Man, still being played, the ring suspended from the ceiling, the hook on the wall. The idea is to swing the ring onto the hook. It is harder than it looks.

*Open: 11.00–23.00 (Mon–Sat), 12.00–22.30 (Sun)*
*Food: 12.00–15.00 (Mon–Sun, winter); 12.00–15.00 and 19.00–21.00 (Mon–Sun, summer)*
*Credit cards: none taken*
*Draught beers: Young's Bitter, Young's Premium, Young's Special, plus a seasonal ale, Castlemaine, Grolsch, London Lager, Guinness, Dry Blackthorn*
*Nearest tube station: Putney Bridge*
*Nearest railway station: Putney*

# The Grenadier

Old Barrack Yard, Wilton Row, SW1. Tel: 0171 235 3074

A smart little pub, a well bred little pub, tucked away in a quiet Knightsbridge mews and keeping up its standards. 'It is house policy', says the notice on the door, 'that customers should be suitably dressed …'

The Duke of Wellington is the presiding spirit in The Grenadier. His officers used it as their mess, he is said to have played cards here himself, his mounting block is outside and his patrician features look scornfully down at you from the walls. The bar is tiny, but happily customers can spill out into the mews if it's fine, and there always seems to be room. The little restaurant at the back, candlelit at night, has crisp white linen cloths, crystal glassware and Beef Wellington on the menu. It can't seat more than 28, so it's best to book. The pewter bar counter has been scrubbed and polished daily since 1827, when the pub was built, and military memorabilia has steadily accumulated. They used to send a man from Wellington Barracks every week to groom the Guardsman's bearskin in the bar. It is made from the pelt of a female Canadian bear which, they say, like fingernails, goes on growing. A Sunday morning Bloody Mary bar is another tradition at the Grenadier. The Bloody Marys are made from a recipe passed from licensee to licensee, and the long-standing record for a single session is 276. Paul Gibb, who runs the pub now, says his customers have come pretty close to this. I've half a mind to assemble my cronies and descend on the place one Sunday to see what we can do about it.

*Open: 12.00–23.00 (Mon–Sat), 12.00–22.30 (Sun)*
*Food: bar 12.00–14.30 and 18.00–22.00 (Mon–Fri), 12.00–22.00 (Sat–Sun); restaurant 12.00–14.00 and 18.00–21.45 (Mon–Sat), 12.00–22.00 (Sun)*
*Credit cards: all major cards*
*Draught beers: Courage Best, Theakston Best, Young's Special, a monthly guest ale, Budweiser, Foster's, Kronenbourg, Guinness, Strongbow*
*Nearest tube station: Hyde Park Corner*

# Greyhound

2 High Street, Carshalton, SM5. Tel: 0181 647 1511

Sit outside this listed building, wait for a lull in the traffic, and there you have it – Carshalton Ponds before your very eyes. If that's not appealing, then go on in, turn left and enter the Swan bar. What's that I've just trodden over? That's Murphy, the Irish wolfhound, who seems more than happy to act out his role as a rug. He belongs to one of the regulars. There's no music in the pub, although this respectful nod to the art of conversation doesn't include abandoning the television. There's a big screen in the bar and preference is given to, well, whatever you ask for, really. More than 200 years ago, racegoers heading for Epsom would call in for refreshments, and the prices are still etched on one of two original panes. They've gone up a bit since then, though. The Greyhound is a homely pub, and should you feel too much at home, you can always stay the night in one of the four bedrooms upstairs. Murphy, I have to say, does not stay the night. He takes his owner for a walk on the way home.

*Open: 10.30–23.00 (Mon–Sat), 12.00–22.30 (Sun)*
*Food: 12.00–14.15 and 18.30–21.00 (Mon–Sat), 12.00–14.30 (Sun)*
*Credit cards: all major cards*
*Draught beers: Young's Bitter, Young's Export, Young's Special, Carling Black Label, Pilsner, Stella Artois, Young's Ramrod Smooth, Guinness, Young's Oatmeal, Dry Blackthorn*
*Wheelchair access to venue*
*Private room: 80 seated, 120 standing*
*Nearest railway station: Carshalton*

# The Greyhound

1 Kensington Square, W8. Tel: 0171 937 7140

Like many pubs, The Greyhound has periodically reorganised itself to meet the changing needs of its local community. In The Greyhound's case, however, change has also been prompted by more dramatic events. It was built in 1899 and replaced an earlier pub on the site. At one time it became famous for billiards, with many leading players gracing the baize of its two full-size tables, including the late, great Joe Davis. In 1975 it became the *Evening Standard* Pub of the Year. In 1979 there was a major gas explosion and the place was all but destroyed. Luckily, it happened at night and, also luckily, no one was sleeping there. The Greyhound today is rather rakish, with a curious clientele of oddball locals, *Daily Mail* staff sneaking in for a quicky, and young office workers, who enjoy the occasional live music.

*Open: 11.00–23.00 (Mon–Sat), 12.00–22.30 (Sun)*
*Food: 12.00–21.00 (Mon–Sun)*
*Credit cards: all major cards*
*Draught beers: Courage Directors, John Smith's Extra Smooth, Theakston Best, Theakston XB, plus a monthly guest ale, Beck's, Foster's, Kronenbourg, Guinness, Scrumpy Jack*
*Wheelchair access to venue*
*Private room: 40 seated, 150 standing*
*Nearest tube station: High Street Kensington*

# The Grid Inn

22 Replingham Road, SW18. Tel: 0181 874 8460

Southfields didn't have a pub until recently, but in 1994 J. D. Wetherspoon bought up an old restaurant and opened it as a pub, to the great relief of those who live in the area. This being Wetherspoon's, there is a large no-smoking area, a cheap pint and no music of any kind. Lots of local history is framed on the walls – pictures of local landmarks and notables. The Grid Inn serves snacks of crab cakes and nachos, main meals of chicken, ham and leek pie, and the famous JDW chilli con carne.

*Open: 11.00–23.00 (Mon–Sat), 12.00–22.30 (Sun)*
*Food: 11.00–22.00 (Mon–Sat), 12.00–21.30 (Sun)*
*Credit cards: all major cards*
*Draught beers: Courage Directors, London Pride, Theakston Best, Younger's Scotch Bitter, Beck's, Foster's, Kronenbourg, McEwan's, Guinness, Dry Blackthorn, Scrumpy Jack*
*Wheelchair access to venue and loo*
*Nearest tube station: Southfields*

# The Ground Floor Bar

186 Portobello Road, W11. Tel: 0171 243 8701

Once the Colville Arms, The Ground Floor Bar incorporates the ever-so-smart First Floor Restaurant. The walls and ceilings are black, the big, golden air-conditioning tubes spiral down, and the music m-o-o-o-ves along – serious, system-driven music from behind the bar – an eclectic mix, including acid jazz, R & B and calypso. The fuller the bar, the louder the sound.

With its high bar counter, towering barstools and great parties, this place is very big at Carnival. Try the restaurant out sometime; it's really rather special.

*Open: 12.00–23.00 (Mon–Fri), 11.00–23.00 (Sat), 12.00–22.30 (Sun)*
*Food: First Floor Restaurant 11.00–15.00 and 19.00–23.00 (Sun–Fri), 11.00–17.00 and 19.00–23.00 (Sat)*
*Credit cards: none taken*

*Draught beers: John Smith's Extra Smooth, Foster's, Kronenbourg, Miller, Guinness, Dry Blackthorn*
*Wheelchair access to venue*
*Private room: 50 seated, 300 standing*
*Nearest tube station: Ladbroke Grove*

## The Grouse and Claret

Little Chester Street, SW1. Tel: 0171 235 3438

During the Blitz an entire row of the pretty mews houses in Little Chester Street was flattened, along with the two pubs at each end. The war over, houses and pubs were rebuilt in a decent neo-Georgian style. Some thought it a great improvement, and you could tell at a glance that The Pig and Whistle had gone up in the world, so much so that the old plebby name seemed quite inappropriate. So it got a name the owners thought would more befit its new station. It became The Grouse and Claret.

This is still a very swanky pub, with a grouse-moor mural over the front door, a public bar on the left and a big handsome saloon bar elaborately fitted with drinking booths on the right. Both are newly carpeted, and gleam with polish in case Her Majesty should call. She lives just round the corner.

There is a flagged cellar bar mostly used for private parties, and a handsome restaurant upstairs serving any amount of claret but no grouse at all. Well, the restaurant is called The Scandinavian. It goes in for smoked reindeer salad and poached kattfisk, with Ärtsoppa every Thursday. Ärtsoppa is Swedish pea soup with gammon, sausage and Swedish mustard. It is served with warm Swedish punch and followed by cakes with jam and cream.

*Open: 11.00–23.00 (Mon–Sat), 12.00–15.00 (Sun)*
*Food: 12.00–15.00 (Mon–Sun)*
*Credit cards: all major cards*
*Draught beers: Badger Bitter, Dempsey's, Tanglefoot, Wadworth 6X, plus a guest ale, Hofbrau Export, Hofbrau Premium, Munchener Pilsner, Guinness, Dry Blackthorn*
*Wheelchair access to venue*
*Three private rooms: 55 seated, 50–120 standing*
*Nearest tube stations: Hyde Park Corner, Victoria*

## The Guinea

30 Bruton Place, W1. Tel: 0171 409 1728

This exclusive little pub tucked down a Mayfair mews is small and dark, richly accoutred and gets packed at lunchtimes. Well, the beer is Young's and the bar food is excellent. The licensee, Carl Smith, has won so many national steak and kidney pie contests that many competitions have asked him not to enter. He judges them now, but still continues to win a plateful of other food awards. His steaks and mixed grills are substantial, and worth the prices, which start at £14.35. Princess Margaret has dined here, as have Mel Gibson, Frank Sinatra, Sylvester Stallone, Jack Nicklaus and King Hussein. There's also a lighter menu for those with lighter appetites. This famous Mayfair pub restaurant is worth any amount of trips.

*Open: 11.00–23.00 (Mon–Fri), 18.30–23.00 (Sat)*
*Food: bar 12.00–14.30 (Mon–Fri); restaurant 12.30–14.30 and 18.30–23.00 (Mon–Fri), 18.30–23.00 (Sat)*
*Credit cards: all major cards*
*Draught beers: Ramrod Smooth, Young's Ordinary, Young's Special, Castlemaine, Grolsch, Young's London Lager, Young's Premium Lager, Guinness*
*Wheelchair access to venue*
*Private room: 30 seated, 50 standing*
*Nearest tube stations: Green Park, Bond Street*

# The Gun

27 Cold Harbour, E14. Tel: 0171 987 1692

This little riverside pub stands at the point where the Thames completes the deep loop enclosing the Isle of Dogs. The Gun may not have seen many admirals in its time, but seamen have always been its customers, as have lightermen and local dockers, river police and customs men. The world's navies still visit the docks, and The Gun always hoists its White Ensign to welcome them. Its three bars all have their mementos of visiting ships. Flags, crests, naval hat bands and paintings of ships hang everywhere. The Gun is a pub with an eventful past, and its future could be bright, too, with the Jubilee Line extension almost in its front garden and the Millennium exhibition directly across the water. The Lady Hamilton Room, now restored to its former elegance, will have an unrivalled view.

*Open: 11.00–23.00 (Mon–Sat), 12.00–22.30 (Sun)*
*Food: bar 11.00–23.00 (Mon–Sat), 12.00–14.30 (Sun); restaurant 12.00–14.30 and 19.00–23.00 (Mon–Sat), 12.00–14.30 (Sun)*
*Credit cards: all major cards*
*Draught beers: Kilkenny, Nelson's Bitter, Tetley's, Carlsberg, Carlsberg Export, Castlemaine, Guinness, Strongbow*
*Wheelchair access to venue*
*Private room seats 40*
*Nearest railway station: Crossharbour (DLR)*

# The Half Moon

93 Lower Richmond Road, SW15. Tel: 0181 780 9383

This large Edwardian pub is a long-established music venue with live bands every night of the week. You could have seen the Rolling Stones here in their day, and Thin Lizzy. These days you can see their tribute counterparts Stone Roses and Limehouse Lizzy. Status Quo, the Police and Dire Straits also played here, and still making history are the Hamsters, Nova, Boogie Brothers, Four Bills and a Ben, Wilko Johnson and Hank Wangford. Most styles of music are performed but they've stopped doing the Irish folk music. 'Nobody came,' says the new manager Bob Brand. A recent quarter of a million pound refit has seen a dramatic transformation to the place and they are keen to promote up and coming bands on the brink of stardom. Recent acts included Soundsville, Imogen Heap, Fridge, Twister and Garageland

*Open: 11.00–23.00 (Mon–Sat), 12.00–22.30 (Sun)*
*Credit cards: all major cards except AmEx*
*Draught beers: Young's Bitter, Young's Special, Castlemaine, London Lager, Grolsch, Tennent's Extra, Guinness, Dry Blackthorn*
*Private room: 80 seated, 500 standing*
*Nearest tube station: Putney Bridge*

# Hamilton Hall

Liverpool Street Station, EC2. Tel: 0171 247 3579

In 1901 the new Great Eastern Hotel built itself a ballroom. It set out to impress, and impress it did. From floor to ceiling it was three storeys high, and it had sumptuous decorations based on an apartment in the Palais Soubise in Paris – nymphs, garlands and cornucopias, marble fireplaces, soaring mirrors, fine paintings, all lit by chandeliers. When war broke out in 1939 it was closed. It stayed closed until the recent renovation of Liverpool Street station, when J. D. Wetherspoon won the contract to take it over. The priceless fittings and decorations were found in a storeroom, and Hamilton Hall started a new life. It is now a remarkable pub, and it sometimes seems that everyone heading for the station is having a drink there first. The usual Wetherspoon's rules apply: no music, big no-smoking areas, cut-price beer.

*Open: 11.00–23.00 (Mon–Sat), 12.00–22.30 (Sun)*
*Food: 11.00–22.00 (Mon–Sat), 12.00–21.30 (Sun)*
*Credit cards: all major cards*
*Draught beers: Caffrey's, Courage Directors, John Smith's Extra Smooth, London Pride, Theakston Best, Theakston XB, Younger's Scotch Bitter, plus five guest beers, Beck's, Foster's, Kronenbourg, Guinness, Dry Blackthorn*
*Wheelchair access to venue and loo*
*Nearest tube station: Liverpool Street*

## The Hand in Hand

6 Crooked Billet, SW19. Tel: 0181 946 5720

A few doors along from the Crooked Billet (qv), facing the same small green, is the Hand in Hand, the *Evening Standard*'s Pub of the Year in 1982.

What you see is four cottages run together with a pretty, south-facing courtyard in front, and a prize-winning riot of hanging baskets and window boxes. A horse chestnut gives shade to the tables, a vine crawls over one wall, and a wooden porch leads into the pub itself.

You find yourself in a popular, busy inn, plainly decorated and simply furnished with carved wooden benches, stools and solid old tables. There is a family room for children, plus games machines and darts, and two television sets. People are very keen on the home-made pasta. The Hand in Hand remains a lovely village pub.

*Open: 11.00–23.00 (Mon–Sat), 12.00–22.30 (Sun)*
*Food: 12.00–14.30 and 19.00–22.00 (Mon–Sat), 12.00–18.00 (Sun)*
*Credit cards: Mastercard, Switch, Visa*
*Draught beers: Young's Bitter, Young's Special, Castlemaine, Grolsch, Young's Oatmeal, Young's Pilsner, Guinness, Scrumpy Jack*
*Wheelchair access to venue*
*Private room seats 20*
*Nearest tube station: Wimbledon*

## Hand and Shears

1 Middle Street, EC1. Tel: 0171 600 0257

John Betjeman, who lived along the way in Cloth Fair, used to pop into this pub sometimes. Overworked doctors and nurses from nearby Barts like it too. There is no music or machines. It has kept its snug, the fire burns at the far end, the service is friendly, and you can get doorstep sandwiches at the bar and a pubby lunch upstairs quite cheaply. The Hand and Shears gets busy at lunchtime and then again in the evening; it closes altogether at weekends.

*Open: 11.30–23.00 (Mon–Fri)*
*Food: 12.00–14.00 (Mon–Fri)*
*Credit cards: all major cards except AmEx*
*Draught beers: Courage Best, Courage Directors, Theakston Best, Foster's, Gillespies, Kronenbourg, Strongbow*
*Private room: 40 seated, 50 standing*
*Nearest tube station: Barbican*

## Hanover Square

25 Hanover Square, W1. Tel: 0171 408 0935

This is the sister bar to Cork and Bottle (qv); it is owned by Don Hewitson, whose name is clearly branded throughout the bar should you be in doubt. The wine list is extensive, with descriptions written by the man himself, although it can be unwieldy if you're not a connoisseur. You have to decide the region you want first, followed by the colour. I suggested to my drinking partner of the evening that problems with the wine list might arise if you didn't agree with the Bacchus incarnate's opinions. His response was, 'Judging by the decor here you're unlikely to agree with anything he says.' He had a point. We couldn't work out what the hideous resting place was in the middle of the floor – a sort of freestanding shelf supported by champagne bottles. In any case, it didn't appear as though many of the clientele cared too much about the wines; most were drinking beers on our visit. Like Cork and Bottle, Hanover Square boasts air conditioning, but it needs turning up a few notches. Staff don't seem to like emptying ashtrays, even in quiet periods, and even when they've just served you food. It's a bar beneath the pavement at the end of the day, and that's exactly what it feels like.

*Open: 11.00–23.00 (Mon–Fri)*
*Food: as opening hours*
*Credit cards: all major cards*
*Nearest tube station: Oxford Circus*

## The Hare and Billet

Hare and Billet Road, SE3. Tel: 0181 852 2352

There has been an ale house on this site under one name or another since the 17th century, which was not the best time to be out and about in Blackheath. It was just heath in those days, and rather nasty heath at that, with cutpurses lurking ready to cut your throat. The lights of the solitary old ale house must have been a welcome sight for travellers on the lonely London to Dover road. London is a mere half-hour away now, and The Hare and Billet is solitary no longer. It is one of Whitbread's Hogshead pubs and takes its beer very seriously. It has ten cask ales on draught and is gradually becoming more food-focused.

*Open: 11.00–23.00 (Mon–Sat), 12.00–22.30 (Sun)*
*Food: 12.00–14.30 (Mon–Fri), 12.00–16.00 (Sat–Sun)*
*Credit cards: none taken*
*Draught beers: Abroad Cooper, Adnams Southwold, Boddingtons, Flowers, Fuggles Imperial IPA, London Pride, Marston's Pedigree, Old Speckled Hen, Young's Special, plus a guest ale, Heineken, Hoegaarden, Stella Artois, Guinness, Murphy's, Merrydown*
*Nearest railway station: Blackheath*

## The Hare and Hounds

216 Upper Richmond Road West, SW14. Tel: 0181 876 4304

Some punters in East Sheen were not best pleased when the faded, rather dingy charm of The Hare and Hounds was swept away in a major renovation a few years back. The newness wore off, and The Hare and Hounds has regained the comfortable, old-fashioned air we liked so much. It kept some of its best bits, anyway – the old bar, the panelling, the huge garden with its vast lawn and, most important, the full-sized snooker table. This being East Sheen, a golf society meets in the pub. The food, they say in The Hare and Hounds, is the cheapest in East Sheen. The pub has a menu that catches the essential spirit of the place – fish and chips, pie and mash, sizzling skillets. On Sundays it does a roast. Dogs are allowed in the public but not the main bar.

*Open: 11.00–23.00 (Mon–Sat), 12.00–22.30 (Sun)*
*Food: 12.00–15.00 and 17.00–21.30 (Mon–Sat), 12.00–15.00 (Sun)*
*Credit cards: all major cards*
*Draught beers: Young's Bitter, Young's London Lager, Young's Premium Lager, Young's Special, Castlemaine, Tennent's Extra, Guinness, Dry Blackthorn*
*Nearest railway station: Mortlake*

# Harvey Floorbangers

1 Hammersmith Road, W14. Tel: 0171 371 4105

Harvey Floorbangers was started by one of the Slug and Lettuce founding fathers. He sold it to Regent Inns, and very handsome it is: a substantial Victorian public house on the busy road opposite Olympia, the even more substantial Victorian exhibition hall. The pub used to be the Hand and Flower, and all its days has found Olympia a most useful neighbour. A big exhibition there can double its trade. It sells big, bold meals on 16-inch plates – scrumptious burgers almost an inch thick. There's a particularly fine function room upstairs, a huge room with nine long windows. Above that they do bed and breakfast, with ten rooms all en suite. A single room is £45, a double £55 and a triple £60, including Continental breakfast.

*Open: 11.00–23.00 (Mon–Sat), 12.00–22.30 (Sun)*
*Food: 12.00–14.30 and 18.30–21.30 (Mon–Sun)*
*Credit cards: all major cards*
*Draught beers: Bass, Brakspear, Caffrey's, Gale's IPA, Theakston, Young's Special, Carling, Foster's, Holsten Export, Kronenbourg, Guinness, Dry Blackthorn*
*Wheelchair access to venue*
*Private room seats 120*
*Nearest tube stations: Olympia, High Street Kensington, Hammersmith*

# Havana

490 Fulham Broadway, SW6. Tel: 0171 381 5005

Take your energy bags with you to this colourful, loud, vibrant Latin American bar, which has helped to pump up the ever-increasing volume in Fulham Broadway. Night after night the bar pulsates with Latin-influenced jazz. There are DJs Tuesday and Wednesday, and live bands Thursday through to Sunday. Every toe in the house taps away to the beat masters of swing, salsa, jive, rumba, tango and acid jazz. There's room to dance, and many do. Some come and dine first in the restaurant area, which offers more than 20 appetisers and main courses, including Havana nachos for two with frijoles negros (£6.45) and marinated sirloin steak with barbecue potatoes and mango salsa (£10.95). Happy hour (6–8pm) knocks £6 off a bottle of wine (except house) and sells cocktails at £3, so there are some bargains to be had. Our man in Havana occasionally charges admission at the door: £3 after 11pm on Thursday, £5 after 10pm Friday and Saturday. Fast, furious and fun.

*Open: 12.00–02.00 (Mon–Sat), 12.00–midnight (Sun)*
*Food: bar 12.00–02.00 (Mon–Sat), 12.00–midnight (Sun); restaurant 12.00–midnight (Mon–Sun)*
*Credit cards: all major cards*
*Nearest tube station: Fulham Broadway*

# Havelock Tavern

57 Masbro Road, W14. Tel: 0171 603 5374

In 1995 Peter Richnall bought a rather down-at-heel pub in West Kensington called the Havelock Tavern. When he closed it to spruce it up, the place was almost falling down around him. By April 1996 all had been sorted, and the Havelock Tavern opened its doors as a well-designed, spacious bar with a strong food focus. The Modern British menu boasts the likes of poached capon, baked skate wing and char-grilled mushrooms (£5–£9), and the blackboard specials display seasonal offerings and chef's favourites. Earlier this year the yard at the back was cleared, decorated with trees and bedding plants, and a pergola and picnic tables were installed. The West Ken trendies shouldn't think of whooping it up here, though. In order to respect the peace of the neighbours, the garden closes at 9.30pm, and they don't allow large gangs of people out there. Wine is as popular as beer, but make sure you stuff your wallet full of cash before you go; they don't take credit cards.

*Open: 11.00–23.00 (Mon–Sat), 12.00–22.30 (Sun)*
*Food: 12.00–21.30 (Mon–Sun)*
*Credit cards: none taken*
*Draught beers: Courage Best, Courage Director's, Marston's Pedigree, Budweiser, Foster's, Kronenbourg, Guinness, Strongbow*
*Wheelchair access to venue*
*Nearest tube station: Olympia*

## The Henry Addington

22–28 Mackenzie Walk, E14. Tel: 0171 512 9022

The view from the Henry Addington is of Heron Quays. 'It's like being on the deck of a luxury liner,' say the licensees Colin and Phyl Romney-Swallow, who have been in the business for 30 years and pride themselves on their real ales and their food. The pub has an airy interior, a 100-foot-long bar, and plenty of terrace seating where you can sip and enjoy the views.

Henry Addington was Prime Minister from 1801 to 1804. In the course of time he became Viscount Sidmouth and gave the go-ahead for a wharf to be built on the Isle of Dogs to receive goodies from the Canary Islands. Hence Canary Wharf.

*Open: 11.00–23.00 (Mon–Fri), 11.00–17.00 (Sat), 12.00–17.00 (Sun)*
*Food: 11.00–21.00 (Mon–Fri), 11.00–16.00 (Sat), 12.00–16.00 (Sun)*
*Credit cards: all major cards*
*Draught beers: Bass, Caffrey's, London Pride, Carling Black Label, Grolsch, Staropramen, Guinness, Red Rock*
*Wheelchair access to venue and loo*
*Private room seats 50*
*Nearest railway station: Canary Wharf (DLR)*

## The Henry Holland

39 Duke Street, W1. Tel: 0171 629 4426

This pleasant old pub is located down a side street opposite Selfridges. It has a good-looking bar downstairs, a fine panelled dining room upstairs, and a general air of having been built by the great 18th-century architect Henry Holland himself. Actually it was built, or anyway rebuilt, by Whitbreads in 1956. It was called The Red Lion before that. This Henry Holland was quite a goer, but he had his setbacks. His new Drury Lane Theatre incorporated all the latest safety devices but burnt down all the same. By then, though, he had designed the first version of the Brighton Pavilion, quite a lot of Knightsbridge and – rather a stroke of luck – Southill Park in Bedfordshire for Mr Samuel Whitbread, the brewer. The present Samuel Whitbread, great-great-great-great-grandson of the founder, lives there still.

*Open: 11.00–23.00 (Mon–Sat), 13.00–21.00 (Sun)*
*Food: 12.00–15.00 (Mon–Sat)*
*Credit cards: Mastercard, Switch, Visa*
*Draught beers: Abbot Ale, Boddingtons, Flowers Original, Marston's Pedigree, Old Speckled Hen, Heineken Export, Stella Artois, Guinness, Murphy's, Strongbow*
*Wheelchair access to venue*
*Private room seats 36*
*Nearest tube stations: Marble Arch, Bond Street*

# Henry J Beans

195 King's Road, SW3. Tel: 0171 352 9255

Henry J Beans is an American vision of a London pub. It has about an acre of floor space, high pedestal tables with swivel-top stools, and wallfuls of enamelled ads, plus a vast paved garden with rows of picnic tables and benches. There's also wall-to-wall music, a video satellite system with 80 channels, and a high-speed kitchen producing burgers, hotdogs, deli sandwiches, Tex-Mex specials and French fries, for which there's a big demand. As for beers, there's Webster's and Foster's on draught, which are possibly the most expensive keg beers in London at £1.25 for a half-pint glass. They don't serve pints but 2-pint pitchers are £4.95. At these prices it's best to go in happy hours when the price of a pitcher drops to a more cheery £3.50. The big thing here is bottled beers, though – beers at the bar, beers out of vending machines, and many a cocktail. Henry J Beans is a My Kinda Town venue now owned by the Capital Radio group.

*Open: 11.45–23.00 (Mon–Sat), 12.00–22.30 (Sun)*
*Food: 11.45–22.45 (Mon–Sat), 12.00–22.00 (Sun)*
*Credit cards: all major cards*
*Draught beers: Webster's, Foster's*
*Nearest tube station: Sloane Square*

# The Hereford Arms

127 Gloucester Road, SW7. Tel: 0171 370 4988

The Hereford Arms is a low building dating from the time of William and Mary. It is painted black with a sweep of windows the full length of the bar. The glass is tinted yellow, creating a sepia glow over the dim interior. The effect is deliberate and comparatively recent, and seems to work. The barmen are friendly and uniformed, the music is quiet, and the food traditional and filling. One part is reserved for waitress service, though you can eat anywhere, and there are half a dozen picnic tables outside. This is a very popular, up-market pub. Rumour has it that Jack the Ripper drank here. During the war American servicemen who played baseball in Hereford Square took a great shine to The Hereford Arms. The outstanding bill for broken windows has yet to be settled.

*Open: 11.00–23.00 (Mon–Sat), 12.00–22.30 (Sun)*
*Food: 12.00–21.00 (Mon–Sun)*
*Credit cards: AmEx, Mastercard, Visa*
*Draught beers: Beamish Red, Courage Best, Theakston Best, Theakston Old Peculier, Wadworth 6X, Beck's, Budweiser, Foster's, Molson, Guinness, Strongbow, Woodpecker*
*Wheelchair access to venue*
*Nearest tube station: Gloucester Road*

# Hillgate Arms

24 Hillgate Street, W8. Tel: 0171 727 8543

This is a very pleasant pub in a quiet backwater off Notting Hill. There is just room for tables and small benches along one outside wall, and it's hard enough getting a seat at any time, let alone when the sun comes out. The Hillgate Arms has luxuriant window boxes, hanging baskets and tubs, plus a cosy little restaurant at the back with very popular home cooking. 'We do a Sunday lunch every day,' says Pat O'Connor, the manager. 'Every day except Sunday.'

*Open: 11.00–23.00 (Mon–Sat), 12.00–22.30 (Sun)*
*Food: bar 12.00–21.30 (Mon–Sat); restaurant 12.00–14.45 (Mon–Sat)*
*Credit cards: all major cards except AmEx*
*Draught beers: Ruddles County, Theakston Best, Wadworth 6X, Webster's*

Yorkshire, Budweiser, Carlsberg, Foster's, Holsten, Guinness, Strongbow
Wheelchair access to venue and loo
Private room: 20 seated, 40 standing
Nearest tube station: Notting Hill Gate

## The Hobgoblin

95 Effra Road, SW2. Tel: 0171 501 9671

Locals often refer to this substantial old pub as The George Canning, which it was for a hundred years or so, but it is The Hobgoblin now. It remains a popular venue with an exceptional variety of entertainment – techno, rap and Latin, occasional tap-dancing, and classical guitar and stand-up comedy every week. The weekend discos remain a big hit. The old car park of George Canning days is now a large beer garden, where you can drink the Dog's Bollocks and watch the traffic roar by.

*Open: 11.00–midnight (Mon–Sat), 12.00–23.00 (Sun)*
*Food: 11.00–23.00 (Mon–Sat), 12.00–23.00 (Sun)*
*Credit cards: none taken*
*Draught beers: Courage Director's, Dog's Bollocks, Hobgoblin Original, Wychwood Special, Beck's, Foster's, Holsten Export, Kronenbourg, Guinness, Strongbow*
*Wheelchair access to venue*
*Private room: 150 seated, 300 standing*
*Nearest tube station: Brixton*

## The Hogshead in St James

11 Dering Street, W1. Tel: 0171 629 0531

This used to be a little Victorian pub called The Bunch of Grapes. Outside it has a smart, glossy black and gold new frontage; inside it seems to belong to a much earlier time. You could be in an 18th-century country taproom, plain and spare, with wooden floors, timber bar fittings and next to no furniture. The pub was given a new name and a new role as one of Whitbread's real-ale pubs, the Hogsheads. New ones are added all the time. This one manages to offer eight cask ales, quite a trick when you have such small cellars. Two come direct from 10-gallon barrels kept in full view behind the bar. They sit there in a chilling unit enjoying the limelight. People find the small room upstairs useful for parties and meetings; when it isn't booked it becomes an overspill from the bar. Who would have thought that so slender a pillar as the one in the bar could keep a Hogshead standing? As I write, The Hogshead is taking over the office space next door. We'll be seeing a much bigger pub in 1998.

*Open: 11.00–23.00 (Mon–Fri), 12.00–16.00 (Sat)*
*Food: 12.00–14.30 (Mon–Sat)*
*Credit cards: all major cards*
*Draught beers: Adnams, Boddingtons, Flowers, London Pride, Old Speckled Hen, Wadworth 6X, plus two weekly guest ales, Heineken, Stella Artois, Guinness, Strongbow*
*Wheelchair access to venue*
*Private room seats 40*
*Nearest tube stations: Bond Street, Oxford Circus*

## The Holly Bush

22 Holly Mount, NW3. Tel: 0171 435 2892

Take the long flight of steps up the hill from Heath Street and you reach one of Hampstead's oldest (1643) and most picturesque pubs. It had seven bars in Victorian times but they must have been exceptionally small. There are four now, including one that used to be the landlord's living room. However, the general look of the place doesn't seem to have changed since the days when they hung a green branch over the door to announce that the beer was ready. The bare boards, the wood and plaster walls, the old wooden furniture are as they ever were – dark brown and nicotine-stained. This is the effect that modern pub designers go for. The Holly Bush has always been like that.

*Open: 12.00–15.00 and 17.30–23.00 (Mon–Fri), 12.00–23.30 (Sat), 12.00–22.30 (Sun)*
*Food: as opening hours (Tues–Sun)*
*Credit cards: AmEx, Visa*
*Draught beers: Benskins, Burton Ale, Tetley's, plus guest ale, Carlsberg Export, Castlemaine, Guinness, Dry Blackthorn*
*Nearest tube station: Hampstead*

## Hollywood Arms

Hollywood Road, SW10. Tel: 0171 349 9274

Hollywood Road is beginning to grow again as a destination for good quality restaurants, cafés and bars. The Hollywood Arms is right in the thick of things, and seems to go in and out of fashion with each passing season. It is a traditional, high-Victorian building with neo-Gothic arched windows – an old coaching house, in fact. Its mainstay is the wonderful walled beer garden at the back, which fills easily on a warm summer's evening. The food, Scottish & Newcastle's sizzling menu, fails to entice enough of the Hollywood Road crowd away from its near neighbours. The Hollywood Arms has a favourite historical figure, one you may not have come across – a certain Jean-Pierre Blanchard, balloonist. In 1784 he took off from the field where the pub now stands and became the first man to cross the English Channel by air. This notable feat is depicted on the inn sign.

*Open: 11.00–23.00 (Mon–Sat), 12.00–22.30 (Sun)*
*Food: 12.00–22.00 (Mon–Sun)*
*Credit cards: Mastercard, Visa*
*Draught beers: Courage Directors, John Smith's Extra Smooth, Theakston Best, Beck's, Foster's, Kronenbourg, Beamish, Strongbow*
*Wheelchair access to venue*
*Private room : 80 seated, 100 standing*
*Nearest tube station: Earls Court*

## The Hoop and Grapes

47 Aldgate High Street, EC3. Tel: 0171 480 5739

A remarkable thing happened to The Hoop and Grapes in 1666. It was *not* burnt down in the Great Fire of London. It escaped by 50 yards, and there it still is, the only surviving 17th-century timber-framed building in the City of London. Everyone used brick after the fire. Until quite recently The Hoop and Grapes leant, creaked, sloped to the east. Everyone liked it that way, but it was getting a bit alarming, so the brewers spent more than a million pounds virtually rebuilding it. The two courtyards of its coaching-inn days are now part of the main bar, which is huge – all exposed timbers and brick with eating areas, drinking areas, and standing-room-only chatting areas.

The Hoop and Grapes looks very old. Well, it *is* very old, and it has never been so popular. Customers stand shoulder-to-shoulder every lunchtime. Totally underpinned, its old frame supported by steel, the pub is good for another 300 years.

*Open: 11.00–22.00 (Mon–Wed), 11.00–23.00 (Thurs–Sat)*
*Food: 12.00–15.00 and 17.30–21.00 (Mon–Fri)*
*Credit cards: all major cards*
*Draught beers: Adnams, Bass, Caffrey's, Hancock's HB, London Pride, Carling Black Label, Grolsch, Staropramen, Guinness, Cidermaster*
*Wheelchair access to venue*
*Nearest tube station: Aldgate*

# The Hope

15 Tottenham Street, W1. Tel: 0171 637 0896

Big notices outside and inside this busy Whitbread pub announce that it is a Sausage and Ale House. The sausages certainly rule okay every lunchtime – there's a choice of 13 very different bangers supplied by the ingenious Simply Sausages. During the BSE scare the lively Portuguese manager, Roger Fonseca, stopped buying sausages containing beef, but this didn't seem to matter, as the others sold just as well. There's a Creole sausage from the States and four sausages for vegetarians. Glamorgan sausage turns out to be made of Caerphilly and leeks. All the sausages are dished up with mash and baked beans, and reinforced with 13 different mustards; food is available at lunchtimes only. As for the ale, you get a choice of ten, eight on the handpumps and two served direct from barrels behind the bar.

*Open: 11.00–23.00 (Mon–Sat), 12.00–22.30 (Sun)*
*Food: 12.00–14.30 (Mon–Fri)*
*Credit cards: all major cards except AmEx*
*Draught beers: Boddingtons, Boddingtons Gold, Flowers Original, Marston's Pedigree, Wadworth 6X, plus four guest ales, Heineken, Heineken Export, Stella Artois, Guinness, Murphy's, Strongbow*
*Wheelchair access to venue*
*Private room: 24 seated, 50–100 standing*
*Nearest tube station: Goodge Street*

# Hope and Anchor

207 Upper Street, N1. Tel: 0171 354 1312

This big Victorian pub on the corner of Upper Street had more than its 15 minutes of fame in the late seventies. It became nationally famous as the leading venue of punk rock, the shock-horror sensation of the day. Just about anyone who was anyone played here: The Clash, The Damned, The Stranglers. The Sex Pistols were here twice. 'Live at the Hope and Anchor' LPs were brought out to prove it. They are great documents of the rough-and-ready quality of the bands and the crowds who came along to cheer them. It all became too much for the neighbours, however. The Environmental Health Authority closed the music room down, and the pub became a squat. For punks, naturally. They moved on after a while, and it reopened, but it was not until last year that the council finally relented and granted another music licence. So, great news, live music can once again be enjoyed at the Hope and Anchor. The music room downstairs has had plenty of money spent on it. It looks good, the sound system is very loud, and during the week you can watch indie and rock bands playing until midnight (1am at weekends). When they really get going, the floorboards in the room above vibrate. There is a big split-level bar on the ground floor with a modicum of charm; on the first floor is a pool room with three tables, and decor reminiscent of the old days when the bands could only play two chords, and bin liners held together with safety pins were the height of fashion.

*Open: 11.00–23.00 (Mon–Sat), 12.00–22.30 (Sun); music room 21.00–midnight (Mon–Thurs), 21.00–01.00 (Fri–Sat)*
*Food: 12.00–15.00 and 18.00–20.00 (Mon–Fri)*
*Credit cards: none taken*
*Draught beers: Abbot Ale, Greene King IPA, Harp, Kronenbourg, Stella Artois, Guinness, Strongbow*
*Nearest tube station: Highbury & Islington*

# The Hop Poles

17 King Street, W6. Tel: 0181 748 1411

The size of this Victorian pub is impressive. It is enormous. The danger of enormous pubs is that they can look empty, but Scottish & Newcastle has done a reasonable job in breaking up the space while retaining the elaborate front, handsome ceilings and etched mirrors. The Hop Poles also has a vast island bar which you can wander around all day if you like, bumping into one old friend after another. The food is unimpressive S & N standard fare but the location and offerings of this pub appeal to the workers and players of Hammersmith.

*Open: 10.00–23.00 (Mon–Sat), 12.00–22.30 (Sun)*
*Food: 10.00–22.00 (Mon–Sat), 12.00–22.00 (Sun)*
*Credit cards: Visa*
*Draught beers: Greene King IPA, John Smith's Extra Smooth, Marston's Pedigree, Theakston Best, Foster's, Holsten, Kronenbourg, Miller, Guinness, Strongbow*
*Wheelchair access to venue and loo*
*Private room seats 100*
*Nearest tube station: Hammersmith*

# Horniman at Hay's

Hay's Galleria, Tooley Street, SE1. Tel: 0171 407 3611

Hay's Galleria – a soaring atrium with shops, galleries and cafés – is a great place for a pub. HMS *Belfast* lies offshore, and Tower Bridge, with its extraordinary power to cheer you up, is just down river. If you have been doing the riverbank walk, you will be in need of a drink at this point. You will be pleased, then, to find Horniman's waiting. This is an expansive, confident and glossy pub. Its long, polished mahogany counter has a choice of five real ales, not to mention all the lagers, and turns into a tea bar that also sells coffee and chilled milk. Then there's the big wide-open café, serving good, reasonably priced fast food, where children are welcome. Part of the gallery upstairs is kept busy with private functions, and there's a non-smoking bit somewhere. The Horniman in question was Mr F. J. Horniman, the Victorian tea importer, and this used to be the wharf where his tea was landed. You can find out more about him at the Horniman Museum in Forest Hill, where he lived. This pub on his quay has many reminders of his life's work, including a set of clocks from his office showing the time in foreign parts. The pub is 11 years old now, and is decorated in a Victorian style – the one, we are told, that beer drinkers prefer above all others.

*Open: 10.00–23.00 (Mon–Fri), 10.00–18.00 (Sat), 10.00–16.00 (Sun)*
*Food: 12.00–14.30 (Mon–Sun)*
*Credit cards: AmEx, Mastercard, Switch, Visa*
*Draught beers: Adnams, Brakspear, Broadside, Calder's Cream Ale, Eldridge Pope, London Pride, Marston's Pedigree, Old Speckled Hen, Tetley's, Timothy Taylor, Carlsberg, Carlsberg Export, Castlemaine, Lowenbrau, Guinness, Olde English*
*Wheelchair access to venue*
*Two private rooms: 60 and 70 seated*
*Nearest tube station: London Bridge*

# The Horse and Groom

68 Heath Street, NW3. Tel: 0171 435 3140

The original Horse and Groom seems to have been just the sort of old pub we now most admire. It was an 18th-century tavern, the kind of inn that appears on Christmas cards, but by the end of the 19th century it must have seemed very rustic in newly fashionable Hampstead. So in 1899 Young's replaced it with this imposing, five-storey public house with a modish striped brick and stone façade and a high decorated gable, the height of late-Victorian taste. It was the tallest building in Heath Street, and still is. The rich Victorian interior has been largely dismantled over the years but bits of it remain. Today there is one long, open-plan room. The front half is where the counter is, the back half where most of the tables are. The Horse and Groom is a friendly local with pleasant girls who bring your lunch to your table, and chat to regulars spending happy, ruminative afternoons on their bar stools. It remains a genuinely Victorian pub. Convincing replicas of Charles I's death warrant and the Act of Union of 1707 are to be found tucked behind a gaming machine.

*Open: 12.00–23.00 (Mon–Sat), 12.00–22.30 (Sun)*
*Food: 12.00–16.00 (Mon–Sun)*
*Credit cards: none taken*
*Draught beers: Young's Bitter, Young's Special, Castlemaine, London Lager, Premium Lager, Tennent's Extra, Guinness, Oatmeal Stout, Dry Blackthorn*
*Wheelchair access to venue*
*Private room: 30 seated, 70 standing*
*Nearest tube station: Hampstead*

## The House They Left Behind

27 Ropemaker's Fields, E14. Tel: 0171 538 5102

The Black Horse was a small, inner-city pub built in 1856, part of a terrace in the heart of a teeming bit of the East End. It is still there, but there is nothing else left of Ropemaker's Fields, not a single house, just this solitary pub – hence its new name, The House They Left Behind. Looking at Limehouse now, it is hard to imagine it as it used to be – the boatyards, the docks, the maze of tenements. For years, public works went on all around the pub. The dump on one side is now a park, and the empty space at the front door has been made into a piazza with benches, young trees and a sculpture of a seagull on a coil of rope. People play boules there all summer. The pub itself has new owners and new managers. It has been painted up and refurbished and, most important of all, a development of 11 flats has brought new neighbours at last. Regulars tell me they keep a pretty decent pint of ale here.

*Open: 12.00–15.00 and 17.00–23.00 (Mon–Thurs), 11.00–23.00 (Fri–Sun)*
*Food: 12.00–18.00 (Mon–Sun)*
*Credit cards: none taken*
*Draught beers: Boddingtons, Courage Best, John Smith's Extra Smooth, Theakston Best, Foster's, Kronenbourg, Miller, Guinness, Strongbow*
*Wheelchair access to venue*
*Nearest railway station: Westferry (DLR)*

## Hung, Drawn and Quartered

26–27 Great Tower Street, EC3. Tel: 0171 626 6123

Yes, I know it should be *Hanged,* Drawn and Quartered, so don't write to me, write to Fuller's, who insist that this is the common usage. Common it may be, but if you look on the outside of this building, I think you might find the answer – there isn't enough room for the word Hanged. This pub was opened in 1996 as a result of yet another conversion from a bank. For those who stray towards Tower Bridge after work, it is now a single-roomed banking hall with a bar in it and, like a bank, just a few places to sit down. Very creditable.

*Open: 11.00–23.00 (Mon–Fri), 12.00–15.30 (Sat)*
*Food: 12.00–15.00 (Mon–Fri), 12.00–14.30 (Sat)*
*Credit cards: all major cards*
*Draught beers: Chiswick Bitter, ESB, London Pride, plus a guest ale, Carling Black Label, Grolsch, Heineken, Stella Artois, Guinness, Murphy's, Scrumpy Jack*
*Wheelchair access to venue and loo*
*Nearest tube stations: Monument, Tower Gateway (DLR)*

# Iberica

295 New King's Road, SW6. Tel: 0171 371 5939

Tapas bar with occasional discos downstairs. Can be quite fun, and the late opening helps. This is Fulham on the pull when they haven't quite managed to pull anywhere else.

*Open: 12.00–15.00 and 18.00–midnight (Mon–Wed), 12.00–01.00 (Thurs–Sat), 12.00–22.30 (Sun)*
*Food: 12.00–15.00 and 18.00–midnight (Mon–Wed), 12.00–15.00 and 18.00–01.00 (Thurs–Sat), 12.00–15.00 and 18.00–22.00 (Sun)*
*Credit cards: all major cards*
*Private room seats 50 seated, 80 standing*
*Nearest tube station: Fulham Broadway*

# Ink Club

541a King's Road, SW6. Tel: 0171 610 6117

This new bar opened in the spring of 1997 sandwiched between Come the Revolution and Shoeless Joe's (qqv) – a great location. The Ink Club has a small bar at the front, a diminutive restaurant at the back, and a petite lounge bar in the basement. It is a members' club, but the restaurant is always open to the public – a Modern British affair that includes roast monkfish with lemon couscous and pimento salsa (£10.75), and venison fillet and celeriac chips with raspberry vinegar and bitter chocolate sauce (£13.50). The problem with the restaurant is the intrusive noise from the bar and downstairs room. The basement lounge, with too few places to sit, is similarly noisy. The bars are supposed to be for members only on Thursday, Friday and Saturday – although on several visits made by this Guide, we gained access quite easily. This, I am assured, is only a temporary measure until the membership builds up. In order to gain membership you need to apply in person (artists will be looked upon favourably), and it's then up to the management whether or not you're likely to be asked to cough up the required £125 membership fee. They're looking for some 500–600 members, which is rather worrying as the capacity of the place is only 100. Should they accept me as a member (and I don't intend to ask), I would be mightily miffed at being refused admission due to a private party booking. I suspect that things will sharpen up a bit, or change drastically in the coming months, but after such a confusing start to life, I hope the Ink Club doesn't continue to blot its own copybook with an arrogance associated with its prime position.

*Open: 12.00–midnight (Mon–Wed), 12.00–02.00 (Thurs–Sat)*
*Food: bar 12.00–midnight (Mon–Wed), 12.00–02.00 (Thurs–Sat); restaurant 12.00–23.00 (Mon–Wed), 12.00–23.30 (Thurs–Sat)*
*Credit cards: all major cards*
*Draught beers: Staropramen, Guinness*
*Nearest tube station: Fulham Broadway*

# The Intrepid Fox

99 Wardour Street, W1. Tel: 0171 287 8359

Loud, heavy and an all-action music venue, The Intrepid Fox is a leading rock, alternative and indie pub, so popular that you sometimes have to queue to get in. It's black leather jackets, ponytails and half-shaved heads in the big downstairs bar these days, and the walls are covered with icons such as Jimi Hendrix, the Rolling Stones and the Who. They have been overtaken by a whole new generation of intrepid foxes, whose music plays all day, getting louder, ever louder – Oasis and Black Grape, Green Day and Offspring, Prodigy, Terrorvision, Rancid, Jane's Addiction, White Zombie, Beastie Boys....

*Open: 12.00–23.00 (Mon–Sat), 15.00–22.30 (Sun)*
*Credit cards: none taken*
*Draught beers: Abbot Ale, Old Speckled Hen, Carlsberg Export, Castlemaine, Lowenbrau, Guinness, Cidermaster*
*Nearest tube station: Piccadilly Circus*

## The Island Queen

87 Noel Road, N1. Tel: 0171 359 4037

Life-sized wooden pirate puppets hang from the ceiling over the horseshoe bar in this agreeably eccentric Islington local. Bare floorboards, ceiling-high Victorian mirrors, a small pool room at the back – people who drink there like it just as it is. For years the original juke box played the magic music of the sixties, thus ensuring a clientele of discrimination. Alas, it became unwell and was pronounced beyond repair. A modern all-singing CD version took its place. Island Queen regulars reluctantly concede that the replacement keeps true to the music, but enough is enough. The thirtysomethings, says manager Garth Foster, would turn in their ashtrays if modernisation went one step further. There is an agreeable restaurant upstairs.

*Open: 12.00–15.00 and 17.30–23.00 (Mon–Thurs), 11.00–23.00 (Fri), 12.00–23.00 (Sat), 12.00–22.30 (Sun)*
*Food: bar 12.20–14.30 (Mon–Fri); restaurant 18.00–midnight (Fri–Sat), 12.00–16.00 (Sun)*
*Credit cards: Mastercard, Visa*
*Draught beers: Bass, Caffrey's, London Pride, Carling Black Label, Grolsch, Guinness, Dry Blackthorn*
*Private room: 50 seated, 100 standing*
*Nearest tube station: Angel*

## Jack Horner

236 Tottenham Court Road, W1. Tel: 0171 636 2868

Fuller's appear to be obsessed with converting banks into pubs. Banks make very good pubs, actually. The old branch of Martin's bank is now a useful new pub called the Jack Horner, after Little Jack Horner, one of the great heroes of English literature. Horner's is a moving story. He was sitting in his corner eating his Christmas pie when, in a dramatic scene, he stuck in his thumb and pulled out a plum. 'What a good boy am I!' he said. You get a very nice pie in the Jack Horner, this being one of Fuller's Ale and Pie pubs, but it does get very busy.

*Open: 11.00–23.00 (Mon–Sat)*
*Food: 11.00–21.00 (Mon–Thurs), 18.00–20.00 (Sat)*
*Credit cards: all major cards*
*Draught beers: Chiswick Bitter, ESB, London Cream, London Pride, plus two guest ales, Carling Black Label, Grolsch, Heineken, Stella Artois, Guinness, Murphy's, Scrumpy Jack*
*Wheelchair access to venue and loo*
*Nearest tube stations: Warren Street, Goodge Street, Tottenham Court Road*

## Jack Straw's Castle

North End Way, NW3. Tel: 0171 435 8885

Almost remote at the top of Highgate Hill is this three-storey inn with a long weatherboard frontage, a parade of bay windows, arched Gothic windows from end to end, and battlements on top. It is looking very spruce now with its refurbished bars, function rooms and *à la carte* restaurant.

There's always lots going on here. There are coach-loads of tour groups, endless wedding receptions, and barbecues most summer evenings in the big courtyard at the back, a pleasant place with brick paving and cobbles, a tree with a tree seat, and lots of wooden tables and benches. The first floor is for private parties and the top floor is the restaurant. Jack Straw's Castle occupies one of the highest points in London, and the restaurant has fine views over Hampstead Heath.

*Open: 11.00–23.00 (Mon–Sat), 12.00–22.30 (Sun)*
*Food: bar 12.00–15.00 (Mon–Fri); restaurant 12.00–14.30 and 18.30–22.00 (Mon–Sat), 12.00–21.00 (Sun)*
*Credit cards: all major cards*
*Draught beers: Bass, Caffrey's, London Pride, Carling Black Label, Grolsch, Staropramen, Guinness, Dry and Sweet Blackthorn*
*Wheelchair access to venue*
*Private room seats 50*
*Nearest tube station: Hampstead*

## Jacs

48 Lonsdale Road, W11. Tel: 0171 792 2838

Jacs's sign hangs in aged, cut-out metal outside this 1930s stone-fronted building close to the Portobello Road and the trendy, well-established drinking dens Beach Blanket Babylon and the Walmer Castle (qqv) on Ledbury Road. You enter through a series of double doors, first wooden then brass, with a tiny porthole window. You need to pause for a moment to absorb the extraordinary decor, which has such an impact on the eye it almost steals your breath. The wall on the left is painted deep red, and softly lit recesses display objets d'art. Walk past the large, circular island bar – note the aquarium, and two more, one on each side of the entrance to the back room, which is also painted deep red and has a massive skylight. Back in the main bar, the opposite wall has pictures interspersed with what looks like a series of book shelves. These are actually trompe l'oeils. You are now at the front of the candlelit bar, with its velvet-draped armchairs, couches and wooden armchairs, and massive old wooden table. This is where you sit to watch the fractal video sequences on the large screen next to the VJ booth. Rising above you, almost cathedral-like, is a striking and effective mirrored gallery.

Jacs is beauty by design, an eclectic blend, visually stimulating. There is almost too much to look at, and I hope that this doesn't become its downfall. The music seems to be a mix of everything, but it returns to the R & B theme after a few excursions into the surreal. It attracts a quite varied, unpretentious Notting Hill crowd, but if the word gets out quick enough, this could be spoilt by the masses from other parts of town who find it trendy to hang out in alternative, ethnic bars. The air conditioning could do with a little help, and there was a poor choice in the white wine range – two, to be exact.

*Open: 18.00–23.00 (Mon–Sat), 19.00–22.30 (Sun)*
*Credit cards: all major cards except AmEx*
*Draught beers: John Smith's Extra Smooth, Foster's, Kronenbourg, Scrumpy Jack*
*Wheelchair access to venue*
*Private room holds 60 standing*
*Nearest tube stations: Ladbroke Grove, Notting Hill Gate*

## Janet's Bar

208 Fulham Road, SW10. Tel: 0171 795 0111

At first sight you would be forgiven for thinking that Janet's is an American-style ice-cream parlour. At second sight, you might think the caricature painted on the sign outside was that of Janet Street-Porter. You would be wrong on both counts – as I was. The face behind the caricature and the bar's namesake is Janet Evans, one half of the husband (David) and wife team of City lawyers whose dream it was to own their own bar. This is the result. What we have is a pink and white sugar-candy-looking façade with pink wicker chairs on the pavement. Inside, a marble-topped bar fills almost half the room, and the stark white walls, pink accessories and humorous collages of Janet failing in a variety of fitness activities stamp the bar with Janet's personal style. Camp is one word to describe it; adventurous and kitsch are others I've heard used. Undeniably self-indulgent is what it actually is.

They don't mess around with food here, although they let you order in from nearby restaurants. The house menu consists of wines, beers, spirits and a variety of coffees. There is no draught beer; bottled beers go for £2.50 each. Janet's claims to be the only place in London to sell Spike – mango- or lemon-flavoured ciders. Wines start at £9.50 for the house Sauvignon blanc or Château rouge but quickly rise to the £20–£40 range. Champagne is also available at £5 per glass. The menu proudly boasts a narrative, apparently from Nigella Lawson: 'A fabulous idea, a bar where anyone can wander in alone and feel deliciously comfortable.' They even go through the harmless process of manufacturing their own reviews, which are then displayed in the window for the world to see. I suggest they use 'Is Chelsea ready for Janet's?'

*Open: 12.00–23.00 (Mon–Sat), 12.00–22.30 (Sun)*
*Credit cards: all major cards*
*Wheelchair access to venue*
*Two private rooms: 50 seated, 100 standing*
*Nearest tube stations: Fulham Broadway, South Kensington*

# Jimmies

18 Kensington Church Street, W8. Tel: 0171 937 9988

Bare boards, wooden tables and church pews: you don't get pampered in this archetypal seventies-style wine bar. *Evening Standard* reporters know it well – this is where they have their farewell binges when they leave. There's live music most nights, and anyone going in nightly has very catholic tastes: indie on Tuesday, Brit-pop Wednesdays, blues Thursdays, acoustic funk Fridays and jazz Saturdays. Sundays are for recovering, so Jimmies doesn't bother opening.

*Open: 12.00–23.00 (Mon), 12.00–01.00 (Tues–Sat)*
*Food: 12.00–16.00 and 19.00–23.00*
*Credit cards: all major cards*
*Nearest tube station: High Street Kensington*

# Jim Thompson's

Jim Thompson was an American who made his fortune in the Bangkok silk trade. More than a quarter of a century ago, he vanished without trace, and he has since been declared legally dead. His reputation has never waned – the best Thai silk still bears his name – and his disappearance has never been explained. This interesting character has lent his name to a small chain of bar/restaurants owned by Tony Carson – and, yes, he is Frank Carson's son. Tony regularly travels to Thailand on buying trips, and his wares decorate and are for sale in all the Jim Thompson's. You'll be delighted to find a decent range of real ales and an Oriental Express menu in the bar should you decide not to go the full monty and dine in the highly praised restaurant.

*Open: 12.00–midnight (Mon–Sat), 12.00–23.00 (Sun)*
*Food: restaurant as opening hours; Oriental Express menu 12.00–19.30*
*Credit cards: all major cards*
*Draught beers: Adnams, Adnams Broadside, Tetley's, Carlsberg, Lowenbrau, Scrumpy Jack*
*Wheelchair access to venue and loo*
*Nearest tube station: Fulham Broadway*

*Branches at:*
**Croydon**: 34 Surrey Street, CR0. Tel: 0181 256 0007
**Putney**: 408 Upper Richmond Road, SW15. Tel: 0181 788 3737
(opens November 1997)

## JJ's

105–109 The Broadway, SW19. Tel: 0181 540 8339

If you've ever been to the Wimbledon Theatre, you'll no doubt be familiar with this bar. Small and intimate, and covered with theatre posters, it is a good way from the top of Wimbledon Hill both in terms of geography and prices. Bottled beers start at £1.90, draughts at £1.80 and wines at £6.95. If you're going to the theatre, it's worth knowing that they cut 50p off the price of a pint between 5pm and 7pm. Don't expect to eat in the evenings, though; food is currently served only at lunchtimes. Main courses start at £4 and include an interesting range of stir-fries, omelettes, salads and pies with mashed potato.

*Open: 11.30–23.30 (Mon–Fri), 16.30–23.30 (Sat), 18.00–22.30 (Sun)*
*Food: 11.30–15.30 (Mon–Fri)*
*Credit cards: all major cards*
*Draught beers: Young's, Young's Original, Young's Ramrod Smooth, Young's Special, Castlemaine, Labatt's, Stella Artois, Young's Pilsner, Guinness, Dry Blackthorn*
*Nearest tube station: South Wimbledon*

## Joe's Wine Bar and Restaurant

33 Lavender Hill, SW11. Tel: 0171 228 2960

Joe's is a place for wine-drinkers. Spirits are not served, and bottled beers are available as support rather than playing the leading role. The Ashby family, who own Joe's, are dedicated wine professionals, and that's the whole point of the place. The decor is simple and comfortable, with exposed brick walls and an unfussy seating arrangement. The menu, which changes every couple of weeks, is reassuringly short. I have been reliably informed that the food is rather good (£3.25 for starters, £7.50 for main courses). House wines start at £8.40 and are available by the glass from £2.20.

*Open: 18.00–23.00 (Tues–Fri), 12.00–23.00 (Sat), 12.00–22.30 (Sun)*
*Food: as opening hours*
*Credit cards: all major cards*
*Wheelchair access to venue*
*Nearest railway station: Clapham Junction*

## John Keats at Moorgate

83 Moorgate, EC2. Tel: 0171 606 4731

This pub has changed beyond recognition since John Keats was born here in 1795. In those days it was called The Swan and Hoop. By the 1830s it had become the Moorgate Coffee House and then it settled down for long years as The Moorgate. Now it is John Keats at Moorgate. What hasn't changed is that for all its long life it has lived flank to flank with a bigger, noisier pub, The Globe Tavern (qv). Today Bass owns them both and they operate under a single licence with the same manager. Nevertheless, the John Keats does its best to hold on to a separate identity. It has its own restaurant and kitchen, its own regulars, its own personality. No music, for instance. But it can never entirely forget its proximity to The Globe. When the two pubs got their shared licence in 1990, an interior door was inserted between them. It is constantly in use, and whenever anyone opens it you get a short sharp blast of noise from the John Keats's more assertive next-door neighbour.

*Open: 11.00–23.00 (Mon–Fri) Closed Sat & Sun*
*Food: bar 12.00–20.00 (Mon–Fri); restaurant 12.00–15.00 (Mon–Fri)*
*Credit cards: all major cards*
*Draught beers: Bass, Caffrey's, London Pride, Carling Black Label, Carling Premier,*
*Grolsch, Guinness, Red Rock*
*Wheelchair access to venue*
*Nearest tube station: Moorgate*

## Jolly Farmers

7 Purley High Street, Purley CR2. Tel: 0181 660 2076

There are precious few drinking places in Purley, but the Jolly Farmers is at the centre of things. Purley grew up around this pub and continues to do so, with new retail developments and new road schemes being built nearby. The pub hasn't been very jolly of late; like most of us it is starting to show its age and would benefit from a bit of a spruce up. Those who use it find it an acceptable little boozer.

*Open: 11.00–23.00 (Mon–Sat), 12.00–22.30 (Sun)*
*Food: 11.00–14.30 (Mon–Fri)*
*Credit cards: none taken*
*Draught beers: Burton, Calder's Cream Ale, Friary Meux, Tetley's, Carlsberg,*
*Castlemaine, Lowenbrau, Guinness, Dry Blackthorn*
*Nearest railway station: Purley*

## Kemia Bar at Momo   EROS AWARD WINNER

25 Heddon Street, W1. Tel: 0171 434 4040

Imagine, if you will, a Bedouin tent in Morocco – incense burning, wailing music, organza drapes, rugs, pouffes, silk cushions and long couches – all, incidentally, made in Morocco. To say this is a beautiful and stylish bar is an understatement. It is irresistible. Close your eyes, inhale the aroma, listen to the music, and you could almost be transported to a sweet, seductive, North African landscape. The hand-painted orange walls glow under filtered light from Moroccan lanterns. The kemia (a Moroccan word meaning light snacks or appetisers) are terrific, even down to the pepper- and garlic-stuffed olives. Borchettes, pastry-wrapped prawns, meat or cheese, are among the offerings at £3.50. Designers of other bars should come here first to see what can be done in the name of authenticity. Kemia is to be applauded for its realism, its individuality and its contribution to the London bar and restaurant scene. Customers eating in the restaurant are eligible to use the bar at all times. The rest of us can only go on Monday, Tuesday and Wednesday. Otherwise it's members only, I'm afraid. Membership is strictly by invitation, but if you go down and plead with them, they might – and I say might – just consider you. They say they don't like people to wear suits. I was told, and I quote, 'You're not likely to enjoy yourself if you're wearing a suit.' Be prepared for changes. If Kemia's popularity persists, which it undoubtedly will, they may make the place members only every night of the week.

*Open: 19.00–01.00 (Mon–Sun)*
*Food: as opening hours*
*Credit cards: all major cards*
*Nearest tube station: Piccadilly Circus*

## Kettner's Champagne Bar

29 Romilly Street, W1. Tel: 0171 437 6437

The champagne bar at Kettner's is an elegant drawing room where, as the name suggests, they only serve champagne. City suits and Soho media darlings with expense accounts seem to occupy most of the bar. The conservatory bar at the back – white walls, white tiled floors, views of the kitchen, and a desperate need for air conditioning – serves normal drinks for the smaller budget, i.e., those of us not on expense accounts. Kettner's always seems busy, but it is an uncomfortable place to wait on your own for a friend – you don't want to buy a bottle of champagne in the lounge or occupy a table in the bar *à la* Billy-no-mates, and there are few comfortable spots in which to lose yourself. Publicity material states that the bar was '...established in 1867 by Auguste Kettner, chef to Napoleon III, and [has been] renowned ever since for superb food and wine'. I'll bet Mr Kettner never thought he'd end up owned by the same people who own the Pizza Express chain.

*Open: 12.00–midnight (Mon–Sun)*
*Food: 12.00–midnight (Mon-Sun)*
*Credit cards: All major cards*
*Private rooms: four rooms: 10–80 seated, up to 100 standing*
*Nearest tube stations: Tottenham Court Road, Leicester Square*

## King of Bohemia

210 Hampstead High Street, NW3. Tel: 0171 435 6513

An attractive, popular pub with glass doors that open the whole frontage to the street in warm weather, the King of Bohemia gets very lively in the evenings. You can have breakfast here from 10am but you have to wait another hour for a drop of the hard stuff. This is a pub for the younger residents of Hampstead – those who enjoy the loud music and sometimes frenetic atmosphere.

*Open: 10.00–23.00 (Mon–Fri), 10.00–23.00 (Sat–Sun)*
*Food: 10.00–16.00 and 18.00–21.00 (Mon–Thurs), 10.00–16.00 (Fri–Sun)*
*Credit cards: all major cards except AmEx*
*Draught beers: Boddingtons, Boston Beer, Flowers IPA, Flowers Original, London Pride, Marston's Pedigree, Heineken, Heineken Export, Stella Artois, Guinness, Murphy's, Merrydown*
*Wheelchair access to venue*
*Nearest tube station: Hampstead*

## The King's Head

4 Fulham High Street, SW6. Tel: 0171 736 1413

The King's Head's claim to be 'London's Premier Live Music Venue' is supported by the regular army of live music followers who pack the place out for secret gigs, record launches and album previews. The sign reading 'Bar closed to public' is the clue that tells you something special is going on. The public need not include you. Secret gigs, like any other, need audiences, so leave your name, address and telephone number in the book at the door and you will be told about it. The admission price varies but starts around £3. Led Zeppelin recorded an album here a couple of years back. A large black room with a bar leads to a smaller black room with a stage and sophisticated equipment. If this is not your scene you can go through the unlabelled connecting door, past the ladies and into the comparatively bright lights of the public bar. This has its own customers. You will find them drinking at a massive U-shaped bar, playing pool, feeding coins into machines, watching music, sport and films on big-screen television and listening to a major juke box in constant use. The bar has its own entrance from the street and one from the beer garden, which seems to have grown. On sunny days 250 people can and do find a seat there. A new barbecue has been installed, and people bring their own sausages and burgers and cook them themselves. 'It's big enough for two sheep at once,' says the licensee, John McKibbin.

*Open: bar 11.00–23.00 (Mon–Sat), 12.00–22.30 (Sun); music room 20.30–midnight (Mon–Sat)*
*Food: barbecue available – bring your own food*
*Credit cards: none taken*

*Draught beers: Caffrey's, Carling Black Label, Tennent's Pilsner, Tennent's Extra,
Guinness, Dry Blackthorn*
*Wheelchair access to venue*
*Private room seats 150*
*Nearest tube station: Putney Bridge*

## The King's Head

115 Upper Street, N1. Tel: 0171 226 1916

There are now at least a dozen theatre pubs in London. This particular example
is a substantial Victorian pile with a busy and in some ways eccentric life of its
own. When the nation went decimal in 1971, the manager, Dan Crawford, was
reluctant to replace his noble Victorian till, so he didn't. The King's Head contin-
ued with the old currency, and it still does. A pint of Guinness costs
£2-4s-0d; a cup of coffee 14s.

The theatre is at the back. The productions staged here get brilliant casts and
national reviews. Many have transferred to the West End. One transferred to
Broadway and won four TONY awards. There is a fair-sized apron stage and a
decent view from just about anywhere. Supper is served at tables in the theatre
before the performance – you don't have to eat there but most people do. A
three-course meal costs £8-10s-0d, and you stay on at your table to watch the
play. Tickets for this cost £10 during the week and £11 on Saturday. The
capacity is 125 with 90 able to eat. Meanwhile the pub will have been filling up
and, the play over, departing theatregoers have to squeeze through a crowded
bar to reach the street. Some stay on for the Adnams and the music which follows the show – there is folk, rock or jazz until midnight.

*Open: 11.00–midnight (Mon–Thurs), 11.00–01.00 (Fri–Sat), 12.00–midnight (Sun)*
*Food: bar as opening hours; pre-theatre dinner 19.00–20.00 (Mon–Sun)*
*Credit cards: all major cards for theatre bookings only*
*Draught beers: Adnams, Benskins, Burton Ale, Carlsberg, Lowenbrau, Guinness,
Olde English*
*Wheelchair access to venue and loo*
*Nearest tube stations: Highbury & Islington, Angel*

## King's Head and Eight Bells

50 Cheyne Walk, SW3. Tel: 0171 352 1820

The King's Head and Eight Bells had modest beginnings, starting life as two
small 15th-century seamen's pubs side by side on the riverbank. The King's
Head was for officers, the Eight Bells for the crews. Eight bells were rung to
summon the men back to their ships. The present pub is no longer on the riverbank, however. The original riverside Cheyne Walk still passes the door, but
Chelsea Embankment long since came between river and pub. The embankment gardens have also intervened. The two old pubs merged in 1580, and the
King's Head and Eight Bells became a local for river boatmen. Today, the big
bar at the front of the pub offers customers a choice of eight cask ales. The bar
opens onto a busy restaurant at the back, where families gather and seem to
enjoy the fare. Both bar and restaurant share a wealth of modern features disguising the long history of this famous pub.

*Open: 11.00–23.00 (Mon–Sat), 12.00–22.30 (Sun)*
*Food: 12.00–15.00 (Mon), 12.00–15.00 and 19.00–22.00 (Tues–Sat), 12.00–14.00
and 19.00–22.00 (Sun)*
*Credit cards: Delta, Mastercard, Switch, Visa*
*Draught beers: Boddingtons, Flowers Original, Old Speckled Hen, Heineken,
Heineken Export, Stella Artois, Murphy's, Scrumpy Jack*
*Wheelchair access to venue*
*Nearest tube station: Sloane Square*

# The King William IV

75 Hampstead High Street, NW3. Tel: 0171 435 5747

The King William IV stands four square on its corner. It is built of yellow London brick and has black shutters, window boxes and hanging baskets bright with flowers. The interior is very smart, the ceiling lincrustaed, the walls sponged, stippled, papered and panelled. There is a substantial island counter and a team of cheerful barmen dealing with four separate drinking areas. Seasoned regulars gather in the small bar at the front. Some have hardly budged in 25 years. Younger customers stick to the big open space at the other end. The upstairs bar is used for functions and a set Sunday lunch (£4.95). The food, which is good, is lunchtime only, but you don't have to go far to find restaurants at other times. The garden – large, pleasant and filled with tables – can always count on a busy and sociable summer.

*Open: 11.00–23.00 (Mon–Sat), 12.00–22.30 (Sun)*
*Food: 12.00–17.00 (Mon–Sun)*
*Credit cards: none taken*
*Draught beers: Brakspear, Courage Best, Courage Directors, John Smith's Extra Smooth, Budweiser, Carlsberg, Foster's, Kronenbourg, Guinness,*
*Wheelchair access to venue*
*Private room: no seating, 60 standing*
*Nearest tube station: Hampstead*

# Kudos

10 Adelaide Street, WC2. Tel: 0171 379 4573

A glass fronted, modern-designed, un-closeted gay café bar, which is fairly quiet during the day and buzzes in the evenings when the suits finish work. Downstairs there is a cruiser room with occasional DJs. Call in to get your queue-jump tickets for Heaven, GAY and The Fridge.

*Open: 11.00–23.00 (Mon–Sat) 12.00–22.30 (Sun)*
*Food: 11.00–17.00 (Mon–Sat), 12.00–17.00 (Sun)*
*Credit cards: all major cards*
*Draught beers: Bombardier, Fresh Lager, Q Lager, Red Stripe*
*Nearest tube station: Charing Cross*

# The Ladbroke Arms

54 Ladbroke Road, W11. Tel: 0171 727 6648

The Ladbroke is a handsome early-Victorian pub that was noticeably unshining when Ian MacKenzie took it over. He gave it a good clean, of course, and did a bit of the old refurbishing, but the key to its renaissance was bright, friendly new staff and a radical change in the kitchen, astonishing the customers with food you actually wanted to eat. There are good cask ales, and the wine list isn't bad either. Classical music or light jazz plays quietly in the background and the raised terrace outside is famously crowded all summer.

*Open: 11.00–15.00 and 17.30–23.00 (Mon–Sat), 12.00–22.30 (Sun)*
*Food: bar 12.00–14.30 and 19.00–21.45 (Mon–Sat), 12.00–21.45 (Sat–Sun)*
*Credit cards: Mastercard, Visa*
*Draught beers: Courage Best, Courage Directors, John Smith's Extra Smooth, Theakston XB, Wadworth 6X, Carlsberg, Holsten Export, Beamish, Guinness, Strongbow*
*Wheelchair access to venue*
*Nearest tube station: Holland Park*

# The Lamb

94 Lamb's Conduit Street, WC1. Tel: 0171 405 0713

The Lamb has long been one of the most admired pubs in London. It was built in the 1720s and twice improved almost beyond recognition by the Victorians, who despised anything 18th century. There were alterations in our own time, too, but thankfully the 1959 restorers left the handsome façade, the etched windows and the splendid U-shaped bar counter, which is ringed by brilliant-cut hinged snob screens. Open them and you are face to face with the barman. Close them and your drink will slide discreetly towards you under the screens. It is all convincingly Victorian – the Spy cartoons, the musical comedy stars, the leather sofas and the splendid Polyphone, great-grandfather of the CD player, with discs going back to 1830. The Lamb belongs to John Young, chairman of the brewers and quite a celeb, making movies and starring in the *Antiques Roadshow*. Put £1 in the charity box and the staff will wind up the Polyphone and let it play. There is a little patio at the back but, whenever they can, regulars at The Lamb like to drink outside in Lamb's Conduit Street.

*Open: 11.00–23.00 (Mon–Sat), 12.00–22.30 (Sun)*
*Food: 12.00–17.00 and 19.00–22.00 (Mon–Sat), 12.00–15.30 (Sun)*
*Credit cards: Mastercard, Visa*
*Draught beers: Young's Ordinary, Young's Special, Young's seasonal ales, Castle-maine, Grolsch, London Lager, Premium Lager, Guinness, Young's Oatmeal Stout, Scrumpy Jack*
*Wheelchair access to venue*
*Nearest tube stations: Russell Square, Holborn*

# The Lamb and Flag

33 Rose Street, WC2. Tel: 0171 497 9504

This small, charming, much-loved pub is tucked away up an alley between Garrick Street and Floral Street and is easily the oldest pub in the area. Half Covent Garden seems to go there for a drink after work. If they can't get in, they drink on the pavement. In the summer when everyone drinks outside you can hardly see the pub for the people. They call the upstairs room the Dryden Room – you get a good straightforward lunch up there, and Dixieland jazz on Sunday nights. Once you've been drinking here for a hundred years or so, they'll mount a brass plaque on the bar in recognition of your service. There are hundreds of them now; some faded, some sparklingly new.

*Open: 11.00–23.00 (Mon–Thurs), 11.00–22.45 (Fri–Sat), 12.00–22.30 (Sun)*
*Food: 12.00–17.00 (Mon–Sat)*
*Credit cards: none taken*
*Draught beers: Courage Best, John Smith's Extra Smooth, John Smith's Yorkshire, Marston's Pedigree, Theakston XB, Foster's, Kronenbourg, Beamish, Guinness, Dry Blackthorn, Scrumpy Jack*
*Nearest tube station: Covent Garden*

# The Lamb Tavern

Leadenhall Market, EC3. Tel: 0171 626 2454

Leadenhall Market is a spectacular sight, with its great stone arches, lofty arcades, stunning cast-ironwork and a couple of pubs – the Lamb Tavern and the New Moon.

The Lamb – a multi-level pub with smoking rooms, non-smoking rooms (the first in the City), a mezzanine and an outside (albeit in the market) drinking area – fills up every lunchtime with energetic City workers, who often come back again in the evening. The main bar is not nearly as impressive as it once was – the result of the installation of the mezzanine floor – but the basement and the upstairs room retain their old style. The Lamb closes at weekends and film crews often move in. John Wayne spent many days there when scenes for *Brannigan* were being shot. Robert Mitchum was there for *The Winds of War* and Tom Selleck for *Magnum*. The BBC shot some of *Bleak House* in The Lamb, and the landlord's children both got parts.

*Open: 11.00–21.00 (Mon–Fri)*
*Food: 11.00–14.30; toasted sandwiches until 21.00*
*Credit cards: all major cards*
*Draught beers: Young's Bitter, Young's Special, Castlemaine, London Lager, Premium Lager, Grolsch, Beamish, Oatmeal, Scrumpy Jack*
*Private room seats 50*
*Nearest tube station: Bank*

## The Latchmere

503 Battersea Park Road, SW11. Tel: 0171 223 3549

This imposing Victorian pub has been thoroughly refurbished in recent years and boasts three separate drinking areas, a walled garden and a 90-seat theatre upstairs with a growing reputation for quality productions with excellent casts. It is called the Grace Theatre at the Latchmere, after Alan Grace, father of the present owner, who is also called Alan. He was a rising young actor at the beginning of a promising career when the war broke out. He was killed in action three months before the birth of his son.

The pub itself has something going on most evenings: games nights, quiz nights, promotional events, jazz.... It claims to be the first pub in the country to offer the Internet to its customers. Surfers may investigate for themselves on http://www.pubnet.uk.com

*Open: 11.00–23.00 (Mon–Sat), 12.00–22.30 (Sun)*
*Food: 12.00–16.00 (Mon), 12.00–20.00 (Tues–Sat), 12.00–16.00 (Sun)*
*Credit cards: Mastercard, Switch, Visa*
*Draught beers: Courage Directors, Greene King, John Smith's, Foster's, Kronenbourg, Miller Pilsner, Guinness, Dry Blackthorn, Scrumpy Jack*
*Nearest railway station: Clapham Junction*

## The Lavender

171 Lavender Hill, SW11. Tel: 0171 978 5242

The Lavender is a home from home for the mixed clientele of young Clapham professionals and street-trendy types. It seems to do very good business as both a restaurant and a bar. It has been around long enough to feel well used, and it's all the better for it. Enormous windows at the front contribute greatly to the feeling of space, and the ceiling fans, spinning alarmingly fast, keep the air circulating on those balmy Battersea evenings. It's £2–£2.50 for bottled beers and £8.50 for the house wines.

*Open: 11.00–23.00 (Mon–Sat), 12.00–22.30 (Sun)*
*Food: 12.00–15.30 and 19.00–23.00 (Mon–Thurs), 12.00–15.30 and 19.00–23.30 (Fri), 12.00–16.00 and 19.00–23.30 (Sat), 12.00–16.00 and 19.00–22.30 (Sun)*
*Credit cards: all major cards*
*Wheelchair access to venue*
*Nearest railway station: Clapham Junction*

## Legless Ladder

339 Battersea Park Road, SW11. Tel: 0171 622 2112

This was the first of the two Legless Ladders in London – the one-time Prince of Wales in Battersea Park Road. It had got tired and dusty, and Jeremy Hampton bought the lease. He turned the three Victorian bars into a big, open-plan space, scrapped the massive old bar counter and brought in lots of pine tables with numbered pews. The new Legless Ladder has become a popular drinking hole for young and sporty Battersea settlers, who go for the big helpings of hearty British food and pints of lager, and also for the big matches prominently featured on screens specially installed for the occasion. Major rugby internationals pack the place with cheering fans.

Sunday lunch is the busiest day in a sport-free week, although you have to be on the ball – they still chuck you out at 3pm.

*Open: 11.00–23.00 (Mon–Sat), 12.00–15.00 and 19.00–22.30 (Sun)*
*Food: 12.00–14.30 and 19.00–22.00 (Mon–Sat), 12.00–15.00 and 19.00–21.30 (Sun)*
*Credit cards: all major cards except AmEx*
*Draught beers: Bass, Courage Directors, John Smith's Extra Smooth, Theakston Best, Budweiser, Foster's, Kronenbourg, Guinness, Dry Blackthorn*
*Wheelchair access to venue*
*Private room seats 100*
*Nearest tube station: Battersea Park*

# Legless Ladder     EROS AWARD WINNER

1 Harwood Terrace, SW6. Tel: 0171 610 6131

Sister-pub of the original Battersea version, this modern, almost circular pub has a central island bar, large wooden tables, stripped pine floors, big windows, and French doors which open out to a large beer garden. The owner is Jeremy Hampton, whose wife Tammy supervises the blackboard-driven menu of sumptuous burgers with real chips, plus pastas, roasts and salads. The pub is slightly difficult to find, being tucked away off the King's Road, but the rather well-heeled folk of Fulham consider it worth hunting down. No doubt there will be more Legless Ladders in the future.

*Open: 12.00–15.00 and 17.00–23.00 (Mon–Thurs), 12.00–23.00 (Fri–Sat), 12.00–22.30 (Sun)*
*Food: 12.00–14.30 and 19.00–22.00 (Mon–Sat), 12.00–15.00 and 19.00–21.30 (Sun)*
*Credit cards: all major cards, except AmEx*
*Draught beers: Bass, Courage Directors, Theakston Best, John Smith's Extra Smooth, Budweiser, Foster's, Kronenbourg, Guinness, Dry Blackthorn*
*Wheelchair access to venue*
*Nearest tube station: Fulham Broadway*

# The Leinster Arms

17 Leinster Terrace, W2. Tel: 0171 723 5757

In the centre of Bayswater, with its communities of transients, visitors and notable personages, is a rather agreeable old coaching house, which looks after its customers well. There are occasions when an ordinary bar becomes something special thanks to the presence of *Mein Host*. Olive McCarthy, the host in question at The Leinster Arms, makes this a most agreeable little local – not a destination, but a local. Olive takes pride in her bar, so much so that she was recently named as the first female Grand Master Cellarman of the Year. If only all locals had an Olive McCarthy.

*Open: 11.00–23.00 (Mon–Sat), 12.00–22.30 (Sun)*
*Food: 11.00–20.00 (Mon–Sat), 12.00–20.00 (Sun)*
*Credit cards: none taken*
*Draught beers: Burton Ale, Kilkenny, Marston's Pedigree, Old Speckled Hen, Tetley, several guest ales, Carlsberg, Castlemaine, Lowenbrau, Guinness, Dry Blackthorn*
*Wheelchair access to venue and loo*
*Nearest tube stations: Lancaster Gate, Paddington, Queensway, Bayswater*

# The London Apprentice

62 Church Street, Isleworth, TW7. Tel: 0181 560 1915

Here is a sports report. In 1828 Luke Walker, the Colliers' Champion, met Ned Donnelly, the Colossal Coal Heaver, in a sensational fist fight. It went on for 37 rounds and left both men covered in blood. Luke Walker won. What he won was The London Apprentice. The idiotic owner had bet it on the other chap. It was, and indeed is, a fine old pub on the river at Old Isleworth. Syon House, the Duke of Northumberland's London home, is next door, and lots of people come to see it, but the London Apprentice considers itself every bit as historic. So there it stands, with its terrace over the river, its conservatory, its ground-floor dining room and the grand à la carte restaurant upstairs, a lovely room with hand-printed wallpaper, a huge oriel window and plaster reliefs more than 300 years old. The two bars seem hardly to have changed at all in that time. Regulars still play darts, shove ha'penny and bar billiards in the old bar at the back. The main bar remains the heart of the pub, with two huge oak posts that keep the whole building up.

*Open: 11.00–23.00 (Mon–Sat), 12.00–22.30 (Sun)*
*Food: bar 11.00–14.30 and 18.00–21.30 (Mon–Sat), 12.00–16.00 (Sun); restaurant 12.00–15.00 and 18.00–21.30 (Mon–Sat), 12.00–17.30 (Sun)*
*Credit cards: all major cards*
*Draught beers: Courage Best, Courage Directors, Theakston Best, Theakston XB, Wadworth 6X, Budweiser, Foster's, Holsten, Guinness, Strongbow*
*Wheelchair access to venue*
*Nearest railway station: Isleworth*

# Longroom

18–20 St John Street, EC1. Tel: 0171 336 6099

The blue and cream painted windows at the front of this bar restaurant provide the only source of natural light in the building. The light is barely assisted by a series of 43 (I was waiting for a friend so I counted) seemingly 2-watt bulbs in the sort of plain metallic shades once manufactured for local-authority use in schools, and nowadays ubiquitous in newly designed bars. The uniformed rows of square tables – placed at an angle to imply dissent – stretch way into the distance, with the ones at the back being reserved for diners. The long spacious bar on the left side serves Adnams and Bitberger beers and a whole host of wines – which was what most people seemed to be drinking. This is clearly a place for having fun, and judging by the City couple heavily involved in a bout of tongue wrestling, a place to be with someone you're not supposed to be with. There's a large-screen TV behind the bar, fairly mellow jazz background music, and too few ceiling fans to control the temperature in a room which desperately needs air conditioning. I am reliably informed that this is a rather decent bar for local suit and skirt wearers and that things can get really wild on Friday nights. Gosh! Do they take their jackets off?

*Open: 12.00–midnight (Mon–Fri)*
*Food: 12.00–23.00 (Mon–Fri)*
*Credit cards: all major cards*
*Draught beers: Adnams Best, Bitberger Pils, Hoegaarden, Murphy's*
*Wheelchair access to venue*
*Nearest tube station: Farringdon*

# The Lord Moon of the Mall

16–18 Whitehall, SW1. Tel: 0171 839 7701

Barclays Bank moved out of this imposing Victorian building next to the White-hall Theatre in 1992 and in came J. D. Wetherspoon with a million pounds to spend on one of the most distinguished buildings on the market. What had been a most superior bank became a most superior public house. Widely spaced tables occupy the one-time banking hall, with its high coffered ceiling and magnificent arched windows. More arches lead from here to the main bar, which has a polished granite counter, and to what was once the partners' room, where dukes awaited an invitation to sit. Anyone can occupy the comfortable chairs here now. Being a Wetherspoon's pub, The Lord Moon has all the well-known Wetherspoon's characteristics – no music, a big no-smoking area, and discounted beers. It is open all the hours permitted and does food all day.

*Open: 11.00–23.00 (Mon–Sat), 12.00–22.30 (Sun)*
*Food: 11.00–22.00 (Mon–Sat), 12.00–21.30 (Sun)*
*Credit cards: all major cards*
*Draught beers: Caffrey's, Courage Directors, London Pride, Theakston Best, Younger's Scotch Bitter, two weekly guest ales, Guinness, Dry Blackthorn, Weston's*
*Wheelchair access to venue and loo*
*Nearest tube station: Charing Cross*

## Lord's Tavern

**EROS AWARD WINNER**

The Grace Gates, St John's Wood Road, NW8. Tel: 0171 266 5980

If you go down to St John's Wood today, you're in for a big surprise. Front Page pubs took over this historic tavern in the summer of 1997 and converted it into one of their up-market foodie pubs. Old taverners won't recognise the Page-ified Inn, with its bright woodwork, big tables, real ales and champagnes, and its modern British menu. The tried-and-tested reputation of the new owners means that the residents of St John's Wood Road now have a real gem on their doorstep. They might want to avoid it when England play at Lord's, as half the stadium seems to pop in for one.

*Open: 11.00–23.00 (Mon–Sat), 12.00–22.30 (Sun)*
*Food: 12.00–14.30 and 18.30–22.00 (Mon–Sun)*
*Credit cards: all major cards*
*Draught beers: John Smith's Smooth, Foster's, Kronenbourg, Miller Pilsner, Guinness, Strongbow*
*Nearest tube stations: Maida Vale, St John's Wood, Warwick Avenue*

## Los Locos Beach Club

14 Soho Street, W1. Tel: 0171 287 0005

If you want to go out and get trashed over a few cocktails with a view to the possibility of getting off with, well, just about anyone, then Los Locos might be the venue for you. Now let's not take this place too seriously. Anyone who calls their bar a Beach Club in the middle of Soho is clearly under the influence of something a little stronger than the cocktails on offer.

Here we go on a bumpy ride through the week. Things get going on Tuesday when there is sixties and seventies music and a happy hour all night, with 'selected' beers and glasses of Le Pré, the internationally renowned house wine, at 99p. Wednesday is Wham! Bam! Thank You, Ma'am, a serious 'Get Your Jugs Out' evening. I am reliably informed, by someone more than a hundred years younger than I, that this refers to the jugs of cocktails, which are £5 all evening. Thursday is Babes night – I understand that one. This involves letting lots of young women in free and plying them with cut-price drinks so that hordes of marauding testosterone-packed office boys can impress them with the size of their expense accounts. Should a babe turn up in her bikini she'll get a free shooter from the bar, and that's probably not all she'll get. Friday (am I only up to Friday?) is just party night, and the same again on Saturday. The cocktail jugs doze Hispanic-style behind the bar on Sunday and Monday, when the bar closes to recover. That's exactly when I'd like to go. Admission is free before 9pm every night, then £5 Tuesday to Thursday and £8 Friday and Saturday. They tell me this is London's only stretch of beach, and having been there, I think they're very probably right.

*Open: 17.30–03.00 (Tues–Sat)*
*Food served: 18.30–21.00 (Tues-Sat)*
*Credit cards: all major cards*
*Nearest tube: Tottenham Court Road*


## Lupo

50 Dean Street, W1. Tel: 0171 434 3399

The bar staff at Lupo are a handsome, trendy bunch of youngsters with hairstyles so fashionable that if my mother were to go in, she would whip out her scissors and give them all a good seeing-to. They seem to have developed their own dialect in this Estuary English-free zone, sort of public school meets ageing hippy: 'Hey Juss-tin, more beeas, yaah?' The owner, Paul-Jean Foster, tells me he would only employ someone who would be happy to drink here. The Soho-media types seem to rub along quite happily with the serious modes and artistically bent. Lupo has wonderful late opening hours, and to control the numbers they charge £5 admission after 11pm from Thursday to Saturday. Three bar areas and two private rooms provide plenty of pocketed places to sit, and the two main bars have a bit of hanging-around space. Concertina walls open up in the summer, when the crowds spill onto the pavement clutching their bottled beers (£2.50) or glasses of wine (from £2.20) and sway to the beat of the acid jazz and dance music. The restaurant serves surprisingly decent food but isn't especially cheap (tuna steak £10.75, duck or lamb £11). The bar gets busy with the after-work crowd and then again with the late-night revellers. As for the name Lupo? 'Latin for wolf,' they told me. I looked it up and found *lupor*, which is something to do with lewd women. I think I prefer that definition.

*Open: 11.30–01.00 (Mon–Wed), 12.00–02.00 (Thurs–Sat)*
*Food: 12.00–15.00 and 18.00–23.30 (Mon–Sat)*
*Credit cards: all major cards*
*Two private rooms: 80 and 120 seated*
*Nearest tube station: Leicester Square*


## McNab's Wine Bar and Restaurant

43 Balham High Road, SW12. Tel: 0181 675 5522

This long-established wine bar and restaurant attracts a loyal following from the residents of SW12. The restaurant is at the rear, but the front and outside seating terrace is very much a bar. You can eat here, of course, but you don't have to. Main courses, which include goat's cheese salad and dim sum, are around £6. Spirits are £4, wine by the glass £3 and bottled beers £2.70. The best nights, if you like live music that is, are Thursday and Sunday, with anything from easy-listening through to R & B. There's a happy hour (yippee!) between 5.30pm and 7.30pm when 25% is knocked off the price of drinks.

*Open: 11.00–23.00 (Mon–Sat), 11.00–22.30 (Sun)*
*Food: 11.30–15.30 and 18.30–23.00 (Mon–Fri), Sat–Sun as opening hours*
*Credit cards: all major cards*
*Draught beers: Fargoe Velvet, Zamek*
*Nearest tube station: Balham*

# The Magdala Tavern

2a South Hill Park, NW3. Tel: 0171 435 2503

On 10 April 1955 Ruth Ellis shot and killed her lover David Blakeley outside this pub.

There are three bullet holes in the cream tiled frontage and a notice explaining how they came to be there. She stood over him putting three more bullets into his body as he lay on the pavement, then quietly waited for the police to come. She was the last woman to be hanged in Britain and she gave this otherwise unmemorable local a sort of macabre glamour. There is a theatrical gloss to it now, with photographs of Alan Bates, John Gielgud and others, but the star, quite rightly, is Ruth Ellis. She stares bleakly from the frame, blonde, ashen, heavily made-up in an open-neck shirt blouse with a silk scarf and a broad belt tightly fastened. With the photograph is a letter she wrote from Holloway and two miniature certificates, the official declaration of execution and the death certificate, signed by the prison surgeon on 13 July 1955.

*Open: 11.00–23.00 (Mon–Sat), 12.00–22.30 (Sun)*
*Credit cards: none taken*
*Draught beers: Caffrey's, Toby Ale, Worthington, Carling Black Label, Guinness, Dry Blackthorn*
*Nearest tube station: Hampstead Heath*

# The Magpie and Stump

442 King's Road, SW10. Tel: 0171 352 5017

A few years ago this rather down-at-heel pub was given a new lease of life when Allied Domecq completely gutted the place and transformed it into what they saw as an up-market bar. It is now a handsome building – large windows, tables outside in the summer and two rooms inside where you can eat all day. It is fair to say that The Magpie has struggled somewhat with its new identity as a bar rather than a pub. The amusement-arcade features in the downstairs bar were largely to blame for this; a new manager, Tim Brown, has come in and removed the majority of them. They have discos now instead. The bar is conveniently situated directly opposite the World's End estate.

*Open: 12.00–23.00 (Mon–Sat), 12.00–22.30 (Sun)*
*Food: 12.00–22.30 (Mon–Sun)*
*Credit cards: all major cards*
*Draught beers: Tetley, Carlsberg, Carlsberg Export, Lowenbrau, Guinness, K6*
*Nearest tube stations: Sloane Square, South Kensington*

# The Magpie and Stump

218 Old Bailey, EC4. Tel: 0171 352 5017

Few London pubs have a more macabre past than this one. It stood facing the gallows of Newgate Jail and would rent out its upper floors for all-night parties before an execution. Vast crowds whooped it up below while the nobs drank, played cards and at dawn watched the wretched prisoner slowly strangling on the gibbet while his relations hung on his legs to hasten his end. The sight gave them a good appetite for The Magpie and Stump's large execution breakfast. After being remodelled in 1931 the pub settled down to a respectable old age as a tourist attraction, and all was well until 1988 when it was sold to a developer and demolished. The deal was that a new Magpie and Stump should be part of the new building. This is it.

The only hint that there might be a pub in Old Bailey is an inn sign oddly attached to what looks like an office wall. The fascia and entrance are hidden away round the corner in an alley called Bishop's Court. Inside, you find a large modern pub on three levels. There's the main bar, a younger, louder bar with big-screen TV on the floor below, and a bar for private hire under that. If you are peckish you can have anything you want as long as it's baguettes or pizzas. The pub is handsomely equipped and fully air conditioned. There is even a lift. But nothing, not even the inn sign, was saved from the historic old tavern.

*Open: 11.00–22.00 (Mon–Wed), 11.00–23.00 (Thurs–Fri),*
*Food: as opening hours*
*Credit cards: all major cards*
*Draught beers: Bass, Caffrey's, London Pride, Carling Black Label, Staropramen, Guinness, Red Rock*
*Wheelchair access to venue and loo*
*Nearest tube station: St Paul's*

## Man in the Moon

392 King's Road, SW3. Tel: 0171 352 5075

This is a splendid Victorian building with a much-acclaimed theatre putting on successful productions back-to-back. By contrast, the pub itself has had a chequered run in recent years but is nonetheless a good venue waiting to happen. In the early nineties the pub was fraught with difficulties until a new landlord came in and banned the pool table. Things improved markedly and the Man in the Moon became a fun, successful, busy pub until the manager, Oisin Rogers, left for the sunnier climes of Richmond (see The Marlborough). Managers then came and left with such frequency that I began to suspect the accommodation was being used as a shelter for lost and stray publicans, as standards began to descend quickly. Then, a ray of hope. In 1995 Scottish & Newcastle spent £250,000 carrying out a sympathetic restoration of the main pub, and converted the cellar into a spanking-new bar to serve the theatre. Sadly, however, the theatre bar rarely opened, and the promises to refit the theatre (possibly the pub's greatest asset) have been 'Dogged by planning restrictions and bureaucratic nonsense,' as the theatre manager says. As I write there is yet another new manager, Mark Lawton, who is trying to get to grips with things. The theatre bar is opening 'occasionally', and future plans are being kept quiet until a midnight licence is approved. Still, people seem to be drifting back in again, and the S & N sizzler menu has made a return. So has the pool table.

*Open: 11.00–23.00 (Mon–Sat), 12.00–22.30 (Sun)*
*Food: 12.00–22.00 (Mon–Sun)*
*Credit cards: none taken*
*Draught beers: Beamish Red, John Smith's Extra Smooth, Beck's, Foster's, Kronenbourg, Guinness, Strongbow*
*Wheelchair access to venue*
*Private room: 80 standing*
*Nearest tube station: Sloane Square*

## The Maple Leaf

41 Maiden Lane, WC2. Tel: 0171 240 2843

The Maple Leaf is the most famous Canadian pub in London, and the flags floating in the breeze outside bear testament to this. It has Canadian beers, Canadian food, and, reassuringly, a Canadian clientele. There is a strong Canadian accent at the bar, too. It is, boasts The Maple Leaf, the only pub in the world outside North America to have draught Molson. Then there is the excellent Canadian food – the burgers and the steaks, the home-made meatloaf with fresh juice, the ham, griddled eggs and hash browns, and the pancakes and maple syrup. There are reminders of Canada everywhere; videos of big ice-hockey matches are flown over every Tuesday and Thursday. This means that you and your mates can sit round the TV in Covent Garden, England, watching the drama on one of the six carefully placed TV screens, with a bucket of chicken wings and another bucket of ice-cold beer.

*Open: 11.00–23.00 (Mon–Sat), 12.00–22.30 (Sun)*
*Food: 12.00–22.00 (Mon–Sun)*
*Credit cards: all major cards*
*Draught beers: Beamish Red, Brakspear, Theakston Best, Beck's, Foster's, Molson Canadian, Beamish, Scrumpy Jack*
*Nearest tube stations: Covent Garden, Charing Cross*

## Market Bar

240a Portobello Road, W11. Tel: 0171 229 6472

Very mixed, young and trendy bar with large draped curtains, candles that have been burning for years, and a serious sound system.

*Open: 11.00–23.00 (Mon–Fri), 11.00–midnight (Sat), 12.00–22.30 (Sun)*
*Food: 12.00–15.30 and 17.30–23.00 (Mon–Sat), 12.00–14.00 (Sun)*
*Credit cards: none taken*
*Wheelchair access to venue*
*Nearest tube stations: Westbourne Park, Ladbroke Grove*

## Market Café Bar

21 The Market, Covent Garden, WC2. Tel: 0171 836 2137

Located above the Market Café on the south-west side of the market, this bar has a rather unimpressive interior but a spectacular terrace which is worth the fight for the space. From here you can watch the buskers on the west piazza, safe in the knowledge that you won't have to pay.

*Open: ground floor 10.00–24.30 (Mon–Sun), upstairs 12.00–02.00 (Mon–Sun)*
*Food: ground floor 10.00–24.00 (Mon–Sun), upstairs 12.00–02.00 (Mon–Sun)*
*Credit cards: all major cards*
*Wheelchairs access to ground level*
*Nearest tube station: Covent Garden*

## The Marlborough

46 Friar Stile Road, Richmond. Tel: 0181 940 0572

This is a particularly good find. Friar Stile Road, off Richmond Hill, is slightly off the beaten track, but it's worth making a detour to visit The Marlborough. The pub begins long and narrow, dividing evenly into three – first the public bar, with wooden floors and high backed settles; then the saloon, carpeted, curtained and set about with green leather chesterfields; and beyond that, a servery with an open grill selling steaks, chops and burgers. What is impressive about the pub is its wonderful walled garden, which seemingly goes on for miles. Children play on the garden furniture far enough away from the drinking area for them not to bother anyone. Picnic tables fill the lawns, and there is an undercover terrace with its own heating system so you can enjoy the garden through the changing seasons. The Marlborough is efficiently run by an erudite Dublin lad named Oisin Rogers, who could win Olympic gold for talking. If you ask, he will undoubtedly talk you into having a home-made beefburger (£5.95), swordfish or tuna loin steak (£6.95) or a mixed charcuterie of European meats, all washed down, of course, with a drop of the black stuff.

*Open: 12.00–23.00 (Mon–Fri), 11.00–23.00 (Sat), 12.00–22.30 (Sun)*
*Food: 12.00–15.00 and 19.00–21.00 (Mon–Sun)*
*Credit cards: all major cards*
*Draught beers: Marston's Pedigree, Old Speckled Hen, Tetley's, Carlsberg Export, Castlemaine, Guinness, Dry Blackthorn*
*Wheelchair access to venue*
*Nearest tube station: Richmond*

# Marquess Tavern

32 Canonbury Street, N1. Tel: 0171 354 2975

Young's took over this high-Victorian pub in 1979, restoring it to its former glory. It has a big, high-ceilinged saloon bar. The adjoining room is impressive, too – a bar-cum-dining room with a fine arched ceiling, booths and big mirrors. This is truly a fine, well-placed pub. The New River, originally designed to bring drinking water to the 17th-century City of London, now brings ducks and river walkers to its door. Picnic tables await them.

*Open: 11.00–23.00 (Mon–Sat), 12.00–22.30 (Sun)*
*Food: 11.00–21.30 (Mon–Sat)*
*Credit cards: none taken*
*Draught beers: Young's Bitter, Young's Premium Lager, Young's Special, Castlemaine, Grolsch, London Lager, Guinness, Dry Blackthorn*
*Wheelchair access to venue*
*Private room seats 80*
*Nearest tube station: Highbury & Islington*

# The Marquis of Granby

51 Chandos Place, WC2. Tel: 0171 836 7657

The Marquis of Granby at the back of the Coliseum has a long, imposing frontage that makes you expect a large, imposing pub, but it proves to be a sliver of a pub – a wedge, all length and no width. At the thin end of the wedge is a very small snug. At the thick end is a rather larger bar parlour. The main bar, getting gradually wider, is in between, and the whole thing has been elaborately refitted. Back bar, bar counter, furniture, everything has been replaced. The renovation has been carefully done, putting to good use a Gothic screen rescued from a demolished church. Rumour has it that Ian Fleming used this pub during the war and that it was here he coined the secret-agent code 007.

*Open: 11.00–23.00 (Mon–Sat), 12.00–22.30 (Sun)*
*Food: 11.00–17.00 (Mon–Sat), 12.00–17.00 (Sun)*
*Credit cards: all major cards*
*Draught beers: Adnams, Calder's Cream Ale, Marquess Bitter, Marston's Pedigree, Tetley's, one guest ale, Carlsberg, Castlemaine, Lowenbrau, Guinness, Olde English*
*Wheelchair access to venue*
*Private room seats 40*
*Nearest tube station: Charing Cross*

# Masons Arms

169 Battersea Park Road, SW8. Tel: 0171 622 2007

There appears to be a new trend in the licensed sector for the offspring of rather well-to-do families to set themselves up in the pub business. Joel Cadbury started out with the Goat in Boots (qv) on the Fulham Road, Lord Fermoy followed a more conventional route into pub management with a Bass training scheme at the Windsor Castle (qv), and now Ewan Guinness, heir to the Guinness empire, has bought himself a pub or two. Three years ago, the Masons Arms was a burnt-out shell of a building near the Dogs' Home on the Battersea Park Road. Guinness and his business partner Matt Jacomb have made a splendid job of bringing the building to life again. It now has one very large, L-shaped room with big, well-spaced tables and a lounge area with chesterfields by the fireplace. The clientele is young but not childish – more Eagles fans than Boy Zone followers. Food is very much the thing here, as the open kitchen near the door suggests. The menu changes every few weeks but on our most recent visit we had char-grilled calamari, chorizo and blackened tomato pancake (£6.50), pan-fried Scottish salmon on rocket and pimento frittata (£7), and a char-grilled beefburger with big chips (£5.80). This was Guinness's first pub. He has another one now, the Stonemasons (qv) in Hammersmith. They serve Guinness in both pubs.

*Open: 11.00–23.00 (Mon–Sat), 12.00–22.30 (Sun)*
*Food: 12.00–22.00 (Mon–Sun)*
*Credit cards: all major cards*
*Draught beers: Boddingtons, Brakspear, Caffrey's, Wadworth 6X, Heineken Export, Hoegaarden, Stella Artois, Guinness, Merrydown, Strongbow*
*Wheelchair access to venue*
*Nearest railway station: Battersea Park*

## The Masons Arms

51 Upper Berkeley Street, W1. Tel: 0171 622 2007

The plaque on the wall of this nice corner pub in W1 tells a romantic though gory tale which not everybody believes. The story is that the pub cellars were originally dungeons where unfortunate persons about to be hanged at Tyburn languished, chained to the walls. A tunnel, it is said, led directly from the cellars to Tyburn just round the corner at Marble Arch.

The executions here were particularly ghastly and much enjoyed by the charming populace; they went on until 1783. As the pub was built around 1780, the dungeon story could be true, and the bright new manager, Sarah Grant, joins in the spirit of the thing by taking occasional parties down there. A candle casts horrid shadows as she points out the old iron fittings on the walls. For the manacles, she says. The Masons Arms is in all other respects a cheerful and agreeable old pub. Its wooden floor is dressed several times a week with fresh sawdust. This is not popular with the cleaners but the visitors like it.

*Open: 11.00–23.00 (Mon–Sat), 12.00–22.30 (Sun)*
*Food: as opening hours*
*Credit cards: all major cards*
*Draught beers: Boddingtons, Brakspears, Caffrey's, Wadworth 6X, Heineken Export, Hoegaarden, Stella Artois, Guinness, Merrydown, Strongbow*
*Wheelchair access to venue and loo*
*Nearest tube station: Marble Arch*

## The Melton Mowbray

18 Holborn, EC1. Tel: 0171 405 7077

The success of The Melton Mowbray took everyone aback, including the people at Fuller's who introduced this modern pub as one of their first Ale & Pie houses. It went from nothing to taking £1 million a year. Workers from every office in sight converged on it – a highly desirable clientele, well mannered, free-spending and, as a rule, quick-eating. The Melton Mowbray became a big place for lunch, and within a year Fuller's was spending more and gaining more tables by opening up a bar downstairs. It too was an instant success. Tables outside gave them more seats still. Almost a thousand people a week are having lunch at the pub now; it gets packed every day, and people arrive at 12.30pm to make sure of a table. So how is it done?

Well, they use the space cleverly, and it is all state-of-the-art in the big cellars, with electronic hoists for the beer and amazing computerised ovens in the kitchens. The steak and ale, and pork and cider pies (£5) rotate behind glass doors and cook in 2 minutes 45 seconds – an arresting bit of kitchen theatre.

*Open: 11.00–23.00 (Mon–Fri)*
*Food: 11.00–20.45 (Mon–Fri)*
*Credit cards: all major cards*

*Draught beers: Chiswick Bitter, Fuller's ESB, London Pride, plus a fortnightly guest ale, Carling, Grolsch, Heineken, Stella Artois, Guinness, Scrumpy Jack*
*Wheelchair access to venue and loo*
*Two private rooms: 25 and 70 seated, 35 and 120 standing*
*Nearest tube station: Chancery Lane*

# El Meson de Los Barriles

8a Lamb Street, E1. Tel: 0171 375 3136

A very authentic tapas bar which does good business with the City folk during the week and the shoppers at Spitalfields market on Sundays. It has a decent-sized bar and a small terrace on the market side. Tapas come in decent portions, most for around £4. Bottled Spanish beers are £2, and the house wine is £8.95 a bottle. Sawdust is sprinkled liberally around the floor, big wooden barrels provide elbow rests, and there is ample seating space.

*Open: 11.00–23.00 (Mon–Fri), 11.00–16.00 (Sun)*
*Food:11.00–23.00 (Mon–Fri), 11.00–16.00 (Sun)*
*Credit cards: all major*
*Wheelchair access to venue*
*Nearest tube station: Liverpool Street*

# MetBar

Metropolitan Hotel, 19 Old Park Lane, W1. Tel: 0171 447 5757

Exclusivity can be a manufactured beast and not, as it should be, the result of a tidal wave of demand to be seen-to-be-there. The MetBar's PR people have gone to arduous lengths to position it as London's latest exclusive venue, claiming that there has been a waiting list for membership since it opened. How can that be? The answer is that the membership opportunities were exhausted in advance by unsolicited invitations to a select group of people. I know for a fact that a number of *Evening Standard* journalists were on that list, so I have reason to suspect their criteria for selection. An inside source told me that one reason for MetBar's strict membership policy is that they don't want it to turn into a knocking shop for rich businessmen from neighbouring hotels. If you do get in, and I'm coming to that, you might be forgiven for thinking that a rich businessman from a neighbouring hotel would be rather a good idea to help with the bill. With house spirits starting at £4.50 (rising rapidly) and a club sandwich at £10.50, a long night on your own credit card is something to be viewed with trepidation. Membership is required only after 6pm, so the bar is open to us hoi polloi for lunch and afternoon tea – should we want to go in daylight hours to a place designed for nightlife. Prompt at six, the flying squad, softened only by their Donna Karan outfits, move in and ever-so-politely chuck you out. The aforementioned *Evening Standard* reprobates were less than complimentary when we descended on the place one evening: 'The red banquettes remind me of a motorway service station,' said one; 'Full of wannabes,' said another; and 'Unappealing and styleless,' added a third. To be a member you must go to the hotel, fill out an application form, let them see the cut-of-your-jib, wait an unspecified period of months, and bingo! – you're in. As a member is allowed to bring a guest, you could try coat-tailing one of the already-in-crowd, or do as I did and gatecrash.

*Open: 09.30–03.00 (Mon–Thurs), 24 hours (Fri–Sat), till 22.30 (Sun)*
*Food: as opening hours*
*Credit cards: all major cards*
*Wheelchair access to venue*
*Nearest tube station: Hyde Park Corner*

## Mezzo

100 Wardour Street, W1. Tel: 0171 314 4000

The bar of the restaurant is undoubtedly a very attractive place to hang out and enjoy the buzz. In stark contrast to the service in the restaurant – push them in, take their order, rush back with the food, remove the plates and get them out in as short a space of time as possible – service in the bar is excruciatingly slow. The concept, surely, is quite simple. If the place is packed, you employ more staff to deal with the demand, right? Not here, I'm afraid. Begging for the eye of the bartender is a local sport with too few winners and as much participant interest as standing in the rain waiting for a bus.

When and if you do get served, the drinks aren't cheap and the house wine (a vin de Pays d'Oc) is of a rather poor quality. Spirits are often completely annihilated by the hosed-in mixers for which they charge a staggering £1.50.

*Open: 12.00–01.00 (Mon–Thurs), 12.00–03.00 (Fri–Sat), 12.00–23.00 (Sun)*
*Credit cards: all major cards*
*Wheelchair access to venue and loo*
*Nearest tube stations: Piccadilly Circus, Tottenham Court Road, Leicester Square*

## The Mitre

24 Craven Terrace, W2. Tel: 0171 262 5240

The Mitre, a much-admired pub in Bayswater and a Grade-2 listed building, emerged from a refurbishment recently. It always was Victorian and it is sort of Victorian still – brand-new, pastiche Victorian, a perfect example of this popular modern pub style. There are three bars, plus a family room and a function room, all beautifully decorated and handsomely furnished in the Victorian manner, hung with portraits and pretty clocks. Two of the bars have marble fireplaces, one has a stag's head, and one a charming skylight that was formerly boarded up. There is no smoking in the family room, which has its own entrance to the hall and so to the street. Down a flight of worn stone steps (an original feature) is the piano bar, again with its own entrance, this time to the little cobbled mews at the side. Here is a maze of drinking areas tucked under low ceilings and arches, with flagged floors, big barrels, and an old kitchen range. It is full of atmosphere and is thought to have a friendly ghost. The new manager, Rob Davey, says that the ghost must be afraid of the dark, as lights turned off at night are on again in the morning.

*Open: 11.00–23.00 (Mon–Sat), 12.00–22.30 (Sun)*
*Food: 12.00–21.30 (Daily)*
*Credit cards: all major cards except AmEx*
*Draught beers: Boddingtons, Flower's IPA, London Pride, Marston's Pedigree, Whitbread, Heineken, Heineken Export, Stella Artois, Murphy's, Guinness, Strongbow*
*Wheelchair access to venue*
*Private room seats 50*
*Nearest tube station: Lancaster Gate*

## Mondo                                   EROS AWARD WINNER

12–13 Greek Street, W1. Tel: 0171 734 7157

Mondo comes to life late in the evening. It doesn't open until 6pm and then goes way into the wee small hours, looking after the night owls until 3am. You go downstairs to find a warren-like bar that is full of grottos, some with entrances so small you have to breathe in before squeezing through. Breaking up the space in this manner means the bar could be completely packed and you'd never see everyone. It is comfortable and relaxed, and the soft lighting adds to the air of intimacy. The leopard-skin-trimmed banquettes are irresistible to stroke. As the night wears on, the young, glam, overtly trendy clientele sashay around with cocktails (from £5), spirits (doubles from £4.50, including mixers) or draught beers (Leffe, £2.70 for a half). There is a restaurant area at the end of the bar on a mezzanine level. We had the Cajun crab cakes (£4), which were far too dry, and looked on enviously at the people eating Phad Thai (£5) – ribbon egg noodles wok-fried with tamarind sauce served up in a brown earthenware bowl. Mondo has a picker on the door; they don't bother with all that dress-code nonsense, but the younger, trendier and more glam you are, the more likely you are to be allowed in.

*Open: 18.00–03.00 (Mon–Fri), 19.00–03.00 (Sat)*
*Food: full menu 18.00–01.00; snacks until 03.00*
*Draught beers: Beck's, Leffe*
*Credit cards: all major cards*
*Nearest tube station: Plccadilly Circus*

## The Monkey Puzzle

30 Southwick Street, W2. Tel: 0171 723 0143

This modern pub on the ground floor of a Bayswater apartment building welcomes its customers in a dozen different languages. There are hotels aplenty in these parts, and the occupants need somewhere to refresh themselves. The pub used to have an old monkey puzzle tree in the garden until the great gale of 1987 blew it down. There is now a replacement growing in a sheltered corner.

*Open: 11.00–23.00 (Mon–Sat), 12.00–22.30 (Sun)*
*Food: 12.00–21.00 (Mon–Sun)*
*Credit cards: all major cards*
*Draught beers: Badger, Dempsey's, Dorset IPA, Gribble Ale, Tanglefoot, Hofbräu, Guinness, Dry Blackthorn*
*Wheelchair access to venue*
*Nearest tube stations: Edgware Road, Paddington*

## Moon and Sixpence

185 Wardour Street, W1. Tel: 0171 734 0037

J. D. Wetherspoon converted this former Barclays Bank into one of its ever-growing number of pubs in London. This is a roomy place with tall arched windows, a no-smoking area and cheap beers. It gets busy at lunchtimes and again in the evenings.

*Open: 11.00–23.00 (Mon–Sat), 12.00–22.30 (Sun)*
*Food: 11.00–22.00 (Mon–Sat), 12.00–21.30 (Sun)*
*Credit cards: all major cards*
*Draught beers: Courage Directors, London Pride, Theakston Best, Younger's Scotch Bitter, Beck's, Foster's, Kronenbourg, Guinness, Dry Blackthorn*
*Wheelchair access to venue*
*Nearest tube stations: Tottenham Court Road, Leicester Square*

## The Moon under Water

28 Leicester Square, WC2. Tel: 0171 839 2837

The Moon under Water used to be an Angus Steak House until 1992 when Wetherspoon's took it over. From being a long thin restaurant with steaks it became a long thin pub with food all day. It specialises in good cask ales, cheaper than most, but Wetherspoon's famous cut-price pint of Younger's Scotch bitter is not quite so cheap here. This being Leicester Square it is £1.50 a pint – still one of the cheapest pints in the West End, however. The Moon under Water has a strong character, won't have music and won't have smoking round the bar. Far from putting anyone off, all this seems to bring more people in, and Wetherspoon's have recently been making a bit more room inside by moving the bar and losing some of the booths. The fickle Westminster Council sometimes allows drinking outside and sometimes won't. At the moment they will, so 12 people can now enjoy refreshments in one of the biggest pedestrianised areas in central London. Very good of you, Westminster.

*Open: 11.00–23.00 (Mon–Sat), 12.00–22.30 (Sun)*
*Food: 11.00–22.00 (Mon–Sat), 12.00–21.30 (Sun)*
*Credit cards: all major cards*
*Draught beers: Courage Directors, London Pride, Theakston Best, Theakston XB, Younger's Scotch Bitter, Foster's, Kronenbourg, Guinness, Dry Blackthorn*
*Wheelchair access to venue and loo*
*Nearest tube station: Leicester Square*

# Morpeth Arms

58 Millbank, SW1. Tel: 0171 834 6442

After a day at the Tate Gallery you might well be in need of a little helper to recover from all that culture. Pop round the corner and you'll find comfort and reassurance in this trusty and dependable Victorian pub. All is traditional and familiar in the Morpeth Arms, and will stay so. It is a listed building now, admired and popular. In summer it gets particularly busy, with stout tables and wooden benches right across the front and down the side. These are regularly filled, particularly at lunchtime. The traffic roars by and you can hardly hear yourself speak, but they do a decent lunch and it's a Young's pub, so the beer is good too.

Don't venture into the cellars, though. They say that soon after the pub was built in 1845 a convict on the run hid in the labyrinth of vaults beneath the pub, lost himself and was never seen again. Visitors to the vaults have felt a hand on their shoulder and have been chilled by an unseen presence dripping water. It has sent them dashing back to the Tate.

Stand with your back to the pub and look across the river. The extraordinary building facing you is the new headquarters of MI5.

*Open: 11.00–23.00 (Mon–Sat), 12.00–22.30 (Sun)*
*Food: 11.00–21.00 (Mon–Sun)*
*Credit cards: all major cards except AmEx*
*Draught beers: Young's Bitter, Young's Special, one seasonal ale, Castlemaine, Grolsch, Young's Premium Lager, Guinness, Oatmeal Stout, Dry Blackthorn*
*Wheelchair access to venue*
*Private room: 36 seated, 60 standing*
*Nearest tube station: Pimlico*

# The Mucky Duck

108 Fetter Lane, EC4. Tel: 0171 242 9518

Partners Gareth Stones and Tony Crowe are proud of the framed seaside postcards at The Mucky Duck. All those bathing belles, landladies, red-nosed drunks, vicars and fat ladies in stripes with all their doubles entendres are worth the detour from Holborn or Fleet Street.

The Mucky Duck has been so named only since July 1993, before which it was The Swan. Upstairs is Annie's Bar. Annie was a previous incumbent. It is a bright room with a busy lunch crowd. Parties are held here. The speciality upstairs as well as down is the Mucky Duck Doorstep, a sandwich measuring 2 inches thick. With the Mucky Duck going strong, Stones and Crowe formed The Mucky Pub Co. and expanded with the acquisition of the Devonshire Arms in Duke Street and the Punch Tavern (qv).

*Open: 11.00–23.00 (Mon–Fri)*
*Food: 11.00–15.00 (Mon–Fri)*
*Credit cards: Mastercard, Visa*

*Draught beers: Bass, Caffrey's, Greene King, London Pride, Young's Special,*
*Carling Black Label, Carling Premier, Beamish, Dry Blackthorn*
*Private room: 35 seated, 60–70 standing*
*Nearest tube station: Chancery Lane*

## Mullins Coffee House

27 The Market, Covent Garden, WC2. Tel: 0171 379 7724

A tiny little coffee shop sits on the south-eastern corner of the market. The entrepreneurial owners concentrate on wines in the evening and have some of the most perfect outside seats on the piazza. Sit for a while, sip on your wine, and the entire world will wander by. There are few better locations in London.

*Open: 08.00 till late (depending on the weather)*
*Food: as opening hours*
*Credit cards: all major cards*
*Wheelchair access to venue*
*Nearest tube station: Covent Garden*

## J. J. Murphy's

48 Beauchamp Place, SW3. Tel: 0171 581 8886

What better address could you have for a pub? Beauchamp Place, Knightsbridge, I think, has the edge on all the others. This was Whitbread's introduction to Irish theme pubs. They converted it from The Grove, Whitbreadified it in an Irish sort of way, installed a new chef, Mohammed, and gave it taped Irish music all day and live music on Sunday afternoons.

Apparently there really was a J. J. Murphy. It was his brewery in County Cork that made the Murphy's stout which is still sold all over London. J. J. Murphy's in Knightsbridge sells Murphy's, of course, and Guinness and Hurley's Irish ale. It is an agreeable pub filled with nooks and crannies, snugs and booths. The food is Irish too – bacon and cabbage, Dublin coddle and the like. Mohammed makes the soda bread fresh every morning.

*Open: 11.00–23.00 (Mon–Sat), 12.00–22.30 (Sun)*
*Food: 11.00–21.30 (Mon–Fri), 11.00–16.00 (Sat)*
*Credit cards: all major cards except AmEx*
*Draught beers: Boddingtons, Hurley's, Wadworth 6X, Heineken, Heineken Export,*
*Stella Artois, Guinness, Murphy's, Strongbow*
*Nearest tube station: Knightsbridge*

## The Museum Tavern

49 Great Russell Street, WC1. Tel: 0171 242 8987

The architect William Finch Hill designed this pub in 1855. It was the third pub on this site and he named it The Museum Tavern in recognition of its cultural neighbour. It had four entrances to five bars, with pool and billiards and rooms for lodgers upstairs. He suspended huge globes from ornate iron fittings above the doors, and gas lamps in every window. It is this building, the outside hardly changed, that you see today. Generations of scholars have crossed the road from the British Museum to drink here. Among them was the museum's most famous student, Karl Marx, who is still suspected by the pub of having broken one of the mirrors in the bar's back fitting. Marx would presumably have approved of what has since happened to the pub interior – all divisions between public bar, private bar, jug bar and bar parlour abolished. No juke boxes or taped music lurk to alarm shy denizens of the British Museum, who still come in. It remains a gentlemanly, scholarly pub surrounded by academic bookshops.

Open: 09.30–23.00 (Mon–Sat), 10.30–22.30 (Sun)
Food: as opening hours
Credit cards: all major cards
Draught beers: Courage Best, Courage Directors, Theakston Best, Theakston Old Peculier, Theakston XB, one monthly guest ale, Foster's, Kronenbourg, Guinness, Strongbow
Wheelchair access to venue
Nearest tube stations: Tottenham Court Road, Russell Square

## The Nag's Head

53 Kinnerton Street, SW1. Tel: 0171 235 1135

The Nag's Head, tucked away in this little mews in the most expensive part of town, is a very chatty pub. It isn't very big and the bar counter is a chatty sort of height, as high as your average kitchen table. The stools round it are the height of kitchen chairs. Kinnerton Street is smart now but it was mostly stables when it started in the 1820s. The Nag's Head was the ostlers' pub. It was tiny, a single bar not much bigger than a horse's stall, and that was how it stayed into the sixties. Len Cole, the formidable landlord of the day, used to say that The Nag's Head was the smallest pub in London and that was how he liked it. However, his successors saw no point in the unused space at the back, and the pub is therefore a bit bigger now and more comfortable. Pictures, photographs and mementos of times past cover the panelled walls; fires are lit in winter, and in the summer people take their drinks into the mews. The front bar is for drinking and talking, and the back bar is for eating and talking, with food from noon to 9.30pm.

Open: 11.00–23.00 (Mon–Sat), 12.00–22.30 (Sun)
Food: 12.00–21.30 (Mon–Sun)
Credit cards: none taken
Draught beers: Adnams, Benskins, Kilkenny, Tetley, Carlsberg, Castlemaine, Lowenbrau, Guinness, Olde English
Nearest tube stations: Hyde Park Corner, Knightsbridge

## The Narrow Boat

119 St Peter Street, N1. Tel: 0171 226 3906

This newly restored pub occupies a lovely site on the bank of the Regent's Canal in Islington. There is a small deck overlooking the water, and a spiral staircase goes down to the towpath. Nautical objects still abound, and the new Narrow Boat attracts a youngish, energetic crowd. There's bar billiards and gaming machines and a Wurlitzer juke box playing everything from Elvis to Oasis. The food is similarly youthful and reasonably priced. Live bands play on Fridays, there's a regular quiz night on Wednesdays, and in the basin beyond, the narrow boats gather, as they always did.

Open: 12.00–23.00 (Mon–Sat), 12.00–22.30 (Sun)
Food: 12.00–15.00 (Mon–Sun)
Credit cards: all major cards except AmEx
Draught beers: Bass, Caffrey's, London Pride, Carling Black Label, Carling Premier, Grolsch, Guinness, Red Rock
Wheelchair access to venue
Private room seats 40
Nearest tube station: Angel

# New Moon

88 Gracechurch Street, EC3. Tel: 0171 626 3625

This handsome, dignified City pub occupies a commanding position in Leaden-hall market, the lofty arcade in the heart of the money market, where you can still find butchers, bakers and candlestick makers.

The high Victorian hall with its long counter fills with brokers when the markets close, and the long downstairs bar gets busy at lunchtimes. This is where the food is served.

*Open: 11.00–23.00 (Mon–Fri)*
*Food: 11.30–14.30 (Mon–Fri)*
*Credit cards: all major cards*
*Draught beers: Boddingtons, Brakspear, London Pride, Marston's Pedigree, Wadworth 6X, Heineken Export, Stella Artois, Guinness, Murphy's, Strongbow*
*Nearest tube stations: Monument, Liverpool Street*

# The Nightingale

97 Nightingale Lane, SW12. Tel: 0181 673 1637

The Nightingale has a delightful and secluded paved garden, the perfect place for a quiet drink on a summer's evening. Borders, window boxes and hanging baskets are all luxuriant. It wins prizes for its flowers.

This is a much-lauded pub. It has an award from Camra for the quality of its beer, and has also received one for the quality of its customers. The Association of London Brewers and Licensed Retailers had a contest to find which pub inside the M25 had raised most money for charity. It turned out to be The Nightingale. It has raised more than £250,000 to date, and this year was nominated once again. Good luck to you, The Nightingale. The pub itself is comfortable and welcoming, with home-made soups, cottage pie and real sausages at lunchtime, and has an impressive wine list – ten reds, nine whites, two sparkling and a good house claret. It is packed in the evening.

*Open: 11.00–15.00 and 17.30–23.00 (Mon–Tues), 11.00–23.00 (Wed–Sat), 12.00–22.30 (Sun)*
*Food: 12.00–14.30 and 19.00–21.15 (Mon–Sat), 12.00–22.30 (Sun)*
*Credit cards: none taken*
*Draught beers: All Young's range, including seasonal ales, Castlemaine, Grolsch, Guinness, Dry Blackthorn*
*Wheelchair access to venue*
*Nearest tube station: Clapham South*

# Notting Hill Arts Club

21 Notting Hill Gate, W11. Tel: 0171 460 4459

Don't worry, it's not in the same vein as the Chelsea Arts Club. This is a club (of sorts) where you can expect almost anything to happen. It is located in a decent-sized air-conditioned basement, where you may well find people playing board games, watching cult movies on a big screen, having dance nights or parties, or reading a book from the Penguin selection available. There are two rooms: one with a large circular island bar, seating booths and some stray sixties and seventies plastic-coated settees. The other room is where the events take place. The Club is a novel idea, well thought-out, and fills a much-needed gap in the market for a young, fashionable clientele. It is helping to make Notting Hill a destination for drinking. Another point to its credit is it doesn't have any of those silly dress codes that so many decent places appear to be adopting.

*Open: 18.00–01.00 (Mon–Sat), 18.00–23.00 (Sun)*
*Food: as opening hours*
*Credit cards: all major cards except AmEx*
*Nearest tube station: Notting Hill Gate*

# O Bar

83 Wardour Street, W1. Tel: 0171 437 3490

Young, energetic and frenetic nights can be had at the O Bar, a glittering, glam arena fuelled by Costa cocktails and strutting its stuff through the nineties, with music thudding, a disco (acid jazz, funk, and every table taken), queues outside, and doormen with headsets and intercoms. It doesn't open until mid-afternoon. It doesn't close until the early hours – 3am Wednesdays to Saturdays. There are three bars now. Downstairs is a grey and silver basement where DJs rule at weekends. The first floor is now a lounge bar with easy chairs and chesterfields and views right up Wardour Street from floor-to-ceiling windows. The main bar on the ground floor is where the action is, though – absolutely packed, music belting, barmen tossing glasses and bottles around.

*Open: 15.00–01.00 (Mon–Tues), 15.00–03.00 (Wed–Sat), 17.00–22.30 (Sun)*
*Credit cards: Visa*
*Wheelchair access to venue*
*Nearest tube stations: Leicester Square, Piccadilly Circus*

# Oblivion     **EROS AWARD WINNER**

7–8 Cavendish Parade, Clapham Common Southside, SW4.
Tel: 0181 772 0303

Bliss! Not just the thinking topers' reaction to the arrival of this bar-eatery but also the name of the woman responsible for bringing it here. Dee Bliss and her cohort designer Jo Laurie (she of Ny:Lon and Babushka (qv) fame) worked flat out for six weeks transforming a rather dull Italian restaurant into this palatial, visually stimulating, up-market venue which opens onto a large sun terrace directly opposite Clapham Common. A large, well-stocked bar of premium spirits, beers and wines is tended by people who know how to pour decent drinks (ask Andrew to mix a cocktail, he makes a mean Bloody Mary), and joy of joys – they do table service. The food confusingly moves between the bar menu and the main menu depending on when you go.

Oblivion is extremely well-presented, creative in design and generally inexpensive. It has proved extraordinarily popular in a short space of time, is always packed, and draws a happy mix of Clapham's professional types and street-trendy clubbers. Misses Bliss and Laurie have moved on now, another project in the offing to watch out for. My only hope is that the very high standards set at Oblivion following its opening don't slip.

*Open: 12.00–23.00 (Mon–Sat), 12.00–22.30 (Sun)*
*Food: à la carte 12.00–19.00 (Mon–Sun), bar food: all opening hours*
*Credit cards: all major cards except AmEx*
*Draught beers: John Smith's Smooth, Beck's, Miller, Guinness*
*Wheelchair access to venue and loo*
*Private room: 40 seated, 75 standing*
*Nearest tube station: Clapham South*

# Office Bar

3–5 Rathbone Place, W1. Tel: 0171 636 1598

We all like to feel good and look the part in preparation for a night on the tiles. When I went to Office recently, the perfectly lit, fully-mirrored stairwell provided a stark reminder of those parts of my body I'd hoped weren't as public as the mirrors reflected. It was quite a relief to get inside the large, colourful, air-conditioned bar, and plonk myself down at one of the well-spaced tables to begin the slow alcoholic descent into memory loss. A pitcher of Alabama Slammer (£11.95) helped, even though I had just missed the half-price happy hour (5–7pm). Wednesday is games night (£5), and from the list of over 100, I found

Ker-Plunk and Connect 4 taxing enough, and decided to steer well clear of a rather intimate young group playing Twister. Office has club nights Thursday to Saturday (prices vary), with live bands, soul, ska and sixties classics. I returned for lunch one day and found it a surprisingly sedate affair – but I'd forgotten about those bloody mirrors.

*Open: 12.00–03.00 (Mon–Sat)*
*Food: as opening hours*
*Credit cards: all major*
*Nearest tube station: Tottenham Court Road*

## O'Hanlon's

18 Tysoe Street, EC1. Tel: 0171 837 4112

There can't be a more Irish pub in London. This has nothing to do with any ersatz sub-genre of Irish theme pubs popping up all over the place. This is an Irish pub that just happens to be in London. John O'Hanlon from County Kerry bought it some five years ago, named it after himself, moved his family in to run the place – and soon had a resounding success on his hands. Inside this little corner pub in Clerkenwell there's a big plain bar where you'll find the man himself pouring out the pints and presiding over the craic. His mother can be found in the kitchen preparing all the home-cooked dishes and baking the soda bread. The beers? Well, they come from a new brewery in London called O'Hanlon's – he brews them himself underneath the arches in Vauxhall. The standard bearer is O'Hanlon's Dry Stout, then there's a wheatbeer he calls Malster's Weiss, an English light ale called Blakely's No. 1, and Myrica Ale, an Irish ale brewed with bog myrtle and honey. So succesful are these brews that many London free houses are now stocking them.

*Open: 11.00–23.00 (Mon–Fri)*
*Food: 12.00–14.30 and 18.00–21.00 (Mon–Fri)*
*Credit cards: none taken*
*Draught beers: Blakely's No. 1, Malster's Weiss, Myrica Ale, O'Hanlon's Red Ale, Carling Black Label, Staropramen, Guinness, O'Hanlon's Dry Stout, O'Hanlon's Smooth Dry Stout*
*Wheelchair access to venue*
*Private room seats 30*
*Nearest tube station: Farringdon*

## Old Bank of England

194 Fleet Street, EC4. Tel: 0171 430 2055

Fuller's, which likes to turn banks into pubs, has excelled itself with this one. It is located in a magnificent Grade-1 listed building which for 87 years was the Law Courts branch of the Bank of England. Now it is one of the most imposing pubs in London. It has noble columns, high Italianate windows, and a magnificent ceiling with chandeliers that have to be winched down from the floor above when a bulb goes. Confidently centre-stage reigns its splendid new bar. You place an order here and it is brought to you or, anyway, to the lawyers and bankers who crowd in at lunchtime. They are back in force on their way home in the early evening.

*Open: 11.00–23.00 (Mon–Fri)*
*Food: 12.00–20.00 (Mon–Fri)*
*Credit cards: all major cards*
*Draught beers: Chiswick Bitter, ESB, Fuller's seasonal ale, London Pride, one guest ale, Carling Black Label, Grolsch, Stella Artois, Guinness, Murphy's, Scrumpy Jack*
*Private room: 20–50 seated, 20–80 standing*
*Nearest tube station: Temple*

# The Old Bell Tavern

95 Fleet Street, EC4. Tel: 0171 583 0070

In the great days of Fleet Street, The Old Bell Tavern was a printers' pub, small but cosy, its bar tucked away behind its off-licence. When the newspapers left in the late eighties it had to find an entirely new clientele, as did all the pubs in Fleet Street. It is now a lawyers' and bankers' pub, and is doing well again.

The Old Bell Tavern was built in 1678 by Sir Christopher Wren as a hostel for his masons, who were rebuilding St Bride's, destroyed in the Great Fire. The off-licence has now disappeared, making the pub a little bigger. In its place is a comfortable snug; a handsome stained-glass window faces the street. Printers taking a trip down memory lane will notice such things and will be pleased to see that the triangular oak stools, a feature of the pub since its early days, are still there. A Nicholson's Heritage Inn.

*Open: 11.00–23.00 (Mon–Fri)*
*Food: 12.00–15.00 (Mon–Fri)*
*Credit cards: all major cards*
*Draught beers: Brakspear, Marston's Pedigree, Pope's Original, Tetley's, a weekly guest ale, Carlsberg, Castlemaine, Guinness, Dry Blackthorn*
*Wheelchair access to venue*
*Private room seats 30*
*Nearest tube station: Blackfriars*

# The Old Bull and Bush

North End Road, NW3. Tel: 0181 455 3685

They say this is probably the most famous pub in the world and they may have a point. It was the song that did it, of course:

> *Come, come, come and make eyes at me*
> *Down at the Old Bull and Bush (ta ra ra ra ra)*
> *Come, come, drink some port wine with me*
> *Down at the Old Bull and Bush....*

The Bull and Bush has a long history. Booklets on the bar tell the story: old farmhouse, Charles I, medicinal springs. Then the pleasure garden and the music licence and concerts and sing-songs and half the East End heading for a day in the country and a good old knees-up down at the Old Bull and Bush. The pub is still going great guns. There were huge changes to it in the twenties and again in the eighties, when it closed for three months for a major rebuilding job. It was changed from top to toe, with new bars, new kitchens, new places to eat, jolly bits and quiet bits. One of the new bars might be a country-house library; it is now used for private parties. It has a piano and every now and then one of the guests will sit down at it and bang out the only possible song all over again.

*Open: 12.00–23.00 (Mon–Sat), 12.00–22.30 (Sun)*
*Food: 12.00–22.00 (Mon–Sat), 12.00–21.30 (Sun)*
*Credit cards: all major cards*
*Draught beers: Calder's Cream Ale, Kilkenny, Marston's Pedigree, Tetley's, a fort-nightly guest ale, Carlsberg, Castlemaine, Guinness, Dry Blackthorn, Addlestones*
*Wheelchair access to venue and loo*
*Nearest tube station: Golders Green*

# The Old Coffee House

49 Beak Street, W1. Tel: 0171 437 2197

The Old Coffee House was a coffee house in the 18th century but didn't see the need to change its name when its primary purpose changed to selling alcohol. The bar is filled with stuffed animals, brass things hanging from the ceiling, and such rare and curious items as the boxing gloves used by Dave Charnley to knock out David 'Darkie' Hughes when defending his lightweight title in 1961. It was the shortest-ever British title fight and lasted 40 seconds. The Old Coffee House is proud of its range of lunches – 20 main courses on offer every day, plus trad pub grub. You can still get coffee in The Old Coffee Shop.

*Open: 11.00–23.00 (Mon–Sat), 12.00–15.00 and 19.00–22.30 (Sun)*
*Food: 12.00–15.00 (Mon–Sat)*
*Credit cards: none taken*
*Draught beers: Courage Best, Courage Directors, Marston's Pedigree, John Smith's Extra Smooth, Budweiser, Foster's, Holsten, Kronenbourg, Guinness, Dry Blackthorn*
*Wheelchair access to venue*
*Private room: 30 seated, 40 standing*
*Nearest tube stations: Piccadilly Circus, Oxford Circus*

## Old Dr Butlers Head

Masons Avenue, EC2. Tel: 0171 606 3504

Masons Avenue is a narrow flagstoned alley with a black and white, five-storey, half-timbered mansion on one side and the Old Dr Butlers Head a few feet away on the other. The pub has one big bar with old timbers, bare floorboards, ancient-looking panelling up to the ceiling, old barrels and stout wooden furniture. Every lunchtime the bar is full of smartly dressed City men and women. Up two steps at the back there are tables and chairs, and girls making good-looking sandwiches, and upstairs are two floors of restaurants, with roasts and Dr Butler's Daily Specialities. Dr Butler was a dreadful old quack who fired off pistols inches away from the ears of his patients to cure epilepsy, and dropped poor souls with ague into the river. The great cure that got him in with King James I was his medicinal ale – good for your tum, he said. He bought several alehouses to sell it in, and got this one in 1616. It is the last remaining of Dr Butler's pubs, but it hasn't sold his ale for 300 years.

*Open: 11.00–23.00 (Mon–Fri)*
*Food: 11.00–14.30 (Mon–Fri)*
*Credit cards: all major cards*
*Draught beers: Boddingtons, Brakspear, Flowers, Marston's Pedigree, Wadworth 6X, Heineken, Stella Artois, Guinness, Murphy's, Strongbow*
*Wheelchair access to venue*
*Private room seats 120*
*Nearest tube station: Moorgate*

## Ye Olde Cheshire Cheese

Wine Office Court, 145 Fleet Street, EC4. Tel: 0171 353 6170

The Cheshire Cheese is one of London's most celebrated taverns. It is the archetypal 17th-century chophouse – small, cosy rooms, black settles, sawdust-covered floors, creaking stairs, open fires and good old boys in the chimney corner. The original tavern burnt down in the Great Fire of London but was rebuilt the following year, and there were no major changes for the next 300 years. The Yorkshire brewers Samuel Smith bought it in 1986 and found it distinctly unsteady on its pins. In 1990 the pub was underpinned and tightened up, totally refurbished and effectively extended. By the time it reopened it had just about doubled in size.

The old tavern now has six separate bars, three restaurants and a private dining room. A modern kitchen on the top floor supplies food to them all, sending it down by dumb waiters. By and large the restoration has been a mannerly one. The pub seems hardly to have changed at all, even keeping the faded gilt notice above the door saying 'Gentlemen Only'. The management hope women customers will ignore this.

*Open: 11.30–23.00 (Mon–Sat), 12.00–17.00 (Sun)*
*Food: bar 12.00–14.30 (Mon–Fri); restaurant 12.00–21.30 (Mon–Sat), 12.00–16.00*
*(Sun)*
*Credit cards: all major cards,*
*Draught beers: Old Brewery, Samuel Smith's Dark Mild, Ayingerbraü, Ayingerbraü*
*Pils, Samuel Smith's Stout, Samuel Smith's Reserve*
*Private room: five function rooms seat 15–120*
*Nearest tube stations: Blackfriars, Chancery Lane*

## Ye Olde Mitre Tavern

Ely Court, Hatton Garden, EC1. Tel: 0171 405 4751

Neatly tucked away in a narrow alley between Hatton Garden and Ely Place, this is one of the most difficult pubs to find in London, and also one of the most picturesque. It stands in the grounds of St Ethelreda's 13th-century church, where until recently the police were not allowed to enter. There's a stone mitre in the wall from the nearby bishops' gatehouse, and the trunk of an ancient cherry tree in a corner of the bar. The present pub dates back to 1772, and consists of two small, dark-panelled rooms with high settles. Upstairs is the Bishop's Room, where there's more chance of a seat; there's also a tiny outside space with barrels for tables if you don't mind standing.

*Open: 11.00–23.00 (Mon–Fri)*
*Food: 11.00–22.00 (Mon–Fri)*
*Credit cards: none taken*
*Draught beers: Burton, Friary Meux, Tetley's, Carlsberg, Castlemaine, Guinness,*
*Dry Blackthorn*
*Private room seats 25*
*Nearest tube station: Chancery Lane*

## Ye Olde Surgeon

183 Tottenham Court Road, W1. Tel: 0171 631 3618

This is a theme pub, and what do you suppose the theme is? An operating theatre. Honestly. It's all *Spitting Image*-type surgeons and patients at Ye Olde Surgeon, jokes involving cutting bits off and sewing bits on, humorous skulls, funny bandaged bits, and real-life ads for Ex-Lax. They used to do a cocktail called Lop It Off and a bar snack called Double Hernia, but they've amputated those now.

*Open: 11.00–23.00 (Mon–Fri), 12.00–22.30 (Sun)*
*Food: as opening hours*
*Credit cards: all major cards except AmEx*
*Draught beers: Courage Directors, Theakston Best, one guest ale, Beck's, Foster's,*
*Kronenbourg, Guinness, Strongbow*
*Wheelchair access to venue*
*Nearest tube stations: Goodge Street, Warren Street*

## Ye Olde Swiss Cottage

98 Finchley Road, NW3. Tel: 0171 722 3487

'Ye Olde' is the new bit in the name of this curious pseudo-Swiss chalet on the extraordinarily busy Finchley Road, which gave its original name to the new bus terminus, then to the Metropolitan Line station, and soon to the entire district. It is an enormous pub with four bars, a private pool club, a terrace with picnic tables, and a deep wooden balcony around three of its sides. Samuel Smith bought it in 1986, and there has been lots of refurbishing since then. The Victoria Bar (with music) and the Albert Bar (without) are now big, comfortable rooms with sofas, armchairs, wing chairs and button-backed chairs, grouped around widely spaced coffee tables. The Tap Room is plain and pleasant, and you could give a ball in the vast upstairs bar, now used as a function room. Just £10 gets you membership of the pool club for life, after which it is 80p a game. The seven tables are permanently occupied every evening.

*Open: 11.00–23.00 (Mon–Sat), 12.00–22.30 (Sun)*
*Food: 12.00–15.00 and 18.00–20.30 (Mon–Sat), 12.00–15.00 (Sun)*
*Credit cards: none taken*
*Draught beers: Old Brewery Bitter, Sovereign Bitter, Ayingerbraü Pils, Ayingerbraü Prinz, Samuel Smith's Extra Stout, Special Reserve*
*Wheelchair access to venue*
*Private room: 150 people standing*
*Nearest tube station: Swiss Cottage*

## The Olde Wine Shades

6 Martin Lane, EC4. Tel: 0171 626 6876

One of only two taverns to have survived the Great Fire (see The Hoop and Grapes), The Olde Wine Shades almost didn't survive at the hands of the developers. A furious battle erupted but this fine pub lives on to tell the tale. It has been in continual use as a pub since 1663, and is owned by El Vino these days. It no longer sells draught beer, but it asks its gentlemen customers to wear jackets and ties, as it has always done, and retains its genteel shabbiness, with its old carpet runner and assorted tables and chairs. The substantial City people who eat and drink here find this all very agreeable. Things don't change much at The Olde Wine Shades. The wine list is as sound, and the food as good, as ever. Victor Little, who runs the pub, has been there since 1961. He is silver-haired and courteous, and an unmistakable figure of authority.

*Open: 11.30–20.00 (Mon–Fri)*
*Food: 12.00–15.00 (Mon–Fri)*
*Credit cards: all major cards*
*Private room seats: 40 people (evenings)*
*Nearest tube station: Cannon Street*

## The Old King Lud

78 Ludgate Hill, EC4. Tel: 0171 329 8517

Whitbread has made the rebuilt King Lud into the most spectacular of their Hogshead pubs, so it is all ancient timbers and old flagstones. There are country benches and old wooden tables, a great gantry is loaded with barrels, and in the far reaches of the vast bar a huge vat labelled Fermenting Vessel No. 1 seems wedged into the corner. Youthful machismo is the keynote here. A minimum of 18 different cask ales are on tap every day, and vast quantities are downed, customers using 2-pint tankards and 4-pint jugs to save time. The staff are young and lively, and throw themselves into the spirit of the thing, particularly on Friday nights, when the place is jumping.

*Open: 11.00–23.00 (Mon–Sat)*
*Food: 12.00–20.00 (Mon–Sat)*
*Credit cards: all major cards except AmEx*
*Draught beers: 18–20 real ales which are changed on a weekly basis, Heineken, Stella Artois, Guinness, Murphy's, Biddenden, Scrumpy Jack*
*Wheelchair access to venue and loo*
*Nearest tube station: Blackfriars*

## The Old Red Lion

72 High Holborn, WC1. Tel: 0171 405 1748

This Red Lion has a rather grisly claim to fame. After the restoration of Charles II it was felt necessary to punish the three men considered most responsible for his father's execution – Oliver Cromwell, his son-in-law Henry Ireton, and the judge who sentenced Charles I to death, John Bradshaw. They were dead already, as it happened, and buried in Westminster Abbey, but they were punished all the same. They were disinterred, taken to Tyburn and strung up. On the way there the cart stopped off at The Red Lion, where the three bodies lay overnight. They can hardly have been very welcome guests. Ireton, the youngest of the three, had been dead ten years. The old pub has been rebuilt, restored and refurbished any number of times since then. The latest renovation closed the pub for six weeks. The good-looking Victorian back bar was retained in the saloon bar, but everything else was replaced. The pub is still Victorian after a fashion, and very comfortable, but brand new. The first floor got a restaurant, lost it and now has a bar with a pool table.

*Open: 11.00–23.00 (Mon–Fri)*
*Food: as opening hours (sandwiches only)*
*Credit cards: all major cards*
*Draught beers: Abbot Ale, Greene King IPA, Greene King seasonal ales, Wexford Irish Cream, Harp, Kronenbourg, Stella Artois, Guinness, Dry Blackthorn*
*Wheelchair access to venue*
*Nearest tube stations: Holborn, Chancery Lane*

# The Old Shades

37 Whitehall, SW1. Tel: 0171 930 4019

The Old Shades is a Grade-2 listed building, which means that you get told off if you pull it down. A long thin pub put up in 1898, it was built in the Flemish-Gothic style, with carved spandrels, cross-mullioned leaded casements and an elongated gable. It seems older than it actually is, and in fact, a tavern stood on this spot long before the present building. I dare say that the crowd that watched the execution of Charles I just up the road came in for a drink afterwards, but The Old Shades believes in letting bygones be bygones. It gets a lot of tourists and welcomes Big Occasions. Almost any parade down Whitehall does wonders for trade.

*Open: 11.00–23.00 (Mon–Sat), 12.00–18.00 (Sun)*
*Food: 12.00–15.00 and 17.00–20.30 (Mon–Fri), 12.00–16.00 and 17.00–20.00 (Sat), 12.00–17.00 (Sun)*
*Credit cards: not AmEx*
*Draught beers: Bass, Caffrey's, London Pride, Carling Black Label, Carling Premier, Grolsch, Guinness, Cidermaster*
*Wheelchair access to venue*
*Private room: 30 seated, 60 standing*
*Nearest tube station: Embankment*

# The Old Ship

25 Upper Mall, W6. Tel: 0181 748 2593

This 17th-century riverside hostelry is probably the oldest pub in Hammersmith. In recent years, though, lessees Paul and Lionel Bann-Murray have changed just about everything: character, appearance, customers, name. Some changes met with fierce local opposition, so the Bann-Murrays have made compromises lately. They have returned the old pub to its original colours, cream and black, and dropped their new name for it, The Ranger on the River. It is The Old Ship again now, and the music has been turned down a bit. It remains a radically altered pub, however, with a big new kitchen, new lavatories and a powerful new sound system. The wide first-floor balcony, once the landlord's private domain, is crowded with lunchers whenever the sun shines. The manager's old sitting room and the old kitchen upstairs are both public dining rooms now, one the Quarter Deck, the other the Mess Room. Both can be hired.

Music remains a major part of life in the new Old Ship, with pop videos and a busy juke box, and there are all the major sporting fixtures on satellite TV. This is certainly the most youthful pub on Hammersmith's riverside.

*Open: 11.00–23.00 (Mon–Sat), 12.00–22.30 (Sun)*
*Food: 10.00 (for breakfast)–22.30 (Mon–Sun)*
*Credit cards: all major cards*
*Draught beers: Flowers Original, John Smith's, Old Speckled Hen, Wadworth 6X, Budweiser, Foster's, Kronenbourg, Guinness*
*Wheelchair access to venue and loo*
*Two private rooms: 50 seated, 70 standing*
*Nearest tube station: Hammersmith*

## Old Thameside Inn

2 Clink Street, SE1. Tel: 0171 403 4243

The Old Thameside Inn is not very old at all. It will have its 13th birthday this year and its luck is changing for the better. Take a look at its neighbours. The *Golden Hinde*, replica of the 16th-century warship, is in dry dock by the entrance, and the new Globe Theatre is just down the way. The remains of the Clink prison – now a museum – are round the back.

A new riverside walk passes between the pub and the river, making it the perfect resting point for walkers, with its picnic tables and views of the river and the City. The Old Thameside used to be a spice warehouse, busy and prosperous at first, abandoned later on. Then it was cleverly converted, the designers keeping the heavy timbers and the old flagstone floor. It could hardly be in a more interesting location.

*Open: 11.00–23.00 (Mon–Fri), 12.00–16.00 (Sat–Sun)*
*Food: 12.00–19.30 (Mon–Fri), 12.00–14.30 (Sat–Sun)*
*Credit cards: all major cards*
*Draught beers: Adnams, Calder's Cream Ale, Marston's Pedigree, Tetley's, five guest ales, Carlsberg Export, Castlemaine, Guinness, Dry Blackthorn*
*Private room: 20–60 seated, 60–150 standing*
*Nearest tube station: London Bridge*

## O'Neill's

The O'Neill's chain is probably one of the best examples of the new generation of Irish theme pubs. In 1994 the Irish Pub Company approached Bass with ideas and designs, and Bass agreed to try them out on one of their struggling pubs, the Tap and Hen in Aberdeen. It was an instant success, and Bass were so pleased they developed O'Neill's as one of their brands. There are now more than 100 up and down the country, 30 of them within the M25 area. People argue that we have enough of them; the matter has even been raised in Parliament. What we might well have enough of are the poorer versions of this ersatz genre, but O'Neill's pubs are certainly not among them. OK, so maybe they don't all look like that in Ireland, but we mustn't rubbish their attempts at authenticity (see the Earl's Court Road O'Neill's, below). We don't live in Ireland for one thing, so I see nothing wrong with the tailoring of a theme to meet the demands of a discerning London market. A representative from the Irish Tourist Board told me, 'If it sells Cork dry gin, Bushmills whiskey and Ballygowan mineral water, its Irish, all right.' O'Neill's sells them all – in fact the pubs stock a rather good range of Irish whiskeys, plus Carrolls and Major cigarettes and Tayto crisps. The menu changes regularly but they retain old favourites such as Irish lamb stew with soda bread, sausage and onion with colcannon (potatoes mixed with cabbage and spring onions and lashings of butter), beef and stout pie, and boxty, a traditional Irish potato pancake. The main meals are usually served at lunchtimes only, with the lite-bite menu of snacks until 7pm.

O'Neill's employ a high proportion of Irish staff, who take the business of not being very serious, very seriously. Don't be surprised if you find them singing or dancing away during their shift – they're encouraged to have fun, and it can be quite contagious. They are generally also quite knowledgeable about the drinks they serve, so don't be afraid to ask, particularly when there are so many whiskeys to choose from. If you're still not convinced about theme bars, bear in mind that with 102 O'Neill's in the country, 102 pubs have been saved from possible closure, creating jobs, stimulating the economy, and most important of all, providing us with choice.

*Branches at:*

**Beckenham**: 9 High Street, BR3. Tel: 0181 650 9831. Nearest railway station: Beckenham Junction

**Blackheath**: 52 Tranquil Vale, SE3. Tel: 0181 852 1121. Nearest railway station: Blackheath

**Camden**: 55 Camden High Street, NW1. Tel: 0171 387 2734. Nearest tube station: Camden Town

**City**: 31–36 Houndsditch, EC3. Tel: 0171 283 5469. Nearest tube station: Liverpool Street

**City**: 64 London Wall, EC2. Tel: 0171 638 1854. Nearest tube station: Moorgate

**City**: 65 Cannon Street, EC4. Tel: 0171 489 1529. Nearest tube station: Cannon Street

**Covent Garden**: 40 Great Queen Street, WC2. Tel: 0171 405 0572. Nearest tube station: Covent Garden

**Covent Garden**: 14 New Row, WC2. Tel: 0171 836 3291. Nearest tube station: Covent Garden

**Croydon**: 1 South End, CR0. Tel: 0181 688 5456. Nearest railway stations: East Croydon, South Croydon

**Earls Court**: 326 Earls Court Road, SW5. Tel: 0171 373 9172. Nearest tube station: Earls Court

**Finchley**: 744 High Road, N12. Tel: 0181 445 5956. Nearest tube station: Woodside Park

**Ilford**: 109 Station Road, IG2. Tel: 0181 478 3297. Nearest railway station: Ilford

**Kingston-upon-Thames**: 3 Eden Street, KT1. Tel: 0181 547 1203. Nearest railway station: Kingston-upon-Thames

**Leytonstone**: 762 Leytonstone High Road, E11. Tel: 0181 532 2692. Nearest tube station: Leytonstone

**Maidstone**: 11 Middle Row, ME14. Tel: 01622 753089. Nearest railway station: Maidstone

**Marylebone**: 56 Blandford Street, W1. Tel: 0171 935 1812. Nearest tube station: Baker Street

**Marylebone**: 4 Conway Street, W1. Tel: 0171 631 5300. Nearest tube station: Great Portland Street

**Marylebone**: 73–77 Euston Road, NW1. Tel: 0171 387 4566. Nearest tube station: King's Cross

**Mayfair**: 21 Old Burlington Street, W1. Tel: 0171 437 8355. Nearest tube station: Oxford Circus

**Mayfair**: 7 Shepherd Street, W1. Tel: 0171 629 3645. Nearest tube station: Green Park

**Mayfair**: 22–23 Woodstock Street, W1. Tel: 0171 495 7624. Nearest tube station: Bond Street

**Muswell Hill**: 291–293 Broadway, N10. Tel: 0181 365 2390. Nearest tube station: Highgate

**Richmond**: 28 The Quadrant, TW9. Tel: 0181 940 2606. Nearest tube station: Richmond

**Slough**: 20 Windsor Road, SL1. Tel: 01753 554877. Nearest railway station: Slough

**Southend-on-Sea**: 119 High Street, SS1. Tel: 01702 335164. Nearest railway station: Southend-on-Sea

**St Albans**: 20–30 London Road, AL1. Tel: 01727 866603. Nearest railway station: St Albans

**Streatham**: 78a Streatham High Road, SW16. Tel: 0181 677 5764. Nearest railway station: Streatham

**Sutton**: 37 High Street, SM1. Tel: 0181 642 3904. Nearest railway station: Sutton

**Upper Holloway**: 456 Holloway Road, N7. Tel: 0171 607 2855. Nearest tube stations: Holloway Road, Finsbury Park

**Upper Norwood**: 98 Church Road, SE19. Tel: 0181 771 5249. Nearest railway station: Crystal Palace

**Wallington**: 89 Manor Road, SM6. Tel: 0181 669 3542. Nearest railway station: Wallington

**Watford**: 66–68 The Parade, WD1. Tel: 01923 242228. Nearest tube station: Watford

**West End**: 34–37 Wardour Street, W1. Tel: 0171 287 4953. Nearest tube station: Leicester Square

**Wimbledon**: 68 The Broadway, SW19. Tel: 0181 543 3771. Nearest tube station: Wimbledon

# O'Neill's

326 Earls Court Road, SW5. Tel: 0171 373 9172

The Irish are particularly good at telling yarns. When I went to meet Eddie Pierce, the manager of this pub, during its internal construction a few years ago, he told me the following tale. 'This was an Irish brewery built in the early 1900s by my grandfather, a master brewer called O'Neill, who came over from County Cork to start a business here. This is where they brewed the beer ...' (referring to the giant copper with pipes stretching up to the floor above), 'over here was the staff dining room, and over here was the storage area. Look, you can see where the walls once were, and notice the way the floors are all different.' It was almost believable. Credit to O'Neill's for building a pub around a yarn. The real story, of course, is somewhat different. The pub started life as The Bolton Hotel, built in 1890, the work of the architect George Whittaker, who designed many of Earls Court's terraces and mansion blocks

The Boltons, as it came to be called, had been a gay pub for years when, in the late eighties, the dealers moved in with the police not far behind. The manager of the day was charged with 'allowing people to be drunk on licensed premises'. Bass closed it down and reopened it as the George Whittaker, a sort of Victorian diner. It was unconvincing and the pub closed again. It cost Bass £500,000 to recreate it as an O'Neill's, and it is one of the best examples of the genre. Food is served until 7pm and you can fax through your order if you're short on time.

*Open: 12.00–23.00 (Mon–Sat), 12.00–22.30 (Sun)*
*Food: 12.00–19.00 (Mon–Sun)*
*Credit cards: all major cards except AmEx*
*Draught beers: Caffrey's, Carling Black Label, Grolsch, Guinness, Cidermaster*
*Wheelchair access to venue and loo*
*Private room: 40 seated, 150 standing*
*Nearest tube station: Earls Court*

# 190

190 Queensgate, SW7. Tel: 0171 581 5666

The bar of the restaurant opens late for members but is also accessible to those who have been dining here. It has been described to me as one of the easiest places to pull in London, and judging by the number of singles and single-sex groups who frequent it, I can see why.

*Open: 11.00–01.00 (Mon–Sat), 11.00–midnight (Sun)*
*Credit cards: all major cards*
*Nearest tube stations: Gloucester Road, South Kensington*

# Orange Brewery

37 Pimlico Road, SW1. Tel: 0171 730 5984

A head of Bacchus looks down from the arch over the corner doorway leading to the bar of the Orange Brewery, a fine four-storey Victorian pub in the bit of London where Chelsea meets Pimlico. The Orange Brewery makes all its own ale in a brewhouse directly underneath the bar. Three main house ales are brewed there: SW1 (3.8%), the pub's best-selling bitter; SW2 (4.8%); and Pimlico Porter (4.5%), a revival of the rich dark ale that was the principal beer drunk in London in the 18th and 19th centuries. Victoria Lager (5%) is, they say, the only house-brewed lager in the country. The bar itself seems hardly to have changed since Victorian times. It even has gas lamps.

*Open: 11.00–23.00 (Mon–Sat), 12.00–22.30 (Sun)*
*Food: 12.00–22.00 (Mon–Sun)*
*Credit cards: all major cards*
*Draught beers: SW1, SW2, Leffe Blonde, Victoria Lager, Pimlico Porter, Scrumpy Jack*
*Wheelchair access to venue*
*Nearest tube station: Sloane Square*

# Orange Tree

45 Kew Road, Richmond. Tel: 0181 940 0944

Large Victorian pub obligingly close to Richmond station, with a fine brick and terracotta façade. It is named after the very first orange tree to be brought to Britain, which was planted at Kew Gardens. The interior has kept its Victorian theme, with big bulbous mahogany pillars and a large L-shaped bar. The pub has a theatre upstairs, and the wine bar and restaurant in the cellars seem to flourish, as does the terrace at the back with its pergola. There are eight tables here and ten at the front, all fully occupied when the weather gets hot. They don't go in for music much at the Orange Tree but they do pull down a large screen for the major sporting events. A former *Evening Standard* Pub of the Year.

*Open: 11.00–23.00 (Mon–Sat), 12.00–22.30 (Sun)*
*Food: bar 12.00–15.00 and 18.00–22.00 (Mon–Sat); restaurant 12.00–15.00 and 18.00–23.00 (Mon–Sat)*
*Credit cards: all major cards*
*Draught beers: Ramrod Smooth, Young's Bitter, Young's Special, Young's London Lager, Young's Premium Lager, Castlemaine, Grolsch, Oatmeal Stout, Guinness, Scrumpy Jack*
*Wheelchair access to venue*
*Private room: 60–70 seated, 100 standing*
*Nearest tube station: Richmond*

# Oriel

50–51 Sloane Square, SW1. Tel: 0171 730 2804

The perfect meeting point for Sloane Square tube and the Royal Court Theatre, this popular bar underwent a bit of a facelift in 1997, involving its temporary closure. It's now all ready for action once again, and the ladies who lunch have returned to their regular nesting spot at the terrace bar. Better use has been made of the remaining space, but the Sloane set who once pervaded the ground-floor bar have been relegated below stairs. The downstairs bar is actually quite comfortable and is still very popular with after-work drinkers and cappuccino sippers. People have been known to travel from the far-flung fields of Putney to take breakfast here at weekends in the belief that this is what Chelsea people do. Chelsea people will probably be in a greasy spoon.

*Open: 12.00–23.00 (Mon–Sat), 12.00–22.30 (Sun)*

*Food: bar as opening hours; restaurant upstairs 08.30–22.45, downstairs*
*08.30–22.00 (Mon–Sun)*
*Credit cards: all major cards*
*Draught beers: Kronenbourg*
*Wheelchair access to venue and loo*
*Private room: 50–60 seated, 130 standing*
*Nearest tube station: Sloane Square*

## The Outpost
Lidlington Place, NW1. Tel: 0171 387 1495

The Outpost is a pub for bikers run by bikers. That doesn't mean to the exclu-
sion of everyone else – in fact, they depend on others, as bikers are not big
drinkers. The kings of the road come and show off their equipment, which they
proudly polish on the road outside. Outpost's bold claim is to be Camden's
best rock pub. It doesn't open until 5pm on weekdays and it has two impossible biker video games. Why not go along for the ride?

*Open: 17.00–23.00 (Mon–Fri), 11.00–23.00 (Sat), 12.00–22.30 (Sun)*
*Food: 12.00–15.00 and 17.00–20.00 (Mon–Fri), 12.00–17.00 (Sun)*
*Credit cards: none taken*
*Draught beers: John Smith's, Foster's, Holsten, Kronenbourg, Guinness, Strongbow*
*Nearest tube stations: Mornington Crescent, Euston, Camden Town*

## Oxo Tower Bar
8th Floor, Oxo Tower Wharf, Barge House Street, SE1.
Tel: 0171 803 3888

The success of the Oxo Tower Bar is down to the happy combination of the
Harvey Nicks elegance and the wonderful panoramic view of London's skyline.
It isn't cheap, and certainly not easy to get to, but worth a punt on a special
occasion.

*Open: 11.00–23.00 (Mon–Sat), 12.00–22.30 (Sun)*
*Credit cards: all major cards*
*Wheelchair access to venue and loo*
*Nearest tube stations: Blackfriars, Waterloo*

## Pals
6 Bridge Street, East Molesey, KT8. Tel: 0181 941 7781

Pals is a grand-looking building on the opposite side of the bridge to The
Gazebo (qv). Its two storeys aim to be all things to all people – a bar, restaurant
and nightclub. The bar can get quite loud, as does the nightclub. Pals is a quiet
place by day, but things start to hot up in the evenings. I hear from a local, reli-
able source that it's a good place to pull.

*Open: 11.00–23.00 (Mon–Wed), 11.00–01.00 (Thurs–Sat), 12.00–22.30 (Sun)*
*Food: 12.00–16.00 and 19.00–21.30 (Mon), 12.00–17.00 and 19.00–21.30*
*(Tues–Thurs), 12.00–17.00 and 19.00–22.30 (Fri–Sat)*
*Credit cards: all major cards*
*Draught beers: Old Speckled Hen, Carlsberg, Carlsberg Export, Castlemaine,*
*Lowenbrau, Guinness, Dry Blackthorn*
*Wheelchair access to venue and loo*
*Club area for hire: 60 seated, 200 standing, 120 for buffet*
*Nearest railway station: Hampton Court*

## Paradise                         EROS AWARD WINNER
19 Kilburn Lane, W10. Tel: 0181 969 0098

The Paradise by way of Kensal Green is the full title of this bar, which has been
quietly beavering away for the past five years, establishing itself as the stamp-

ing ground for urban, street trendies in this otherwise venue-desolate part of north-west London. The bar is owned by Frank Ormonde, whose Portobello Road gallery supplies the interior furnishings. The upstairs Oriental room holds artefacts from the Tang Dynasty, and a pair of Indonesian pillars seemingly support the entire building. This is where you might find the live music, the DJs, the poetry readings or the comedy nights. Everything But The Girl's Ben Watt is a regular, and is known to DJ and jam here occasionally. The restaurant room opens out to a garden patio with space enough for 30 people. Although the Modern British fare is of good quality, I hear the service can be quite slow. As I write, the Paradise is only open in the evenings (apart from Sundays when roast lunches are on offer at £5.80), but plans are afoot to make it an all-day venue. It's a real find, a good starting point for the Cobden Club, and worth any number of detours for a buzzing night out.

*Open: 17.00–23.00 (Mon–Sat), 17.00–22.30 (Sun)*
*Food: 19.30–midnight (Mon–Sat), 19.30–23.30 (Sun)*
*Credit cards: all major cards*
*Draught beers: John Smith's Extra Smooth, Webster's, Holsten, Kronenbourg, Miller, Beamish Red, Guinness*
*Wheelchair access to venue*
*Private room: 20 seated, 30 standing*
*Nearest tube station: Kensal Green*

## The Pavilion

Finsbury Circus Gardens, Finsbury Circus, EC2. Tel 0171 628 8224

Clompity-clomp, clompity-clomp! That's the wooden-floored pavilion at the City of London Bowling Club for you. It's very small, but situated as it is in the gardens of Finsbury Square, it provides a much-needed respite for the workers in nearby offices.

*Open: 11.30–22.00 (Mon–Fri)*
*Food: as opening hours*
*Credit cards: all major cards*
*Nearest tube stations: Moorgate, Liverpool Street*

## Paxton's Head

153 Knightsbridge, SW1. Tel: 0171 589 6627

Sir Joseph Paxton was the Victorian landscape gardener who designed and built the Crystal Palace. He would surely have approved of the brilliant decorated mirrors that cover the walls of the bar here. Some have had to be replaced with plain glass but most of the originals have survived and sparkle as they always did. The polished mahogany bar counter and the listed ceiling are terrific too. Sadly, the huge Victorian mantle clock, which stood on the fireplace for so many years, has now gone 'missing'.

*Open: 11.00–23.00 (Mon–Sat), 12.00–22.30 (Sun)*
*Food: 12.00–19.00 (Mon–Sun)*
*Credit cards: all major cards*
*Draught beers: Brakspear, Tetley's, two guest ales, Carlsberg, Castlemaine, Lowenbrau, Guinness, Olde English Cider*
*Wheelchair access to venue*
*Private room: 50 seated, 100 standing*
*Nearest tube station: Knightsbridge*

## La Perla                    EROS AWARD WINNER

28 Maiden Lane, WC2. Tel: 0171 240 7400

You might be surprised to discover that La Perla is part of a chain – the newest addition from the Café Pacifico Group – as it bears none of the corporate hallmarks of some other theme bars. La Perla is as authentically Mexican as you're likely to get in London, and it is worth any number of visits to get through its comprehensive menu of drinks and food. It has 16 beers, nine of which are imported from Mexico – including the wonderful Negra Modela, an exotic Hispanic rendition of Guinness, only lighter. It also has an eclectic range of 16 wines, but that isn't the point here – you should really tackle the tequilas, margaritas, daiquiris and cocktails. The food is excellent, and you can choose from the botanas (appetisers) or the main meals of platillos exquisitos. Over the course of several visits, I tried, and recommend, the fajitas chiquitas with chicken (£6.50) or prawns (£6.95); the buritto especial, which includes a flour tortilla filled with beans, cheese, onions and peppers, covered in a mild tomato sauce, and served with refried beans and rice; the vegetarian dish of the day; and the sirloin, chicken and honey roast pork (to £8.95). I could go on for ever! If you call in on a hot summer's day, sit with a margarita and a plate of quesadillas and close your eyes – you could almost be in Mexico. Did I mention the service? It is extraordinarily efficient and friendly, and given the number of bars I've been to this year, I ought to know.

*Open: 12.00–23.45 (Mon–Sat), 12.00–22.30 (Sun)*
*Food: bar 12.00–22.45 (Mon–Sat), 12.00–22.00 (Sun); restaurant 12.00–23.45 (Mon–Sat), 12.00–22.30 (Sun)*
*Credit cards: all major cards*
*Draught beers: Red Stripe*
*Wheelchair access to venue*
*Nearest tube stations: Covent Garden, Leicester Square*

# Pharaoh & Firkin

90 Fulham High Street, SW6. Tel: 0171 731 0732

Formerly the old Temperance Billiard Hall, the Pharaoh & Firkin in Fulham High Street has become one of London's biggest and most successful pubs, with its own brewhouse producing vast quantities of ale in what used to be the temperance kitchen. The size, height and spread of the place astonishes customers, and you can get an astonishing number of customers in there – 800 and more partying the weekend away to the live music. Firkin food is sold all day. There's a window to the brewhouse to let you see the Pharaoh Ale, the Cam Ale and the Dogbolter being brewed. It takes a big effort to keep up with the demand.

*Open: 12.00–23.00 (Mon–Sat), 12.00–22.30 (Sun)*
*Food: 12.00–23.00 (Mon–Thurs), 12.00–21.00 (Fri–Sat), 12.00–22.00 (Sun)*
*Credit cards: all major cards*
*Draught beers: Cam Ale, Dogbolter, Pharaoh Ale, Carlsberg Export, Castlemaine, Lowenbrau, Guinness, Weston's Old Rosie*
*Wheelchair access to venue and loo*
*Nearest tube station: Putney Bridge*

# The Phene Arms

9 Phene Street, SW3. Tel: 0171 352 3294

When Dr Samuel Phene built this pub and the streets around it back in 1851 he couldn't possibly have imagined that they would sit so unhappily side by side. Recent years have seen The Phene being dragged through the courts by its neighbours on the grounds of noise pollution. Is this a disco pub? Does it have heavy rock nights? Certainly not. It doesn't have any music at all, and not even a gaming machine. The problem was people chattering in the garden. This otherwise unimpressive local in the quiet backwaters of Chelsea has a wonderful, well-used, well-liked (on the most part) garden, which people flock to on a warm summer's evening. The neighbours revolted, are still revolting, and the latest thing is that the garden must be cleared by 10.40pm. Happily, this doesn't apply to the roof terrace, where 14 people can while away the evening to their hearts' content, telling people to shush! in the garden below.

*Open: 11.00–23.00 (Mon–Sat), 12.00–22.30 (Sun)*
*Food: bar 11.00–23.00 (Mon–Sat), 12.30–22.30 (Sun); restaurant 12.00–15.00 and*
*19.00–22.30 (Mon–Sat), 12.30–16.00 and 19.30–22.00 (Sun)*
*Credit cards: all major cards except Switch*
*Draught beers: Adnams, Courage Best, Courage Directors, Old Speckled Hen,*
*Webster's, Budweiser, Carlsberg, Coors, Foster's, Holsten, Kronenbourg, Guin-*
*ness, Scrumpy Jack, Strongbow*
*Wheelchair access to venue*
*Private room seats 80*
*Nearest tube station: Sloane Square*

## The Phoenix

162–164 Lower Richmond Street, SW15. Tel: 0181 780 3131

This much-loved, pristine, white-painted restaurant in the somewhat uncharted
waters of the Lower Richmond Road has a bar that – unlike the restaurant –
simply doesn't work. Its position doesn't help. It is sandwiched between the
restaurant and the kitchen so that all you can see is the waiters negotiating
their orders. I'm not even sure they're taking the bar seriously. It has a small
(i.e., five) scattering of two-seater tables in a room devoid of any atmosphere.

*Open: 12.30–14.30 and 19.30–23.00 (Mon–Fri), 19.30–23.30 (Sat), 12.00–15.00*
*and 19.00–22.00 (Sun)*
*Credit cards: all major cards*
*Wheelchair access to venue and loo*
*Nearest tube station: Putney Bridge*

## The Phoenix & Firkin

Windsor Walk, SE15. Tel: 0171 701 8282

The Phoenix used to be a railway station, and a good-looking station at that.
The Times once described it as a glorious 1866-vintage Tuscan palazzo. One
night early in 1980 some rotter almost burnt it down. Phoenix-like, and indeed
Firkin-like, it rose from the ashes to start a new chapter, this time as a lively and
popular public house. So there it is, straddling the railway line at Denmark Hill, a
Tuscan palazzo with a classic London, Chatham and Dover interior that is also
classic Firkin – bare boards, plain furniture, a big, practical 58-foot bar, and a
good view of platforms 1, 2, 3 and 4. The Phoenix does good plain food, as
Firkins do, but what is really special is the beer. They brew it themselves in a
brewhouse in the cellar. So while you drink your ale, think of the big vats of
English beer coming silently to fruition beneath your feet – the famous Dogbolter, the Firkin Mild and the Phoenix Rail Ale, which is the pub's best seller.

*Open: 11.00–23.00 (Mon–Sat), 12.00–22.30 (Sun)*
*Food: restaurant 12.00–15.00 and 18.00–20.30 (Mon–Sun); sandwiches*
*15.00–18.00 (Mon–Sun)*
*Credit cards: all major cards*
*Draught beers: Dogbolter, Golden Glory, Phoenix Rail Ale, Carlsberg Export, Carls-*
*berg Pilsner, Lowenbrau, Dry Blackthorn, Scrumpy Jack*
*Wheelchair access to venue and loo*
*Nearest railway station: Denmark Hill*

## Pickled Pelican

22 Waterford Road, SW6. Tel: 0171 736 1023

This was perhaps the first of the modern-day breed of bars to arrive in Fulham.
It opened in 1989 as a result of a conversion and buy-out from the Waterford
Arms. The Pickled Pelican consists of one bright room, with a raised seating
area with large windows, and a floor area with plenty of space for people to
crowd into in the evenings. It was an immediate success, and it is still going

strong as a popular meeting place for young boozers and wine tipplers, who like the loud music, social intercourse, and burger and snack menu. In the words of the manager, 'You don't get a big bill at the Pelican.' Yes, I know, but it's well worth a try. A very decent, trouble-free bar which is ever-so-slightly starting to look its age.

*Open: 11.00–15.30 and 17.30–23.00 (Mon and Thurs), 11.00–23.00 (Tues, Wed, Fri and Sat), 12.00–22.30 (Sun)*
*Food: 11.00–15.00 and 17.00–22.00 (Mon–Sun)*
*Credit cards: all major cards*
*Draught beers: Boddingtons, Marston's Pedigree, Old Speckled Hen, Wadworth 6X, Budweiser, Foster's, Holsten Export, Guinness, Strongbow*
*Nearest tube station: Fulham Broadway*

## Pitcher & Piano

69–70 Dean Street, W1. Tel 0171 434 3585

In 1986 Crispin Tweddell decided that there were too few places in London for people like him to drink and enjoy themselves. So he did the obvious thing and opened up a bar on the far-flung reaches of the Fulham Road. The light, bright rooms with big windows and polished woodwork were to become the blueprint for all Pitcher & Pianos to follow. They have a limited drinks range, but Marston's features highly on the ale front, and you can buy pitchers, of course. There are eight Pitcher & Pianos now in London, and the Soho branch is possibly the most impressive. It is housed in a rather fine, white stucco building in Dean Street, has a palatial interior with a galleried upper floor, and – needless to say – a piano. Mr Tweddell's original philosophy was to provide 'somewhere to meet and talk'. You can do that during the day over lunch or a late-afternoon snifter, and they even offer table service, so it's remarkably civilised. In the evenings, however, the serious music systems encourage a party atmosphere. If I ever get to meet Crispin Tweddell, I think I'll ask him to turn the music down just a teeny bit.

*Open: 11.00–23.00 (Mon–Sat), 12.00–22.30 (Sun); Dean Street closed Sun*
*Food: 12.00–22.30 (Mon–Sat), 12.00–22.00 (Sun)*
*Draught beers: Marston's Pedigree, Marston's Smooth, Kronenbourg, Labatt's, Beamish, ScrumpyJack*
*Credit cards: all major cards*
*Nearest tube station: Piccadilly Circus*

*Branches at:*

**Chelsea**: 214 Fulham Road, SW10. Tel: 0171 352 9234. Nearest tube station: South Kensington
**Chiswick**: 18–20 Chiswick High Road, W4. Tel: 0181 742 7731. Nearest tube stations: Stamford Brook, Turnham Green
**Clapham**: 8 Balham Hill, SW12. Tel: 0181 673 1107. Nearest tube station: Clapham South
**Fulham**: 871–873 Fulham Road, SW6. Tel: 0171 736 3910. Nearest tube station: Parsons Green
**Islington**: 68 Upper Street, N1. Tel: 0171 704 9974. Nearest tube station: Angel
**Trafalgar Square**: 40–42 William IV Street, WC2. Tel: 0171 240 6180. Nearest tube station: Charing Cross
**Wimbledon**: 4–5 High Street, SW19. Tel: 0181 879 7020. Nearest tube station: Wimbledon

## PJs

52 Fulham Road, SW3. Tel: 0171 581 0025

An extraordinarily popular bar-brasserie in an area of South Kensington full of boutiques and restaurants, PJs looks like a rather up-market pub, with its big, imposing bar. It was formerly a pub. You may remember it as The Cranley

Arms. The white linen-covered tables are reserved for people eating, but you can perch at the bar and wonder why they have a huge aeroplane propeller suspended from the gallery above. PJs is on the expensive side of drinking, but the Kensington and Chelsea darlings who go here don't worry about that. They occasionally put a menacing person on the door. Menacing people in South Kensington are rather snotty, actually.

*Open: 12.00–23.30 (Mon–Sat), 12.00–23.00 (Sun)*
*Food: as opening hours (Mon–Sat), 12.00–22.30 (Sun)*
*Credit cards: all major cards*
*Wheelchair access to venue*
*Private room: 40 seated, 80 standing*
*Nearest tube station: South Kensington*

## Plumbers Arms

14 Lower Belgrave Street, SW1. Tel: 0171 730 4067

On a rainswept night in November 1974, Lady Lucan stumbled into this pub, bleeding and soaked to the skin. She had a shocking story to relay. An intruder had murdered her nanny, Sandra Rivett, and then attacked her. He was still in the house. The police were called and the nanny was found dead in the basement of the Lucan family home opposite. Later that night Lord Lucan turned up briefly at a friend's house in Sussex before disappearing. He has never been seen since. The murder has still not been resolved.

The Plumbers Arms is a pleasant single-bar pub with a lincrusta ceiling, a splendid mahogany bar counter, old plates and prints, and smart barmen in white shirts and grey waistcoats polishing up the gleaming beer pulls. It has well-kept cask ales, and denizens of Lower Belgrave Street find it a very good place for lunch.

*Open: 11.00–23.00 (Mon–Fri), 12.00–15.00 (Sat)*
*Food: as opening hours*
*Credit cards: all major cards*
*Draught beers: Courage Directors, John Smith's Extra Smooth, Theakston Best, one guest ale, Foster's, Gillespies, Kronenbourg, Scrumpy Jack*
*Wheelchair access to venue*
*Private room: 25 seated, 30–40 standing*
*Nearest tube station: Victoria*

## The Polar Bear

30 Lisle Street, WC2. Tel: 0171 437 3048

In New Zealand, The Polar Bear is the one London pub everyone has heard of, and young New Zealanders arriving in London head straight for it. There is a Kiwi advice centre upstairs, with a noticeboard offering accommodation and information on all kinds of activities. The pub has three bars nowadays: the main bar on the ground floor, which gets very lively, the quieter upstairs bar, and the late-night cellar bar. New Zealanders seem to like late-night cellar bars. Almost anything goes in this place so long as it's rugby and drinking related. They wouldn't want you to miss a moment of rugger, so there are six TV screens in the main bar, two big screens and four small ones in the cellar bar, and another big screen and a small one in the quieter bar upstairs. There's also a papier-mâché figure of Jonah Lomu. He hasn't been here yet, but I'm sure he will.

*Open: main bar 11.00–23.00 (Mon–Sat), 12.00–22.30 (Sun); upstairs bar 16.00–23.00 (Mon–Sat); basement bar 20.00–03.00 (Mon–Sat)*
*Food: 12.00–15.00 and 18.00–21.00 (Mon–Sun)*
*Credit cards: all major cards except AmEx*
*Draught beers: Caffrey's, Carling Black Label, Grolsch, Guinness, Red Rock*
*Wheelchair access to venue*
*Nearest tube station: Leicester Square*

# Po Na Na

316 King's Road, SW3. Tel: 0171 352 4552

This funky, friendly pleasure basement on the happening end of the King's Road is known essentially as a late-night drinking venue which gets packed with Sloanes and other interesting types eager to make new acquaintances. The appearance, says owner Christian Arden – a man whose name could easily be used to market a pair of jeans, a bottle of perfume or a handbag – is that of an authentic souk bar. Not being sure how many bars there are in Muslim marketplaces, I'll take his word for it. The name Po Na Na is completely made up, so I don't think we need bother ourselves too much with the authenticity of the design. The trendy people who come here are more intent on having a good time, getting it on with the opposite sex and sinking a few drinks. Bottled beers (£2–£2.50), house wine (£10) and champagne (from £25) are staple drinks, but the house speciality is a vodka Red Bull (£3.50), a caffeine-loaded cocktail to keep you going. There's no charge for admission but the scary doorman frightens off unruly gangs and, when the place is full, controls entry on a one-out, one-in basis. To get the best tables and avoid the queues, you should arrive before the pubs shut.

*Open: 20.30–01.00 (Mon–Sat)*
*Credit cards: all major cards*
*Nearest tube stations: Sloane Square, Fulham Broadway*

*Branches at:*

**Chelsea**: The Fez Club, 222 Fulham Road, SW10. Tel: 0171 352 5978. Nearest tube station: South Kensington
**Croydon**: 32–34 High Street, Croydon. Tel: 0181 681 1066. Nearest railway station: Norwood Junction
**Islington**: 259 Upper Street, N1. Tel: 0171 359 6191. Nearest tube station: Angel

# Porters

16 Henrietta Street, WC2. Tel: 0171 836 6466

Lord Bradford has recently opened this bar on two floors next to his long-established restaurant in Covent Garden. I was able to make only a few visits before the Guide went to print, but Porters promises to be a useful addition to Covent Garden's drinking scene. Lord Bradford's thinking is, 'Customers deserve better, and I'm going to see that they finally get a quality bar.' Despite a few shortcomings, he's not that far away from realising his ambition. The air-conditioned rooms are decorated in the modern style; purple and white feature predominantly. The ground level isn't really designed for seating but the lower floor rectifies this, with ample tables and chairs. I was delighted to find so many cask ales on tap, and also to note that, unlike many West End bars, Porters has resisted the temptation to have fast-pouring keg beers. There are no great surprises in the list of 13 bottled beers, but all 18 wines from the list are available by the glass. Bar food is served until half an hour before closing time, and includes sandwiches (£5.75), savoury pancakes (£6.50) and kebabs (£6.95). For chips or salad, add an extra £1.50. Premium spirits include Bombay Sapphire gin, which, alas, is completely destroyed with hosed-in tonic from a gun. A Bombay gin and hosed-in? I don't think so.

*Open: 11.00–23.00 (Mon–Sat), 12.00–22.30 (Sun)*
*Food: 11.00–22.30 (Mon–Sat), 12.00–22.00 (Sun)*
*Credit cards: all major cards*
*Draught beers: Boddingtons, Bombardier, Eagle, Manchester Gold, Marston's Pedigree, Old Speckled Hen, Wadworth 6X, Heineken, Stella Artois, Guinness, Strongbow*
*Wheelchair access to venue*
*Nearest tube stations: Covent Garden, Leicester Square*

# The Prince Alfred

Formosa Street, W9. Tel: 0171 286 3027

One of the most splendid examples of a Victorian pub in London, The Prince Alfred has barely changed since it opened its various doors in 1862. They have kept everything – the beautiful curved and etched glass, the towering centre-piece, the massive mahogany counter, and best of all, the splendid carved and glazed partitions. These divide the space into five separate bars: the Public, the Gentlemen's, the Ladies', the Private and the Snug, into which one has to duck. There are little doors in the partitions, but once in there you are assured of perfect privacy. Rotating snob screens hide you from even the bar staff.

The Prince Alfred has a sixth bar now, bigger than all the others, open-plan in the modern way, and kitted out with a pool table and gaming machines. It is an incongruous mix.

*Open: 12.00–15.00 and 17.30–23.00 (Mon–Thurs), 12.00–23.00 (Fri–Sat), 12.00–22.00 (Sun)*
*Food: 12.00–14.45 (Mon–Thurs), 12.00–18.00 (Fri–Sun)*
*Credit cards: none taken*
*Draught beers: Calder's Cream Ale, Marston's Pedigree, Prince Alfred's House Bitter, Tetley's, Young's, Carlsberg Export, Castlemaine, Lowenbrau, Guinness, Addlestones*
*Nearest tube station: Warwick Avenue*

# The Prince Bonaparte

80 Chepstow Road, W2. Tel: 0171 229 5912

Beth Coventry and Phillip Wright bought a rough old pub a few years ago and have succeeded in bringing it immeasurably up-market. It is now well estab-lished as a foodie pub of the nineties. The two old bars are as one, light floods through the restored conservatory roof, and a splendid open kitchen offers dishes such as aubergine tagine, roast duck leg and grilled tuna (from £3.75 to £9.50). They serve five reasonably priced white wines and seven reds; two of each by the glass. The Prince Bonaparte has a growing reputation for quality food, but declines to call itself a bar or a bistro. It remains a pub. There is draught ale and draught lager on the hand pumps, you can't book a table, they don't take credit cards, and you order your food at the bar. The good news is that Phillip Wright and Mark Harris, the manager, are planning a new project together, close to the Princess Alexandra on Westbourne Park Road.

*Open: 12.00–23.00 (Mon and Wed–Sat), 17.00–23.00 (Tues), 12.00–22.30 (Sun)*
*Food: 12.00–22.30 (Mon–Sat), 12.00–22.00 (Sun)*
*Credit cards: none taken*
*Draught beers: Boddingtons IPA, Caffrey's, London Pride, Worthington, Carling Black Label, Grolsch, Staropramen, Guinness, Scrumpy Jack*
*Wheelchair access to venue*
*Nearest tube station: Notting Hill Gate*

# The Prince of Teck

161 Earls Court Road, SW5. Tel: 0171 373 3107

Earls Court has long been the stamping ground for travelling Australians. Parts of it are so Australian you wonder why they bothered to leave home at all. Here in the centre of their community, as a pub should be, is The Prince of Teck. It is a handsome pub with gargoyles on the outside. Inside, there's a map and boomerangs, and a stuffed and very male kangaroo. For those who've been away from home too long, there's also a handy glossary of the language – gid-day, cow's hoof, djavagidweegend? There are no carpets and there is very little furniture. The lager is cold. Upstairs is the Princess Lounge, a complete con-trast to the rest of the pub. It has a fitted carpet, comfy seats and swagged curtains. Curtains? You're sure this bit isn't for cow's hoofs, Bruce?

*Open: 11.00–23.00 (Mon–Sat), 12.00–22.30 (Sun)*
*Food: 11.00–15.00 and 17.00–21.00 (Mon–Sat), 12.00–20.00 (Sun)*
*Credit cards: none taken*
*Draught beers: Courage Best, John Smith's Yorkshire Bitter, Theakston XB,*
*Young's Bitter, Young's Special, Beck's, Foster's, Kronenbourg*
*Wheelchair access to venue*
*Nearest tube station: Earls Court*

## The Prince of Wales

38 Clapham Old Town, SW4. Tel: 0171 622 4789

This is the floodlit building opposite The Sun (qv). It has fairy lights round the doors and windows, a Union Jack flying from the flagpole, and a model of an old sailor keeping watch from the roof over the Old Town. Looking at the Prince of Wales, you might suspect that you are about to enter somewhere quite eccentric – you'd be right. Duck your head on your way in to avoid the vast amount of antiques and junk suspended from the ceiling and covering every available inch of wallspace. There are traffic lights, trolley carts, military uniforms, masses of pots and pans, music sheets.... I even tried to put money in the juke box, only to be told by the landlord that it was not functional and belonged to the collection. 'I knew that', I lied, moving quickly off to another part of the pub. They still play the rousing 'Land of Hope and Glory' here at closing time.

*Open: 12.00–23.00 (Mon–Sat), 12.00–22.30 (Sun)*
*Food: sandwiches 12.00–19.00 (Mon–Sat); hot food 12.00–16.00 (Sun)*
*Credit cards: none taken*
*Draught beers: Boddingtons Gold, Flowers, one guest ale, Heineken, Heineken*
*Export, Stella Artois, Guinness, Murphy's, Scrumpy Jack*
*Wheelchair access to venue*
*Nearest tube station: Clapham Common*

## The Princess Louise

121 High Holborn, WC2. Tel: 0171 405 8816

An exceptional Victorian pub which has one large room with a massive mahogany bar occupying centre stage. The polished granite pillars, richly engraved windows, gilt mirrors, elaborate tiling, fine plaster ceilings and plush banquettes have all survived any threats of redevelopment. The Princess Louise is now a listed building, so redevelopment will be kept at bay for some time to come. Even the gents' toilets are listed. I don't often recommend an inspection of pub loos, but in this case you should make the effort. The Princess Louise has always been famous for its quality real ales but the former operators, Regent Inns, have now had to relinquish the lease to the freeholders, Sam Smith's. As I write, changes are taking place but, as Sam Smith won't talk to the press, it is difficult to obtain any information. We may well see a drastic change in the ales being offered at The Princess Louise.

*Open: 11.00-23.00 (Mon-Fri)*
*Draught beers: see above*
*Nearest tube station: Holborn*

## The Princess of Wales

1a Montpelier Row, Blackheath, SE3. Tel: 0181 297 5911

The Princess of Wales stands out on the edge of Blackheath as a hugely popular Georgian pub with three bars that get so crowded that they have given up on food in the evening. You'll do very well earlier in the day, though, when hearty pub lunches are served in the stylish conservatory and the beer garden at the back. All summer the heath on the other side of the road is dotted with customers from this pub. What could be nicer on a sunny day than to take your drink onto this agreeable common? There are rules, however. Plastic glasses only on the grass, and the heath must be cleared 20 minutes after last orders.

*Open: 11.00–23.00 (Mon–Sat), 12.00–22.30 (Sun)*
*Food: 12.00–15.00 (Mon–Sat), 12.00–17.00 (Sun)*
*Credit cards: all major cards except AmEx*
*Draught beers: Bass, Caffrey's, London Pride, two weekly guest ales, Carling Premier, Grolsch, Guinness, Dry Blackthorn*
*Wheelchair access to venue*
*Nearest railway station: Blackheath*

## Prospect of Whitby

57 Wapping Wall, E1. Tel: 0171 481 1095

The Prospect of Whitby is the oldest riverside pub in London and probably the most famous. Its flagstoned bar with its pewter-topped counter sitting on old barrels must have been used by half London in its long day. There's a separate section for bar snacks now, a good restaurant up creaking stairs, and a jolly riverside terrace with picnic tables under an old weeping willow. The inn was built around 1520 and was, from the start, a haunt of smugglers, thieves and other low lifers. Indeed, it boldly called itself the Devil's Tavern. Misbehaving sailors were hanged along the low-water mark, a popular entertainment drawing big crowds. The pub was burnt down, rebuilt, changed its name – the *Prospect* (from Whitby) was a merchant ship which moored nearby – and, slowly, slowly, it started to get respectable. It is very respectable now, as you can see from the two chairs by the dining-room door. A notice on one of them reads: 'This chair was occupied by HRH Princess Margaret when dining here on June 26, 1949.'

It was as well she was not dining here on 14 January 1953, when Robert Harrington 'Scarface' Sanders and his Red Scarf Gang raided the Prospect of Whitby, where a certain Captain John Cunningham was giving a small dinner party. He and his guests were relieved of their watches, jewellery and money at pistol point. Scarface was caught soon afterwards when, doing another job, he shot at a policeman. He got life.

*Open: 11.30–15.00 and 17.30–23.00 (Mon–Fri), 11.30–23.00 (Sat), 12.00–22.30 (Sun)*
*Food: bar 12.00–14.30 and 18.00–21.30 (Sat), 12.00–15.00 and 19.00–21.00 (Sun); restaurant 19.00–21.00 (Sat), 12.00–14.30 (Sun)*
*Credit cards: all major cards*
*Draught beers: Courage Best, Courage Directors, Theakston Best, Theakston XB, Foster's, Holsten, Kronenbourg, Molson, Guinness, Strongbow*
*Wheelchair access to venue*
*Private room: 50 seated, 80 standing*
*Nearest tube station: Wapping*

## Punch and Judy

40 The Market, Covent Garden, WC2. Tel: 0171 379 0923

This modern pub at the end of the piazza in Covent Garden is now called The World Famous Punch and Judy. It used to be a section of the old overnight vegetable store, and its flagged floor and vaulted arches make a perfect cellar bar that opens onto a courtyard in the glass-roofed arcade. You can sit and drink there whatever the weather and still think you are in the open air. The staff speak lots of languages and need them; the food remains hearty and traditional, and the lager sales are phenomenal. Business is booming.

*Open: 11.00–23.00 (Mon–Sat), 12.00–22.30 (Sun)*
*Food: 11.30–17.00 (Mon–Sat), 12.00–15.00 (Sun); sandwiches available till closing time*

*Credit cards: all major cards except AmEx*
*Draught beers: Beamish Red, Courage Best, Courage Directors, Theakston Best,*
*Theakston XB, Foster's, Kronenbourg, Beamish, Strongbow*
*Nearest tube station: Covent Garden*

## Punch Tavern

99 Fleet Street, EC4. Tel: 0171 353 6658

This pub, the informal Fleet Street headquarters of *Punch* magazine since
1841, closed last year following a bitter dispute between the owners. It was the
Crown and Sugarloaf until, 150 or so years ago, the staff of *Punch* all became
regulars; the pub changed its name to acknowledge its literary clientele. The
complicated history goes as follows: in 1896, Bass, freeholders of the pub,
bought a 100-year lease on the smaller pub next door, which was owned by
Allied, in order to create one large venue. In September 1996 the lease expired
and Allied sold the freehold to Samuel Smith. What that led to was one pub
with two freeholds. Bass offered to buy a new lease from Sam Smith, but they
weren't having any of it, and built a wall along the original dividing lines of the
property. The result? Neither pub was viable. The Punch was left with an
entrance only in Fleet Street, no windows, and no access to its cellar. As it was
a listed building, English Heritage got involved, and in fact have given Bass
listed-building consent to make the place viable again. They are currently
restoring the albeit smaller pub to its original splendour, and furnishing it with
*Punch* memorabilia. Sam Smith won't say what they intend to do with the
remainder, but the Punch Tavern will live to entertain again.

*Open: 11.00–23.00 (Mon–Fri), 12.00–18.00 (Sat–Sun)*
*Draught beers: Bass, Caffrey's, Greene King IPA, London Pride, Young's Special,*
*Carling Black Label, Carling Premier, Beamish, Dry Blackthorn*
*Wheelchair access to venue*
*Nearest tube station: Temple*

## Putney Bridge

Embankment, SW15. Tel: 0181 781 1811

Pride of place for the start of the Boat Race has been nicked by this bar, a new
development on the wedge-shaped piece of land on Putney Embankment. The
architecture is apparently up for some awards, but from a distance it looks
rather like a bus shelter. The bar is on the ground floor, long, narrow and almost
ship-shape. There's a food servery at the far end, with limited offerings, including smoked salmon and cucumber salad (£7.50), cheese and pickle sandwiches (£3.20), and six rock oysters with pumpernickle bread (£7.80). The ultra-
modern design lacks both spirit and atmosphere, but there are great views of
the river. Like everywhere around here, this bar will make a fortune on Boat
Race days.

*Open: 11.00–23.00 (Mon–Sat), 12.00–22.30 (Sun)*
*Food: bar 11.00–15.00 (Mon–Sat), 10.00–15.00 (Sun); restaurant 12.00–15.00 and*
*18.00–23.00 (Mon–Sat), 12.30–15.00 and 19.00–22.30 (Sun)*
*Credit cards: Mastercard, Delta, Switch, Visa*
*Draught beers: Boddington's Gold, Wadworth 6X, Heineken, Hoegaarden, Stella*
*Artois, Guinness*
*Wheelchair access to venue and loo*
*Nearest tube station: Putney Bridge*

## The Queens

49 Regent's Park Road, NW1. Tel: 0171 586 0408

The young entrepreneurs who have made The Chelsea Ram (qv) such a pleasant place now have The Queens in their small portfolio. It has a very smart
cream-and-green painted bar with modish, old-fashioned floorboards. The

clientele are friendly and span a wide age range. Upstairs there is a very agreeable balcony bar with a modern open kitchen serving up delicious salads, fresh fish and pasta dishes.

*Open: 11.00–23.00 (Mon–Sat), 12.00–22.30 (Sun)*
*Food: bar 12.30–14.30 and 19.00–21.45 (Mon–Sat), 12.00–20.45 (Sun)*
*Credit cards: all major cards except AmEx*
*Draught beers: Ramrod Smooth, Young's Bitter, Young's Special, Castlemaine, Grolsch, Young's London Lager, Young's Premium Lager, Guinness, Oatmeal Stout, Strongbow*
*Wheelchair access to venue*
*Nearest tube station: Chalk Farm*

## Queens Head

25–27 Tryon Street, SW3. Tel: 0171 589 0262

Long-established gay local with Dolly Daydream staff. There's nothing threatening or heavy about the pub, which is in fact hetero-friendly.

*Open: 10.00–23.00 (Mon–Sat), 12.00–22.30 (Sun)*
*Food: bar 12.00–16.00 (Mon–Sun); snacks 16.00–20.00 (Mon–Sun)*
*Credit cards: all major cards*
*Draught beers: Courage Best, Courage Directors, Theakston XB, one guest ale, Foster's, Holsten Export, Kronenbourg, Beamish, Guinness, Scrumpy Jack, Strongbow*
*Nearest tube station: Sloane Square*

## Quo Vadis

26–29 Dean Street, W1. Tel: 0171 437 9585

The entrance to Quo Vadis bar and restaurant scores about zero on my design scale. It is as welcoming as a government building for illegal immigrants, and the staff who greet you contribute little to the warmth. The bar upstairs is spacious while having hardly anywhere to sit. Too much of the space has been given over to the art (if we can call it that) of Damien Hirst, and even if you're standing (which you inevitably will be), there isn't a single place to rest your drink. Frankly, it's not my idea of fun to pay for expensive drinks only to have to look at some decomposing animal's head in a glass case. There are skeletons in the cupboard (literally) at Quo Vadis – you might mistake them for the waiting staff.

*Open: 11.00–23.00 (Mon–Sat))*
*Restaurant food: 12.00–15.00 and 18.00–midnight (Mon–Sun)*
*Credit cards: all major cards*
*Nearest tube station: Tottenham Court Road*

## The Racing Page

2 Duke Street, Richmond. Tel: 0181 940 1257

This big sporty pub in Richmond has a racing scene across the top of the bar, with cantering horses, led by Desert Orchid. Below is a fine selection of beers, wines and champagnes. The Racing Page is owned by Front Page Pubs, which means a few things. Stylewise, it has highly varnished wood, well-spaced tables and chairs, and plenty of room for milling about in. Most of the major sporting events are broadcast on a large-screen TV, and quality bar food is available at inexpensive prices.

*Open: 11.00–23.00 (Mon–Sat), 12.00–22.30 (Sun)*
*Food: 12.00–14.30 and 17.30–19.30 (Mon–Sat)*
*Credit cards: Mastercard, Visa*
*Draught beers: Brakspear, Carlsberg, Theakston XB, Foster's, Holsten, Guinness, Strongbow*
*Wheelchair access to venue*
*Nearest tube station: Richmond*

# Rack and Tenter

45 Moorfields, EC2. Tel: 0171 628 3675

If you turn up at the Rack and Tenter wearing jeans they won't let you in. You need to know this. I didn't!

*Open: 11.30–23.00 (Mon–Fri)*
*Food: 11.30–15.00 (Mon–Fri)*
*Credit cards: AmEx, Visa*
*Draught beers: Bass, Boddingtons, Brakspear, Greene King IPA, Wadworth 6X, Foster's, Heineken, Kronenbourg, Stella Artois, Guinness, Dry Blackthorn*
*Wheelchair access to venue*
*Nearest tube station: Moorgate*

# Railway

18 Clapham High Street, SW4. Tel: 0171 622 4077

A bright, airy, spacious and colourful bar which is just a little bit too convenient for Clapham North tube or Clapham High Street railway station. The young-ish clientele spill out onto the pavement, proving that there *is* life outside the Old Town. To walk past the Railway would be something of a missed opportunity, as they know what they're doing in Clapham these days. The bar is owned by Ann and Tom Halpin – creators of The Sun and The Falcon (qqv) – who are almost entirely responsible for the renaissance of Clapham as an eating and drinking destination. Here, you can opt for a range of baguettes (£3), and a number of small but interesting main courses, which include boiled bacon and cabbage (£4.95), chicken with tarragon (£5.50), and Japanese beef with ratatouille (£6.50). Japanese beef? I never heard the like....

*Open: 12.00–23.00 (Mon–Sat), 12.00–22.30 (Sun)*
*Food: 12.00–16.00 and 18.00–21.30 (Mon–Sun)*
*Credit cards: all major cards*
*Draught beers: Caffrey's, Worthington's Best, Grolsch, Staropramen, Tennent's Extra, Tennent's Pilsner, Guinness, Dry Blackthorn*
*Restaurant can be hired as a private room*
*Nearest tube station: Clapham North*

# The Railway Tavern

15 Liverpool Street, EC2. Tel: 0171 283 3598

This Railway Tavern has been so much a part of Liverpool Street station for so many years that it has become known as Platform 19. 'Meet you on Platform 19,' say older commuters, showing they know a thing or two. Liverpool Street, you will gather, has 18 platforms. The Tavern has a big, impressive, high-ceilinged bar with recent Victorian fittings, an island of booths in the middle, and partitions around the outside walls. There is a Pizza Hut franchise upstairs and a small wine bar with Moulin Rouge murals on the ground floor. You generally get served within minutes. The staff know that customers either have a job to go to or a train to catch.

*Open: 11.00–23.00 (Mon–Fri), 12.00–17.00 (Sat)*
*Food: 11.00–21.00 (Mon–Fri)*
*Credit cards: all major cards*
*Draught beers: Boddingtons, Boston, Flowers Original, London Pride, Manchester Gold, Heineken, Heineken Export, Stella Artois, Guinness, Murphy's, Scrumpy Jack, Strongbow*
*Wheelchair access to venue*
*Two private rooms: 20 and 60 seated, 40 and 100 standing*
*Nearest tube station: Liverpool Street*

# The Rat and Carrot

60 Chelsea Manor Street, SW3. Tel: 0171 352 0725

Mel and Irene Barnett (see The Admiral Codrington) took over The Rat and Carrot early in 1996, and this once sleepy, gloomy pub seemed to come to life again almost overnight. There has barely been a quiet night since, as the young 'uns of Chelsea hang around the pool table smacking gum, chatting each other up and arranging dates in trendy clubs for later on. There is an attractive garden at the back which draws them out in the summer, but Mel draws them back in again at 9.30pm – must respect the neighbours. Do they do food? I do believe they do, but with all those young people there, the thought of food didn't cross my mind.

*Open: 11.00–23.00 (Mon–Sat), 12.00–22.30 (Sun)*
*Food: 12.00–15.00 (Mon–Sat)*
*Credit cards: all major cards except AmEx*
*Draught beers: Abbot Ale, Boddingtons, Courage Directors, Greene King IPA, London Pride, Wexford Irish Cream Ale, Budwar, Carlsberg, Foster's, Kronenbourg, Stella Artois, Guinness, Strongbow*
*Wheelchair access to venue*
*Nearest tube stations: Sloane Square, South Kensington*

# Rat & Parrot

Branding, as it is generally referred to by the breweries, is a way of theming a series of pubs, usually in terms of style and decor, food and drink, and – less commonly – the facilities they offer. Along with Finnegan's Wake (qv), Rat & Parrots are Scottish & Newcastle's attempts at creating a brand. The Rat & Parrot chain was started in 1988, and the first one was in Covent Garden. It was based on a relatively new concept, offering all-day facilities and opening at 8am for breakfast. There are 20 of them now, spread around London from Harrow to Croydon and Ealing to Chelmsford. A standard fare is on offer throughout the chain, and the locations are carefully chosen.

Covent Garden, as you might expect, gets fairly wild on a Friday night. The Fulham branch does well on summer evenings, while Gloucester Road can be a fairly sedate affair, and Kensington Church Street is a bit rakish. You're supposed to get table service, although in our experience this rarely happens. The staff are attired in the ubiquitous white tops, black bottoms that you see so often in those B-road diners that are pretending to be up-market; these uniforms look like something their mothers have run up the night before. Rats, long-tailed rodents of an unsavoury kind, are way down on my list of delightful animals. Rat & Parrots are way down on my list of acceptable pubs. Researchers for this Guide have had consistent problems in finding something complimentary to say about the food (see the Rat & Parrot, Gloucester Road, below). It's such a shame that an organisation that pretends to focus on food serves up such poor quality offerings at prices that aren't even cheap. There really is no excuse for this when the general quality of food in pubs has risen dramatically in recent years. Come on Rats, you're letting the side down!

*Branches at:*

**Bayswater**: 99 Queensway, W2. Tel: 0171 727 0259. Nearest tube station: Bayswater
**Beckenham**: 157 High Street, BR3. Tel: 0181 658 9618. Nearest railway station: Beckenham Junction
**Belgravia**: 4 Elizabeth Street, SW1. Tel: 0171 730 3952. Nearest tube station: Victoria
**Camden**: 25 Parkway, NW1. Tel: 0171 482 2309. Nearest tube station: Camden Town

**Chelmsford**: Duke Street, CM1. Tel: 01245 256752. Nearest railway station: Chelmsford

**Chiswick**: 122 High Road, W4. Tel: 0181 995 4392. Nearest tube station: Stamford Brook

**Covent Garden**: 63–66 St Martin's Lane, WC2. Tel: 0171 836 2990. Nearest tube station: Leicester Square

**Croydon**: 24 Park Street, CR0. Tel: 0181 688 2607. Nearest railway station: East Croydon

**Ealing**: 23 High Street, W5. Tel: 0181 567 3228. Nearest tube station: Ealing Broadway

**Earls Court**: 123 Earls Court Road, SW5. Tel: 0171 370 2760. Nearest tube station: Earls Court

**Fulham**: 704 Fulham Road, SW6. Tel: 0171 736 3014. Nearest tube station: Parsons Green

**Hampstead**: 250 Haverstock Hill, NW3. Tel: 0171 431 0889. Nearest tube station: Belsize Park

**Harrow**: 84 St Ann's Road, Harrow, HA1. Tel: 0181 427 0552. Nearest tube station: Harrow-on-the-Hill

**Notting Hill**: 206 Kensington Church Street, W8. Tel: 0171 229 8421. Nearest tube station: Notting Hill Gate

**Putney**: 160 Putney High Street, SW15. Tel: 0181 780 1282. Nearest tube station: Putney Bridge

**Soho**: 77 Wardour Street, W1. Tel: 0171 439 1274. Nearest tube station: Piccadilly Circus

**Sutton**: 33–35 High Street, SM1. Tel: 0181 642 4930. Nearest railway station: Sutton

**West Hampstead**: 100 West End Lane, NW6. Tel: 0171 624 7611. Nearest tube station: West Hampstead

# Rat & Parrot

25 Gloucester Road, SW7. Tel: 0171 589 0905

This building has just come out of a complete refurbishment, revealing the Rat & Parrot to Gloucester Road after a long time behind scaffolding. There it is, bright and cheery. It's recently been refurbished inside, too, and is looking not bad for a pub that likes heavily patterned carpets. Like all Rat & Parrots, it opens at 8am for breakfast. I have been lucky enough to have some great food in London's pubs and bars over the past year and, indeed, some rather disappointing food. None can compare, however, to a stomach-churning disaster I had here recently. Considering myself something of a connoisseur of burgers, I opted for their 'prime 6oz beefburger served with curly fries, coleslaw and a choice of toppings'. When it arrived, it was clear that the poor thing had endured only a minor detour between freezer and plate. It was about half an inch thick and had the texture of thick-set paste, with little to remind me that I was eating a beefburger. I couldn't imagine what it might be made of, and a passing thought concerning the name of the pub stayed with me longer than was comfortable. As for the curly fries, I've never really understood how these are made but I have a theory that they start life in the kitchen as straight-cut chips and turn in on themselves in sheer horror when they're popped on a plate next to the burger. I am an animal lover. If I weren't, I'd have given my food to the dog. Lucky for dogs they're not allowed in.

*Open: 08.00–23.00 (Mon–Sat), 10.00–22.30 (Sun)*
*Food: 08.00–22.00 (Mon–Sat), 10.00–22.00 (Sun)*
*Credit cards: all major cards*
*Draught beers: Directors, John Smith's Smooth, Theakston Best, Theakston XB, Beck's, Castlemaine, Gillespies, Kronenbourg, Strongbow*
*Wheelchair access to venue*
*Nearest tube station: Gloucester Road*

# R Bar

4 Sydney Street, SW3. Tel: 0171 352 3433

Newly refurbished trendy bar beneath the L'Altro restaurant which is always useful for a night on the pull. Its late-night opening is the big attraction and it hosts a plethora of corporate and promotional events. This is a decent-quality basement bar and deserves any praise it gets.

*Open: 17.30–23.00 (Mon–Wed), 17.30–midnight (Thurs–Sat)*
*Food: as opening hours*
*Credit cards: all major cards*
*Nearest tube station: South Kensington*

# Red Lion

Crown Passage, SW1. Tel: 0171 930 4141

This tiny, timber-fronted pub with its leaded glass windows, hanging baskets and antique lanterns looks too picturesque to be true, but it is every bit as old as it seems. It has been there for more than 400 years, has the second-oldest beer licence in London, and is still very much in business.

The small, panelled bar is open all day and fills up quickly at lunchtime and again when people finish work. There is a pleasant room upstairs that serves good plain pub food. On the last Saturday of every January the pub is packed with splendidly attired Cavaliers. They come together to mark the execution of their hero, King Charles I, on 30 January 1649. The Red Lion remembers this well, but it knew King Charles II better, or so legend has it. He lived in St James's Palace over the road, and his lively mistress Nell Gwynne lived round the corner at 79 Pall Mall. Some discretion seemed appropriate, so Nell would slip into the Red Lion, go down the cellar steps and through a tunnel. At the other end the King would be waiting. Is this true? We like to think so.

*Open: 11.00–23.00 (Mon–Sat), 12.00–22.30 (Sun)*
*Food: 12.00–14.30 (Mon–Sun)*
*Credit cards: none taken*
*Draught beers: John Smith's, London Pride, Ruddles County, Carlsberg, Foster's, Kronenbourg, Guinness, Strongbow*
*Restaurant for hire: 20–40 seated, 30 standing*
*Nearest tube stations: Piccadilly Circus, Green Park*

# Red Lion

Duke of York Street, SW1. Tel: 0171 930 2030

This is the most glittering of Red Lions – brilliant-cut and bevelled glass flashes and sparkles on all sides. The pub is small – there is just 300 square feet of it – and in summer it spills onto the pavement. The rest of the year sees Londoners reverting to one of their most profoundly held beliefs: there's always room for one more inside. Michael Browne, who has run the pub for 11 years, likes to see it really full. He will tell you that the Red Lion sells more beer per square foot than any other pub in Piccadilly.

In the pub's bohemian past, Jermyn Street flower girls would offer their services for 2d a time in the private bar. The Red Lion, robbed of its private bar, is the height of respectability these days. Unexpected people are sometimes seen pushing through the crush: Clint Eastwood, for example, and Andrew Lloyd Webber, who is said to like it because there is never any music of any sort.

*Open: 12.00–23.00 (Mon–Sat)*
*Food: 12.00–14.30 (Mon–Sat)*
*Credit cards: none taken*
*Draught beers: Burton, Tetley's, four regular guest ales, Carlsberg Export, Castle-maine, Lowenbrau, Guinness, Dry Blackthorn*
*Nearest tube stations: Green Park, Piccadilly Circus*

# Red Lion

318 High Street, Brentford, TW8

I'm completely cheating by making reference to this pub, as it doesn't exist any more, but I know there are many of you who like to monitor the progress of famous pubs that have been featured in this Guide for many years. In 1967 the Red Lion became the very first winner of the *Evening Standard* Pub of the Year competition. It soldiered on for 30 years, hitting various highs and lows, and in the nineties it found a new lease of life as a major rock venue. Things went badly west in 1996, however, and Fuller's, clearly tired of propping the place up, sold it. Tragic, but there's worse to come. It was bought by McDonald's, who demolished the pub and built a drive-through burger bar. Let this be a lesson to all those gloomy people who complain about the growth of theme bars. One of the reasons themes exist is to provide a new image, new life, new markets for those pubs that have run out of steam. I'd rather see a themed rock venue in Brentford High Street any day than a drive-through McDonald's.

*Drinks available: milk shakes, over-iced sodas, teas and coffees*

# Red Lion

48 Parliament Street, SW1. Tel: 0171 930 5826

Of all the Red Lions, this one lies nearest to the corridors of power. Around it are great ministries of state. Across the road lives the Prime Minister. Round the corner are the Houses of Parliament themselves. This is the MP's pub, the one they nip into before some brisk legislating.

The Red Lion is a handsome pub, a Grade-2 listed building and historical in spades. Its style is eclectic Flemish Baroque, as you can see. The original pub was built on this site in 1733 and was nervously visited by Charles Dickens when he was only 11. The adventure appears in *David Copperfield*:

*'What is your best – your VERY BEST – ale a glass?' [...] 'Twopence-halfpenny,' says the landlord, 'is the price of the Genuine Stunning ale.' 'Then,' says I, producing the money, 'just draw me a glass of the Genuine Stunning, if you please....'*

They pulled Dickens's Red Lion down in 1899 during the great pub boom and built this one in its place, a superior pub, no cost spared. It has changed hardly at all since then. It has most of the original fittings, and the bar walls are covered in drawings, cartoons and photographs of famous politicians, mostly long departed. There's a nice old-fashioned dining room upstairs, with old-fashioned English food and a cable television set tuned into the Parliamentary channel, letting Members keep an eye on their colleagues at work. There's another screen in the bar. Bar and restaurant both have division bells.

The Red Lion also has a comfortable cellar bar. The Parachute Regiment holds reunions here, and back in the eighties it was much liked by demonstrating miners. The licensee liked them right back. 'Top quality customers,' he recalls. The pit banners they presented to the pub are now part of its history.

*Open: 11.00–23.00 (Mon–Sat), 12.00–22.30 (Sun)*
*Food: bar 11.00–15.00 (Mon–Sun); restaurant 12.00–14.30 (Mon–Sun)*
*Credit cards: all major cards except AmEx*
*Draught beers: Burton, Kilkenny, Red Lion Bitter, Tetley's, Carlsberg, Castlemaine, Lowenbrau, Guinness, Dry Blackthorn*
*Wheelchair access to venue*
*Private room seats 35*
*Nearest tube station: Westminster*

# Riki Tik

23–24 Bateman Street, W1. Tel: 0171 437 1977

Exceptionally modish lounge bar where suits are certainly not *de rigueur*. The strict door policy enforces this, as Quentin Tarantino was to discover. Such a policy is most irritating when you want to meet up with a group of friends, but can't co-ordinate your wardrobes to the liking of the Door Whores (the rather unkind name given to bouncers these days). If you make it inside, you'll find the atmosphere very laid back.

*Open: 12.00–01.00 (Mon–Sat)*
*Food: 12.00–18.00 (Mon–Sat)*
*Credit cards: all major cards except AmEx*
*Wheelchair access to venue*
*Nearest tube stations: Tottenham Court Road, Leicester Square*

# The Ring

72 Blackfriars Road, SE1. Tel: 0171 928 2589

As the name suggests, The Ring is a boxers' pub. It is run by Neville Axford, a one-time army champion, who had 25 professional fights and is still in the game. He's a coach now, with young boxers in training. They work in the gym over the bar – no frills up there, just a ring, some well-used punchbags, and young hopefuls toiling and pummelling. From the gym windows you can see the corner of the crossroads where the Blackfriars Ring once stood. 'London's Premier Arena' said the posters. 'Turbulent Centre of Boxing' said the papers of the day. It was run for many years by Bella Burge, the world's only woman boxing promoter, but in 1940 it was reduced to rubble in an air raid, and after the war an office block replaced it. That is what you see now, together with Southwark tube station, soon to be opened on the Jubilee Line extension.

*Open: 11.00–23.00 (Mon–Sat), 12.00–22.30 (Sun)*
*Food: 12.00–15.00 (Mon–Sat), 12.00–17.00 (Sun)*
*Credit cards: none taken*
*Draught beers: Burton's, Calder's Cream Ale, Tetley's, Young's Bitter, Carlsberg, Castlemaine, Lowenbrau, Guinness, Dry Blackthorn*
*Nearest tube station: Waterloo*

# The River Rat

2 Lombard Road, SW11. Tel: 0171 978 4167

Only ten years old, this very pleasant pub on Battersea's new river walk, looking across the river to Chelsea Harbour and the marina, had a rather dodgy start to life as The Chandler. Things plummeted so far downhill that the brewery closed it in 1993 for almost a year. Then Dennis and Denise Timms from The Water Rat (qv) in Chelsea took it over and installed their son Gavin as the manager. Now to look at Gavin, you can see why the place has gone stratospherically up-market. He's a strapping lad that you wouldn't want to argue with. When he said the pool tables had to go, they probably left of their own accord. The same applied to the pinball machines and all the other games he didn't like. The people who wanted to have lunch, dinner or just drinks on the terrace flocked in. Gavin's happy again. If Gavin's happy, I'm happy.

*Open: 11.00–23.00 (Mon–Sat), 12.00–22.30 (Sun)*
*Food: 12.00–21.00 (Mon–Sun)*
*Credit cards: Mastercard, Visa*
*Draught beers: Bass, Caffrey's, London Pride, Wadworth 6X, Carling Black Label, Grolsch, Staropramen, Guinness, Dry Blackthorn*
*Wheelchair access to venue and loo*
*Nearest railway station: Clapham Junction*

# Robert Browning

15 Clifton Road, W9. Tel: 0171 286 2732

Now owned by Samuel Smith's, this pub was transformed from The Eagle several years ago, and changed its name to commemorate the poet who was once its neighbour. The main bar downstairs is where the serious drinking is; the first-floor bar might have appealed more to Robert and Elizabeth Barrett Browning. It is a comfortable Victorian sitting room with long windows, button-backed leather sofas, mahogany tables, lamps, mirrors and portraits.

*Open: 11.30–23.00 (Mon–Sat), 12.00–22.30 (Sun)*
*Food: 12.00–14.30 (Mon–Sat), 17.30–21.00 (Sun)*
*Credit cards: Mastercard, Visa*
*Draught beers: Old Brewery Bitter, Sovereign, Ayingerbraü Pils, Ayingerbraü Prinz, Samuel Smith's Extra Stout, Special Reserve*
*Wheelchair access to venue*
*Private room seats 30*
*Nearest tube station: Warwick Avenue*

# The Rose and Crown

55 High Street, SW19. Tel: 0181 947 4713

The Rose and Crown in Wimbledon Village is one of south London's great pubs. The *Evening Standard* Pub of the Year judges thought so, and gave it the crown in 1970. It was built in 1640 and retains a powerful appeal for generation after generation. Inside are old maps of Wimbledon and a complete set of Hogarth's *Idle Prentice*, adding to the pub's historical feel.

   The bar still draws crowds. There is a small no-smoking area now, a light, plain lounge, and a buttery serving hot and cold food. A conservatory leads to a little garden, paved, ivy-walled and thoroughly charming, where families recuperate after constitutionals on the Common, young lovers seek a quiet table, and people read papers and chat.

*Open: 11.00–23.00 (Mon–Sat), 12.00–22.30 (Sun)*
*Food: 11.00–22.00 (Mon–Sat), 12.00–16.30 (Sun)*
*Credit cards: none taken*
*Draught beers: Young's Bitter, Young's Special, Castlemaine, Grolsch, Young's London Lager, Young's Premium Lager, Guinness, Dry Blackthorn*
*Wheelchair access to venue*
*Nearest tube station: Wimbledon*

# Rose and Crown

2 The Polygon, Clapham Old Town, SW4. Tel: 0171 720 8265

Together with The Sun and The Prince of Wales (qqv), the Rose and Crown makes up a triangle of pubs in Clapham Old Town, and it would be churlish not to mention it in this Guide. It is a traditional Victorian pub with one room and a couple of snugs. Should you want to get away from the madding crowds of the Old Town, then this pub will offer you the necessary respite.

*Open: 11.00–23.00 (Mon–Sat), 12.00–22.30 (Sun)*
*Food: 12.00–14.30 (Mon–Sat), 12.00–16.00 (Sun)*
*Credit cards: none taken*
*Draught beers: Abbot Ale, Greene King IPA, Wexford Irish Cream, three guest ales, Harp, Kronenbourg, Stella Artois, Guinness, Strongbow*
*Nearest tube station: Clapham Common*

# The Rose of York

Petersham Road, Richmond, TW10. Tel: 0181 948 5867

A most appealing country pub with a big comfortable bar and good traditional food, The Rose of York has a lovely sheltered courtyard and a view of Petersham meadows and the bend in the Thames so beautiful that it has been painted by almost everyone. It was once an old cavalry barracks, so there was quite a lot of space to utilise. It now has 12 bedrooms with en-suite bathrooms. It was the *Evening Standard* Pub of the Year in 1980.

*Open: 11.00–23.00 (Mon–Sat), 12.00–22.30 (Sun)*
*Food: 12.00–15.00 and 18.30–21.30 (Mon–Sat), 12.00–15.30 (Sun)*
*Credit cards: none taken*
*Draught beers: Old Brewery Bitter, Ayingerbraü, Ayingerbraü Pils, Ayingerbraü Prinz, Samuel Smith's Extra Stout, Special Reserve*
*Wheelchair access to venue*
*Nearest tube station: Richmond*

# The Round House

1 Garrick Street, WC2. Tel: 0171 836 9838

The Round House, the substantial Victorian pub on the corner of Garrick Street, acquired a bit of a bad name for itself, so Scottish & Newcastle closed it down, gave it a new interior and reopened it as the first of their new real ale houses. This meant a nice wooden floor, plain wooden furniture, eight draught ales on the hand pumps, and pies with puff-pastry tops floating up from the kitchen. It also meant short shrift for troublesome customers. Troublesome customers weren't keen on any of this, particularly the short shrift, and agreeable new customers replaced them. These days, people spill out into the street when Westminster City Council allows them, and they're no trouble.

*Open: 11.00–23.00 (Mon–Sat), 12.00–22.30 (Sun)*
*Food: 12.00–15.30 (Mon–Sun)*
*Credit cards: none taken*
*Draught beers: Abbot Ale, John Smith's, Marston's Pedigree, Old Speckled Hen, Theakston Best, Theakston Hogshead, Theakston Old Peculier, Beck's, Bombardier, Foster's, Guinness, Strongbow*
*Wheelchair access to venue*
*Nearest tube stations: Leicester Square, Covent Garden*

# The Round Table

St Martin's Court, WC2. Tel: 0171 836 6436

This is a civil, good-looking pub with downstairs and upstairs bars, both very busy at times. The landlord, Norman Gregory from Manchester, uses a doorman to discourage any unruly gangs that might scare his laid-back customers. The Round Table has become known for its cask ales. Big blackboards display lists of the guest beers coming soon. Knowledgeable barmen wear grandfather shirts and aprons, and happily guide you through the ales on tap. For serious beer drinkers, there are 2- or 4-pint jugs. Beer festivals are held four times a year, during which The Round Table has been known to get through 50 guest ales in 14 days. It is a reasonable place to eat, too. Great pies.

*Open: 11.00–23.00 (Mon–Sat), 12.00–22.30 (Sun)*
*Food: 12.00–15.00 and 18.00–21.00 (Mon–Sun)*
*Credit cards: none taken*
*Draught beers: Abbot Ale, Marston's Pedigree, Theakston Best, Theakston Old Peculier, Beck's, Foster's, Guinness, Bulmer's*
*Wheelchair access to venue*
*Private room: 20 seated, 30 standing*
*Nearest tube station: Leicester Square*

# Rupert Street

50 Rupert Street, W1. Tel: 0171 734 5614

One of the most recent and positive additions to the gay scene is this well-designed, bright and cheery, air-conditioned bar. It has a large hanging-around bit, a comfort zone at the back furnished with comfortable sofas and armchairs, and a constant flow of traffic between the two. Food here ranges from moules (£5.50) through a wide range of Modern British fare to a Mediterranean puff of cheeses and vegetables (£6.95). They would serve all evening if they could, but the sheer enormity of the night-time crowds means last orders is at 7pm. Did I mention the loos? Here are some of the most dramatic loos of any pub or bar in London. Ladies' cubicles have their own washbasins, men's have plenty of sprucing-up space, and there is an extra communal washing area with a water fountain. Little backpacks seem to be the essential accoutrements and, thanks to the air conditioning, you won't leave with your clothes smelling of cigarette smoke. The hefty aroma of aftershaves, however, can linger for days after a visit.

*Open: 09.00–23.00 (Mon–Sat), 12.00–22.30 (Sun)*
*Food: 12.00–19.00 (Mon–Sun)*
*Credit cards: all major cards except AmEx*
*Draught beers: Caffrey's, Carling Black Label, Carling Premier, Grolsch, Guinness, Red Rock*
*Wheelchair access to venue and loo*
*Private room: 32 seated, 300 standing*
*Nearest tube station: Piccadilly Circus*

# Saint

8 Great Newport Street, WC2. Tel: 0171 240 1551

A wide, sweeping staircase takes you down into this spacious, futuristic bar. A small bar on the left is followed by a row of mauve booths, a larger eating area to the right, and the massive island bar serving bottled beers, wines and cocktails. Saint has that 'something special' feel, but if you're not comfortable with a young, overtly trendy clientele, this isn't the place for you. Getting in is a real trial. They employ a very selective door policy, which I've now nearly cracked. When I was first turned away, I was told that it was due to a no-suits policy. I subsequently got in – obtaining membership through the back door – and nearly everyone was wearing a suit. Looking around, it became evident that their criteria for selection is down to your looks, and I interpret their idea of good looks as follows. Girls: blonde and young, fashion air-head. Boys: short hair, taut and tight, new interrogationist. On my most recent visit, the picker was a rather camp little queen done up like a Christmas tree with a waist size I haven't had since I was seven years old. He seemed genuinely surprised that I had a membership card – but hey, I'm sorry, I never intended to be a target market. I hear tell that Paul Smith was turned away one night. If you see him, tell him to book a table to eat next time. That's the easy way to get in.

*Open: 12.00–01.00 (Mon–Thurs), 12.00–02.00 (Fri), 19.00–02.00 (Sat)*
*Food: bar as opening hours; restaurant 19.30–01.00 (Mon–Thurs), 17.30–02.00 (Fri –Sat)*
*Credit cards: all major cards*
*Wheelchair access to venue and loo*
*Nearest tube station: Leicester Square*

# St John

26 St John Street, EC1. Tel: 0171 251 0848

The St John restaurant has been much written about for its adventurous menu and celebrity diners. What is less well known is that there is quite a useful bar here, too. You enter through an enclosed passageway, widening as you reach the double-height bar, to be greeted by the aroma of freshly baked bread. The room is stark, white-painted and airy, with lots of natural light. It sounds bland but it really works. The place has a functional, workshop feel to it, and the clientele is quite unpretentious, bearing in mind the adjacent restaurant. There is no music of any kind, and the wine list, which most people opt for, is comprehensive and starts at £10.

*Open: 11.00–23.00 (Mon–Fri), 18.00–23.00 (Sat)*
*Food: 12.00–15.00 and 18.00–23.00 (Mon–Fri), 18.00–23.00 (Sat)*
*Credit cards: all major cards*
*Draught beers: Boddingtons, Wadworth 6X, Budwar, Heineken, Hoegaarden, Stella Artois, Guinness*
*Wheelchair access to venue and loo*
*Private room seats 20*
*Nearest tube station: Farringdon*

## St Paul's Wine Vaults

229 Knightrider Street, EC4. Tel: 0171 236 1013

This wine bar was until recently known as The Horn Tavern. Eldridge Pope spent a lot of money doing it up, and the long, narrow ground-floor bar is now looking very smart, with its varnished wood furniture. There's a basement bar too – great for private parties or just to dine by candlelight in the evenings. Although Eldridge Pope brew beers, they're no longer sold here. The emphasis is very much on good wine, with over 100 on the list, starting at £6.95.

*Open: 11.00–20.00 (Mon–Fri)*
*Food: 12.00–15.00 (Mon–Fri)*
*Credit cards: all major cards*
*Private room seats 16*
*Nearest tube station: Mansion House*

## The Salisbury

90 St Martin's Lane, WC2. Tel: 0171 836 5863

The Salisbury is sometimes said to be the most beautifully preserved Victorian public house in London. It has lovely windows, brilliant cut, acid-etched and delicately engraved. It also has a lincrusta ceiling, Art Nouveau bronze figures of alluring maidens, and flower stalks out of which light bulbs grow. You have to go early, however, to get a proper look at this famous pub, as it is packed to the doors a lot of the time. Every evening, and often at lunchtimes, doormen check who comes in. On occasion, they also check who goes out, an anti-riff-raff move, apparently.

*Open: 11.00–23.00 (Mon–Sat), 12.00–22.30 (Sun)*
*Food: 12.00–19.00 (Mon–Sat), 12.00–15.00 (Sun)*
*Credit cards: all major cards*
*Draught beers: Calder's Cream Ale, Kilkenny, Marston's Pedigree, Theakston Best, Carlsberg, Carlsberg Export, Lowenbrau, Guinness, Olde English*
*Wheelchair access to venue*
*Nearest tube station: Leicester Square*

## The Salutation Inn

154 King Street, W6. Tel: 0181 748 2365

In what is a fairly unattractive street, you will find this old coaching inn, which has a bar, a conservatory and a beautiful walled garden. Its tranquillity may well surprise you – this is a perfect place to hide from the harsh realities of worka-day Hammersmith. The garden has earned The Salutation many accolades:

Fuller's Garden of the Year seven times, and numerous London in Bloom awards. Such is its reputation that in 1989, Her Majesty Queen Elizabeth, the Queen Mother came to see it in her capacity as Patron of the Royal Horticultural Society. She was delighted. She even pulled a few pints.

*Open: 11.00–23.00 (Mon–Sat), 12.00–22.30 (Sun)*
*Food: 11.00–14.00 (Mon–Fri), 11.00–15.00 (Sat), 12.00–15.00 (Sun)*
*Credit cards: none taken*
*Draught beers: Chiswick Bitter, Fuller's ESB, London Pride, Carling Black Label, Castlemaine, Grolsch, Tennent's Extra, Heineken, Stella Artois, Guinness, Murphy's, Strongbow*
*Wheelchair access to venue*
*Nearest tube stations: Ravenscourt Park, Hammersmith*

## S Bar

37 Battersea Bridge Road, SW11. Tel: 0171 223 3322

Something quite interesting might – and I say might – be happening in Battersea, with the opening of the S Bar (so named in the absence of any other ideas). It is large and visually quite appealing, with big, canopied windows, a long, copper-topped bar, and a pebble-dashed fireplace with dripping candles. They say the fish tank was designed by Tom Dixon. Fish tank? Designed? I thought you just bought them from Homebase and chucked in a few stones. It's very pretty, though. People who like mirrors will love the enormous one at the back of the room – it's very regal but when you're in its path, it serves as an uncomfortable reminder of what other people have to look at when you're hanging around a bar. The bar staff also look designed: their garb is pseudo-Vivienne Westwood, crossed with the brains of Tara What's-herface. The hybrid looks good, but so does a rather expensive, well-designed bottle-opener I carry around, and that doesn't work properly, either. Still, this is a decent-enough bar, and I just hope that it doesn't get so style-conscious that it loses touch with the ordinary Battersea drinker.

*Open: 11.00–23.00 (Mon–Sat), 11.00–22.30 (Sun)*
*Food: 12.00–15.00 and 19.00–23.00 (Mon–Sat), 12.00–16.00 (Sun)*
*Credit cards: all major cards*
*Draught beers: Beamish Red, London Pride, Foster's, Kronenbourg, Guinness, Dry Blackthorn*
*Wheelchair access to venue and loo*
*Private room: 50 standing*
*Nearest railway station: Clapham Junction*

## The Scarsdale

23a Edwardes Square, W8. Tel: 0171 937 1811

You need to look carefully for this pub as it is tucked away in a corner of Edwardes Square to the south of Kensington High Street. People warm to the pub as soon as they see it. Its impeccable Georgian façade is covered in flowers and greenery, and it is just as attractive inside, with high ceilings, wooden fans, a rich gleam of mahogany and brass, and the original etched glass. The Scarsdale's traditional pub food is very popular, and people travel for miles to sample it. It is one of London's most admired pubs, has no music at all, and has been an *Evening Standard* Pub of the Year.

*Open: 12.00–23.00 (Mon–Sat), 12.00–22.30 (Sun)*
*Food: 12.00–14.30 and 18.30–21.45 (Mon–Sat), 12.30–15.30 (Sun)*
*Credit cards: Mastercard, Visa*
*Draught beers: Courage Directors, Theakston Best, Theakston XB, three weekly guest ales, Beck's, Foster's, Kronenbourg, Guinness, Strongbow*
*Nearest tube stations: High Street Kensington, Earls Court*

# Scotts

20 Mount Street, W1. Tel: 0171 629 5248

Scotts has been given a new lease of life, fully refurbished and stylishly redesigned by its new owners, Chez Gerard. It looks the business: slick and sophisticated. On my visit, the clientele included a group of Japanese businessmen, a City gathering quaffing champagne, a genteel elderly couple drinking wine, and a rather glamorous foursome meeting for what appeared to be pre-supper drinks.

Then there was yours truly, markedly under-dressed, having a bad face day and looking like a character from *Manon des Sources*. Do you know what? They didn't mind in the slightest. The ultra-efficient bar staff have many years' experience behind them – and it showed. They know how to put someone at their ease, how to chat, what to say, what not to say, and most of all, how to pour a decent drink. I ordered a G & T, and it was among the best presented I've had in London – not too much ice, a large gin, a slice of freshly cut lemon, and a premium tonic from an individual bottle with only a little added to the drink (£5.50). Wine prices are actually surprisingly low, with house wines (albeit La Croix) at £8.95; the most expensive bottle is a Chablis at £23. The surroundings are similar to the Savoy but with the addition of booths with drapes which can be drawn. Before you ask, people do actually draw them. A 25-foot frieze behind the bar depicts the glamour, opulence and decadence of thirties London. Scotts is not without its modernity – a large, bubbling, water-filled tubular glass obelisk acts as the core of the spiral staircase, which leads up to the restaurant. There is the most wonderful private room for dining, plus lavatories I'd be happy to see anywhere (no menacing staff demanding money). If any of you have been wondering whatever happened to the pianist Bobby Crush, I think I've found him (or a lookalike, at least) – he tinkles the ivories here most evenings.

*Open: 17.30–23.00 (Mon–Sat)*
*Food: as opening hours*
*Credit cards: all major cards*
*Two private rooms: 14 and 22 seated, up to 40 standing*
*Nearest tube stations: Green Park, Bond Street*

# Scruffy Murphy's

Scruffy Murphy's is Allied Domecq's vision of an Irish theme pub; the Denman Street branch is perhaps the most Irish in the chain. You see them all over town – there's often an old grocer's bicycle leaning against the outside wall. While many people criticise such pubs, they certainly inject a new lease of life into tired old venues. There are currently ten Scruffy Murphy's in London, and we probably won't be seeing any more for the time being. You may well spot one on your foreign travels, however. There's a Scruffy Murphy's in Norway, one in Poland, and three in Sweden! There's even one in Dublin, where they converted The Hive, a pub in the heart of the fair city, into an Irish theme bar. The cheek of it! London Scruffys all serve Irish food, English cider and Danish lager brewed in England. They're not particularly good examples of the genre, and with so many Irish theme bars saturating the market, such places need to be a little bit special to become a venue of choice.

*Branches at:*

**Brentwood**: 161 Kings Road, CM14. Tel: 01277 212860. Nearest railway station: Brentwood

**Bromley**: 10 Widmore Road, BR1. Tel: 0181 460 4828. Nearest railway station: Bromley North

**Chelsea**: 451 Fulham Road, SW10. Tel: 0171 352 8636. Nearest tube station: Earls Court

**City**: 142 Fleet Street, EC4. Tel: 0171 353 2451. Nearest tube station: Temple

**Guildford**: 9 Millmead, GU2. Tel: 01483 572160. Nearest railway station: Guildford

**Soho**: 15 Denman Street, W1. Tel: 0171 437 1540. Nearest tube station: Piccadilly Circus

**Sutton**: 67 High Street, SM1. Tel: 0181 770 0009. Nearest railway station: Sutton

**Uxbridge**: 8 Windsor Street, UB8. Tel: 01895 233919. Nearest tube station: Uxbridge

**West Hampstead**: 283–285 West End Lane, NW6. Tel: 0171 794 7817. Nearest tube station: West Hampstead

**Whetstone**: 1262 High Road, N20. Tel: 0181 445 1110. Nearest tube station: Totteridge and Whetstone

## Secrets

62 Glenthorne Road, W6. Tel: 0181–563 7974

Table dancing, I am reliably informed, is about to take Britain by storm. This is not your average strip-joint but more of an upmarket eating and drinking venue where people take their clothes off to dance. There are plenty of rules to follow: no jeans or trainers, over 21s only, remain seated, £10 for every dance they do especially for you, £5 for each track when they sit at your table, no physical contact (except to place money in their garters), and no propositioning, shouting or profane language. Your £10 admission gives you a £5 discount on food and drinks. Plans are afoot for a ladies night on Mondays with male dancers going the full monty.

*Open: 17.30–02.00 (Tues-Fri), 20.00–02.00 (Sat)*
*Food: 17.30–01.00 (Tues-Fri), 20.00–01.00 (Sat)*
*Credit cards: all major*
*Wheelchair access to venue*
*Nearest tube station: Hammersmith*

## The Sekforde Arms

34 Sekforde Street, EC1. Tel: 0171 253 3251

Clerkenwell is currently undergoing a bit of a renaissance, and this pleasant little village pub plays a central part in local life. Staff and students from the City University seem to do a lot of research here, and its prosperous new neighbours find it a real treat.

*Open: 11.00–23.00 (Mon–Sat), 12.00–16.00 (Sun)*
*Food: bar 12.00–21.00 (Mon–Sun); restaurant 12.00–21.00 (Mon–Sat), 12.00–14.30 (Sun)*
*Credit cards: all major cards except AmEx*
*Draught beers: Young's Bitter, Young's Special, one guest ale, Grolsch, London Lager, London Premium, Guinness, Dry Blackthorn*
*Private room: 38 seated, 50 standing*
*Nearest tube station: Farringdon*

## Selfridges

Oxford Street, W1. Tel: 0171 629 1234

The enormous Oxford Street emporium for the fashion-conscious need not be such an arduous visit for those dragged along by the credit cards to offer advice and support and to feign interest in the activities of enthusiastic shopaholics. Such is the enormity of Selfridges you can do your very own bar crawl along the miles of floor space. Gordon's Bar on the first floor shields you from the shoppers behind a curved wooden wall. The interior is modern and has a substantial no-smoking area. The Balcony Bar is a bijou terrace over the wine department on the ground floor, and the Oyster Bar in the foodhall seats eight for champagne and oysters. Only the Balcony Bar is not accessible with a wheelchair.

*Open: 10.00–19.00 (Mon–Wed), 10.00–20.00 (Thurs–Fri), 10.00–19.00 (Sat), 12.00–18.00 (Sun)*
*Nearest tube station: Bond Street*

## Le Shaker

159 Old Brompton Road, SW5. Tel: 0171 373 1926/7

The unusual combination of serious cocktail drinking with fine Vietnamese dining can be found on this unlikely stretch of the Old Brompton Road as you head away from Chelsea towards Earls Court. The cocktails might well be expensive at around £8, but they're very strong, very large (without the tacky accoutrements of fiddly umbrellas and plastic sticks), and when they're shaken under the professional eye of Mark Boccard Schuster – many times a world-champion cocktail shaker – you might feel that your money is well spent. Le Shaker has one long bar, where you can sit (if you get there early enough) and watch the theatre of the cocktail making. The barmen seem to enjoy their work, although they appear slightly miffed when asked the predictable question, 'Ooh! What's in that one, then?' The clientele don't generally care about the prices – serious money earners and sun-bed-tanned lottery winners don't worry about such things.

*Open: 18.30–23.30 (Mon–Sat)*
*Food: as opening hours*
*Credit cards: all major cards*
*Nearest tube stations: South Kensington, Earls Court*

## Sheila's Bar Barbie

41 King Street, WC2 Tel: 0171 240 8282

Walking through Covent Garden one day I couldn't resist popping into this bar. It pretends to be everything Australian, and judging by the audible accents, it is. What I can't work out is why people fly halfway round the world and go somewhere that reminds them of home. This bar is surely poking fun at the Australian culture, implying that life down under is macho-orientated and trashy. Sheila's has fake corrugated-steel walls, Aussie flags and pictures, and – what a surprise – a boomerang directing you into the barbie. Beer can be sunk in pitchers – they like that. Food includes baguettes called husband-beaters, plus bushman's brekkie (bacon, egg, beans, tomato, mushrooms, lamb chop, a kind of sausage called a snagette, and toast and coffee) for £4.95, and a bushman's veggie brekkie. Veggie brekkie? For bushmen? I don't think so. They advertise a five-course meal: four tinnies and a waggle pie – now that's more like a bushman's brekkie. As for a waggle pie, don't ask the staff, they're not really sure, but I am reliably informed that it contains diced lamb in puff pastry. If this is authentically Australian, I think an Australian might be a little embarrassed.

*Open: 11.30–23.00 (Mon–Sat), 12.00–22.30 (Sun)*
*Food: as opening hours*
*Credit cards: all major cards*
*Draught beers: Castlemaine, Foster's*
*Wheelchair access to venue and loo*
*Nearest tube station: Covent Garden*

## Sherlock Holmes

10–11 Northumberland Street, WC2. Tel: 0171 930 2644

The Sherlock Holmes is a smartly turned-out pub in the modern Victorian style with a comfortable restaurant, a hidden verandah and a unique tourist attraction: Holmes's study as it appeared one foggy night in *The Empty House*, every item supplied by the Conan Doyle family. It attracts a seemingly endless supply of tourists, who turn up with their cameras and snap away happily all day. They then lunch or dine in the upstairs restaurant, which has a no-smoking bit. There is a picture of Peter Cushing, a famous Sherlock Holmes, on the inn sign. The tourists snap that too.

*Open: 11.00–23.00 (Mon–Sat), 12.00–22.30 (Sun)*
*Food: bar 12.00–22.30 (Mon–Sun); restaurant 12.00–15.00 and 17.30–22.45 (Mon–Thurs), 12.00–22.30 (Fri–Sun)*
*Credit cards: all major cards*
*Draught beers: Boddingtons, Flower's Original, Old Speckled Hen, Sherlock Holmes Ale, a weekly guest ale, Heineken, Stella Artois, Murphy's, Merrydown, Strongbow*
*Wheelchair access to venue*
*Private room seats 40*
*Nearest tube station: Embankment*

## The Ship

10 Thames Bank, SW14. Tel: 0181 876 1439

Boat Race day is when it all happens at The Ship, the closest pub to the finishing post. It has a substantial bar, a patio that can seat 300 people, and a garden with children's games. This is a handsome, fun pub that is always ready to celebrate any occasion. St Patrick's Day sees session musicians; on Burns Night they bring out the haggis. They also have regular beer festivals, quiz nights and barbecues.

*Open: 11.00–23.00 (Mon–Sat), 12.00–22.30 (Sun)*
*Food: 12.00–14.30 and 18.00–21.30 (Mon–Sat), 12.00–21.00 (Sun)*
*Credit cards: all major cards*
*Draught beers: Courage Best, Courage Directors, John Smith's Extra Smooth, one guest ale, Foster's, Budweiser, Kronenbourg, Guinness, Strongbow*
*Wheelchair access to venue*
*Nearest railway station: Mortlake*

## Ship Inn

41 Jews Row, SW18. Tel: 0181 870 9667

This is such an unlikely location for a successful pub. Jews Row is the last possible turning as you approach Wandsworth Bridge from the south side of the river. Its neighbours include a cement works, a bus depot and a car park. There's a public bar at the front where dogs doze happily on the floor while their owners enjoy the Young's ales. There's a big conservatory overlooking the garden and an attractive restaurant with a long open kitchen producing Modern British dishes at high speed and served by a small army of waiting staff. You can eat out in the garden on warm days, and hundreds of people do just that. A new wooden bar has been opened in the garden, the Doolali bar, which takes the pressure off the main bar when this is busy or when barbecues are on. There's also a riverside marquee which is often used for raucous parties. More than a thousand people have been known to gather around the large-screen TV they erect for the Last Night of the Proms. The other big night is Guy Fawkes' Night, which packs them in for a massive fireworks display. The Ship Inn is a wonderful pub sandwiched between unwonderful buildings, but this doesn't matter when there's a party going on. It was the *Evening Standard* Pub of the Year in 1991.

*Open: 11.00–23.00 (Mon–Sat), 12.00–22.30 (Sun)*
*Food: bar as opening hours; restaurant 12.00–15.00 and 19.00–22.30 (Mon–Sun)*
*Credit cards: all major cards*
*Draught beers: Ramrod Smooth, Young's Bitter, Young's Special, Castlemaine,*

*Young's Export, Young's Pilsner, Beamish, Guinness, Scrumpy Jack*
*Wheelchair access to venue*
*Two private rooms: 10 seated, 30–150 standing*
*Nearest railway station: Wandsworth Town*

## Shoeless Joe's

555 King's Road, SW6. Tel: 0171 384 2333

On big sporting occasions, you must book your table at Shoeless Joe's a month in advance for the downstairs bar. Televised events can only be truly appreciated when you're watching the thing on a 16-foot video wall with an endless supply of chilled beers. The clue is to start early and order food to put a decent lining on your stomach before getting on with the unruly (but gentlemanly) behaviour of screaming your rocks off during the match. I had a sumptuous burger and fries (£7) but had to wait for ever for the limited-choice relish. My companions had a chicken tortilla sandwich (£6) and an 8oz New York strip with potatoes (£11). Try and book one of the raised booths (some have their own TV) or one of the row of tables on the balcony level. Those who don't book take their chances on the floor space, which can fill up very quickly. On Friday and Saturday nights there are fairly wild but fun discos, with screens displaying fractal videos (a sort of nineties high-tech lava lamp). The ground-floor restaurant has recently been reorganised and is focusing on the bar more than the food these days. It's much quieter than the basement, but don't opt for the table on its own in the corner – the waiting staff can't see you, and it seems to be a case of 'can't see, won't serve'. Service is included in the final bill, but when we each threw in a credit card to divide up the bill, they told me they would be rounding each payment up to the nearest 10p. Call me mean, but if you multiply all those ten pences by the number of people who share their bills over the course of a year, then I think it's just a little too much in their pockets rather than ours. Anyway, I refused, and they gave in with just a little bit of a sulk. Having had my moan, I should add that I think Shoeless Joe's is one of the best additions to this stretch of the King's Road. It provides a complete mix of entertainment, from quiet drinks to full meals and a party atmosphere.

And as the holiday-camp man Fred Pontin used to say, 'Remember, book early.'

*Open: bar 12.00–midnight (Mon–Sat), 12.00–18.00 (Sun); club 21.00–01.00 (Thurs–Sat)*
*Food: 12.00–midnight (Mon–Sat), 12.00–22.30 (Sun)*
*Credit cards: all major cards*
*Draught beers: Freedom Ale, Marston's Smooth Ale, Kronenbourg, Labatt's, Guinness*
*Wheelchair access to venue*
*Two private rooms: 30–70 seated, 60–200 standing*
*Nearest tube station: Fulham Broadway*

## Shuckburgh Arms

47 Denyer Street, SW3. Tel: 0171 589 8382

When Scottish & Newcastle converted the Shuckburgh Arms into a Finnegan's Wake in October 1996, throwing the baronet's coat of arms into a skip, they hadn't bargained on the dramatic reaction. Sir Rupert Shuckburgh, whose ancestors occupied the building in the last century, was incensed: 'My family has been proud to be associated with this pub for more than a hundred years, and I have often visited it. I think its new name is a silly name, I will never go there again and I hope that no one else does.' As if to fulfil this aristocratic prophecy, the people of Chelsea stayed away, forcing S & N into an embarrassing U-turn. 'It just wasn't doing any business as a Finnegan's Wake, so the brewery decided to put things back as they were,' says manager Jason Gregory. When the *Evening Standard* informed Sir Rupert that the pub was to revert to its former name, complete with a new coat of arms which S & N claimed had been 'painstakingly recreated', he agreed to go along to the opening night. There were some nervous moments as Sir Rupert and Lady Shuckburgh inspected the premises before delivering their verdict. 'We like the pub, but they've used the wrong coat of arms.' The nice people at S & N are 'looking into the matter'.

*Open: 11.00–23.00 (Mon–Sat), 12.00–22.30 (Sun)*
*Food: 11.00–21.00 (Mon–Sun)*
*Credit cards: all major cards*
*Draught beers: Greene King IPA, John Smith's Smooth, Theakston Best, one guest*
*ale, Beck's, Foster's, Kronenbourg, Guinness, Scrumpy Jack*
*Wheelchair access to venue*
*Private room seats 30*
*Nearest tube station: South Kensington*

## Slap Harry's

1–3 Warwick Street, W1. Tel: 0171 734 4409

Slap Harry's, a minute or so from Piccadilly Circus, is what is known as a late-night venue. It is comparatively quiet during the day, and in the summer it is light and airy, with a wall of windows that concertinas back, opening one side of the bar to the tables and chairs on the pavement. A transformation occurs in the evening, however. Doors and windows close, down come the blinds to black the place out, and in come the doormen. The sound inside starts to rise. At around 9pm a DJ takes over in the main bar, and the volume increases with every record played. By 11pm, when it costs £2 to get in, four giant Roboscans are producing sensational lighting effects and the place is thumping. It costs you more in the basement, but then it's even louder down there. The DJs here play soul, reggae and R & B, and the music ricochets off the walls. This bar has Roboscans too, and a massive air-conditioning system keeps the sweat levels down. There's not a chair in sight but you don't come here to sit down. The fun-loving, Spandex-clad clientele suck beer from bottles and gyrate to the beat. They're too grown-up for grunge, and training shoes are a complete no-no.

*Open: main bar 12.00–01.00 (Mon–Wed), 12.00–03.00 (Thurs), 12.00–04.00*
*(Fri–Sat), 17.00–22.30 (Sun); basement bar 20.00–01.00 (Tues–Wed), 21.00–03.00*
*(Thurs), 21.00–04.00 (Fri–Sat), 19.00–22.30 (Sun)*
*Food: 12.00–15.30 (Mon–Sat)*
*Credit cards: none taken*
*Draught beers: Caffrey's, Carling Black Label, Carling Premier, Guinness, K6*
*Two private rooms: 60–80 seated, 60–200 standing*
*Nearest tube station: Piccadilly Circus*

## Slug and Lettuce

Slug and Lettuces have done a great job injecting new leases of life into some of London's fading pubs. There are 12 of them now in the capital, and this number is slowly increasing as they identify new outlets. There's a rather splendid one by the river in Richmond, a popular one in St Martin's Lane, a locals' local in Bayswater, and one for young Fulham on the pull. The good thing about Slug and Lettuces is that they don't seem to be afraid to change, and are constantly evolving. Only a few years ago they all got a bit of a spruce up, and they are now looking lighter and brighter. They have a standard offering, which means similar ales and fare throughout the chain, and the staff have been trained, they tell me, to very high standards in customer service. In this Guide's experience, their politeness almost makes up for their sometimes indifferent attitude to table care. The menu looks and generally is very inviting. The Cajun spiced chicken burger got the thumbs-up, as did the linguini with bacon, peas, herbs, wine and cream (both £5.75). We all moaned about the fries, though, which, for some completely illogical reason, arrived coated with more than enough salt to put an end to any slug trail. (See also Slug and Lettuce, Putney, below.)

*Branches at:*

**Battersea**: 4 St John's Hill, SW11. Tel: 0171 924 1322. Nearest railway station: Clapham Junction

**Bayswater**: 47 Hereford Road, W2. Tel: 0171 229 1503. Nearest tube station: Bayswater

**Covent Garden**: 114 Upper St Martin's Lane, WC2. Tel: 0171 379 4880 Nearest tube station: Leicester Square

**Fulham**: 474 Fulham Road, SW6. Tel: 0171 385 3209. Nearest tube station: Fulham Broadway

**Islington**: 1 Islington Green, N1. Tel: 0171 226 3864. Nearest tube station: Angel

**Kingston-upon-Thames**: Turks Boatyard, Thameside, KT1. Tel: 0181 547 2323. Nearest railway station: Kingston-upon-Thames

**Pimlico**: 11 Warwick Way, SW1. Tel: 0171 834 3313. Nearest tube station: Pimlico

**Richmond**: Riverside House, Water Lane, TW9. Tel: 0181 948 7733. Nearest tube station: Richmond

**Soho**: 80–82 Wardour Street, W1. Tel: 0171 437 1400. Nearest tube station: Leicester Square

**Walton-on-Thames**: Thameside, KT12. Tel: 01932 223996. Nearest railway station: Walton-on-Thames

**Wandsworth**: 21 Alma Road, SW18. Tel: 0181 874 1833 Nearest railway station: Wandsworth Town

# Slug and Lettuce

14 Putney High Street, SW15. Tel: 0181 785 3081

The White Lion in Putney High Street roared for the last time in 1993 when the Slug brought in its Lettuce and completely restyled the place. Its front windows now have clear glass, and the interior colour scheme of cream, orange and blue brightens the spirits of its customers. The new pub is firmly food-focused, and offers dishes such as Cumberland sausage, Thai chicken curry and tagliatelle with red pepper pesto. There's champagne on the wine list and an up-to-the-minute coffee-making machine on the bar.

A watering hole of quality for Putney's young money spenders.

*Open: 11.00–23.00 (Mon–Sat), 12.00–22.30 (Sun)*
*Food: 12.00–22.00 (Mon–Sun)*
*Credit cards: all major cards*
*Draught beers: Courage Directors, Wadworth 6X, a weekly guest ale, Kronenbourg, Miller, Guinness, Red Rock*
*Wheelchair access to venue*
*Two private rooms: 70 and 100 seated*
*Nearest tube station: Putney Bridge*

# Smithfield Free House

334 Central Market, EC1. Tel: 0171 248 5311

The Smithfield Free House occupies a prime site in the old Smithfields market. What the market traders would make of the place now, I'm sure I can't say. This youthful pub has pool tables and non-stop music increasing in volume hour after hour. At 10pm the music takes over completely, and kids come from all over London for the nightly disco.

*Open: pub 12.00–23.00 (Mon), 11.00–23.00 (Tues–Fri); club 22.00–01.00*
*(Tues–Thurs), 21.00–15.30 (Fri–Sat)*
*Food: 12.00–14.30 (Mon–Fri)*
*Credit cards: none taken*
*Draught beers: Bass, Caffrey's, Stones, Worthington Best, Carling Black Label,*
*Carling Premier, Grolsch, Staropramen, Guinness, Strongbow*
*Wheelchair access to venue*
*Nearest tube stations: Chancery Lane, Farringdon*

## Sofa Bar at The Drawing Room

103 Lavender Hill, SW11. Tel: 0171 350 2564

The Drawing Room is a restaurant but if you go through the doors and turn right, you'll find the Sofa Bar. No prizes for guessing what you'll be sitting on. It's small, cosy, and a perfect respite from the frenetic activity of the main road. Clocks feature largely, for no other reason than the owner has a collection of them and this seemed an ideal place to display them. Low-level lighting, table service and plenty of foliage help to create a relaxed atmosphere. Drinks will be brought to your table. Very civilised.

*Open: pub 1700-midnight (Mon-Sat), 11.00-19.00 (Sun)*
*Food: As opening hours*
*Credit cards: All major except AmEx*
*Wheelchair access to venue*
*Nearest railway station: Clapham Junction*

## Soho Soho

11–13 Frith Street, W1. Tel: 0171 494 3491

The ground floor of this noisy, busy brasserie has a bar with limited seating potential, but that doesn't seem to bother the crowds of after-work drinkers who happily squeeze together to allow a few more in. It's fun, young, and on a summer's eve you can sit and breathe in the air of traffic-ridden Frith Street.

*Open: 12.00–23.00 (Mon–Sun)*
*Food: as opening hours*
*Credit cards: all major cards*
*Wheelchair access to venue and loo*
*Nearest tube stations: Tottenham Court Road, Leicester Square*

## Soho Spice

124–126 Wardour Street, W1. Tel: 0171 434 0808

No, this is not a new member of the uniquely talented singing troupe. Soho Spice is a rather attractive bar beneath the restaurant of the same name. The heat and dust of an Indian bazaar may be missing, but the colourful decor, burning incense sticks, spicy snacks and khurta-clad staff help to evoke dreamy images from the subcontinent. You know you're in London, though – the modern, air-conditioned bar serves draught Kronenbourg (£1.75 for a half pint) and an Indian beer, Kingfisher (brewed in Kent). Thankfully, there is also an Indian-import beer, Cobra (£4 for 65cl), and they spice up the cocktails with aromatic infusions of cinnamon, cumin, fennel or ginger-stuffed apricot (£4.95). Bar snacks include the ones you might expect, but also chaat (chicken in a pepper sauce), and crisp mini-pooris with a yoghurt sauce (all £2.95). With most drinking joints in this part of town bursting at the seams, it made a pleasant change to find this under-used, perfectly agreeable bar that might be just a little too posh for Posh Spice.

*Open: 12.00–midnight (Mon–Thurs), 12.00–00.30 (Fri–Sat)*
*Food: as opening hours*

*Credit cards: all major cards*
*Draught beers: Kingfisher, Kronenbourg*
*Nearest tube stations: Piccadilly Circus, Tottenham Court Road*

## The Spaniards Inn

Spaniards Road, NW3. Tel: 0181 455 3276

This is the 16th-century weatherboarded building on the road that cuts through Hampstead Heath, and none of the many additions and alterations has spoilt it in any way. The saloon bar has low ceilings, old panelling and cosy alcoves. Bar stools surround the old wooden bar, and there is a charming panelled room upstairs with original beams and shutters and a splendidly sloping floor. There are real fires in winter, and in the summer you can enjoy one of the best pub gardens you will ever find, with its raised lawn and roses, its fine pergola and big terrace with picnic tables. At the bottom of the garden more than 100 budgies lead busy lives in a big aviary. Children love them and are welcome here. It is a pub worth making any sort of detour to visit. Mind the tollgate.

*Open: 11.00–23.00 (Mon–Sat), 12.00–22.30 (Sun)*
*Food: 12.00–21.30 (Mon–Sun)*
*Credit cards: all major cards*
*Draught beers: Adnams, Bass, Caffrey's, Hancocks, London Pride, Worthington, Carling Black Label, Staropramen, Tennent's Extra, Guinness, Dry Blackthorn*
*Wheelchair access to venue*
*Private room seats 30*
*Nearest tube station: Hampstead, Golders Green*

## The Sporting Page

6 Camera Place, SW10. Tel: 0171 376 3694

The Sporting Page sits happily tucked away in a quiet little side street, sheltered from the endless roar of the traffic on the King's Road and Fulham Road. It is a small, whitewashed pub with a rather smart interior of varnished pine and rosewood, and murals depicting sporting scenes from yesteryear. Big red canopies featuring the Bollinger trademark hint at what goes on inside: this pub sells more Bollinger than any other pub in the country and is second only to The Lanesborough among retail outlets. The quaffing clientele pile in from the City after work, along with the old military brigade and public-school types, for evenings of antics and tomfoolery. On rugby occasions, the big screen comes down and the crowds don their designer rugby attire to cheer on the action. The Modern British menu, more adventurous than the usual pub fare, is very popular, and includes traditional comfort foods such as bangers and mash. As The Sporting Page can be very busy in the evenings, the smart time to go is during the day and (unsurprisingly for this area) on Saturday evenings, when the locals pack up their picnic hampers and disappear off to the country for the weekend. Back to the Bolly: a bottle is remarkably good value at £30 (NV), a jeroboam is £135, and a Methuselah £300. They don't yet stock a Nebuchadnezzar, but should you want one, have a word with Kerry Ennis – the manager, who takes no prisoners – she'll sort you out. For those who like to know these things, the order of bottle sizes for champagne is as follows: quarter (20cl), half (37.5cl), bottle (75cl), magnum (2 bottles), jeroboam (4), rehoboam (6) Methuselah (8), Salmanazar (12), Balthazar (16) and Nebuchadnezzar (20).

*Open: 11.00–23.00 (Mon–Sat), 12.00–22.30 (Sun)*
*Food: 12.00–14.30 and 19.00–22.00 (Mon–Sat), 12.00–14.30 and 19.00–21.30 (Sun)*
*Credit cards: Eurocard, Mastercard, Visa*
*Draught beers: Brakspear, John Smith's Extra Smooth, Theakston XB, Foster's, Holsten Export, Kronenbourg, Miller, Guinness, Strongbow*
*Wheelchair access to venue*
*Nearest tube station: Fulham Broadway*

## Sports Academy

24 King William Street, EC4. Tel: 0171 623 0714

A remarkable conversion from a tired old wine bar resulted in this handsome, state-of-the-art sports bar, owned by ever-experimenting Bass, which could be the first of a new brand of themed venue. For the sports enthusiasts in the City, this is a mecca. On the ground floor there's a squeaky-clean, air-conditioned room with large windows looking out onto King William Street, which is so bright it seems an unlikely venue in which to watch broadcast sport. The action, however, proves to be downstairs. There's a large video wall behind the bar, TV monitors throughout, blue-baized pool tables and an ever-growing collection of sporting memorabilia. Cheers to it.

*Open: 11.00–23.00 (Mon–Fri)*
*Food: 11.00–21.00 (Mon–Fri)*
*Credit cards: all major cards except AmEx*
*Draught beers: Caffrey's, Carling Black Label, Carling Premier, Grolsch, Guinness, Cidermaster*
*Wheelchair access to venue and loo*
*Nearest tube station: Monument*

## Sports Café

80 Haymarket, SW1. Tel: 0171 839 8300

This is a much better example of a themed sports bar than its near neighbour Football Football (qv). The Sports Café has been designed in the American big-bar style, with the large spaces broken up carefully so you don't quite feel like you're in a scrum. There are two bars downstairs and one bar upstairs, where they hold sports-related promotional events. Drinks are not cheap (£2.65 for a pint of Foster's), but then they never are in places like this. There are plenty of TV screens and a large screen visible from the restaurant area.

*Open: 12.00–02.00 (Mon–Thurs), 12.00–03.00 (Fri–Sat), 12.00–23.00 (Sun)*
*Food: 12.00–midnight (Mon–Sun); bar snacks after midnight (Mon–Thurs and Sun), 12.00–01.00 (Fri–Sat)*
*Credit cards: all major cards*
*Draught beers: Boston, Foster's, Heineken, Miller, Stella Artois, Murphy's, Max Dry, Strongbow*
*Wheelchair access to venue and loo*
*Private room: 50 seated, 70 standing*
*Nearest tube station: Piccadilly Circus*

## The Spot

29 Maiden Lane, WC2. Tel: 0171 379 5900

The Spot is a collection of bars occupying a prime position in growing-ever-popular Maiden Lane. There's a couple of bars on the ground floor, a tatty one on the right and the main bar on the left. You go up to the Oval Room, which is kind of oval. This is where the serious action is – it has a large screen, a party atmosphere, and loud music, an eclectic mix of soul, R & B, house and garage. Monday night is comedy night (£4 or £8 including dinner). The Spot is open late but they charge £4 admission after 11pm on Fridays and Saturdays.

*Open: 11.30–midnight (Mon–Sun)*
*Food: as opening hours*
*Credit cards: Mastercard, Switch, Visa*
*Draught beers: Caffrey's, Carling Black Label, Carling Premier, Grolsch, Guinness, Dry Blackthorn*
*Wheelchair access to venue*
*Nearest tube stations: Covent Garden, Charing Cross*

# Springbok

20 Bedford Street, WC2. Tel: 0171 379 1734

Here's a zoological piece. A springbok is a graceful, strikingly marked gazelle-like antelope of the *Bovidae* family. It is native to the open, tree-less plains of southern Africa and once roamed in such dense masses it destroyed the area over which it passed. When alarmed or excited it makes a series of stiff-legged vertical leaps more than 3 metres off the ground, known as pronking. A certain amount of pronking goes on in this basement bar. The phenomenon of global grouping continues unabated in London, and most of the punters here have some connection with South Africa. It's high energy, loud music, TV screens and video games, with loud talking, fast-living boozers downing the Castle lager. There's a quieter bar, the Tunnel Bar, at the back; it has tables and chairs where you can relax – a little – and think of home.

*Open: 12.00–23.00 (Sun–Wed), 12.00–midnight (Thurs–Sat)*
*Food: 12.00–17.00 (Mon–Sun)*
*Credit cards: all major cards except AmEx*
*Draught beers: Beamish Red, Foster's, Kronenbourg, Guinness, Dry Blackthorn*
*Wheelchair access to venue*
*Nearest tube stations: Covent Garden, Charing Cross, Leicester Square*

# The Star Tavern

6 Belgrave Mews West, SW1. Tel: 0171 235 3019

The Star Tavern was built for the household servants of the nobility of 19th-century Belgravia. It is agreeably old fashioned. On winter evenings you can sit at a table near one of the open fires, and on summer evenings customers like to take their drinks into the mews, where there are tubs of geraniums and hanging baskets of lobelia. They say the upstairs room was where the Great Train Robbers planned their deed, and that Christine Keeler often held court in the main bar. Ther food is still a big attraction, as are the Fuller's ales. The Star Tavern was the *Evening Standard* Pub of the Year in 1992.

*Open: 11.30–15.00 and 17.00–23.00 (Mon–Thurs), 11.30–23.00 (Fri), 11.00–23.00 (Sat), 12.00–15.00 and 19.00–22.30 (Sun)*
*Food: 12.00–14.30 and 18.30–20.45 (Mon–Fri)*
*Credit cards: none taken*
*Draught beers: Chiswick Bitter, Fuller's ESB, London Pride, Carling Black Label, Grolsch, Heineken, Guinness,*
*Private room: 45–50 seated, 90–100 standing*
*Nearest tube station: Knightsbridge*

# Stonemasons

54 Cambridge Grove, W6. Tel: 0181 748 1397

Located just off Glenthorne Road in Hammersmith, this is a new, well-designed bar with a strong food focus. It has probably been saved by the intervention of Ewan Guinness and Matt Jacomb (see Masons Arms), who came across a rather gloomy saloon bar, The Cambridge Arms, bought it, all but demolished the interior, added a room at the back, gave it a skylight, big windows, bare-board flooring and big tables to eat at, and installed an open kitchen. It's early days yet but the Stonemasons seems to have lost itself somewhere in the dictionary between a bar and a restaurant. It is clearly a bar where you can go for a pint but it also serves up some reasonable quality food from a barely legible handwritten, badly photocopied menu. This includes crocodile with New Zealand mussels in a Thai red curry (£7.50), pan-fried calves' liver in sage and onion mash (£6.50), Cumberland sausages with mash and gravy (£5.10), and plenty of vegetarian alternatives. The problem with open kitchens is that they should be a spectacle in themselves, a form of theatre. This one lacked drama, and the chefs busying away in the middle of it all looked like suitably cast extras from *Trainspotting*, so it came as something of a surprise when we got our food and discovered how delicious it all was. The bar service is painfully slow, tables are often littered with the debris of previous occupants, and if you ask the rarely-to-be-found waitress, who might just happen to stray by, for more drinks, she'll reiterate the house policy, 'Please order at the bar.'

*Open: 11.00–23.00 (Mon–Sat), 12.00–22.30 (Sun)*
*Bar: 12.00–22.00 (Mon–Sat), 12.00–21.30 (Sun)*
*Credit cards: all major cards*
*Draught beers: Boddingtons, Boston, Wadworth 6X, Heineken, Hoegaarden, Stella Artois, Guinness, Strongbow*
*Nearest tube station: Hammersmith*

## The Sun

47 Clapham Old Town, SW4. Tel: 0171 622 4980

A rather fine Victorian building takes pride of place in the Old Town and is one of the most popular meeting points in Clapham. It seems that you don't need the might of a giant brewer behind you to transform an old pub into the kind of venue the public clearly wants. Ann and Tom Halpin, a couple who were weaned on the pub scene in Ireland, bought the lease of The Sun from Bass. After such an extravagant purchase, they needed to get the place up and running as soon as they could. They all but gutted the building and let loose a couple of artists, Caroline Ward and John Hammond, to create an effective and handsome interior of distressed green and yellow paintwork, spruced-up woodwork and bizarre, rain-forest-decorated loos. There is ample space for relaxed lunching, and good quality, well-presented food. The 'lunch for a fiver' deal offers an ever-changing selection of dishes, includes a glass of wine or beer, and is available until the late afternoon, when the place fills up with Clapham's twenty- and thirtysomethings returning from work. The evening crowds occupy every available inch of floor space, and the large garden at the side, which now has its own bar, is as likely to be packed in February as it is in August (they use garden heaters). You needn't be put off by the vast numbers who congregate here – they are fun, friendly and street-fashionable, and the fast and efficient bartenders ensure that getting a drink is an easy trip.

*Open: 11.00–23.00 (Mon–Sat), 12.00–22.30 (Sun)*
*Food: 12.30–21.30 (Mon–Sun)*
*Credit cards: all major cards except AmEx*
*Draught beers: Bass, Caffrey's, London Pride, Grolsch, Staropramen, Tennent's Extra, Tennent's Pilsner, Guinness, Dry Blackthorn*
*Wheelchair access to venue*
*Private room seats 100*
*Nearest tube station: Clapham Common*

## The Sun and Doves    EROS AWARD WINNER

61–63 Coldharbour Lane, SE5. Tel: 0171 733 1525

A ray of hope now shines in Camberwell, whose residents have for far too long been denied any decent drinking venues. In September 1995 Mark Dodds, then a landscape gardener but with considerable experience in the food and drink industry, negotiated with Inntrepreneur to obtain the lease of this sleepy little local just a few hundred yards from Camberwell Green. His vision was to retain the pub as the focal point of the community while providing a modern bar in line with contemporary expectations. He closed the old place down, gutted it, refurnished and redecorated it on a very tight budget, and three months later opened the doors to the people of Camberwell. As if to illustrate the dictum that nature abhors a vacuum, it filled up quickly, becoming an almost instant success and proof positive that you don't need to spend the fantastic sums now being sloshed around by the big breweries on refurbishment projects to give the punters what they want.

The Sun and Doves has one large, brightly coloured room with painted floor-boards scratched almost clear again with wear. Rickety old furniture provides plenty of seating space, and there's a raised area where the leopard-skin seats are – that's the sexy corner! A simple curtain partitions the restaurant area, which leads on to a rather handsome patio garden at the back. The bohemian atmosphere is supported with works of art on the walls, which change monthly, providing a showcase for new artists. Two years on and the place is thriving, nearly all the profits have been put back into the pub, enabling them to update the furniture, add a smoke-extraction system, and so forth. There are clearly some very good-looking people in Camberwell, and it seems they are more than happy to spend their leisure time in The Sun and Doves.

*Open: 11.00–23.00 (Mon–Fri), 12.00–23.00 (Sat), 12.00–22.30 (Sun)*
*Food: bar 11.00–22.30 (Mon–Fri), 12.00–22.30 (Sat–Sun); restaurant 12.00–15.00 and 18.30–22.00 (Mon–Thurs), 12.00–15.00 and 18.30–22.30 (Fri–Sat), 12.00–21.30 (Sun)*
*Credit cards: all major cards except AmEx*
*Draught beers: Courage Directors, John Smith's Extra Smooth, Foster's, Kronenbourg, Guinness, Scrumpy Jack*
*Wheelchair access to venue*
*Private room: 40 seated, 50–80 standing*
*Nearest tube station: Oval*
*Nearest railway station: Denmark Hill*

## Sun & Thirteen Cantons   EROS AWARD WINNER

21 Great Pulteney Street, W1. Tel: 0171 734 0934

There has been a pub on this site for more than 300 years, and the first of these started life simply as The Sun. In the late 1600s many Soho pubs adopted the name Thirteen Cantons to recognise the mostly Protestant Swiss community that had settled in the area. In Switzerland, a canton is a political division, and at the end of the Thirty Years War in 1648, thirteen cantons were declared free from the rule of the Holy Roman Emperor. A further religious war in Switzerland in 1656 resulted in victory for the Catholics, leading to the oppression of the Protestant communities. Many Protestants made their way to London and congregated in Soho, still expressing their allegiance to their cantons.

The old Sun and Thirteen Cantons survived until 1882 when it was demolished and rebuilt as the pub we see today standing square on the corner of Great Pulteney Street and Beak Street. Goldcrest Films bought the building about five years ago, as well as the brasserie next door. They gutted everything and created a much bigger pub with a comforting green and cream decor. On warm days the first thing you notice is the crowds of people spilling out onto the pavement; on colder days they all snuggle into the small main bar. There is a much bigger room, which was the brasserie, with wooden wall panels, framed mirrors, marble-topped tables and a very discreet large-screen TV which rolls down from the ceiling for major sporting events. By day this room is used as a restaurant serving a constantly changing menu of pastas, salads and chef's specials (the Toulouse sausages are a good bet). In the evenings the local businesses release their media executives, and they all seem to come to this pub. You're likely to overhear conversations about media awards and web sites, and find the clientele dressed in designer suits rather than City suits, and carrying portfolios rather than attaché cases. You can tell they're media people, as even the over-35s are trendy. Go downstairs, past the loos, and you'll find another big room with its own bar – much darker than upstairs, and illuminated with red lights. This is a great venue for parties, and is the scene of many events organised by the amiable young manager, Justin Mallett.

*Open: 11.00–23.00 (Mon–Sat), 12.00–22.30 (Sun); sometimes open till midnight*
*Food: bar 12.00–22.00; restaurant 12.00–17.00*
*Credit cards: all major cards*
*Draught beers: Boddingtons, Boston, Heineken, Stella Artois, Murphy's, Strongbow*
*Wheelchair access to venue*
*Private room: 60–70 standing*
*Nearest tube station: Piccadilly Circus*

## The Sun Inn

Church Road, SW13. Tel: 0181 876 5256

Barnes Green is a spectacular location in a prosperous part of south-west London that has all the ingredients of the perfect village – a pond with a family of ducks gliding by, a brook with a willow tree, an avenue of horse chestnuts, and The Sun Inn, a pretty Georgian building with a mansard roof, a pergola, window boxes and hanging baskets. It has a charming warren of little rooms, a jumble of nooks and snugs divided by rails, pillars, stained-glass panels and curious sliding leaded windows. There are wooden floors on different levels, beams, low ceilings, stuffed owls, a piano, a huge stuffed pike, old prints, old bottles, old rugs, bric-a-brac of all sorts and a ghost who alters the clocks. It gets very lively, and the traditional Sunday roast is particularly popular with young and old alike.

*Open: 11.00–23.00 (Mon–Sat), 12.00–22.30 (Sun)*
*Food: 12.00–14.45 (Mon–Sat), 12.00–16.00 (Sun)*
*Credit cards: none taken*
*Draught beers: Adnams, Burton Ale, Calder's Cream Ale, Marston's Pedigree, Pope's Traditional, Tetley's, Carlsberg, Castlemaine, Lowenbrau, Guinness, Taunton*
*Wheelchair access to venue*
*Nearest railway station: Barnes Bridge*

## The Surprise

6 Christchurch Terrace, SW3. Tel: 0171 352 4699

The surprise about The Surprise is finding it. Time and again I seem to lose this handsome little local pub, tucked away as it is in a peaceful square behind the Royal Hospital Road. Quiet is the location and quiet is the pub. It has no music, ever. A black oak bar with a painted frieze serves both the public and saloon bars. There is a dartboard and shove-halfpenny. Umbrellas shade the tables outside, although the church opposite blocks out most of the sun. They worship something else in the pub – a quiet pint!

*Open: 12.00–23.00 (Mon–Sat), 12.00–22.30 (Sun)*
*Food: 12.00–14.30 (Mon–Sat)*
*Credit cards: all major cards except AmEx*
*Draught beers: Bass, Caffrey's, Hancock HB, Worthington Best, Carling Black Label, Grolsch, Guinness, Red Rock*
*Wheelchair access to venue*
*Nearest tube station: Sloane Square*

# The Sussex

20 Upper St Martin's Lane, WC2. Tel: 0171 836 1834

On 12 October 1992 the IRA planted a bomb in this pub, in the men's lavatory. Five customers were injured, one died days later.

The Sussex replaced its windows, mended its shattered bar and got on with it. The pub has just emerged from a £250,000 refit which has given it a bright new interior, new windows, new most things. There it is in the heart of the West End, everywhere just a short walk away. Tourists love this pub. So do Londoners.

*Open: 11.00–23.00 (Mon–Sat), 12.00–22.30 (Sun)*
*Food: 11.00–20.00 (Mon–Sat), 12.00–18.00 (Sun)*
*Credit cards: all major cards*
*Draught beers: Beamish Red, Courage Best, Courage Directors, John Smith's, Foster's, Miller, Kronenbourg, Guinness, Strongbow*
*Nearest tube stations: Leicester Square, Covent Garden*

# The Swan

66 Bayswater Road, W2. Tel: 0171 262 5204

The Swan is genuinely pretty and genuinely old. It was there in the 18th century, or anyway some of it was, and it takes care to look its age. It was built as a coaching inn, then became the Floral Tea Gardens, then happily returned to being a tavern. Today, though bigger, it is still a nice manageable size – just two storeys, with a handsome swan painted on the stucco, and lanterns and hanging baskets. It also has a terrace with tables and chairs – a tremendous asset. The terrace extends to the pavement, and much of it is sheltered by a glass canopy, so let it rain, and let the traffic roar by, you can eat here undisturbed. The food is comfortably English. They serve a hearty English breakfast from 10am every morning, and there's a roast on the menu every lunchtime. While you're there, have a look at the big old painting in the room at the back, a typically English scene. There is the Swan and there is Bayswater Road, and those kindly Redcoats are allowing felons one last drink before hanging them at Tyburn. The locals used to enjoy that. Entertainment is still provided at the Swan; there's a typical English singsong in the back room every night, and everyone, whether they are from Tokyo, Texas or the Tottenham Court Road, ends up joining in. Tourists love it.

*Open: 10.00–23.00 (Mon–Sat), 10.00–22.00 (Sun)*
*Food: 10.00–22.00 (Mon–Sat), 10.00–21.30 (Sun)*
*Credit cards: all major cards*
*Draught beers: Courage Directors, John Smith's Extra Smooth, Theakston Best, Beck's, Foster's, Kronenbourg, Beamish, Strongbow*
*Wheelchair access to venue*
*Nearest tube station: Lancaster Gate*

# The Swan

77–80 Gracechurch Street, EC3. Tel: 0171 283 7712

This might well be the smallest pub in the City. Imagine, if you will, being aboard the *Orient Express* and walking up to the buffet car for some refreshments, squeezing past first one person, then another. Should you get yourself a place at the bar, keep it. There's more room upstairs, relatively speaking, but this is not somewhere to organise an office party. Stand and have a jar or two, sit around one of the very few tables or pull up a bar stool, and admire this splendid example of a Victorian parlour.

*Open: 11.00–23.00 (Mon–Fri)*
*Food: as opening hours*
*Credit cards: AmEx, Mastercard, Visa*

*Draught beers: Chiswick Bitter, ESB, London Pride, one guest ale, Grolsch,*
*Heineken, Tennent's Extra, Guinness, Scrumpy Jack*
*Wheelchair access to venue*
*Nearest tube stations: Monument, Bank*

# SWX1

8 Battersea Square, SW11. Tel: 0171 924 2288

This seems to be something of a jinxed site. In recent years it has been
Nachos, then B Square, and now that Joel Cadbury has his hands on it he's
renamed it SWX1. Can you remember what B Square looked like? I can't see
any difference myself, although that isn't a negative point. The large horseshoe-
shaped bar is almost too big, but space isn't really a problem here. There are
three rooms, two of them given over to the restaurant. The drinks area is on the
right as you go in; it has some of the most uncomfortable seating possible.
Shabbily put-together bar menus display the happy-hour jugs of cocktails (£6).
You don't get table service in the bar, which makes you feel like a second-class
customer as you see the staff bustling around the restaurant area. The big windows allow you to observe all the other, much busier, cafés around the square.

*Open: 18.00–23.00 (Mon–Fri), 12.00–23.00 (Sat), 12.00–22.00 (Sun)*
*Food: 18.00–midnight (Mon–Sat), 12.00–23.00 (Sun)*
*Credit cards: all major cards*
*Nearest railway station: Clapham Junction*

# Tactical Café

27 D'Arblay Street, W1. Tel: 0171 287 2823

Two shops knocked together have realised a student's fantasy: poetry and
book readings, specialist jazz nights, light shows, and DJs with visuals. The
decor is a complete mix from the two old shops – a granite-tiled floor and metal
tables and chairs in one half, wooden floors and coloured plastic in the other.
Bookcases separate the two halves – the books are for sale, by the way. When
I was a student I wanted to open a bar that did everything. I didn't, of course,
but the Tactical Café is trying to do just that.

*Open: 09.00–23.00 (Mon–Fri), 11.00–23.00 (Sat), 12.00–22.30 (Sun)*
*Food: as opening hours*
*Credit cards: none taken*
*Private room seats 20*
*Nearest tube station: Oxford Circus*

# The Talbot Tavern

Little Chester Street, SW1. Tel: 0171 235 1639

The Talbot is a big, modern, jolly sort of pub just a short distance away from the
Queen's garden wall. It attracts a lively young crowd from the local offices at
lunchtime and in the evening. The one-time car park is now a terrace with lots
of tables and chairs, very popular in the summer.

*Open: 11.00–23.00 (Mon–Fri)*
*Food: 11.00–22.00 (Mon–Fri)*
*Credit cards: AmEx, Mastercard, Visa*
*Draught beers: Brakspear, Courage Best, Courage Directors, John Smith's Extra*
*Smooth, Theakston Best, Beck's, Foster's, Holsten, Guinness, Strongbow*
*Wheelchair access to venue*
*Nearest tube station: Hyde Park Corner (exit 5)*

# The Tattershall Castle

King's Reach, Victoria Embankment, SW1. Tel: 0171 839 6548

The *Tattershall Castle*, a coal-fired paddle steamer, used to make eight trips a day between Hull and New Holland, carrying up to l,000 people plus cars and livestock. A million pounds was spent on her by Scottish & Newcastle to make her ship-shape and ready for a new career as a floating pub. Her taste for nightlife has not gone unnoticed. The nightclub in the stern is open Thursday (until 2am), Friday and Saturday (3am) and Sunday (midnight). The pub can't keep traditional ales, but two lagers and a bitter are piped into ten big tanks in the barge moored alongside. These have to be refilled twice a week in the summer when the decks are crowded and the demand for lager seems insatiable. There is a buffet downstairs, snacks in the bar, a barbecue on deck (weather permitting), and in the afternoons they do teas. There is another refurbishment planned for late 1997. Two new bars will be added – one on the deck and one down below. A heating system will be installed on the deck and a canopy will skirt the entire length of the boat for sheltered drinking. This should help business in the winter. The Tattershall is moored at Victoria Embankment near Waterloo Bridge.

*Open: 11.00–03.00 (Mon and Thurs–Sat), 11.00–23.00 (Tues–Wed), 12.00–22.30 (Sun)*
*Food: 12.00–04.00 (Mon and Thurs–Sat), 12.00–21.00 (Tues–Wed and Sun)*
*Credit cards: AmEx, Mastercard, Visa*
*Draught beers: John Smith's Extra Smooth, Foster's, Kronenbourg, Beamish, Strongbow*
*Nearest tube station: Embankment*

# Three Greyhounds

25 Greek Street, W1. Tel: 0171 287 0754

The Three Greyhounds is the Tudor-looking building on the corner of Greek Street and Old Compton Street, a genuinely old pub with half-timbering that was added in the twenties. The interior was faked up a few years ago to recreate Ye Olde England, but that doesn't matter either. What matters is the romantically named Roxy Beaujolais, who took over the place in 1992, bringing a touch of glamour and style previously lacking at this fine Soho watering hole. Nobody misbehaves in the Three Greyhounds any more now that this is Roxy's place – she won't have any music or gangs of lads. She's a very good cook, too, and if you're lucky enough to go there, you'll find out for yourself. If you can't make it in person, you can still find out what I mean, as she recently published her own cook book, *Home from the Inn Contented*. So go there, have a few real ales, sample the food and chat to Roxy, and you too will be able to go home from the inn contented.

*Open: 11.00–23.00 (Mon–Sat), 12.00–22.30 (Sun)*
*Food: 12.00–16.00 (Mon–Sat)*
*Credit cards: none taken*
*Draught beers: Adnams Bitter, Adnams Broadside, Marston's Pedigree, Tetley's, one guest ale, Carlsberg, Castlemaine, Guinness, Addlestone's*
*Wheelchair access to venue*
*Nearest tube station: Leicester Square*

# The Tottenham

6 Oxford Street, W1. Tel: 0171 636 7201

This is the only pub left on Oxford Street. It is busy enough. By day it gets tourists and shoppers. By night young bloods heading for the clubs cram the two bars, take over the pinball and gaming machines, and rock along with the music. It's just opposite Tottenham Court Road tube station.

*Open: 11.00–23.00 (Mon–Sat), 12.00–22.30 (Sun)*
*Food: bar 11.00–15.00 (Mon–Fri), 12.00–17.00 (Sat–Sun); sandwiches available till closing time*
*Credit cards: all major cards*
*Draught beers: Burton, Kilkenny, six guest ales, Carlsberg, Carlsberg Export, Castlemaine, Guinness, Dry Blackthorn*
*Wheelchair access to venue*
*Private room seats 30*
*Nearest tube station: Tottenham Court Road*

## The Trafalgar

200 King's Road, SW3. Tel: 0171 352 1076

This is a pub for teenagers of all ages. Big-screen TV, smaller TVs everywhere, darts, arcade games, beefburgers, potato skins, steakwiches, chips (and extra chips) with everything. The Mancunian manager Tony McDonnell has been making great efforts to clean the place up following some stormy years. He seems to be succeeding. They now provide table service for drinks and food, but as it still gets packed in the evenings, this sometimes gets a little unworkable. There's a disco on Friday nights and bouncers on the door at weekends.

*Open: 11.00–23.00 (Mon–Sat), 12.00–22.30 (Sun)*
*Food: 11.00–20.00 (Mon–Sun)*
*Credit cards: all major cards except AmEx*
*Draught beers: Bass, Caffrey's, Worthington, Carling Black Label, Carling Premier, Grolsch, Guinness, Dry Blackthorn*
*Wheelchair access to venue*
*Nearest tube station: Sloane Square*

## The Trafalgar Tavern

Park Row, SE10. Tel: 0181 858 2437

The Trafalgar was built in 1837 in the dashing Regency style to attract free-spending grandees from London, which indeed it did. It was one of a number of what were called whitebait taverns, noted for their whitebait dinners, hugely popular and very expensive in their day. No one did them better or charged so much for them as The Trafalgar Tavern. The whitebait taverns had a good run, but with the turn of the century they went out of business one by one. The Trafalgar lasted longer than most, but in the end it succumbed too, and for the next 50 years it was used as a home for old seamen and as a working men's club. Then in 1965 it was restored, relicensed and reopened, and here it is, full of swank and swagger again.

The Nelson Room is a vast room of quite astonishing splendour with its classical mouldings, elegant windows and curved wrought-iron balconies overlooking the river. It has elaborate swagged curtains and no fewer than ten chandeliers. It is currently painted burgundy and is much in demand for wedding receptions, but most of the action is in the lofty main bars downstairs. The Trafalgar places a strong emphasis on food, and whole families seem to unite over Sunday lunch. It was the *Evening Standard* Pub of the Year for 1996.

*Open: 11.30–23.00 (Mon–Sat), 12.00–22.30 (Sun)*
*Food: bar 12.00–20.00 (Mon–Sat); restaurant 12.00–15.00 (Mon–Sun)*
*Credit cards: all major cards except AmEx*
*Draught beers: Courage Best, Courage Directors, John Smith's Extra Smooth, Marston's Pedigree, Old Speckled Hen, Beck's, Foster's, Kronenbourg, Guinness, Scrumpy Jack*
*Wheelchair access to venue*
*Nearest railway stations: Greenwich, Maze Hill*

# Trinity

108–110 New King's Road, SW6. Tel: 0171 731 2142

Fun bar which gets packed at weekends – very trendy Fulham on the pull.

*Open: 11.00–23.00 (Mon–Sat)*
*Food: as opening hours*
*Credit cards: all major cards except AmEx*
*Draught beers: Boddingtons, Freedom, Heineken, Stella Artois, Murphy's, Merrydown*
*Wheelchair access to venue*
*Private room: 55 seated, 140 standing*
*Nearest tube station: Parsons Green*

# Tut 'n' Shive

235 Upper Street, N1. Tel: 0171 359 7719

The problem for the management of themed pubs is that they have to maintain the image or the entire concept goes awry. This appears to have happened at this once-fun pub in Islington. The Tut 'n' Shive is losing it. The railway track around the ceiling remains, but the trains don't run, the quirky jokes have all been removed, and Frankenstein's monster and the open coffin look like they might be the next to go. The way this pub looked when it opened – old doors holding the counter up, graffiti on peeling paint, and corrugated iron sheets – is now starting to look like neglect.

*Open: 11.00–23.00 (Mon–Sat), 12.00–22.30 (Sun)*
*Food: 12.00–15.00 (Mon–Fri)*
*Credit cards: none taken*
*Draught beers: Boddingtons, Boddingtons Gold, Boston, Flowers Original, Old Speckled Hen, Whitbread Trophy, Heineken, Heineken Export, Hoegaarden, Stella Artois, Guinness, Murphy's, Merrydown*
*Wheelchair access to venue*
*Nearest tube station: Highbury & Islington*

# The Two Chairmen

39 Dartmouth Street, SW1. Tel: 0171 222 8694

Sedan chairs were the taxis of their day. They were slow and swayed a lot, and the men who carried them were often drunk, but the streets were foul and dangerous, and people threw unspeakable things from the upper windows. The chairmen picked up fares at fixed points in London, and this pub was one of them. Most of one wall in the bar is covered by a large painting showing a customer being given a bad time by two red-faced chairmen dressed in the traditional green greatcoats. Those chairmen wouldn't be allowed in the Two Chairmen nowadays, not in that state. It is a well-mannered, up-market pub in the heart of St James's, frequented almost entirely by civil servants. Quiet conversation is the thing. You get the agreeable impression that little has happened there lately, at least not since 1756 when it was rebuilt. There it is, then, a quiet, dignified pub, at ease among its government offices. The small restaurant upstairs is popular at lunchtimes. Few pubs sell more pink gins.

*Open: 11.00–23.00 (Mon–Fri)*
*Food: bar 11.00–22.30 (Mon–Fri); restaurant 12.00–15.00 (Mon–Fri)*
*Credit cards: none taken*
*Draught beers: Courage Directors, John Smith's Extra Smooth, Theakston Best, one guest ale, Foster's, Gillespies, Holsten, Kronenbourg, Strongbow*
*Wheelchair access to venue*
*Nearest tube station: St James's Park*

# The Two Chairmen

1 Warwick House Street, SW1. Tel: 0171 930 1166

It's difficult to find this pub, which is almost in Trafalgar Square. You can see the entire length of Nelson's column from one end of the little street, but the only people likely to stumble over it are those who pop into the National Lottery office to claim their millions. The Two Chairmen has been there since 1684 and is by far the oldest building in the street, but it looks very well, a narrow four-storeyed house with a cosy, panelled bar on the ground floor and an inn sign showing two sleek fellows carrying a sedan chair. Mrs Rhona Barnett, a life-long publican, signed a 20-year lease on the pub when she was 75, and there she is, at 81, with every intention of signing a new lease in 2011. She pays so much rent – £50,000 a year – and the pub is so small that it is hard to make a profit, but she says it is a pleasure to be there. Indeed it is!

*Open: 11.00–23.00 (Mon–Sat), 12.00–15.00 (Sun)*
*Food: 12.00–15.00 (Mon–Sat)*
*Credit cards: none taken*
*Draught beers: Courage Best, Courage Directors, John Smith's Extra Smooth, Old Speckled Hen, Young's Special, Foster's, Kronenbourg, Miller's, Guinness, Dry Blackthorn*
*Wheelchair access to venue*
*Nearest tube station: Charing Cross*

# Two Floors

3 Kingly Street, W1. Tel: 0171 439 1007

Give this place a chance. It takes a few minutes to get used to the feeling that you're in a bar rather than an empty shop. There is no sign outside and the spartan room – lime-green decorated walls, scruffy seats and slashed bar stool covers – can be off-putting. That isn't the point, however. This bar on two floors is for the young and alternatively trendy with a certain amount of street cred – quite good-lookers too! There are no draught beers but it stocks a decent range of bottles. Don't ask for a glass; you suck your beer from the bottle, that's the cool thing. Spirits are excellent; free-poured doubles (and they are large doubles) are served in large glasses, nicely presented with lots of ice and decent quality mixers included in the £3.50 asking price (£4 for premium brands). The downstairs bar is decorated in stripes of orange, brown and cream and has very large cushions where you can sit cross-legged, lie on your belly, or recline in the lap of another. Very laid back.

*Open: 11.00–23.00 (Mon–Sat)*
*Food: 12.00–16.00 (Mon–Sat),*
*Credit cards: none taken*
*Private room: 90 standing*
*Nearest tube station: Oxford Circus*

# dell'Ugo

56 Frith Street, W1. Tel: 0171 734 8300

This building has a huge bust outside, hanging precariously over the crowds who congregate on the pavement. The ground floor is the bar area – small, not very comfortable and not very clean the last time I was there. So stained were the glasses I had to send two consecutive ones back.

*Open: 12.00–23.00 (Mon–Sat)*
*Food: 12.00–15.00 and 17.30–midnight (Mon–Sat); restaurant 12.00–15.00 and 19.00–midnight (Mon–Sat)*
*Credit cards: all major cards*
*Wheelchair access to venue*
*Two private rooms: 8 and 16 seated*
*Nearest tube station: Tottenham Court Road*

# Vic Naylor

38–40 St John Street, EC1. Tel: 0171 608 2181

Useful after-work bar with jazz background music and live bands on a Saturday.

*Open: 12.00–midnight (Mon–Fri), 19.00–01.00 (Sat)*
*Food: 12.00–22.30 (Mon–Thurs), 11.30–midnight (Fri–Sat)*
*Credit cards: all major cards*
*Nearest tube stations: Farringdon, Barbican*

# Victoria

68 Pages Walk, SE1. Tel: 0171 237 3248

In 1972 a couple of likely lads from Bermondsey were watching the extraordinary scenes going on at this rather splendid pub. The event was the presentation of the *Evening Standard* Pub of the Year award. Brothers Pat and Mike McKenna grew up to own the lease on the Victoria, which is still proving to be a very popular venue. It has a 66-foot horseshoe-shaped bar offering a decent range of traditional ales, but what they're really famous for are the pan-fried steaks, cooked by the McKennas' aunt, available all day during the week. The Victoria normally has quiet background music, but things liven up a little at weekends, when a disco takes over until 1am. You won't have a problem getting there in a black cab – the Victoria is a point on the Knowledge.

*Open: 11.00–midnight (Mon–Thurs), 11.00–01.00 (Fri), 20.00–01.00 (Sat),*
*12.15 and 19.30–22.30 (Sun)*
*Food: 12.00–15.00 (Mon–Sun)*
*Credit cards: none taken*
*Draught beers: Navigator, Ruddles, Webster's, Carlsberg, Foster's, Holsten Pils,*
*Guinness, Strongbow*
*Nearest tube station: Elephant & Castle*

# Walkabout

11 Henrietta Street, WC2. Tel: 0171 379 5555

This is possibly the most Australian of all the Australian pubs in London. It was well known as The Outback until recently when it had to change its name, as another company had legally registered it. So the Walkabout it is now. It has plain wooden floors, stout wooden tables, squat wooden stools, and a bar counter that looks as if it was knocked together last night. There's a drinking bit, an eating bit and a huge games bar in the basement. Videos of all major sporting events back home are flown over straight after the match, and enthralled crowds watch them on big screens upstairs and down. There is live music five nights a week and cold lager all day and every day. You don't have to be an Aussie or indeed a Kiwi to drink in the Walkabout, but it helps.

*Open: 12.00–23.00 (Mon–Sat), 12.00–22.30 (Sun)*
*Food: 12.00–20.00 (Mon–Sun)*
*Credit cards: all major cards*
*Draught beers: Caffrey's, John Smith's Extra Smooth, Foster's, Kronenbourg,*
*Guinness, Dry Blackthorn*
*Wheelchair access to venue*
*Private room: 100 standing*
*Nearest tube stations: Covent Garden, Charing Cross*

# Walkabout

58 Shepherd's Bush Green, W12. Tel: 0181 740 4339

A colossal music venue on an Australasian theme has recently opened up in Shepherd's Bush, with a 20,000-watt sound system, a 32-track mixing desk, and a 200-CD computerised interchange system which could easily shatter the rafters of the bar and its close neighbours at the Shepherd's Bush Empire. If this wasn't enough, there is a 15 x 20-foot large-screen monitor (one of the biggest in the country inside a bar) showing tapes of Australasian sports flown in on an almost daily basis. Should you not be able to see the screen, which is unlikely, there are a further 24 TV monitors throughout the bar. The food is substantial enough to soak up any amount of beers. The breakfast of steak, bacon, sausage, eggs, chips, baked beans, mushrooms, tomatoes and toast (phew!) is £5.50, crocodile steak with salad and fries is £6.20, and kangaroo kebabs with salad and a fruit relish £5.75. They have a range of bottled beers, including Stein lager, Victoria bitter, Crown lager and Lion Red, which will appeal to any homesick Aussie or Kiwi. Occasionally – at weekends after 9pm and when there's a big sporting event – they levy a small cover charge of £2–£3. They tell me the sound system can be isolated in three different zones within the bar, offering a choice of music along with the DJs and live bands that play there six nights a week – I'll believe that when I hear it.

*Open: 11.00–midnight (Mon–Sat), 10.00–22.30 (Sun)*
*Food: 11.00–20.30 (Mon–Sat), 10.00–20.30 (Sun)*
*Credit cards: all major cards*
*Draught beers: Caffrey's, John Smith's Extra Smooth, Foster's, Kronenbourg, Guinness, Dry Blackthorn*
*Wheelchair access to venue and loo*
*Nearest tube station: Shepherd's Bush*

## Walmer Castle

Ledbury Road, W11. Tel: 0171 229 4620

This high-Victorian, distinctly impressive three-storey building about halfway down Ledbury Road is where the good-looking people of Notting Hill chill out. It has a bright, clean and impressive main bar, a smaller, charming little lounge at the back, and a Thai restaurant upstairs, owned and operated by the Pelican Group. You can get some of the menu downstairs: spicy chicken wings (£5.95), dim sum (£7.95) and vegetarian Thai dishes (£5.50). They have an English menu in the bar, which offers a brie and avocado baguette (£3.50) before listing more traditional English fare such as Cumberland sausage, mash and beans (£5.95), and ham, egg and chips (£4.50). The Walmer Castle is not far off being a traditional English pub but with a more modern feel to it. It buzzes at weekends.

*Open: 11.00–23.00 (Mon–Sat), 12.00–22.30 (Sun)*
*Food: bar 11.00–22.30 (Mon–Sat), 12.00–22.30 (Sun); restaurant 12.00–14.30 and 18.00–22.30 (Sun–Thurs), 18.00–23.30 (Fri–Sat)*
*Credit cards: all major cards*
*Draught beers: Abbot Ale, Boddingtons, Tetley's, Heineken, Heineken Export, Stella Artois, Guinness, Cidermaster, Dry Blackthorn*
*Wheelchair access to venue*
*Nearest tube stations: Notting Hill Gate, Westbourne Park*

## The Water Rat

1 Milmans Street, SW10. Tel: 0171 351 4732

This pub has a beautiful exterior. The white stucco, three-storey building is covered with such masses of flowers spilling from window boxes, baskets and tubs that the Royal Borough of Kensington and Chelsea gives it prizes.

Inside there is a big bar, taped music and Sky TV for major sports events. It is a free house, so real ales rule. Absolut Vodkas are big there, too, with homemade variations – Absolut Hot Chilli Pepper, Absolut Raspberry and Absolut Mars Bar, £1.30 a slam on Friday and Saturday nights. They certainly get things going. People from the nearby estates seem to love the Water Rat.

*Open: 11.00–23.00 (Mon–Sat), 12.00–22.30 (Sun)*
*Food: 12.00–14.30 (Mon–Fri)*
*Credit cards: none taken*
*Draught beers: Beamish Red, John Smith's Extra Smooth, Theakston Best, Young's Special, one guest ale, Foster's, Holsten Export, Kronenbourg, Guinness, Strongbow*
*Nearest tube station: Sloane Square*

## The Water Rats

328 Grays Inn Road, WC1. Tel: 0171 837 7269

By day The Water Rats is a conventional King's Cross local, used by unsuspecting office workers. At the stroke of eight it becomes one of the most influential venues in the music business. Formerly The Pindar of Wakefield, it was taken over by the Grand Order of Water Rats in 1985 and duly renamed. For the next six years it played host to a live version of *The Good Old Days*.

It was not the hottest ticket in town, so the management switched from music hall to indie and alternative music. King Rats withdrew to their HQ upstairs, leaving the stage to a younger generation, and the influential venue now known as the Splash Club was born. The vaudeville drapes still hang above the stage, and the chandeliers remain, giving the music room a unique appeal to platinum-selling bands like Bush, who came here fresh from 4,000-seater stadiums in the US. Young indie bands on the way up can be seen here seven nights a week. On a good night, when the buzzing atmosphere in the front bar is picked up by a band enjoying itself in the music room at the back, there is nowhere better in London for live music. Absolut vodkas are £1.30 every night.

*Open: 11.00–midnight (Mon–Fri), 20.00–midnight (Sat)*
*Food: 12.00–18.00 (Mon–Fri)*
*Credit cards: none taken*
*Draught beers: Courage Best, Courage Directors, John Smith's Extra Smooth, Foster's, Holsten Export, Kronenbourg, Guinness, Dry Blackthorn*
*Nearest tube station: King's Cross*

## The Waterside

82 York Way, N1. Tel: 0171 837 7118

In the middle of a red brick development at the back of King's Cross station is something of a pleasant surprise – a large 19th-century Hereford barn, with an oak frame, roof beams, timber and brick walls, an old black plank floor, and plain tables and benches made from leftover timber. Go through the big doors at the end and you make another welcome discovery – The Waterside is indeed on the waterside. Beyond the brick terrace covered in picnic tables is a wide spread of glossy water. This is Battlebridge Basin, a working siding for canal boats. The terrace narrows and follows the basin to its junction with the Grand Union Canal. Behind the railings, men and boys sit fishing.

The Waterside has a Berni Inns food servery in the bar and a barbecue on the terrace on sunny Sundays. It is an unexpected pub which greatly cheers a glum bit of London.

*Open: 11.00–23.00 (Mon–Sat), 12.00–22.30 (Sun)*
*Food: 12.00–14.30 and 18.00–21.00 (Mon–Fri), 12.00–14.30 and 18.00–20.00 (Sat), 12.00–19.00 (Sun)*
*Credit cards: Mastercard, Switch, Visa*
*Draught beers: Boddingtons, Flowers IPA, Marston's Pedigree, Young's Special, Heineken, Heineken Export, Stella Artois, Murphy's, Guinness, Strongbow*
*Wheelchair access to venue*
*Private room: 22 seated, 30–40 standing*
*Nearest tube station: King's Cross*

# Waxy O'Connor's

14–16 Rupert Street, W1. Tel: 0171 287 0255

The interior of this cavernous pub is an Irish Gothic fantasy, 9,000 square feet of bars, galleries, saloons and snugs, each built round the interiors of goodness knows how many Irish churches. There are carved screens, arches, finials, friezes, panels, choir stalls and pulpits. One anteroom has a confessional and a pavement of tombstones. Every space is at a different level. In one, the ceiling is so low you have to duck; in another the ceiling is two storeys high. The bleached remains of an ancient Irish beech tree soar skyward. Waxy O'Connor's was an instant success when it opened, and continues to be so. It is quieter in the afternoons, but the design is such that it never feels empty. In the evenings you often have to queue to get in. Irish music is piped through the pub all day, and Irish musicians play five nights a week. The food is Irish, the whiskey is Irish, the poteen is so Irish it is banned in Ireland. It's the most spectacular of all the Irish theme bars and the service is unpretentious yet efficient.

*Open: 11.00–23.00 (Mon–Sat), 12.00–22.30 (Sun)*
*Food: bar 12.00–18.00 (Mon–Sun); restaurant 18.00–23.00 (Mon–Sun)*
*Credit cards: all major cards*
*Draught beers: Caffrey's, Kilkenny, Carling Premier, Carlsberg Export, Foster's, Guinness, Murphy's, Dry Blackthorn*
*Private room seats 75*
*Nearest tube stations: Leicester Square, Piccadilly Circus*

# The Westbourne    EROS AWARD WINNER

101 Westbourne Park Villas, W2. Tel: 0171 221 1332

This big, good-looking pub in deepest Notting Hill is far enough away from the trend-setters to be stylish in its own right. There isn't a quiet spot in the house, so people stand, sit, eat and drink where they can, many flowing over into the delightful forecourt on a sunny day. This is one of the new generation of bistro pubs. It was created by Oliver Daniaud and Sebastian Boyle from a run-down pub located in a run-down part of town, and it opened to astonishing success in 1985, just a few weeks after its near-neighbour The Cow (qv). It has lifted the area and put it on the map as a destination rather than a place to be avoided. It's worth any number of detours to go there now.

*Open: 17.00–23.00 (Mon), 12.00–23.00 (Tues–Fri), 11.00–23.00 (Sat), 12.00–22.30 (Sun)*
*Food: 19.00–22.15 (Mon), 13.00–15.30 and 19.00–22.15 (Tues–Sat), 19.00–21.30 (Sun)*
*Credit cards: all major cards except AmEx*
*Draught beers: Kilkenny, Dortmunder Union, Heineken, Kronenbourg, Leffe Blonde, Stella Artois, Guinness*
*Wheelchair access to venue*
*Nearest tube stations: Notting Hill Gate, Royal Oak*

# The Westminster Arms

9 Storey's Gate, SW1. Tel: 0171 222 8520

Until the new Queen Elizabeth Conference Centre was built, The Westminster Arms had a clear view of Big Ben and Westminster Abbey. Now what it sees is the side of the conference centre – not a good swap. On the other hand, it gets wave after wave of custom from the new building. In fact, it is extraordinarily busy most of the time. MPs can find safety here in numbers, and reassurance from the division bell in the bar.

The main bar, crowded most of the day, looks much as it did when the pub was rebuilt in 1913. The cellar bar was thoroughly done over in the modern manner recently, and looks a great deal older. It is now back in the 1850s, with a flagstone floor, drinking booths round the walls, old panelling, benches and wooden tables. There is a pleasant restaurant upstairs, a wine bar downstairs, and tables and chairs on the pavement outside. The Westminster Arms is a free house and has seven real ales on the hand pumps. A pint of Westminster Best, the one the pub has specially brewed, is £1.75.

*Open: 11.00–23.00 (Mon–Sat), 12.00–18.00 (Sun)*
*Food: bar 12.00–21.30 (Mon–Fri), 11.00–17.00 (Sat), 12.00–17.00 (Sun); restaurant 12.00–14.30 (Mon–Fri)*
*Credit cards: AmEx, Mastercard, Visa*
*Draught beers: Abbot Ale, Bass, Brakspear PA, Brakspear Special, Caffrey's, Theakston XB, Wadworth 6X, Westminster Bitter, Young's, Carling Premier, Foster's, Stella Artois, Tennent's Pilsner, Guinness, Dry Blackthorn, Strongbow*
*Wheelchair access to venue*
*Private room seats 40*
*Nearest tube station: Westminster, St James's Park*

# J. D. Wetherspoon

Disillusioned with London pubs, Tim Martin founded the Wetherspoon chain in 1979. His first pub was in Muswell Hill, and it created the blueprint for all Wetherspoons to come. They are rarely pub conversions; you are more likely to find that in a previous existence the place was a car showroom, a bank, a cinema or even a supermarket. Martin, a New Zealander, borrowed the name Wetherspoon from his former, slightly nutty schoolteacher; the J. D. was added for a certain amount of kudos. Moons appear in many of the names – The Moon under Water (qv), JJ Moons and the Moon and Sixpence (qv). The first of these comes from a short story by George Orwell, who described his perfect pub as a place where he could have a quiet pint with good conversation. Orwell named this fictitious pub The Moon under Water. The other names tend to recognise local history or the previous use of the building, so Bankers Drafts were formerly banks, The Gatehouse (qv) is in Highgate, and 179 Upper Street is, well, at 179 Upper Street, of course. There is a strict rule throughout Wetherspoon's pubs: no music of any kind. Even the sound of the gaming machines is muted, and there is no darts, pool or pinball. Each pub stocks several real ales, including Fuller's London Pride – clearly a selling point. Wetherspoons are also air conditioned, with big no-smoking areas and cut-price beer. Food is served all day and, although hardly Marco Pierre-White, the menu includes substantial dishes at extraordinarily reasonable prices: oven-baked potatoes with a variety of fillings (from £2.75), hot or cold baguettes (from £1.95), burgers and chips (from £2.95), and a Sunday roast at £4.45.

*Branches at:*

**Acton**: Red Lion and Pineapple, 281 High Street, W3. Tel: 0181 896 2248. Nearest tube station: Acton Town

**Anerley**: Moon and Stars, 164–166 High Street, SE20. Tel: 0181 776 5680. Nearest railway station: Penge East

**Balham**: The Moon under Water, 194 Balham High Street, SW12. Tel: 0181 673 0535. Nearest tube station: Balham

**Barking**: Barking Dog, 61 Station Parade, IG11. Tel: 0181 507 9109. Nearest tube station: Barking

**Barkingside**: New Fairlop Oak, Fencepiece Road, IG11. Tel: 0181 500 2217. Nearest railway station: Fairlop

**Barnet**: The Moon under Water, 148 High Street, EN5. Tel: 0181 441 9476. Nearest tube station: High Barnet

**Bethnal Green**: Camden's Head, 456 Bethnal Green Road, E2. Tel: 0171 613 4263. Nearest tube station: Bethnal Green

**Bexley Heath**: Wrong 'Un, 234–236 The Broadway, DA6. Tel: 0181 298 0439. Nearest railway station: Bexley Heath

**Borehamwood**: Hart and Spool, 148 Shenley Road, WD6. Tel: 0181 953 1883. Nearest railway stations: Elstree, Borehamwood

**Brixton**: Crown and Sceptre, 2a Streatham Hill, SW2. Tel: 0181 671 0843. Nearest tube station: Brixton

**Camberwell**: Fox on the Hill, 149 Denmark Hill, SE5. Tel: 0171 738 4756. Nearest railway station: Denmark Hill

**Camden**: Man in the Moon, 40–42 Chalk Farm Road, NW1. Tel: 0171 482 2054. Nearest tube station: Chalk Farm

**Catford**: Tiger's Head, 350 Bromley Road, SE6. Tel: 0181 698 8645. Nearest railway station: Catford

**Chingford**: King's Ford, 250–252 Chingford Mount Road, E4. Tel: 0181 523 9365. Nearest railway station: Chingford

**Chiswick**: JJ Moon's, 80–82 Chiswick High Road, W4. Tel: 0181 742 7263. Nearest tube station: Stamford Brook

**City**: Hamilton Hall, Liverpool Street Station, EC2. Tel: 0171 247 3579. Nearest tube station: Liverpool Street

**City**: Masque Haunt, 168–172 Old Street, EC2. Tel: 0171 251 4195. Nearest tube station: Old Street

**City**: Sir John Oldcastle, 29–35 Farringdon Road, EC1. Tel: 0171 242 1013. Nearest tube station: Farringdon

**Cricklewood**: Beaten Docket, 50–56 Cricklewood Broadway, NW2. Tel: 0181 450 2972. Nearest tube station: Kilburn

**Croydon**: George, 17–21 George Street, CR0. Tel: 0181 649 9077. Nearest railway station: East Croydon

**Crystal Palace**: Postal Order, 33 Westow Street, SW19. Tel: 0181 771 3003. Nearest railway station: Crystal Palace

**Dagenham**: Lord Denman, 270–272 Heathway, RM10. Tel: 0181 984 8590. Nearest tube station: Dagenham Heathway

**Dartford**: Paper Moon, 55 High Street, DA1. Tel: 01322 281127. Nearest railway station: Dartford

**East Ham**: Millers Well, 419–421 Barking Road, E6. Tel: 0181 471 8404. Nearest tube station: East Ham

**Edgware**: Blacking Bottle, 122–126 High Street, HA8. Tel: 0181 381 1485. Nearest tube station: Edgware

**Edmonton**: Lamb, 52–54 Church Street, N9. Tel: 0181 887 0128. Nearest railway station: Edmonton Green

**Eltham**: Bankers Draft, 80 High Street, SE9. Tel: 0181 294 2578. Nearest railway station: Eltham

**Enfield**: The Moon under Water, 116–117 Chaseside, EN2. Tel: 0181 366 9855. Nearest railway station: Enfield Chase

**Feltham**: Moon on the Square, Unit 30 The Centre, Wilton Road, TW13. Tel: 0181 893 1293. Nearest railway station: Feltham

**Finchley**: Tally Ho, 749 High Road, N12. Tel: 0181 445 4390. Nearest tube station: Finchley Central

**Finsbury Park**: Old Suffolk Punch, 10–12 Grand Parade, N4. Tel: 0181 800 5912. Nearest tube station: Manor House

**Finsbury Park**: White Lion of Mortimer, 125–127 Stroud Green Road, N4. Tel: 0171 281 4773. Nearest tube station: Finsbury Park

**Forest Hill**: Bird in Hand, 35 Dartmouth Road, SE23. Tel: 0181 699 7417. Nearest railway station: Forest Hill

**Hampstead**: Three Horseshoes, 28 Heath Street, NW3. Tel: 0171 431 7206. Nearest tube station: Hampstead

**Harrow**: JJ Moon's, 20 The Broadwalk, Pinner Road, HA2. Tel: 0181 424 9686. Nearest tube station: North Harrow

**Harrow**: JJ Moon's, 3 Shaftesbury Parade, Shaftesbury Circle, HA2. Tel: 0181 423 5056. Nearest tube station: South Harrow

**Harrow**: Moon on the Hill, 373–375 Station Road, HA1. Tel: 0181 863 3670. Nearest tube station: Harrow-on-the-Hill

**Harrow**: New Moon, 25–26 Kenton Park Parade, Kenton Road, HA3. Tel: 0181 909 1109. Nearest tube station: Harrow-on-the-Hill

**Hayes**: The Moon under Water, 10–11 Broadwater Parade, Coldharbour Lane, UB3. Tel: 0181 813 6774. Nearest railway station: Hayes & Harlington

**Hayes End**: Moon and Sixpence, 1250–1256 Uxbridge Road, UB8. Tel: 0181 561 3541. Nearest railway station: Hayes & Harlington

**Heathrow Airport**: JJ Moon's, Terminal 4 Airside, Heathrow Airport, TW6. Tel: 0181 759 0355. Nearest tube station: Heathrow (Terminal 4)

**Heathrow Airport**: Wetherspoon's, Terminal 4 Landside, Heathrow Airport, TW6. Tel: 0181 759 2906. Nearest tube station: Heathrow (Terminal 4)

**Highgate**: Gatehouse, 1 North Hill, N6. Tel: 0181 340 8054. Nearest tube station: Highgate

**Holloway**: Coronet, 338–346 Holloway Road, N7. Tel: 0171 609 5014. Nearest tube station: Holloway Road

**Hornchurch**: JJ Moon's, 46–62 High Street, RM12. Tel: 01708 478 410. Nearest tube station: Hornchurch

**Hornsey**: Elbow Room, 22 Topsfield Parade, N8. Tel: 0181 340 3677. Nearest tube station: Turnpike Lane

**Hornsey**: Tollgate, 26–30 Turnpike Lane, N8. Tel: 0181 889 9085. Nearest tube station: Turnpike Lane

**Hounslow**: The Moon under Water, 84–86 Staines Road, TW3. Tel: 0181 572 7506. Nearest tube station: Hounslow Central

**Ilford**: Great Spoon of Ilford, 114–116 Cranbrook Road, IG1. Tel: 0181 518 0535. Nearest railway station: Ilford

**Islington**: 179 Upper Street, N1. Tel: 0171 226 6276. Nearest tube station: Highbury & Islington

**Kingsbury**: JJ Moon's, 553 Kingsbury Road, NW9. Tel: 0181 204 9675. Nearest tube station: Kingsbury

**Kingsbury**: The Moon under Water, 10 Varley Parade, NW9. Tel: 0181 200 7611. Nearest tube station: Colindale

**Leyton**: Drum, 557–559 Lea Bridge Road, E10. Tel: 0181 539 6577. Nearest tube station: Leyton

**Loughton**: Last Post, 227 High Street, IG10. Tel: 0181 532 0751. Nearest tube station: Loughton

**Mitcham**: White Lion of Mortimer, 223 London Road, CR4. Tel: 0181 646 7332. Nearest railway station: Tooting Junction

**Morden**: Wetherspoon's, 33 Aberconway Road, SM4. Tel: 0181 540 2818. Nearest tube station: Morden

**New Barnet**: Railway Bell, 13 East Barnet Road, EN4. Tel: 0181 449 1369. Nearest railway station: New Barnet

**North Cheam**: Wetherspoon's, 552–556 London Road, SM3. Tel: 0181 644 1808. Nearest railway station: Cheam Village

**Northwood**: Sylvan Moon, 27 Green Lane, HA6. Tel: 01923 820760. Nearest tube station: Northwood

**Orpington**: Harvest Moon, 141 High Street, BR6. Tel: 01689 876931. Nearest railway station: Orpington

**Palmers Green**: Whole Hog, 430–434 Green Lanes, N13. Tel: 0181 882 3597. Nearest railway station: Palmers Green

**Petts Wood**: Sovereign of the Seas, 109–111 Queensway, BR5. Tel: 01689 891606. Nearest railway station: Petts Wood

**Pinner**: Moon and Sixpence, 250 Uxbridge Road, HA5. Tel: 0181 420 1074. Nearest railway station: Hatch End

**Pinner**: Village Inn, 402–408 Rayners Lane, HA5. Tel: 0181 868 8551. Nearest railway station: Rayners Lane

**Purley**: Foxley Hatch, 8–9 Russell Hill Road, CR8. Tel: 0181 763 9307. Nearest railway station: Purley

**Putney**: Railway, 202 Upper Richmond Road, SW15. Tel: 0181 788 8190. Nearest railway station: Putney

**Romford**: Moon and Stars, 99–103 South Street, RM1. Tel: 01708 730117. Nearest railway station: Romford

**Ruislip Manor**: JJ Moon's, 12 Victoria Road, HA4. Tel: 01895 622373. Nearest tube station: Ruislip Manor

**Shepherd's Bush**: Moon on the Green, 172–174 Uxbridge Road, W12. Tel: 0181 749 5709. Nearest tube station: Shepherd's Bush

**Soho**: Moon and Sixpence, 183 Wardour Street, W1. Tel: 0171 734 0037. Nearest tube station: Tottenham Court Road

**Southfields**: Grid Inn, 22 Replingham Road, SW18. Tel: 0181 874 8460. Nearest tube station: Southfields

**Southgate**: Bankers Draft, 36–38 Friern Barnet Road, N11. Tel: 0181 361 7115. Nearest tube station: Arnos Grove

**Southgate**: New Crown, 80–84 Chase Side, N14. Tel: 0181 882 8758. Nearest tube station: Southgate

**Staines**: George, 2–8 High Street, TW18. Tel: 01784 462181. Nearest railway station: Staines

**Stanmore**: Man in the Moon, 1 Buckingham Parade, HA7. Tel: 0181 954 6119. Nearest tube station: Stanmore

**Stockwell**: Beehive, 407–409 Brixton Road, SW9. Tel: 0171 738 3643. Nearest tube station: Brixton

**Stoke Newington**: Rochester Castle, 145 High Street, N16. Tel: 0171 249 6016. Nearest railway station: Stoke Newington

**Stratford**: Golden Grove, 146–148 The Grove, E15. Tel: 0181 519 0750. Nearest tube station: Stratford

**Streatham**: The Moon under Water, 1327 London Road, SW16. Tel: 0181 765 1235. Nearest railway station: Norbury

**Sutton**: Moon on the Hill, 5–9 Hill Road, SM1. Tel: 0181 643 1202. Nearest railway station: Sutton

**Tooting**: JJ Moon's, 56a High Street, SW17. Tel: 0181 672 4726. Nearest tube station: Tooting Broadway

**Tottenham**: Elbow Room, 503–505 High Road, N17. Tel: 0181 801 8769. Nearest railway station: Tottenham Hill

**Tottenham**: New Moon, 413 Lordship Lane, N17. Tel: 0181 801 3496. Nearest tube station: Wood Green

**Twickenham**: The Moon under Water, 53–57 London Road, TW1. Tel: 0181 744 0080. Nearest railway station: Twickenham

**Upper Holloway**: Dog, 17–19 Archway Road, N19. Tel: 0171 263 0429. Nearest tube station: Archway

**Uxbridge**: Good Yarn, 132 High Street, UB8. Tel: 01895 239852. Nearest tube station: Uxbridge

**Victoria**: Wetherspoon's, Victoria Station, SW1. Tel: 0171 931 0445. Nearest tube station: Victoria

**Wallington**: Whispering Moon, 25 Ross Parade, Woodcote Road, SM6. Tel: 0181 647 7020. Nearest railway station: Wallington

**Walton-on-Thames**: Regent, 19 Church Street, KT12. Tel: 01932 243980. Nearest railway station: Walton-on-Thames

**Wandsworth**: Spotted Dog, 72 Garratt Lane, SW18. Tel: 0181 875 9531. Nearest railway station: Wandsworth Town

**Wanstead**: George, High Street, E11. Tel: 0181 989 2921. Nearest tube station: Wanstead

**Watford**: The Moon under Water, 44 High Street, WD1. Tel: 01923 223559. Nearest railway station: Watford High Street

**Wealdstone**: Sarsen Stone, 32 High Street, HA3. Tel: 0181 863 8533. Nearest tube station: Harrow and Wealdstone

**Wembley**: JJ Moon's, 397 High Road, HA9. Tel: 0181 903 4923. Nearest tube station: Wembley Central

**West End**: The Moon under Water, 105–107 Charing Cross Road, WC1. Tel: 0171 287 6039. Nearest tube station: Leicester Square

**West End**: The Moon under Water, 28 Leicester Square, WC2. Tel: 0171 839 2837. Nearest tube station: Leicester Square

**West Hendon**: White Lion of Mortimer, 3 York Parade, NW9. Tel: 0181 202 8887. Nearest railway station: Hendon

**Whitehall**: Lord Moon of the Mall, 16–18 Whitehall, SW1. Tel: 0171 839 7701. Nearest tube station: Charing Cross

**Willesden**: Coliseum, Manor Park Road, NW10. Tel: 0181 961 6570. Nearest tube station: Willesden Junction

**Willesden**: Outside Inn, 312–314 Neasden Lane, NW10. Tel: 0181 452 3140. Nearest tube station: Neasden

**Wimbledon**: Wibbas Down Inn, 6–12 Gladstone Road, SW19. Tel: 0181 540 6788. Nearest tube station: South Wimbledon

**Winchmore Hill**: Half Moon, 749 Green Lanes, N21. Tel: 0181 360 5410. Nearest railway station: Winchmore Hill

# Wetherspoon's

Victoria Station, SW1. Tel: 0171 931 0445

This is a pub built in the nineties in the style of the nineties. It is light, leafy and minimalist. There is a remarkably lifelike hologram of Queen Victoria outside it. She liked trains, though possibly not pubs.

The pub is in the middle of Victoria station on the first floor of a new building it shares with W. H. Smith. It has its own short escalators to take you up and bring you down again, and if you don't like escalators there's a lift. It has a terrace on both sides. From one side you look down on the South Central concourse and get a full view of the departure board, and from the other you can look down on platforms 6, 5, 4 and 3 and watch your train leaving without you. An unexpectedly quiet and civilised spot in this hectic place.

*Open: 11.00–23.00 (Mon–Sat), 12.00–22.30 (Sun)*
*Food: 11.00–22.00 (Mon–Sat), 12.00–21.30 (Sun)*
*Credit cards: Delta, Mastercard, Switch, Visa*
*Draught beers: Beck's, Courage Directors, Theakston Best, Younger's Scotch Bitter, Guinness, Dry Blackthorn*
*Wheelchair access to venue and loo*
*Nearest tube station: Victoria*

# The White Cross     EROS AWARD WINNER

Water Lane, Richmond, TW9. Tel: 0181 940 6844

They don't call it Water Lane for nothing. The Thames regularly creeps up to the doorway of this riverside pub in Richmond, flooding the lane outside. The floodgates on the cellar flaps and the tidal valves in the drains prevent the pub's cellar from flooding so long as the staff remember to activate them. 'We've had some pretty close shaves,' says the manager, Quentin Thwaites, 'but our neighbour, Bamber Gascoigne, provides us with a set of tide tables every year, and we have to monitor them quite closely.' The pub itself is up a flight of stairs so it always remains dry, and it has stayed virtually unchanged since it was built in 1835. The saloon bar has a fireplace under the window, which makes everyone wonder where the chimney is. Upstairs is a particularly splendid bar with the tiniest of balconies commanding a spectacular view of the garden and the river. Snacks include jumbo sausage with crusty bread (£2.60) and Cornish or cheese and onion pasty with baked beans (£2.75). Sunday roasts have proved very popular at £6.25. A delightful, deeply traditional pub.

*Open: 11.00–23.00 (Mon–Sat) 12.00– 22.30 (Sun)*
*Food: 12.00–15.00 (Mon–Sun); snacks available till 19.00*
*Draught beers: Ramrod Smooth, Young's Bitter, Young's Special, Young's Wheatbeer, Castlemaine, London Lager, Premium Lager, Stella Artois, Guinness, Oatmeal Stout, Dry Blackthorn*
*Credit cards: Mastercard, Visa*
*Nearest tube station: Richmond*

# The White Horse

1 Parson's Green, SW6. Tel: 0171 736 2115

The White Horse should get a mention in any book, article or conversation relating to pubs. It is an extrovert, cheerful place with a distinctly Sloaney clientele. It is known locally as the Sloaney Pony. It has a big, comfortable, U-shaped bar, leather sofas, eating booths, a patio at the front overlooking Parson's Green, and a very efficient troupe of bar staff.

The White Horse is expertly run by Rupert Reeves and Mark Dorber, the latter still leading his double life, by day successful City analyst, by night White Horse cellarman. The food is to be taken seriously – it gets better all the time and is now among the best in London's pubs and bars. A lot goes on at The White Horse. Big beer festivals have spread its reputation far beyond London, and its cellars are remarkable. It claims to be the only place in the world to offer all fifteen Trappist brewed beers, houses many European lagers and has up to a hundred wines on its wine list. It should almost go without saying that it is an *Evening Standard* Pub of the Year.

*Open: 11.00–23.00 (Mon–Sat), 12.00–22.30 (Sun)*
*Food: 11.00–15.00 and 18.00–22.00 (Mon–Fri), 11.00–22.00 (Sat–Sun)*
*Credit cards: all major cards*
*Draught beers: Adnams Extra, Bass, Harvey's Sussex, Highgate Mild, Carling Black Label, Grolsch, Staropramen, Guinness, Strongbow*
*Wheelchair access to venue*
*Private room: 60 seated, 120 standing*
*Nearest tube station: Parson's Green*

# The White Swan

Old Palace Lane, Richmond, TW9. Tel: 0181 940 0959

The White Swan, painted white like the cottages in the lane that leads down to it, draws you inside on a cold day, with its fires, dark panelling, low ceilings and old settles. It could hardly be more picturesque. It has a small conservatory, a flagged garden with picnic tables, and it doesn't go in for music and the usual pub noises. The noise is on the outside – trains thunder by and planes roar overhead. Despite this, it's still a delightful pub.

*Open: 11.00–15.00 and 17.30–23.00 (Mon–Fri), 11.00–23.00 (Sat), 12.00–22.30 (Sun)*
*Food: 12.00–14.30 (Mon), 12.00–14.30 and 18.00–22.00 (Tues–Sun)*
*Credit cards: none taken*
*Draught beers: Courage Best, Courage Directors, John Smith's Extra Smooth, one guest ale, Foster's, Kronenbourg, Guinness, Dry Blackthorn*
*Wheelchair access to venue*
*Private room: 35 seated, 50 standing*
*Nearest tube station: Richmond*

# The White Swan

The Riverside, Twickenham, TW1. Tel: 0181 892 2166

The White Swan has been sitting on the riverside since 1690. Outside it has terraces and balconies, crooked windows, hanging baskets and troughs of flowers; inside it's all old wood and real ale. Bizarre collections cover the walls but the star exhibits are in the rugby room at the back – pictures of scrums and celebrated tries, shirts of the great and ties of the famous, autographed oval balls, and Paul Ackford's shorts. Rugger men are trenchermen, and food is important at The White Swan. At lunchtimes a buffet is laid out on a huge table with a great ham cooked on the premises. On summer evenings and Sunday lunchtimes landlord Steve Roy mans the barbecue, and in the winter he cooks a corking Sunday lunch.

The best table is the triclinium. A triclinium, explains Steve, is a room with three walls, the fourth being open, or a table that has seats on three sides. The

one in the main bar of The White Swan, with its view of the river and the terraces, is an excellent example of both. After brave resistance, a TV set has now
been allowed into the bar of the pub. For the rugby, of course. For other kinds
of football the sound doesn't seem to work.

*Open: 11.00–23.00 (Mon–Sat), 12.00–22.30 (Sun)*
*Food: 12.00–15.00 and 19.00–21.00 (Mon–Fri), 12.00 and 15.00 (Sat–Sun)*
*Credit cards: Mastercard, Visa*
*Draught beers: Courage Best, Marston's Pedigree, Theakston XB, Wadworth 6X,*
*Webster's Yorkshire Bitter, Budweiser, Carlsberg, Foster's, Holsten, Guinness,*
*Scrumpy Jack, Strongbow*
*Private room: 20–30 seated*
*Nearest railway station: Twickenham*

## The White Swan

555 Commercial Road, E14. Tel: 0171 780 9870

They may well mount one of London's blue plaques on the exterior of this popular gay venue. It could read: 'On this site, in August 1995, Michael Barrymore
came out.'

*Open: 21.00–02.00 (Mon–Thurs), 21.00–03.00 (Fri–Sat), 17.30–01.00 (Sun)*
*Draught beers: Courage Best, Carlsberg, Foster's, Holsten, Kronenbourg, Guin-*
*ness, Dry Blackthorn*
*Wheelchair access to venue*
*Nearest tube station: Aldgate East*
*Nearest railway station: Limehouse (DLR)*

## Williamson's Tavern

1 Groveland Court, EC4 (Off Bow Lane). Tel: 0171 248 6280

This pub is in the exact centre of the City of London's square mile. A stone in
what was the parlour marks the spot. It started off as a grand private house, so
grand that it was the official residence of successive Lord Mayors. In 1739
Robert Williamson converted it into an hotel.

The Williamson's is now a distinctly superior pub, with a library, two fine
panelled bars and the general air of a gentlemen's club. It is very popular with
City gents and City women, who like its unpubby atmosphere. Between them
they fill all three big bars at lunchtime. There is a charcoal grill in one of these,
and some say its steak sandwiches are the best in London. The pub is very
peaceful in the afternoon, when everyone goes back to work. Then it wakes up
again as people look in for a snifter on their way home. It closes at about 9pm
as most city pubs do. Like most city pubs, too, it stays closed at weekends.

*Open: 11.30–21.00 (Mon–Fri)*
*Food: 11.30–14.45 (Mon–Fri)*
*Credit cards: all major cards*
*Draught beers: Adnams, Brakspear, Calder's Cream Ale, Eldridge Pope, Marston's*
*Pedigree, Tetley's, Carlsberg, Castlemaine, Guinness*
*Two private rooms: 80–200 standing*
*Nearest tube station: Mansion House*

## The Windmill on the Common

Clapham Common Southside, SW4. Tel: 0181 673 4578

The Windmill is in terrific form. It has a big, wandering bar with tropical fish in
tanks, a spacious conservatory for non-smokers, an excellent restaurant, and
an adjoining hotel that gets three stars and a rosette from the AA and a highly
commended from the English Tourist Board. Things are always going on at The
Windmill – live music, fiesta nights, opera in the conservatory. In the summer,
drinkers spill out onto the Common, and in the winter there's an open fire in the
bar. There are cask ales, draught lagers and a plentiful wine list – six reds, eight
whites, two rosés and three champagnes. The head chef of the attached

restaurant does the bar food. The Windmill gets packed in the evenings and at weekends, and no wonder.

*Open: 11.00–23.00 (Mon–Sat), 12.00–22.30 (Sun)*
*Food: 12.00–14.30 and 19.00–22.00 (Mon–Sat), 12.00–15.00 and 19.00–21.00 (Sun)*
*Credit cards: all major cards*
*Draught beers: Young's Bitter, Young's Special, Young's seasonal ale, London Lager, Young's Premium, Guinness, Scrumpy Jack*
*Wheelchair access to venue and loo*
*Two private rooms: 28–45 seated, 35–65 standing*
*Nearest tube station: Clapham Common*

## Windows on the World

London Hilton, 22 Park Lane, W1. Tel: 0171 493 8000

Twenty-eight floors above Park Lane you will find what has to be one of the most fabulous views of London from any public observatory. Included in the view is the back garden of Buckingham Palace, which apparently makes the Queen so furious that she has refused to enter the place since it opened back in 1963. You can come here for breakfast, but the night-time views are the best, and it's a great place to take a date and hope to impress. If the date isn't going that well, just look over their shoulder at the view – it will bring a childish thrill to even the most hardened cynic. The novelty value of this bar dies hard and it's always a surprise to find it so under-used.

*Open: 12.00–15.00 and 17.30–02.00 (Mon–Sun)*
*Food: as opening hours*
*Credit cards: all major cards*
*Nearest tube station: Hyde Park Corner*

## The Windsor Castle

114 Campden Hill Road, W8. Tel: 0171 727 8491

The Windsor Castle is part of the Eton drinking round, one of a handful of London pubs where Old Etonians meet, and is one of the most up-market pubs in London. It gets extraordinarily busy. The garden is open all year long, and in the summer the capacity of the pub trebles. The Windsor Castle's kitchen has a high reputation. There is a roster of cooks producing pesto salad, vegetable couscous and such, and from Monday to Saturday there's food all day. On Sundays you can have a traditional roast lunch or just snack on the sausages and mustard, and there is a no-smoking section in the Campden bar at lunchtimes. A remarkable story is told about The Windsor Castle. When Tom Paine, author of *The Rights of Man*, died in America in 1809, the journalist and social reformer William Cobbett had his bones shipped back to England. Cobbett himself died before he could put up his planned memorial to Paine, and left the bones to his son, who, years later, traded them to the landlord of The Windsor Castle to settle a beer debt. They were then lodged in one of the cellars, which was subsequently filled in.

*Open: 12.00–20.30 (Mon–Sat), 12.00–22.30 (Sun)*
*Food: 12.00–22.45 (Mon–Sat), 12.00–22.15 (Sun)*
*Credit cards: all major cards*
*Draught beers: Bass, Caffrey's, London Pride, one guest ale, Carling Black Label, Staropramen, Guinness, Red Rock*
*Wheelchair access to venue*
*Nearest tube station: Notting Hill Gate*

# The Woodman

60 Battersea High Street, SW11. Tel: 0171 229 2968

There is in Battersea High Street a little country pub called The Woodman. It is at number 60. A few doors along, at number 44, is another little country pub. It is called The Original Woodman. This Woodman is the pretty one, with a cottage frontage and hanging baskets, and it is much the bigger. First comes a public bar with a sawdust floor, full of real ale and character. Behind it is a saloon bar with a carpet and traditional games – bar billiards, table football, shove-ha'penny. Then comes a much newer bit with a modern food counter, and beyond that is a pleasant paved garden with a large pull-out awning. It is an interesting, lively pub. Its regulars send it postcards when they go on their hols; there is a pub football team; empty champagne bottles commemorate marriages and births; and local horses go there for carrots and Guinness every Christmas morning.

*Open: 11.00–23.00 (Mon–Sat), 12.00–22.30 (Sun)*
*Food: 12.00–22.00 (Mon–Sat), 12.00–21.30 (Sun)*
*Credit cards: Mastercard, Switch, Visa*
*Draught beers: Badger Best, Blackadder, Dempsey's, Dorset IPA, Gribble Best, Reggie's Tipple, Tanglefoot, Hofbrau Export, Hofbrau Pils, Hofbrau Premium, Guinness, Taunton Somerset*
*Wheelchair access to venue*
*Nearest railway station: Clapham Junction*

# World's End

174 Camden High Road, NW1. Tel: 0171 482 1932

The lively and thirsty young customers of World's End are prodigious drinkers of lager; they have helped this pub achieve its record of selling more beer than any other pub in the country. A million pints a year certainly takes some getting through, but then, this is a huge pub with an atrium tagged on at the back and a big mezzanine gallery.

There's hardly any furniture. Furniture takes up valuable standing-around and milling-about space. Down below there's the famous Underworld – usually packed – with live bands (some of them very big). Five nights a week at 11pm, one of five different clubs takes over, each with its own style and audience. The Underworld is now considered one of London's top ten venues, and consequently, the World's End is under siege as the weekend approaches, with doormen highly visible at all three doors.

*Open: pub 11.00–23.00 (Mon–Sat), 12.00–22.30 (Sun); club 19.30–22.30 and 23.00–03.00 (Mon and Wed–Sat)*
*Food: 12.00–15.00 (Mon–Fri), 12.00–18.00 (Sat–Sun)*
*Credit cards: none taken*
*Draught beers: Bass, Boddingtons, Caffrey's, Courage Best, Courage Directors, John Smith's Extra Smooth, Kilkenny, Ruddles, Tetley's, Webster's, Carlsberg Pilsner, Carling Black Label, Carlsberg Export, Foster's, Holsten, Lowenbrau, Guinness, Dry Blackthorn*
*Nearest tube station: Camden Town*

# The World's End

459 King's Road, SW10. Tel: 0171 376 8946

The World's End is a bus terminus, a garden centre, a council estate, a district and, of course, the pub that gave them all its name. When The World's End was built in 1890 it was called the World's End Distillery, a name which still appears on the oldest of the surviving windows, suggesting the downward path to Gin Lane. It has had many ups and downs since then, and many owners too, some of whom soon decided that this was indeed the world's end. A couple of years ago it became a Harvey Floorbangers but it was soon taken on by Badger Inns and got its historic name back. For many years now it has had one big bar with an island counter, leaving lots of room for the pinball machine, the table football and the gaming machines. Fresh sawdust is strewn across the floor every day, just as it's always been. Youngsters on their way to clubs in Chelsea and Fulham meet here for a drink, and the music is pumped up late in the evening to get them in the mood. You can get burgers and chips all day.

*Open: 11.00–23.00 (Mon–Sat), 12.00–22.30 (Sun)*
*Food: 12.00–15.00 (Mon–Sun)*
*Credit cards: AmEx, Mastercard, Visa*
*Draught beers: Badger, Dempsey's, Dorset IPA, Tanglefoot, Kronenbourg, Guinness, Dry Blackthorn*
*Wheelchair access to venue*
*Private room seats 30*
*Nearest tube stations: Sloane Square, Earls Court*

## The Yard

57 Rupert Street, W1. Tel: 0171 437 2652

A doorway in Rupert Street leads into a courtyard fronting this two-storey gay bar. The downstairs bar has a café feel to it – doors opening out onto the courtyard, a scattering of tables and chairs, and people hanging around reading newspapers. Go through the courtyard, up a staircase, and you find a platform where you can lean and keep your eye on who you want to keep your eye on down below. The bar upstairs is more relaxed, with comfortable chairs and armchairs and even more hanging-around space. Unlike some gay venues, The Yard doesn't have a 'heavy' atmosphere, which is probably down to the clientele, who seem to be mainly suits after work. Stick to beers, the wine is unmentionable.

*Open: 12.00–23.00 (Mon–Sat)*
*Food: 12.00–17.00 (Mon–Sat)*
*Credit cards: all major cards (over £10 only)*
*Wheelchair access to venue*
*Private room: 100 standing*
*Nearest tube station: Piccadilly Circus*

## Yates's Wine Lodge

Mattock Lane, Ealing Green, W5. Tel: 0181 840 0988

Yates's have come a long way since opening their first branch in Oldham in 1884. Gone are the old spit-and-sawdust rough boozers often found near railway stations. In has come a new style of venue. Unfortunately, its progress seems to have got stuck somewhere in the seventies. The Ealing Yates's has a rather pleasant courtyard outside, filled with tables and parasols, which on a summer's day looks very inviting. Inside the two-level bar is a riot of contrasting colours and designs. The cluttered bar back is so busy with signs, promotions, drinks and gimmicks that it's difficult to know what you're looking at. I suspect the designers were given the brief of transforming the place beyond recognition, and have gone crazy, filling every available space with jokey notices and *objet crap*. The last notice you see as you leave reads 'Mind how you go'. If I were the signwriter, it'd say, 'Mind you don't come back'.

*Open: 11.00–23.00 (Mon–Sat), 12.00–22.30 (Sun)*
*Food: 12.00–18.00 (Sun–Thurs), 12.00–17.00 (Fri–Sat)*
*Credit cards: all major cards*

*Draught beers: Bass, John Smith's Smooth, Budweiser, Carling Black Label, Carling Premier, Foster's, Kronenbourg, Beamish, Dry Blackthorn, Woodpecker*
*Wheelchair access to venue and loo*
*Nearest tube station: Ealing Broadway*

*Branches at:*

**Croydon**: 3–11 High Street, CR0. Tel: 0181 681 8219. Nearest railway stations: East Croydon and West Croydon
**Harrow**: 269–271 Station Road, HA1. Tel: 0181 863 9470. Nearest tube station: Harrow-on-the-Hill
**Hounslow**: 1–3 Bath Road, TW3. Tel: 0181 570 0091. Nearest tube station: Hounslow Central
**Lewisham**: 67–71 High Street, SE13. Tel: 0181 318 6192. Nearest railway station: Lewisham

# Zd

289 Kilburn High Road, NW6. Tel: 0171 372 2544

The designer frontage of plate glass, wood pillars and copper-clad entrance entices you into this air-conditioned, night-time dance venue. It's part of the Mean Fiddler organisation so you can be sure there's always something going on. Magic Monday is indie, pop, dance and trance. Tuesday's Heatwave is soul, funk and hip-hop. Wednesday and Thursday's Hot Tub is for DJ promo, soul and big house anthems. Friday goes Supersonic, with DJs Danny and Jon playing an eclectic mix of Brit-pop, funk and a 'Pop 'n' Punk' fusion. Saturday sees Climax with DJ L-Tel, featuring vocal and underground garage. On Sunday, All Things End With A Zed, and there's soul, R & B, funk and acid jazz. With cheap drinks, free admission and an impressive light and sound system, this has to be a great deal for the youth of NW6.

*Open: 17.00–01.00 (Mon–Thurs), 17.00–02.00 (Sat), 17.00–22.30 (Sun)*
*Food: 17.00–01.00 (Mon–Thurs), 17.00–22.00 (Fri–Sun)*
*Credit cards: None taken*
*Draught beers: Kilkenny, Carlsberg, Carlsberg Export, Lowenbrau, Guinness, Blackthorn*
*Wheelchair access to venue and loo*
*Nearest tube station: Kilburn*

# Zilli Bar

40 Dean Street, W1. Tel: 0171 734 1853

If you own a bar and your ego's big enough, you make sure that your name is plastered all over it. Aldo Zilli is the man who owns this place. His world-famous restaurant has been feeding visitors to Soho for the past 12 years or so; he acquired the next-door unit about three years ago and opened this bar. I called in when it first opened and didn't go back again for a long time. A mistake. I had been missing out! This is rather a fine bar, attracting a loyal following of Soho media moguls and once-upon-a-time television stars, who help to create a party atmosphere in the evenings. When Italy are playing football, it's almost a carnival. Drinks are ever so slightly on the expensive side, but those who stay until 1am don't mind too much.

*Open: 12.00–01.00 (Mon–Sat)*
*Credit cards: all major cards*
*Nearest tube: Piccadilly Circus*

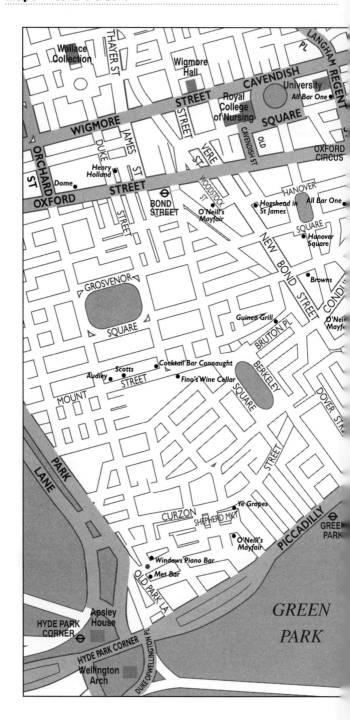

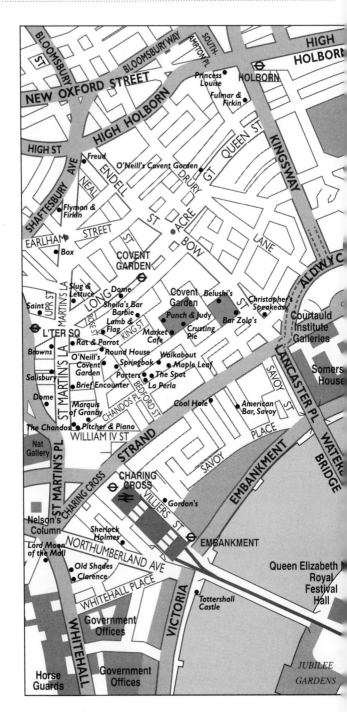

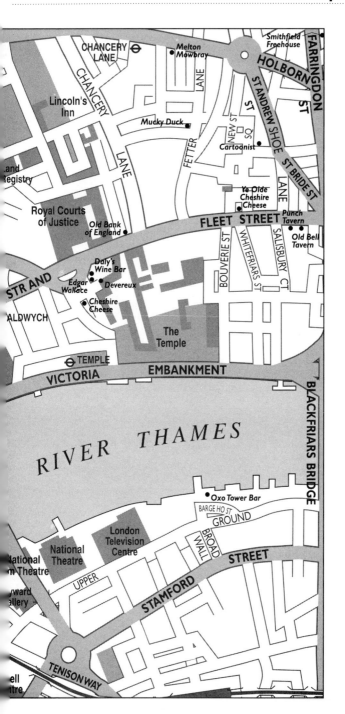

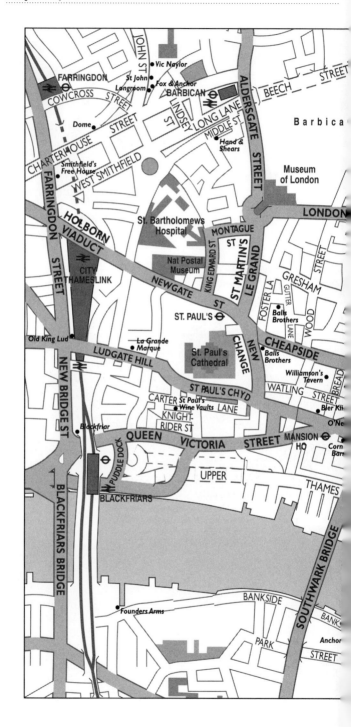

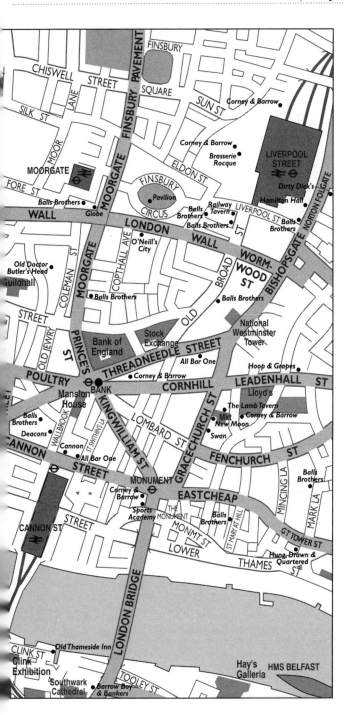

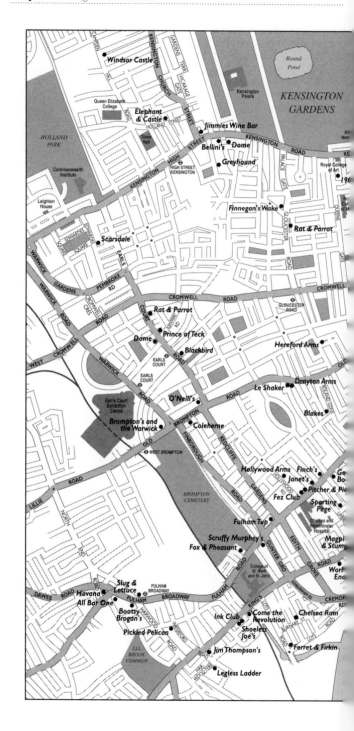

Windsor Castle

Queen Elizabeth College

Elephant & Castle

Jimmies Wine Bar

KENSINGTON GARDENS

Round Pond

Kensington Palace

HOLLAND PARK

Town Hall

Bellini's    Dome
Greyhound

Commonwealth Institute

Leighton House

HIGH STREET KENSINGTON

Royal College of Art

Finnegan's Wake

Rat & Parrot

Scarsdale

CROMWELL    ROAD

CROMWELL

GLOUCESTER ROAD

Rat & Parrot
Prince of Teck
Dome    Blackbird

Hereford Arms

WEST    CROMWELL

EARLS COURT

EARLS COURT

Le Shaker    Drayton Arms

Earl's Court Exhibition Centre

O'Neill's

Blakes

Brompton's and the Warwick
Coleherne

WEST BROMPTON

BROMPTON    CEMETERY

Hollywood Arms    Finch's
Janet's
Fez Club    Pitcher & Pie

Sporting Page

Fulham Tup

Chelsea and Westminster Hospital

Scruffy Murphey's
Fox & Pheasant

Magpie & Stump

College of St. Mark and St. John

World's End

Slug & Lettuce
Havana    FULHAM    BROADWAY
All Bar One
Bootsy Brogan's

Pickled Pelican

FULHAM

CREMORNE

Ink Club    Come the Revolution    Chelsea Ram

Shoeless Joe's

Ferret & Firkin

Jim Thompson's

LLL BROOK COMMON

Legless Ladder

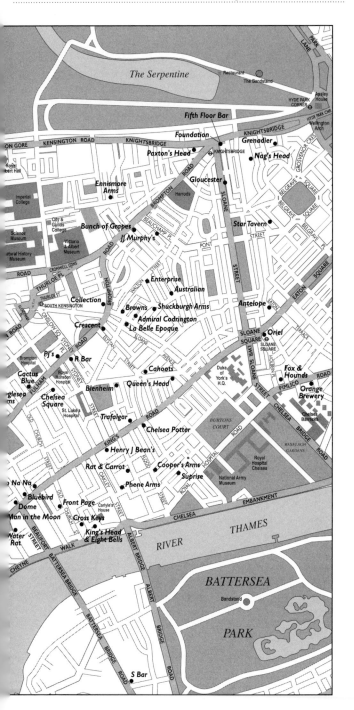

The Serpentine

Restaurant

The Bandstand

Apsley House

HYDE PARK CORNER

HYDE PARK CNR

Wellington Arch

Fifth Floor Bar

Foundation

KNIGHTSBRIDGE

Grenadier

Paxton's Head

KNIGHTSBRIDGE

Nag's Head

ON GORE

KENSINGTON ROAD

KNIGHTSBRIDGE

Royal Albert Hall

Gloucester

Ennismore Arms

BROMPTON

Harrods

SLOANE

BELGRAVE SQUARE

BELGRAVE

Imperial College

Science Museum

City & Guilds College

Bunch of Grapes

BEAUCHAMP PL

Star Tavern

BELGRAVE

STREET

JJ Murphy's

Victoria & Albert Museum

ROAD

Natural History Museum

CROMWELL GDNS

PONT

THURLOE PL

WALTON

Enterprise

STREET

EATON SQUARE

THURLOE ST

SOUTH KENSINGTON

Collection

BROMPTON

Australian

Antelope

ONSLOW SQ

STONEY

ROAD

Browns

Shuckburgh Arms

EATON

Crescent

Admiral Codrington

La Belle Epoque

SLOANE

Oriel

ROAD

BEUFAN

SLOANE SQUARE

TERRACE

Brompton Hospital

PJ's

SLOANE

SLOANE SQUARE

ALBERT

Cactus Blue

R Bar

Cahoots

Fox & Hounds

ROAD

Royal Marsden Hospital

SYDNEY

AVENUE

Duke of York's H.Q.

LWR SLOANE

PIMLICO

Orange Brewery

glesea ms

Blenheim

Queen's Head

Chelsea Square

STREET

ROAD

STREET

CHELSEA

Chelsea Barracks

St. Luke's Hospital

Trafalgar

KING'S

ROAD

BURTONS COURT

BRIDGE

RANELAGH GARDENS

ROAD

Chelsea Potter

Henry J Bean's

OAKLEY

ROAD

Cooper's Arms

HOSPITAL

Royal Hospital Chelsea

Na Na

Rat & Carrot

Suprise

ROYAL

National Army Museum

Bluebird

Phene Arms

Dome

Front Page

Carlyle's House

EMBANKMENT

Man in the Moon

Cross Keys

CHELSEA

THAMES

Water Rat

STREET

King's Head & Eight Bells

ALBERT BRIDGE

RIVER

CHEYNE

BATTERSEA BRIDGE

WALK

BATTERSEA

BEAUFORT

BATTERSEA BRIDGE

ALBERT

Bandstand

ROAD

BRIDGE

PARK

S Bar

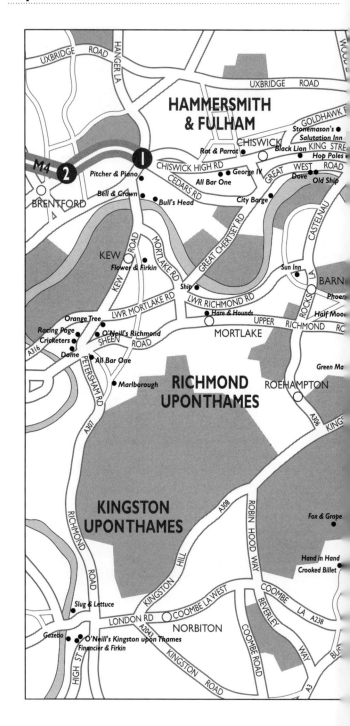

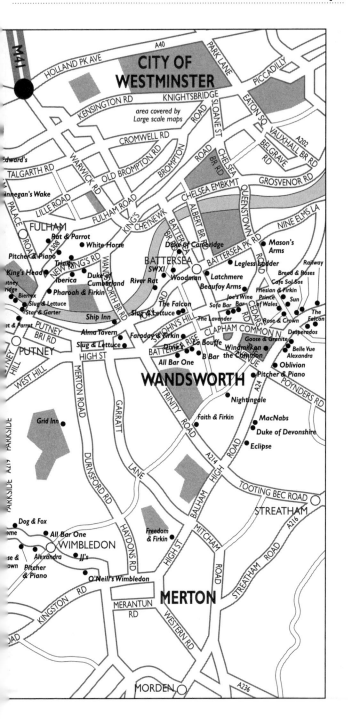

M41

HOLLAND PK AVE

A40

CITY OF
WESTMINSTER

PARK LANE

PICCADILLY

KNIGHTSBRIDGE

KENSINGTON RD

SLOANE ST

EATON SQ

area covered by
Large scale maps

CROMWELL RD

BELGRAVE RD

VAUXHALL BR RD

A202

BROMPTON RD

CHELSEA BR RD

dward's

TALGARTH RD

WARWICK RD

OLD BROMPTON RD

GROSVENOR RD

innegan's Wake

LILLE ROAD

CHELSEA EMBKMT

QUEENSTOWN RD

NINE ELMS LA

PALACE ROAD

FULHAM ROAD

KINGS CHEYNE WK

ALBERT BR

BATTERSEA BR

Rat & Parrot

FULHAM

A308

White Horse

Duke of Cambridge

BATTERSEA PK RD

Mason's
Arms

Pitcher & Piano

NEW KING'S RD

Trinity

BATTERSEA

Legless Ladder

Railway

WANDSWORTH BR RD

SW XI

Bread & Roses

King's Head

Duke of
Cumberland

River Rat

Woodman

Latchmere

Cafe Sol Sos

utney
idge

Iberica

Beaufoy Arms

Friesian & Firkin

Bierrex

Pharoah & Firkin

The Falcon

Joe's Wine
Bar

Prince
of Wales

Sun

Slug & Lettuce

Ship Inn

Slug & Lettuce

Sofa Bar

The
Falcon

Star & Garter

The Lavender

Rose & Crown

t & Parrot

PUTNEY

JOHN'S HILL

CLAPHAM COMMON N

Desperados

BRI RD

Alma Tavern

Faraday & Firkin

Goose & Granite

NEY HILL

PUTNEY

Slug & Lettuce

BATTERSEA RISE

Dusk

La Bouffe

Windmill on
the Common

Belle Vue

Alexandra

HIGH ST

B Bar

Oblivion

WEST HILL

All Bar One

Pitcher & Piano

MERTON ROAD

WANDSWORTH

A24

POYNDERS RD

GARRATT

TRINITY ROAD

Nightingale

Grid Inn

Faith & Firkin

MacNabs

PARKSIDE A219 PARKSIDE

DURNSFORD RD

Duke of Devonshire

A314

Eclipse

BALHAM HIGH ROAD

MITCHAM ROAD

TOOTING BEC ROAD

LANE

STREATHAM

Dog & Fox

HAYDONS RD

A216

STREATHAM ROAD

ome

All Bar One

Freedom
& Firkin

WIMBLEDON

se &
own

Alexandra

JJ's

HIGH ST

Pitcher
& Piano

O'Neill's Wimbledon

KINGSTON RD

MERANTUN
RD

MERTON

WESTERN RD

OAD

MORDEN

A236

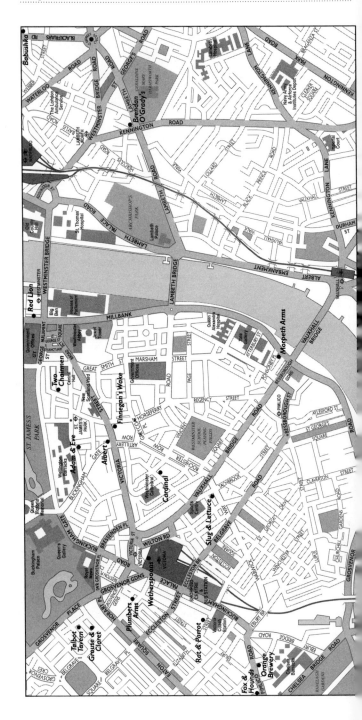

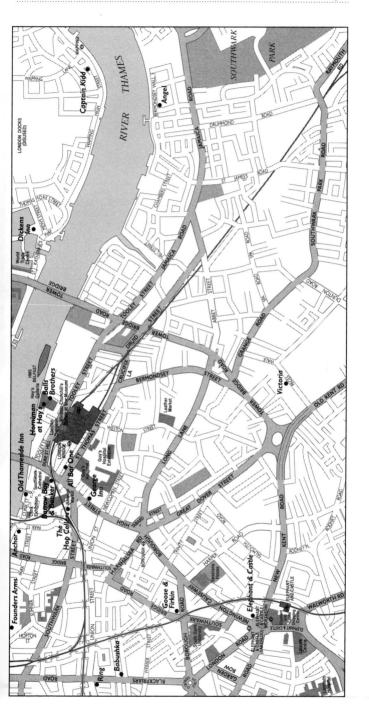

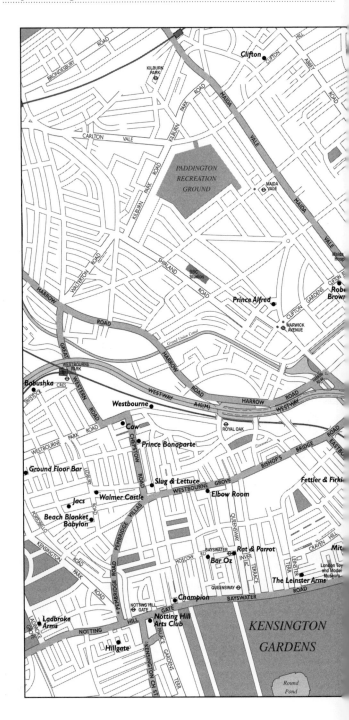

Clifton

KILBURN
PARK

BROADSBURY

CARLTON VALE

PADDINGTON
RECREATION
GROUND

MAIDA
VALE

SHIRLAND

BBC
Studios

Prince Alfred

Rob
Brown

WARWICK
AVENUE

HARROW

ROAD

Grand Union Canal

HARROW

ROAD

Bobushka

WESTBOURNE
PARK

WESTWAY

Westbourne

A40(M)

WESTWAY

ROYAL OAK

Caw

Prince Bonaparte

BISHOP'S

BRIDGE

WESTBOURNE PARK

Fettler & Firki

Ground Floor Bar

Slug & Lettuce

GROVE

WESTBOURNE

Elbow Room

Jacs

Walmer Castle

QUEENSWAY

Beach Blanket
Babylon

PEMBRIDGE VILLAS

BAYSWATER

Rat & Parrot

CRAVEN HILL

Mit

MOSCOW

Bar Oz

INVER
PL

London Toy
and Model
Museum

KENSINGTON
PARK
ROAD

QUEENSWAY

The Leinster Arms

Champion

BAYSWATER

Ladbroke
Arms

NOTTING HILL
GATE

Notting Hill
Arts Club

KENSINGTON
GARDENS

NOTTING

HILL

Hillgate

KENSINGTON CH ST

Round
Pond

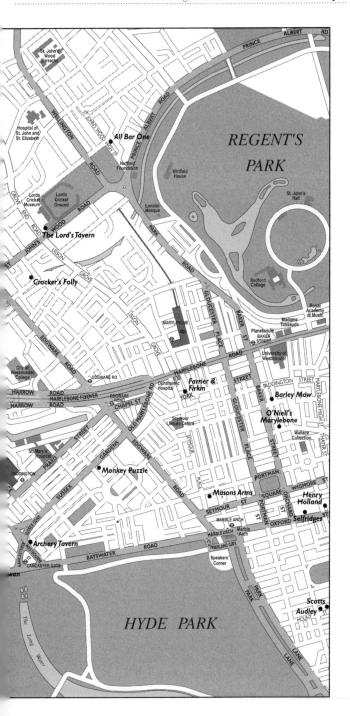

REGENT'S
PARK

HYDE PARK

St John's
Wood
Barracks

Hospital
of St John and
St Elizabeth

All Bar One

Nuffield
Foundation

Winfield
House

London
Mosque

St John's
Hall

Lords
Cricket
Museum

Lords
Cricket
Ground

The Lord's Tavern

Crocker's Folly

Bedford
College

Royal
Academy
of Music

MARYLEBONE

Madame
Tussauds

Planetarium
BAKER
STREET

University of
Westminster

City of
Westminster
College

EDGWARE RD

MARYLEBONE FLYOVER

Ophthalmic
Hospital
YORK

Farrier &
Firkin

Barley Mow

O'Niell's
Marylebone

Wallace
Collection

HARROW      ROAD

HARROW      ROAD

CHAPEL ST

Seymour
Leisure Centre

St Mary's
Hospital

PADDINGTON

Monkey Puzzle

Masons Arms

SEYMOUR

MARBLE ARCH

Marble
Arch

PORTMAN

SQUARE

WIGMORE   ST

Henry
Holland

OXFORD

Selfridges

Archery Tavern

LANCASTER GATE

BAYSWATER        ROAD

MARBLE ARCH

CUMBERLAND GATE

Speakers'
Corner

wan

The
Long
Water

Scotts

Audley

MOUNT   ST

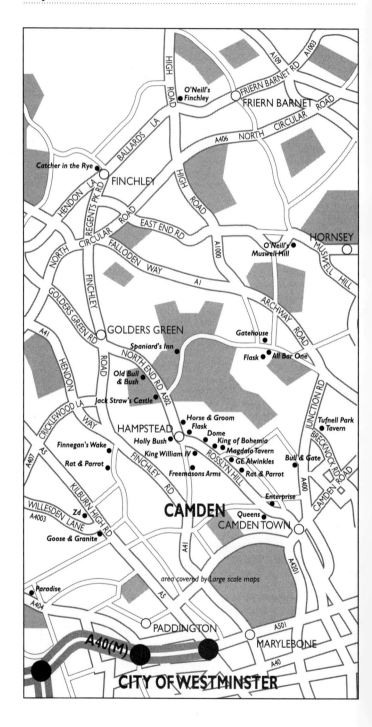

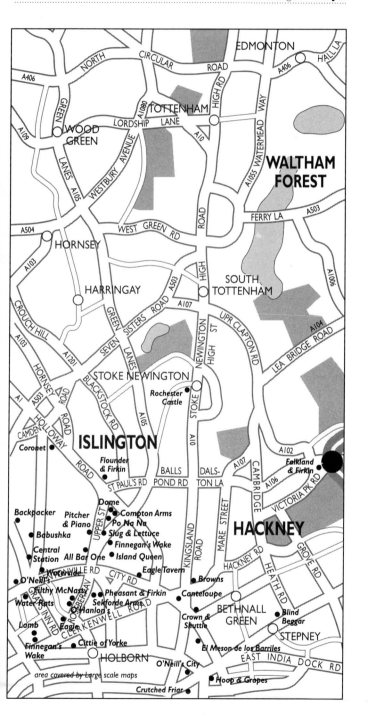

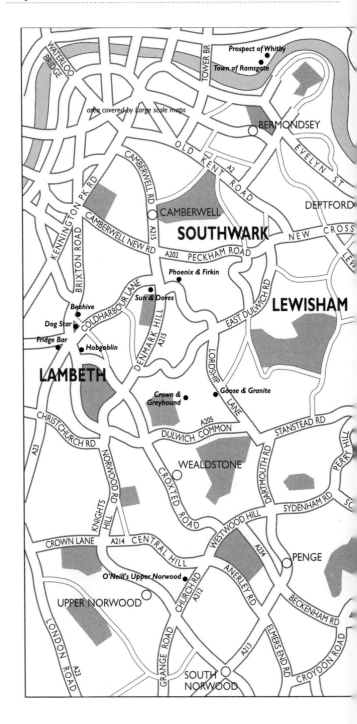

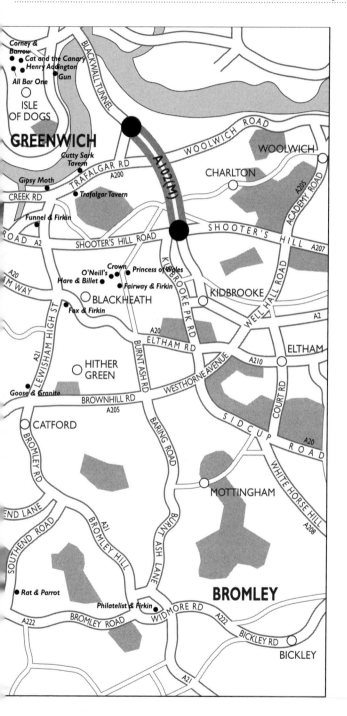

Corney &
Barrow
Cat and the Canary
Henry Addington
Gun
All Bar One

ISLE
OF DOGS

GREENWICH

Cutty Sark
Tavern

Gipsy Moth

TRAFALGAR RD
A200

CREEK RD

BLACKWALL TUNNEL

Trafalgar Tavern

Funnel & Firkin

ROAD  A2

SHOOTER'S HILL ROAD

A20

M WAY

O'Neill's
Hare & Billet

Crown  Princess of Wales

Fairway & Firkin

BLACKHEATH

Fox & Firkin

A20

ELTHAM RD

A205

LEWISHAM HIGH ST

A21

HITHER
GREEN

BURNT ASH RD

Goose & Granite

BROWNHILL RD

CATFORD

A205

BROMLEY RD

SOUTHEND ROAD

END LANE

BARING ROAD

A21

BROMLEY HILL

Rat & Parrot

Philatelist & Firkin

BROMLEY ROAD

A222

A102(M)

WOOLWICH ROAD

WOOLWICH

CHARLTON

SHOOTER'S  HILL

A207

ACADEMY ROAD

A205

KIDBROOKE PK RD

KIDBROOKE

WELL HALL ROAD

A2

ELTHAM

A210

WESTHORNE AVENUE

COURT RD

SIDCUP  ROAD

A20

MOTTINGHAM

BURNT ASH LANE

WHITE HORSE HILL

A208

BROMLEY

WIDMORE RD

A222

BICKLEY RD

BICKLEY

A21

# By area

**Balham**
Duke of Devonshire
  39 Balham High Rd, SW12
Eclipse
  157 Balham High Rd, SW12
McNab's Wine Bar & Restaurant
  43 Balham High Rd, SW12
Nightingale
  97 Nightingale La, SW12
Pitcher & Piano
  8 Balham Hill, SW12

**Barnes**
Sun Inn
  Church Rd, SW13

**Battersea**
All Bar One
  32–38 Northcote Rd, SW11
B Bar
  94 Northcote Rd, SW11
Beaufoy Arms
  18 Lavender Hill, SW11
La Bouffe
  11–13 Battersea Rise, SW11
Dixie's
  25 Battersea Rise, SW11
Duke of Cambridge
  228 Battersea Bridge Rd,
  SW11
Falcon
  2 St John's Hill, SW11
Faraday & Firkin
  66a Battersea Rise, SW11
Joe's Wine Bar & Restaurant, 33
  Lavender Hill, SW11
Latchmere
  503 Battersea Park Rd, SW11
Lavender
  171 Lavender Hill, SW11
Legless Ladder
  339 Battersea Park Rd, SW11
The Masons Arms
  169 Battersea Park Rd, SW8
River Rat
  2 Lombard Rd, SW11
S Bar
  37 Battersea Bridge Rd, SW11
Slug and Lettuce
  4 St John's Hill, SW11
Sofa Bar
  103 Lavender Hill, SW11
SWXI
  8 Battersea Sq, SW11
Woodman
  60 Battersea High St, SW11

**Bayswater**
Archery Tavern
  4 Bathurst St, W2
Bar Oz
  51 Moscow Rd, W2
Champion
  1 Wellington Terrace, Bayswater
  Rd, W2
Cow
  89 Westbourne Park Rd, W2

Elbow Room
  103 Westbourne Grove, W2
Fettler & Firkin
  15 Chilworth St, W2
Leinster Arms
  17 Leinster Terrace, W2
Mitre
  24 Craven Terrace, W2
Monkey Puzzle
  30 Southwick St, W2
Prince Bonaparte
  80 Chepstow Rd, W2
Rat & Parrot
  99 Queensway, W2
Slug and Lettuce
  47 Hereford Rd, W2
Swan
  66 Bayswater Rd, W2
Westbourne
  101 Westbourne Park Villas,
  W2

**Beckenham**
O'Neill's
  9 High St, Beckenham
Rat & Parrot
  157 High St.,Beckenham

**Belgravia (including Sloane St and Knightsbridge)**
Antelope
  22 Eaton Terrace, SW1
Fifth Floor Bar, Harvey Nichols
  Knightsbridge, SW1
Foundation, Harvey Nichols
  Knightsbridge, SW1
Fox and Hounds
  29 Passmore St, SW1
Gloucester
  187 Sloane St, SW1
Grenadier, Old Barrack Yard
  Wilton Row, SW1
Grouse and Claret
  Little Chester St, SW1
Nag's Head
  53 Kinnerton St, SW1
Oriel
  50–51 Sloane Sq, SW1
Paxton's Head
  153 Knightsbridge, SW1
Plumbers Arms
  14 Lr. Belgrave Sq, SW1
Star Tavern
  6 Belgrave Mews West, SW1
Talbot Tavern
  Little Chester St, SW1

**Blackheath**
Crown
  49 Tranquil Vale, SE3
Fairway & Firkin
  16 Blackheath Village, SE3
The Hare and Billet
  Hare and Billet Rd, SE3
O'Neill's
  52 Tranquil Vale, SE3

Princess of Wales
  1A Montpelier Row, SE3

**Bow**
Flautist & Firkin
  588 Mile End Rd, E3

**Brentwood**
Scruffy Murphy's
  161 Kings Rd, Brentwood

**Brixton**
The Dog Star
  388 Coldharbour La., SW9
Fridge Bar
  1 Town Hall Parade, SW2
Hobgoblin
  95 Effra Rd, SW2

**Bromley**
Philatelist & Firkin
  27–28 East St
Scruffy Murphy's
  10 Widmore Rd

**Camberwell**
The Sun and Doves
  61–63 Coldharbour La, SE5

**Camden**
The Black Cap
  171 Camden High St, NW1
Dome
  18 Chalk Farm Rd, NW1
The Dublin Castle,
  94 Parkway, NW1
Edward's
  1 Camden High St, NW1
Engineer
  65 Gloucester Ave, NW1
Friar and Firkin
  120 Euston Rd, NW1
Fusilier & Firkin
  7–8 Chalk Farm Rd, NW1
O'Neill's
  73–77 Euston Rd, NW1
O'Neill's
  55 Camden High St, NW1
The Outpost
  Lidlington Pl, NW1
The Queens
  49 Regents Park Rd, NW1
Rat & Parrot
  25 Parkway, NW1
T.E.Dingwalls
  11 Camden Lock Pl, NW1
The World's End
  174 Camden High Rd, NW1

**Canary Wharf Area**
All Bar One
  42 Mackenzie Walk E14
Barley Mow
  Narrow St, E14
The Cat and the Canary, 1–24
  Fisherman's Walk, E14
Corney and Barrow
  9 Cabot Sq,E14
Davys
  31–35 Canary Wharf, E14

Grapes
76 Narrow St, E14
Gun
27 Cold Harbour, E14
The Henry Addington, 22–28
Mackenzie Walk, E14
The House They Left Behind, 27
Ropemaker's Fields, E14
The White Swan
555 Commercial Rd, E14

**Carshalton**
The Fox & Hounds
41 The High St,
The Greyhound
2 The High St

**Catford**
Goose and Granite
88 Rushey Green, SE6

**Chelmsford**
Rat & Parrot
Duke St, Chelmsford

**Chelsea**
Admiral Codrington
17 Mossop St, SW3
Australian
29 Milner St, SW3
La Belle Epoque
151 Draycott Avenue, SW3
Blenheim
27 Cale St, SW3
Bluebird
350 King's Rd, SW3
Browns
114 Draycott Ave, SW3
Bunch of Grapes
207 Brompton Rd, SW3
Cactus Blue
86 Fulham Rd, SW3
Cahoots
2 Elystan St, SW3
Chelsea Potter
119 King's Rd, SW3
Chelsea Ram
32 Burnaby St, SW10
Chelsea Sq
145 Dovehouse St, SW3
Collection, 264 Brompton Rd,
SW3
Coopers' Arms
87 Flood St, SW3
Crescent
99 Fulham Rd, SW3
Cross Keys
1 Lawrence St, SW3
Dome
354 King's Rd, SW3
Enterprise
35 Walton St, SW3
Ferret & Firkin
114 Lots Rd, SW10
Fez Club
220 Fulham Rd, SW10
Finch's
190 Fulham Rd, SW10
Fox and Pheasant
1 Billing Rd, SW10
The Front Page
35 Old Church St, SW3

Fulham Tup
268 Fulham Rd, SW10
Goat in Boots
333 Fulham Rd, SW10
Henry J Beans
195 King's Rd, SW3
Hollywood Arms
Hollywood Rd, SW10
J J Murphy's
48 Beauchamp Pl, SW3
Janet's
208 Fulham Rd, SW10
The King's Head and Eight Bells
50 Cheyne Walk, SW3
Magpie & Stump
442 King's Rd, SW10
The Man in the Moon
392 King's Rd, SW3
The Phene Arms
9 Phene St, SW3
Pitcher & Piano
214 Fulham Rd, SW10
PJ's
52 Fulham Rd, SW3
Po Na Na
316 Kings Rd, SW3
Queen's Head
25–27 Tryon St, SW3
Rat and Carrot
60 Chelsea Manor St, SW3
R Bar
4 Sydney St, SW3
Scruffy Murphy's,
451 Fulham Rd, SW10
The Shuckburgh Arms,
47 Denyer St, SW3
Sporting Page
6 Camera Pl, SW10
The Surprise
6 Christchurch Tce, SW3
The Trafalgar
200 Kings Rd, SW3
Water Rat
1 Milmans St, SW10
World's End
459 King's Rd, SW10

**Chiswick**
All Bar One
197–199 Chiswick High Rd,
W4
Bell and Crown
72 Strand on the Green, W4
City Barge
27 Strand on the Green, W4
George IV
185 High Rd, W4
Pitcher & Piano
18–20 High Rd, W4
Rat & Parrot
122 High Rd, W4

**City EC1**
Coates,
46 Cowcross St
Davys
15/17 Long La
DCO
84–86 Rosebery Avenue

Dome
57–59 Charterhouse St
The Eagle
159 Farringdon Rd
Filthy McNasty
68 Amwell St
The Fox and Anchor
115 Charterhouse St
The Hand and Shears
1 Middle St
The Longroom
18–20 St John St
The Melton Mowbray
18 Holborn
O'Hanlon's
18 Tysoe St
Pheasant & Firkin
166 Goswell Rd
The Sekforde Arms
34 Sekforde Street
Smithfield Free House
334 Central Market
St John
26 St John St
Vic Naylor
38–40 St.John St
Ye Olde Mitre Tavern
Ely Court, Hatton Garden

**City EC2**
All Bar One
34 Threadneedle St
Balls Brothers
Carey La (off Gutter La)
Balls Brothers
Moor House, London Wall,
Balls Brothers, Great Eastern
Hotel, Liverpool St
Balls Brothers
Kings Arms Yard
Balls Brothers
6–8 Cheapside
Balls Brothers
11 Bloomfield St
Balls Brothers
42 Threadneedle St
Balls Brothers
Gows Restaurant, 81–82 Old
Broad St
Bill Bentley's
18 Old Broad St
Brasserie Rocque
37 Broadgate Circle
Cantaloupe Bar & Grill
35 – 42 Charlotte Rd
City Tup
66 Gresham St
Coates
45 London Wall
Corney and Barrow
2B Eastcheap
Corney and Barrow
5 Exchange Sq, Broadgate
Corney and Barrow
19 Broadgate Circle
Davys at Russia Row, Ale & Port
House, Russia Court, Russia
Row
Davys at Russia Row, Wine Rooms,
Russia Court, Russia Row

Dirty Dick's
  202 Bishopsgate
The Globe
  83 Moorgate
Hamilton Hall
  Liverpool St Station
John Keats at Moorgate
  83 Moorgate
The Old Dr Butlers Head,
  Masons Avenue
O'Neill's
  64 London Wall
The Pavilion
  Finsbury Circus Gardens
  Finsbury Circus
The Rack and Tenter
  45 Moorfields
The Railway Tavern
  15 Liverpool St

**City EC3**
Balls Brothers
  St Mary at Hill
Balls Brothers
  Mark La
Balls Brothers
  52 Lime St
Bill Bentley's
  5 The Minories
Bill Bentley's
  1 St George's La
Caravaggio
  107–112 Leadenhall St
Corney and Barrow
  1 Leadenhall Pl
Corney and Barrow
  16 Royal Exchange
Crutched Friar
  39–41 Crutched Friars
The Hoop and Grapes
  47 Aldgate High St
The Hung, Drawn and Quartered
  26/27 Great Tower St
The Lamb Tavern, Leadenhall
  Market
The New Moon
  88 Gracechurch St
O'Neill's
  31/36 Houndsditch
The Swan
  77–80 Gracechurch St
Willy's Wine Bar
  107 Fenchurch St

**City EC4**
All Bar One
  44–46 Ludgate Hill
All Bar One
  103 Cannon St
Balls Brothers, Bucklersbury
  House, Cannon St
Bier Klinik
  74 Queen Victoria St
BierRex
  2–3 Creed La
Blackfriar
  174 Queen Victoria St
The Cannon
  95 Cannon St

The Cartoonist
  76 Shoe La
The City Page
  2a Suffolk La
Corney and Barrow
  3 Fleet Pl
Corney and Barrow
  44 Cannon St
Davys, 10 Creed La
Deacons,
  Walbrook
La Grande Marque
  47 Ludgate Hill
Magpie and Stump
  218 Old Bailey
Mucky Duck
  108 Fetter La
The Old Bank of England, 194
  Fleet St
The Old Bell Tavern
  95 Fleet St
Olde Wine Shades
  6 Martin La
The Old King Lud
  78 Ludgate Hill
O'Neill's
  65 Cannon St
The Punch Tavern
  99 Fleet St
Scruffy Murphy's
  142 Fleet St
Sports Academy
  24 King William St
St Paul's Wine Vaults
  229 Knightrider St
Williamson's Tavern
  1 Groveland Court
Ye Olde Cheshire Cheese, Wine
  Office Court
  145 Fleet St

**Clapham**
The Alexandra
  14 Clapham Common
  Southside, SW4
The Belle Vue
  1 Clapham Common
  Southside, SW4
The Bread and Roses
  68 Clapham Manor St, SW4
Cafe Sol Dos
  56 Clapham High St, SW4
Desperados Bourbon Bar, 127
  Clapham High St, SW4
The Falcon
  33 Bedford Rd, SW4
Friesian & Firkin
  87 Rectory Grove, SW4
Fringella & Firkin
  762–764 High Rd, SW4
The Goose and Granite
  196 Clapham High St, SW4
Oblivion
  7–8 Cavendish Parade
  Clapham Common Southside,
  SW4
Prince of Wales
  38 Clapham Old Town, SW4
Railway
  18 Clapham High St, SW4

The Rose & Crown
  2 The Polygon, Clapham Old
  Town, SW4
The Sun
  47 Clapham Old Town, SW4
The Windmill on the Common,
  Clapham Common Southside,
  SW4

**Colchester**
Faunus & Firkin
  128 High St, Colchester

**Covent Garden and
  Leicester Sq**
All Bar One
  48 Leicester Sq, WC2
American Bar
  Savoy Hotel Strand, WC2
Bar Zola's
  33 Wellington St, WC2
Belushi's
  9 Russell St, WC2
Box, 32–34
  Monmouth St, WC2
Brief Encounter
  42 St Martin's La, WC2
Browns
  82–84 St Martins La, WC2
The Chandos
  29 St Martin's La, WC2
The Cheshire Cheese
  5 Little Essex St, WC2
Christopher's Speakeasy
  18 Wellington St, WC2
The Cork and Bottle
  44 Cranbourn St, WC2
The Crusting Pipe
  27 The Market, WC2
Daly's Wine Bar
  210 The Strand, WC2
The Devereux
  Devereux Mews, WC2
Dome
  8 Charing Cross Rd, WC2
Dome
  32 Long Acre, WC2
The Edgar Wallace,
  40 Essex St, WC2
Fashion Cafe
  3-4 Coventry St, W1
Flyman and Firkin
  166–170 Shaftesbury Avenue,
  WC2
Freud
  198 Shaftesbury Ave, WC2
Fulmar and Firkin
  51 Parker St, WC2
Gordon's
  47 Villiers St, WC2
Kudos
  10 Adelaide St, WC2
Lamb and Flag
  33 Rose St, WC2
La Perla
  28 Maiden La, WC2
The Maple Leaf
  41 Maiden La, WC2
The Market Cafe Bar
  21 The Market, WC2

The Marquis of Granby
51 Charnos Pl, WC2
The Moon Under The Water, 28 Leicester Sq, WC2
The Mullins Coffee House, 27 The Market, WC2
O'Neill's
14 New Row, WC2
O'Neill's
40 Great Queen St, WC2
Polar Bear,
30 Lisle St, WC2
Porters
16 Henrietta St, WC2
Pitcher & Piano,
40–42 William IV St, WC2
Princess Louise
208 High Holborn, WC2
Punch and Judy
40 The Market, WC2
Rat & Parrot
24 Tavistock St, WC2
Rat & Parrot
63 St Martin's La, WC2
The Round House
1 Garrick St, WC2
The Round Table
St Martin's Court, WC2
Saint
8 Great Newport St, WC2
Salisbury
90 St Martin's La, WC2
Sherlock Holmes
10–11 Northumberland St, WC2
Slug and Lettuce
114 Upp St Martins La, WC2
Spot
29 Maiden La, WC2
Springbok
20 Bedford St, WC2
Sussex
20 Upp. Martin's La, WC2
TS Queen Mary,
Victoria Embankment, WC2
Walkabout
11 Henrietta St, WC2
Sheila's Bar Barbie
41 King's St, WC2
Faun & Firkin
18 Bear St, WC2

**Croydon**
Fiddler & Firkin
14 South End, Croydon
Jim Thompsons
34 Surrey St, Croydon
O'Neill's
1 South End, Croydon
Po Na Na,
The Arcade 32–34 High St.
Rat & Parrot
24 Park St, Croydon
Yates's Wine Lodge
3–11 High St, Croydon

**Dulwich**
Crown and Greyhound
73 Dulwich Village, SE21

Goose and Granite
381 Lordship La, SE22

**Ealing**
Edward's
28–30 New Broadway, W5
Finnegan's Wake
The Green Ealing, W5
Photographer & Firkin, 23–25 High St, W5
Rat & Parrot
23 High St, W5
Yates's Wine Lodge
Mattock La, Ealing Green, W5

**Earls Court**
The Blackbird
209 Earls Court Rd, SW5
Brompton's and the Warwick Bar, 294 Old Brompton Rd, SW5
The Coleherne,
261 Old Brompton Rd, SW5
Dome
194 Earls Court Rd, SW5
The Drayton Arms
153 Old Brompton Rd, SW5
Le Shaker
159 Old Brompton Rd, SW5
O'Neill's
326 Earls Court Rd, SW5
Prince of Teck
161 Earls Court Rd, SW5
Rat & Parrot
123 Earl's Court Rd, SW5

**East Molesey**
Pals
2–6 Bridge St, East Molesey

**Epping**
Forest & Firkin
High St, Epping

**Epsom & Ewell**
Favel & Firkin
4 East St, Epsom
Friend & Firkin
High St, Ewell

**Fulham**
All Bar One
587–591 Fulham Rd, SW6.
Bootsy Brogan's
1 Fulham Broadway, SW6
Come the Revolution
541 King's Rd, SW6
Duke of Cumberland,
235 New King's Rd, SW6
Havana
490 Fulham B'way, SW6
Iberica
295 New King's Rd, SW6
Ink Club
541a King's Rd, SW6
Jim Thompson's
617 King's Rd, SW6
The King's Head
4 Fulham High St, SW6
Legless Ladder
1 Harwood Terrace, SW6

Pharaoh & Firkin
90 Fulham High St, SW6
Pickled Pelican
22 Waterford Rd, SW6
Pitcher & Piano
871–873 Fulham Rd, SW6
Rat & Parrot
704 Fulham Rd, SW6
Shoeless Joe's
555 King's Rd, SW6
Slug and Lettuce
474 Fulham Rd, SW6
Trinity
108 New King's Rd, SW6
The White Horse
1 Parson's Green, SW6

**Greenwich**
Cutty Sark Tavern
Ballast Quay, SE10
Davys Wine Vaults
161 Greenwich High Rd, SE10
Davys Wine Vaults
65 Greenwich High Rd, SE10
Funnel & Firkin
Greenwich High Rd, SE10
Gipsy Moth
60 Greenwich Church St, SE10
Trafalgar Tavern,
Park Row SE10

**Guildford**
Forger & Firkin
55–56 Woodridge Rd
Scruffy Murphy's
9 Millmead

**Hackney**
Browns
1 Hackney Rd, E2

**Hammersmith**
Black Lion
2 South Black Lion La, W6
Blue Anchor
13 Lower Mall, W6
Bulls' Head
Strand on the Green, W6
Dove
19 Upper Mall, W6
Edward's
40 Hammersmith Broadway, W6
Finnegan's Wake
48 Fulham Palace Rd, W6
Hop Poles
17 King St, W6
Old Ship
25 Upper Mall, W6
Salutation Inn
154 King St, W6
Secrets
62 Glenthorn Rd, W6
Stonemasons
54 Cambridge Grove, W6

**Hampstead**
Dome
58–62 Heath St, NW3
The Enterprise
2 Haverstock Hill, NW3

# Indices By area

The Flask
14 Flask Walk, NW3
The Freemasons Arms
32 Downshire Hill, NW3
G.E.Aldwinkles
154 Fleet Rd, NW3
The Holly Bush
22 Holly Mount, NW3
The Horse and Groom
68 Heath St, NW3
Jack Straw's Castle
North End Way, NW3
The King of Bohemia
210 Hampstead High St, NW3
The King William IV, 75
Hampstead High St, NW3
The Magdala Tavern
2a South Hill Park, NW3
The Old Bull and Bush, North
End Rd, NW3
Rat & Parrot
250 Haverstock Hill, NW3
The Spaniard's Inn, Spaniard's
Rd, NW3
Ye Olde Swiss Cottage
98 Finchley Rd, NW3

**Harrow**
Rat & Parrot
84 St Ann's Rd, Harrow
Yates's Wine Lodge, 269–271
Station Rd
Fornax & Firkin
Northolt Rd

**Highgate**
All Bar One
1–1A Highgate, N6
The Flask
77 Highgate West Hill, N6
The Gatehouse
North Rd, N6

**Holborn to Strand**
The Cittie of Yorke
22 High Holborn, WC1
The Coal Hole
91 The Strand, WC1
Finnegan's Wake
63 Lambs Conduit St, WC1
The Lamb
94 Lambs Conduit St WC1
The Museum Tavern
49 Gt Russell St, WC1
The Old Red Lion
72 High Holborn, WC1
The Water Rats
328 Grays Inn Rd, WC1

**Holloway**
The Coronet
338 Holloway Rd, N7
Flounder & Firkin
54 Holloway Rd, N7
O'Neill's,
456 Holloway Rd, N7

**Homerton**
Falcon & Firkin
360 Victoria Park Rd, E9

**Hounslow**
Yates's Wine Lodge
1–3 Bath Rd, Hounslow

**Ilford**
O'Neill's
109 Station Rd, Ilford

**Isleworth**
London Apprentice
62 Old Church St

**Islington**
The Albion
10 Thornhill Rd, N1
All Bar One
1 Liverpool Rd, N1
babushka
125 Caledonian Rd, N1
Backpacker
126 York Way, N1
Camden Head
Camden Walk, N1
The Central Station
37 Wharfdale Rd, N1
The Compton Arms,
4 Compton Avenue, N1
The Crown
116 Cloudesley Rd, N1
Dome
341 Upper St, N1
The Eagle Tavern
2 Shepherdess Walk, N1
Finnegan's Wake
2 Essex Rd, N1
Finnock & Firkin
100 Upper St, N1
The Hope and Anchor
207 Upper St, N1
The Island Queen
87 Noel Rd, N1
The King's Head
115 Upper St, N1
The Marquess Tavern,
32 Canonbury St, N1
The Narrow Boat
119 St Peter St, N1
Pitcher & Piano,
68 Upper St, N1
Po Na Na
259 Upper St, N1
Slug and Lettuce
1 Islington Green, N1
Tut 'n' Shive
235 Upper St, N1
The Waterside
82 York Way, N1

**Kensal Rise**
Paradise
19 Kilburn La, W10

**Kensington**
Bellini's
47 Kensington Court, W8
Dome
Kensington Court, 35a
Kensington High St, W8
Elephant & Castle
40 Holland St, W8
Greyhound
1 Kensington Sq, W8

Hillgate Arms
24 Hillgate St, W8
Jimmies Wine Bar
18 Kensington Church St, W8
Rat & Parrot, 206 Kensington
Church St, W8
Scarsdale
23a Edwardes Sq, W8
Windsor Castle
114 Campden Hill Rd, W8

**Kentish Town**
Bull and Gate
389 Kentish Town Rd, NW5

**Kew**
Flower and Firkin
Kew Gardens Station

**Kilburn**
Finnegan's Wake
37 Fortune Green Rd, NW6
Goose and Granite
155 Kilburn High Rd, NW6
Rat & Parrot
100 West End La, NW6
Scruffy Murphy's
283 West End La, NW6
Zd Bar
289 Kilburn High Rd, NW6

**Kingston-upon-
Thames**
Financier & Firkin
43 Market Pl
Gazebo
Kings Passage
O'Neill's
3 Eden St
Slug and Lettuce
Turks Boatyard Thameside

**Lewisham**
Fox & Firkin
316 Lewisham High St, SE13
Yates's Wine Lodge
67–71 High St

**Leytonstone**
O'Neill's
762 High Rd, E11

**Maida Vale**
Prince Alfred
Formosa St, W9
Robert Browning
15 Clifton Rd, W9

**Maidstone**
O'Neill's
11 Middle Row, Maidstone

**Mayfair**
All Bar One
289 Regent St, W1
All Bar One
3–4 Hanover St, W1
The Audley
41 Mount St, W1
Browns
47 Maddox St, W1
Cocktail Bar, Connaught Hotel,
16 Carlos Pl, W1

Dover St Wine Bar, 8–9 Dover
St, W1
Fino's Wine Cellar
123 Mount St, W1
The Guinea
30 Bruton Pl, W1
Hanover Sq
25 Hanover Sq, W1
Kemia Bar at Momo
25 Heddon St, W1
The Masons Arms,
51 Upper Berkeley St, W1
MetBar
19 Old Park La, W1
O'Neill's,
21 Old Burlington St, W1
O'Neill's
22 Woodstock St, W1
O'Neill's
7 Shepherd St, W1
Scotts
20 Mount St, W1
Windows Piano Bar
28th Floor Hilton Hotel Park La,
W1
Ye Grapes
16 Shepherd Market, W1

**Mortlake**
Hare and Hounds
216 Upper Richmond Rd West,
SW14
Ship
10 Thames Bank, SW14

**Muswell Hill**
O'Neill's
291–293 Broadway, N10

**North of Oxford St**
The Barley Mow
8 Dorset St, W1
The Champion
12/13 Wells St, W1
Dome
400 Oxford St, W1
Fanfare & Firkin
38 Gt Marlborough St, W1
Farrier & Firkin
74–76 York St, W1
Fitz & Firkin
240 Great Portland St, W1
Flintlock & Firkin
108a Tottenham Court Rd, W1
The Hope
15 Tottenham St, W1
Jack Horner
236 Tottenham Court Rd, W1
Marylebone Tup
93 Marylebone High St, W1
Office Bar
3–5 Rathbone Pl, W1
Ye Olde Surgeon, 183
Tottenham Court Rd, W1
O'Neill's
56 Blandford St, W1
O'Neill's
4 Conway St, W1
Selfridges
Oxford St, W1

The Tottenham
6 Oxford St, W1

**North Finchley**
O'Neill's
744 High Rd, N12

**Norwood**
O'Neill's
98 Church Rd, SE19

**Notting Hill**
All Bar One
126 Notting Hill Gate, W11
Babushka
41 Tavistock Cres, W11
Beach Blanket Babylon
45 Ledbury Rd, W11
Frog & Firkin
96 Ladbroke Grove, W11
Ground Floor Bar
186 Portobello Rd, W11
Jacs
48 Lonsdale Rd, W11
The Ladbroke Arms
54 Ladbroke Rd, W11
The Market Bar
240a Portobello Rd, W11
Notting Hill Arts Club
21 Notting Hill Gate, W11
The Walmer Castle
58 Ledbury Rd, W11

**Peckham**
Phoenix & Firkin
Windsor Walk, SE15

**Pimlico**
Morpeth Arms
58 Millbank, SW1
Orange Brewery
37 Pimlico Rd, SW1
Slug and Lettuce
11 Warwick Way, SW1

**Pinner**
Frothfinders & Firkin
Marsh Rd, Pinner

**Plaistow**
The Duke of Edinburgh
299 Green St, E13

**Purley**
The Jolly Farmers
Purley High St, Purley
Las Fuentes Tapas Bar, 36–40
High St, Purley

**Putney**
Bar M
4 Lwr Richmond Rd, SW15
BierRex
22 Putney High St, SW15
Green Man
Putney Heath, SW15
Half Moon
93 Lwr Richmond Rd, SW15
Jim Thompson's
408 Upp Richmond Rd, SW15
Phoenix Bar & Grill
162 Lwr Richmond St, SW15
Putney Bridge
Embankment, SW15

Rat & Parrot
160 Putney High St, SW15
Slug and Lettuce
14 Putney High St, SW15

**Regent's Park Rd**
The Catcher in the Rye
317 Regents Park Rd, N3

**Richmond**
All Bar One
9 Hill St, Richmond
The Cricketers
The Green, Richmond
Dome
26 Hill St, Richmond
Flicker & Firkin
Dukes Yard 1 Dukes St,
The Marlborough
46 Friar Stile Rd
O'Neill's,
28 The Quadrant
The Orange Tree
45 Kew Rd
The Racing Page
2 Duke St, Richmond
The Rose of York
Petersham Rd
Slug and Lettuce
Riverside House, Water La
The White Cross
Riverside, Water La
The White Swan
Old Palace La

**Rotherhithe**
The Angel
101 Bermondsey Wall East,
SE16

**St Albans**
O'Neill's
20–30 London Rd

**St James's including
Haymarket**
Balls Brothers
20 St James's St (entrance
Ryder St), SW1
Football Football
57–60 Haymarket, SW1
The Golden Lion
25 King St, W1
Henry Holland
39 Duke St, W1
The Hogshead in St James
11 Dering St, W1
Red Lion
Crown Passage, SW1
Red Lion
Duke of York St, SW1
Sports Café
80 Haymarket, SW1
Two Chairman
1 Warwick House St, SW1

**Shepherd's Bush**
Albertine
1 Wood La, W12
Edward's
170 Uxbridge Rd, W12

Fringe & Firkin
  2 Goldhawk Rd, W12
Walkabout
  58 Shepherds Bush Green,
  W12

**Slough**
O'Neill's
  20 Windsor Rd, Slough

**Southend–on–Sea**
O'Neill's
  119 High St, Southend on Sea

**Soho**
All Bar One
  Dean St, W1
Alphabet,
  61–63 Beak St, W1
The Argyll Arms
  18 Argyll St, W1
Atlantic Bar and Grill
  20 Glasshouse St, W1
The Back Bar
  8–10 Brewer St, W1
The Blues Bar,
  Kingly St, W1
Cafe Boheme
  13 Old Compton St, W1
Cafe Latino
  25 Frith St, W1
Cairo Jack's
  10 Beak St, W1
Clachan
  34 Kingly St, W1
Coach and Horses
  29 Greek St, W1
Crown and Two Chairman, 31
  Dean St, W1
De Hems, 11 Macclesfield St,
  W1
dell'Ugo
  56 Frith St, W1
Dog & Duck
  18 Bateman St, W1
The Dog House
  187 Wardour St, W1
Dome
  57–59 Old Compton St, W1
Edge
  11 Soho Sq, W1
Est,
  54 Frith St, W1
Freedom
  60–66 Wardour St, W1
The French House
  49 Dean St, W1
The Golden Lion
  51 Dean St, W1
The Intrepid Fox
  99 Wardour St, W1
Kettners Champagne Bar,
  29 Romilly St, W1
Latino
  25 Frith St, W1
Los Locos Beach Club
  14 Soho St, W1

Lupo
  Dean St, W1
Mezzo
  100 Wardour St, W1
Mondo
  12–13 Greek St, W1
The Moon and Sixpence, 185
  Wardour St, W1
O Bar
  83 Wardour St, W1
The Old Coffee House, 49 Beak
  St, W1
O'Neill's
  34–37 Wardour St, W1
Pitcher & Piano
  69 Dean St, W1
Quo Vadis
  26–29 Dean St, W1
Rat & Parrot
  77 Wardour St, W1
Riki Tik
  23–34 Bateman St, W1
Rupert St
  50 Rupert St, W1
Scruffy Murphy's
  15 Denman St, W1
Slap Harry's
  1–3 Warwick St, W1
Slug and Lettuce
  80–82 Wardour St, W1
Soho Soho
  11–13 Frith St, W1
Soho Spice
  124 Wardour St, W1
The Sun and Thirteen Cantons
  21 Great Pulteney St, W1
Tactical
  27 D'Arblay St, W1
The Three Greyhounds
  25 Greek St, W1
Two Floors
  3 Kingly St, W1
Waxy O'Connor's, 14–16 Rupert
  St, W1
Yard
  57 Rupert St, W1
Zilli Bar
  40 Dean St, W1

**St John's Wood**
All Bar One, 60 St John's Wood
  High St, NW8
The Clifton
  96 Clifton Hill, NW8
The Crocker's Folly
  24 Aberdeen Pl, NW8
The Lord's Tavern
  St John's Wood Rd, NW8

**South Kensington**
The Anglesea Arms
  215 Selwood Terrace, SW7
Blakes
  33 Roland Gardens, SW7
Finnegan's Wake
  34 Gloucester Rd, SW7
Hereford Arms
  127 Gloucester Rd, SW7
Rat & Parrot
  25 Gloucester Rd, SW7

190
  190 Queensgate, SW7

**Southwark**
All Bar One
  28 London Bridge St, SE1
The Anchor, Bankside
  234 Park St, SE1
Babushka
  173 Blackfriars Rd, SE1
Balls Brothers, Hay's Galleria
  Tooley St, SE1
Balls Brothers
  The Hop Cellars 24 Southwark
  St, SE1
Barrow Boy and Banker, Bank
  Chambers, 6 Borough High St,
  SE1
Brendan O'Grady's
  67 Kennington Rd, SE1
The Elephant and Castle,
  Newington Causeway, SE1
The Founders Arms
  52 Hopton St off Southwark St,
  SE1
The George Inn
  77 Borough High St, SE1
Goose & Firkin
  47–48 Borough Rd, SE1
Horniman at Hay's
  Hay's Galleria, Tooley St, SE1
The Old Thameside Inn
  2 Clink St, SE1
Oxo Tower Bar, 8th Floor Oxo
  Tower Wharf Barge House St,
  SE1
The Ring
  72 Blackfriars Rd, SE1
Victoria
  68 Pages Walk, SE1

**Stepney**
The Blind Beggar
  337 Whitechapel Rd, E1
The Captain Kidd
  108 Wapping High St, E1
The Crown and Shuttle,
  Shoreditch High St, E1
The Dickens Inn
  St Katherine's Way, E1
El Meson de los Bariles
  8a Lamb St, E1
The Prospect of Whitby
  57 Wapping Wall, E1

**Streatham**
O'Neill's
  78a Streatham High Rd, SW16

**Sutton**
All Bar One
  2 Hill Rd, Sutton
Chicago Rock Café, Throwley
  Rd, Sutton
Goose and Granite
  2 Dunstan's Hill, Sutton
Rat & Parrot
  33–35 High St, Sutton
Scruffy Murphy's
  67 High St, Sutton

**Sydenham**
Fewterer & Firkin
313 Kirkdale, Sydenham

**Theydon Bois**
The Bull
Coppice Row, Theydon Bois

**Tooting**
Faith & Firkin
1 Bellevue Rd, SW17
Freedom & Firkin
196 Tooting High St, SW17

**Twickenham**
The White Swan
The Riverside, Twickenham

**Upminster**
The Essex Yeoman
70 Station Rd, Upminster

**Victoria**
Adam and Eve
81 Petty France, SW1
Albert
52 Victoria St, SW1
Cardinal
23 Francis St, SW1
Finnegan's Wake
2 Strutton Ground, SW1
Rat & Parrot
4 Elizabeth St, SW1
Two Chairmen
39 Dartmouth St, SW1
Westminster Arms,
9 Storey's Gate, SW1
Wetherspoons
Victoria Station, SW1

**Wallington**
O'Neill's
89 Manor Rd, Wallington

**Walthamstow**
The Central Station
80 Brunner Rd, E17

Goose and Granite
264 Hoe St, E17

**Walton-on-Thames**
Slug and Lettuce, Thameside

**Wandsworth**
All Bar One
Old York Rd, SW18
Alma Tavern
499 York Rd, SW18
Grid Inn
22 Replingham Rd, SW18
Ship Inn
41 Jews Row, SW18
Slug and Lettuce
21 Alma Rd, SW18

**Watford**
O'Neill's
66-68 The Parade, Watford

**Wembley**
Bootsy Brogan's
86 East La, Wembley

**West Kensington**
Frigate & Firkin
Blythe Rd, W14
Harvey Floorbangers
1 Hammersmith Rd, W14
Havelock Tavern
57 Masbro Rd, W14

**Weybridge**
Formula & Firkin
Heath Rd, Weybridge

**Whetstone**
Scruffy Murphy's
1262 High Rd, N20

**Whitehall**
Clarence
53 Whitehall, SW1

Lord Moon of the Mall, 16–18
Whitehall, SW1
Old Shades
37 Whitehall, SW1
Red Lion
48 Parliament Sq, SW1
Tattershall Castle
King's Reach
Victoria Embankment, SW1

**Wood Green**
Goose and Granite
203 High Rd, N22

**Wimbledon**
Alexandra
33 Wimbledon Hill Rd, SW19
All Bar One
37 Wimbledon Hill Rd, SW19
Crooked Billet
14 Crooked Billet, SW19
Dog and Fox
224 Wimbledon High St, SW19
Dome
91 High St, SW19
Fox and Grapes
Camp Rd, SW19
Hand in Hand
6 Crooked Billet, SW19
JJ's
159 The Broadway, SW19
O'Neill's
68 The Broadway, SW19
Pitcher & Piano
4–5 High St, SW19
Rose and Crown
55 High St, SW19

**Woking**
Fahrenheit & Firkin
Chobham Rd, Woking

## Late-openers

Atlantic Bar and Grill, W1
Babushka, SE1
Babushka, N1
Backpacker, N1
B Bar, SW11
The Beaufoy Arms, SW11
Belushi's, WC2
Black Cap, NW1
Blues Bar, W1
Brendan O'Grady's, SE1
Brompton's and The Warwick
Bar, SW5
Browns, E2
Browns, SW3
Browns, W1
Browns, WC2
Cactus Blue, SW3
Café Bohème, W1

Café Latino, W1
Café Sol Dos, SW4
Cairo Jacks, W1
Cantaloupe Bar and Grill, EC2
Central Station, E17
Central Station, N1
Chicago Rock Café, Sutton
Cork and Bottle, WC2
The Crescent, SW3
De Hems, W1
The Dog Star, SW9
Dover Street Wine Bar, W1
Dublin Castle, NW1
Duke of Devonshire, SW12
The Edge, W1
Est, W1
Fashion Café, W1
Football Football, W1

Freedom, W1
Friar & Firkin, NW1
Fridge Bar, SW2
Havana, SW6
The Hobgoblin, SW2
Iberica, SW6
Ink Club, SW6
Jim Thompson's, SW6
JJ's, SW19
Kemia Bar at Momo, W1
Kettner's Champagne Bar, W1
King's Head, N1
The Longroom, EC1
Los Locos Beach Club, W1
Lupo, W1
Market Bar, W11
Market Cafe Bar, WC2
MetBar, W1

Mondo, W1
Notting Hill Arts Club, W11
O Bar, W1
Office Bar, W1
Pals, East Molesey
La Perla
The Polar Bear, WC2
Po Na Na, SW3
Po Na Na, N1
Po Na Na, Croydon

Po Na Na Fez Club, SW10
R Bar, SW3
Riki Tik, W1
Saint, WC2
Shoeless Joe's, SW6
Slap Harry's, W1
Soho Spice, W1
Sports Café, SW1
The Spot, WC2
Springbok, WC2

Tattershall Castle, SW1
dell'Ugo, W1
Vic Naylor, EC1
Victoria, SE1
Walkabout, W12
Water Rats, WC1
White Swan, E14
Windows on the World, W1
Zd, NW6
Zilli Bar, W1

## ...with outside space

Albion, N1
Alexandra, SW19
Anchor, Bankside, SE1
Angel, SE16
Anglesea Arms, SW7
Audley, W1
Australian, SW3
B Bar, SW11
Babushka, N1
Babushka, SE1
Barley Mow, E14
Beaufoy Arms, SW11
Bell and Crown, W4
Bellini's, W8
Belushi's, WC2
BierRex, EC4
BierRex, SW15
Bill Bentley, EC2 1DP
Black Cap, NW1
Black Lion, W6
Blenheim, SW3
Blind Beggar, E1
Blue Anchor, W6
Bluebird, SW3
Bootsy Brogan's, HA0 3NJ
Bouffe, La, SW11
Box, WC2
Brasserie Rocque, EC2
Bread and Roses, SW4
Brendan O'Grady's, SE1
Brief Encounter, WC2
Bull and Gate, NW5
Bulls' Head, W6
Cafe Boheme, W1V
Camden Head, N1
Captain Kidd, E1
Cartoonist, EC4
Cat and the Canary, E14
Catcher in the Rye, N3
Central Station, N1
Champion , W2
Champion, The, W1
Chelsea Potter, SW3
Chelsea Ram, SW10
Chicago Rock Café, SM1
City Barge, W4
Clarence, SW1
Clifton, NW8

Compton Arms, N1
Corney and Barrow, E14
Corney and Barrow, EC2
Corney and Barrow, EC4
Cow, W2
Cricketers
Crooked Billet, SW19
Crown, N1
Crown, SE3
Crown and Greyhound, SE21
Crown and Two Chairmen, W1
Crutched Friar, EC3
Cutty Sark Tavern, SE10
Daly's Wine Bar, WC2
DCO, EC1
De Hems, W1
Dickens Inn, E1
Dixie's, SW11
Dog and Fox, SW19
Dog Star, SE5
Dove, W6
Drayton Arms, SW5
Duke of Cambridge, SW11
Duke of Cumberland, SW6
Duke of Devonshire, SW12
Duke of Edinburgh, E13
Eagle, EC1
Eagle Tavern, N1
Eclipse, SW12
Edge, The, W1
Elephant and Castle, SE1
Engineer, NW1
Enterprise, SW3
Falcon, The, SW4
Filthy McNasty, EC1
Finnegan's Wake, SW1
Flask, N6
Flask, NW3
Flower and Firkin,
Founders Arms, SE1
Fox & Hounds, SM5
Freemasons Arm, NW3
Friar and Firkin, NW1
G.E.Aldwinkles, NW3
Gatehouse, N6

Gazebo, Kingston
George Inn, SE1
George IV, W4
Gipsy Moth, SE10
Goose & Firkin, SE1
Goose and Granite, SE22
Goose and Granite, SW4
Grapes, E14
Green Man, SW15
Grenadier, SW1
Greyhound, SM5
Greyhound, W8
Gun, E14
Half Moon, SW15
Hamilton Hall, EC2
Hand in Hand, SW19
Hare and Hounds, SW14
Havelock Tavern, W14
Henry Addington, E14
Henry Holland, W1
Henry J Beans, SW3
Hereford Arms, SW7
Hillgate Arms, W8
Hobgoblin, SW2
Hollywood Arms, SW10
Holy Drinker, SW11
Hope, W1
Horniman at Hay's, SE1
House They Left Behind, E14
Hung, Drawn and Quartered
J J Murphy's, SW3
Jack Horner, W1
Jack Straw's Castle, NW3
Jacs, W11
Janet's, SW10
Jim Thompsons, SW6
JJ Murphy's, SW3
Jolly Farmers, Purley
King of Bohemia, NW3
King's Head, SW6
King William IV, NW3
Ladbroke Arms, W11
Lamb, WC1
Lamb and Flag, WC2

Latchmere, SW11
Lavender, The, SW11
Legless Ladder, SW11
Legless Ladder, SW6
Leinster Arms, W2
London Apprentice,
Longroom, EC1
Lord's Tavern, The, NW8
Lupo, W1
MacNabs, SW12
Magpie & Stump, SW10
Maple Leaf, WC2
Market Cafe Bar, WC2
Marlborough, Richmond
Marquess Tavern, N1
Masons Arms, W1
Melton Mowbray, EC1
Mitre, W2
Monkey Puzzle, W2
Moon Under The Water, WC2
Morpeth Arms, SW1
Mullins Coffee House, WC2
Narrow Boat, N1
Oblivion, SW4
O'Hanlon's, EC1
Old Bull and Bush, NW3
Old Dr Butlers Head, EC2
Old King Lud, EC4
Old Ship, W6
Old Thameside Inn, SE1
O'Neill's, E11
O'Neill's, SE3

Orange Brewery, SW1
Orange Tree,
Oriel, SW1
Pals, KT8
Paradise, W10, 30
Phene Arms, SW3
Phoenix Bar & Grill, SW15
Plumbers Arms, SW1
Prince of Wales, SW4
Prince of Wales, WC1
Princess of Wales, SE3
Prospect of Whitby, E1
Punch and Judy, WC2
Queen's Head, SW3
Rack and Tenter, EC2
Red Lion, SW1
River Rat, SW11
Robert Browning, W9
Rose and Crown, SW19
Rose & Crown, SW4
Rose of York,
Round Table, WC2
Salisbury, WC2
Salutation Inn, W6
Scarsdale, W8
Scotts, W1
Scruffy Murphy's, W1
Sekforde Arms, EC1
Sheila's Bar Barbie, WC2E
Sherlock Holmes, WC2
Ship, SW14
Ship Inn, SW18

Shuckburgh Arms, SW3
Slap Harry's, W1
Slug and Lettuce, SW15
Smithfield Free House, EC1
Spaniard's Inn, NW3
Sporting Page, SW10
Sun Inn, SW13
Surprise, SW3
Sussex, WC2
Swan, W2
Talbot Tavern, SW1
Tattershall Castle, SW1
T.E.Dingwalls, NW1
TS Queen Mary, WC2
Tut 'n' Shive, N1
Two Chairmen, SW1
Walmer Castle, W11
Water Rat, SW10
Waterside, N1
Westbourne, W2
Westminster Arms, SW1
Wetherspoons, SW1
White Horse, SW6
White Swan, Twickenham
White Swan, Richmond
Windsor Castle, W8
Woodman, SW11
Yard, The, W1
Yates's Wine Lodge
Ye Olde Mitre Tavern, EC1
Ye Olde Surgeon, W1
Ye Olde Swiss Cottage, NW3

# ...with accommodation

Brewers Inn,
 147 East Hill, Wandsworth, SW18.
 Tel: 0181 874 4128
Bull's Head, Royal Parade,
 Chislehurst, Kent, BR7. Tel: 0181 467 1727
Clarence,
 Park Rd, Teddington, TW11. Tel: 0181 977 8025
Coach & Horses
 8 The Green, Teddington, TW11.
 Tel: 0181 940 1208
Fox & Goose
 Hanger La, Ealing, W5.
 Tel: 0181–998 5864
Gorsvenor Arms
 204 Garratt La, Wandsworth, SW18
 Tel: 0181 874 2709
Greyhound
 2 High St, Carshalton, SM5.
 Tel: 0181 647 1511
Harvey Floorbangers
 1 Hammersmith Rd, W14.
 Tel: 0171 371 4105

King's Arms
 19 Boston Manor Rd, Brentford, TW8.
 Tel: 0181 560 5860
King's Arms
 254 Edgware Rd, W2.
 Tel: 0171 262 8441
Mary Rose
 40 High St, St Mary Cray, Orpington, BR5
 Tel: 01689 817917
Mitre Inn
 Greenwich High Rd, SE10.
 Tel: 0181 355 6760
Oxford Arms
 21 Halliford St, Islington.
 Tel: 0171 226 6629
Plough Inn
 42 Christchurch Rd, East Sheen, SW14.
 Tel: 0181 876 7833
Swan Hotel
 The Hythe, Staines, TW18.
 Tel: 01784 452494

Wellington
81–83 Waterloo Rd, SE1.
Tel: 0171 928 6083

Windermere
Windermere Ave, S Kenton, Wembley, HA9.
Tel: 0181 904 7484

Windmill on the Common
Southside, Clapham, SW4.
Tel: 0181 673 4578

Windsor Castle
415 Brighton Rd, South Croydon, CR2.
Tel: 0181 680 4559

# Gay venues

The Back Bar
8–10 Brewer Street, W1

Black Cap
171 Camden High Street, NW1

Box
Seven Dials, 32–34 Monmouth Street, WC2

Brief Encounter
42 St Martin's Lane, WC2

Brompton's and the Warwick Bar
294 Old Brompton Road, SW5

Central Station
80 Brunner Road, E17

Central Station
37 Wharfdale Road,N1

Champion
1 Wellington Terrace,  Bayswater Road, W2

Coleherne
261 Old Brompton Road, SW5

The Edge
The,11 Soho Square, W1

Freedom
60-66 Wardour Street, W1

Fridge Bar
1 Town Hall Parade, Brixton, SW2

Kudos
10 Adelaide Street, WC2

Queens Head
27 Tryon St, SW3

Rupert Street
50 Rupert Street, W1

White Swan
555 Commercial Road, E14

The Yard
57 Rupert Street, W1

# Waterside venues

Docklands: Dickens Inn, E1
Docklands: Prospect of Whitby, E1
Docklands: Barley Mow, E14
Docklands: Cat and the Canary, E14
Docklands: Grapes, E14
Docklands: Gun, E14
Islington: Babushka, N1
Islington: Waterside, N1
Kingston: Gazebo
Richmond: Slug and Lettuce

Richmond: White Cross
SE1: Anchor Bankside
SE1: Founders Arms
SE1: Horniman at Hay's
SE1: Old Thameside Inn
SE1: Oxo Tower Bar
SE10: Cutty Sark Tavern
SE10 : Trafalgar Tavern
SE16: Angel
SW1: Tattershall Castle
SW11: River Rat

SW14: Ship
SW15 : Bar M
W4: Bell and Crown
W4: City Barge
W6: Black Lion
W6: Blue Anchor
W6: Bulls' Head
W6: Dove
W6: Old Ship
WC2: Daly's Wine Bar

# … to play darts

Australian
29 Milner Street,SW3

Bulls' Head
Strand on the Green,W6

Cardinal
23 Francis St,SW1

Cat and the Canary
1-24 Fisherman's Walk,E14

Champion
12/13 Wells Street,W1

Chandos
29 St Martin's Lane,WC2

Cheshire Cheese
5 Little Essex Street,WC2

Clachan
34 Kingly Street,W1

Duke of Devonshire
39 Balham High Road,SW12

Duke of Edinburgh
299 Green Street,E13

Flask
14 Flask Walk,NW3

George IV
185 High Road, Chiswick,W4

George Inn
77 Borough High Street,SE1

Green Man
  Putney Heath,SW15
Greyhound
  2 The High Street, Carshalton,SM5
Gun
  27 Cold Harbour,E14
Hand in Hand
  6 Crooked Billet,SW19
Hare and Hounds
  216 Upper Richmond Road West,SW14
Jolly Farmers
  Purley High Street, Purley,
King's Head
  115 Upper Street,N1
Lamb Tavern
  Leadenhall Market,EC3
Leinster Arms
  17 Leinster Terrace,W2London Apprentice
  62 Old Church Street, Isleworth,
Ye Olde Cheshire Cheese
  Wine Office Court, 145 Fleet Street,EC4

Outpost
  Lidlington Place,NW1
Paxton's Head
  153 Knightsbridge,SW1
Pharaoh and Firkin
  90 Fulham High Street,SW6
Plumbers Arms
  14 Lower Belgrave Square,SW1
Princess of Wales
  1A Montpelier Row, Blackheath,SE3
Rose of York
  Petersham Road, Richmond,
Ship Inn
  41 Jews Road,SW18
Surprise
  6 Christchurch Terrace,SW3
Ye Olde Swiss Cottage
  98 Finchley Road,NW3
Trafalgar
  200 Kings Road,SW3
World's End
  459 King's Road,SW10

# What was it called before?

| | |
|---|---|
| Bar Coast, 13 Maiden Lane, WC2 | The Pineapple |
| Bootsy Brogan's, 1 Fulham Broadway, SW6 | The Swan |
| Brendan O'Grady's, 67-69 Kennington Road,SE1 | The Three Stags |
| Cactus Blue, 86 Fulham Road,SW3 | The Rose |
| Cartoonist, 76 Shoe Lane,EC4 | The Cartoon Page |
| Chelsea Square, 145 Dovehouse Street,SW3 | The Princess of Wales |
| Dog Star,389 Coldharbour Lane,SW9 | The Atlantic |
| Edward's,170 Uxbridge Road,W12 | The Beaumont Arms |
| Edward's,28-30 New Broadway,W5 | Fiddler's Three |
| Edward's,1 Camden High St,NW1 | The Southampton Arms |
| Edward's,1 Hammersmith Broadway,W6 | The Swan |
| Filthy McNasty & the Whiskey Cafe, 68 Amwell Street, EC1 | The Fountain |
| Finnegan's Wake,48 Fulham Palace Road,W6 | The Duke of Cornwall |
| Finnegan's Wake,2 Strutton Ground,SW1 | Graftons |
| First and Last,Little Somerset St,EC1 | The Duke of Somerset |
| Friar & Firkin,120 Euston Road,NW1 | The Rising Sun |
| Front Page,35 Old Church St,SW3 | The Black Lion |
| Fulmar & Firkin,51 Parker St,WC2 | The Kingsway Tavern |
| Fusilier & Firkin,7-8 Chalk Farm Road,NW1 | The Caernarvon Castle |
| G E Aldwinkles,154 Fleet Road,NW3 | The White Horse |
| Goose & Firkin,47-48 Borough Road,SE1 | The Duke of York |
| Goose & Granite,155 Kilburn High Road,NW6 | The Earl Derby |
| Goose & Granite,264 Hoe Street,E17 | Flanagan's Tower |
| Goose & Granite,248 North End Road,SW6 | The Fulham Tap |
| Goose & Granite,2 St Dunstan's Hill,Sutton | The Gander |
| Goose & Granite,231 Marchmont St,WC1 | The Marquis Cornwallis |
| Goose & Granite,203 High Road,N22 | The Nags Head |
| Goose & Granite,196-198 Clapham High St,SW4 | The Plough |
| Goose & Granite,381 Lordship Lane,SE22 | The Plough |
| Goose & Granite,88 Rushey Green,SE6 | The Rising Sun |
| Goose & Granite,264 Hoe St,E17 | The Tower Hotel |
| Ground Floor Bar,186 Portobello Road,W11 | The Colville Arms |
| Grouse & Claret,Little Chester Street,SW1 | The Pig & Whistle |
| Harvey Floorbangers,1 Hammersmith Road,W14 | The Hand and Flower |
| Henry Holland,39 Duke Street,W1 | The Red Lion |
| Henry J Beans,195 Kings Road,SW3 | The Six Bells |
| Hobgoblin,95 Effra Road,SW2 | The George Canning |

| | |
|---|---|
| Hogshead in St James,11 Dering Street,W1 | The Bunch of Grapes |
| House They Left Behind,27 Ropemaker's Fields,E14 | The Black Horse |
| Legless Ladder,339 Battersea Park Road,SW11 | The Prince of Wales |
| Legless Ladder,1 Harwood Tce,SW6 | The Rose |
| MacDonalds,318 High Street,Brentford | The Red Lion |
| Manhattan,268 Fulham Road,SW10 | The Fulham Tup |
| Maple Leaf,41 Maiden Lane,WC2 | The Bedford Head |
| McDonalds,318 High St,Brentford | The Red Lion |
| Mucky Duck,108 Fetter Lane,EC4 | The Swan |
| Museum Tavern,49 Great Russell Street,EC2 | The Dog and Duck |
| O Bar,83 Wardour Street,W1 | The Round House |
| O'Neill's,364 Earls Court Rd,SW5 | The George Whittaker |
| Old King's Head, 173 Blackfriars Road, SE1 | Babushka |
| The Outback,11 Henrietta Street,WC2 | The Rickshaw |
| Outpost,Lidlington Place,NW1 | The Russell Arms |
| Pharaoh & Firkin,90 Fulham High St,SW6 | Temperance Billiard Hall |
| Prince Bonaparte,80 Chepstow Road,W2 | The Artesian |
| Punch Tavern,99 Fleet St,EC4 | The Crown and Sugarloaf |
| Racing Page,2 Duke Street,Richmond | The Cobwebs |
| Raj,40 Holland Park Ave,W11 | The Mitre |
| Rat and Carrot,60 Chelsea Manor Street,SW3 | The Beehive |
| The River Rat,2 Lombard Road,SW11 | The Chandler |
| Robert Browning,15 Clifton Road,W9 | The Eagle |
| Rose of York,Petersham Road,Richmond | The Tudor Close |
| Secrets, 62 Glenthorne Road, W6 | The Royal Oak |
| Scruffy Murphy's,283-295 West End Lane,NW6 | The Arkwright's Wheel |
| Scruffy Murphy's,1262 High Road,N20 | The Griffin |
| Scruffy Murphy's,451 Fulham Rd,SW10 | The Gunter Arms |
| Scruffy Murphy's,142 Fleet St,EC4 | The King & Keys |
| Scruffy Murphy's,15 Denman Street,W1 | The Queen's Head |
| Shuckburgh Arms,47 Denyer Street,SW3 | Finnegan's Wake |
| Sporting Page,Camera Place,SW10 | The Red Anchor |
| Tut 'n' Shive,235 Upper Street,N1 | The Angel and Crown |
| Walkabout,58 Shepherd's Bush Green,W12 | The Bottom Line |
| Walkabout,11 Henrietta Street,WC2 | The Outback Inn |

## Pool Tables

| | |
|---|---|
| Bar Oz,51 Moscow Rd, W2 | Island Queen,87 Noel Rd, N1 |
| Beaufoy Arms,18 Lavender Hill, SW11 | Jolly Farmers,Purley High St, Purley |
| Browns,1 Hackney Rd, E2 | King's Head,4 Fulham High St, SW6 |
| Bull and Gate,389 Kentish Town Rd, NW5 | Magpie & Stump,442 King's Rd, SW10 |
| Bunch of Grapes,207 Brompton Rd, SW3 | Magpie and Stump,218 Old Bailey, EC4 |
| Cardinal, 23 Francis St, SW1 | Man in the Moon, 392 Kings Rd, SW3 |
| Cheshire Cheese,5 Little Essex St, WC2 | Museum Tavern, 49 Great Russell St, WC1 |
| Crown and Shuttle,Shoreditch High St, E1 | Old Red Lion,72 High Holborn, WC1 |
| Deacons,Walbrook, EC4 | Ye Olde Swiss Cottage,98 Finchley Rd, |
| Duke of Edinburgh,299 Green St, E13 | NW3Outpost,Lidlington Pl, NW1 |
| Elbow Room,103 Westbourne Grove, W2 | Prince Alfred,Formosa St, W9 |
| Elephant and Castle,Newington Causeway, SE1 | Rat and Carrot,60 Chelsea Manor St, SW3 |
| Falcon, 33 Bedford Rd, SW4 | Smithfield Free House,334 Central Market, EC1 |
| Gazebo,Kings Passage, Kingston, KT1 1PG | Springbok,20 Bedford St, WC2 |
| Hare and Hounds,216 Upper Richmond Rd West, | Sports Academy, 24 King William St, EC4 |
| SW14 | Trafalgar,200 Kings Rd, SW3 |
| Hope and Anchor,207 Upper St, N1 | |

## Bar Billiards

| | | |
|---|---|---|
| Cat and the Canary E14 | Inn, SE1 | Nightingale, SW12 |
| Eagle Tavern. N1 | London Apprentice  Isleworth | Rose of York, Richmond |
| Fox & Hounds, SuttonGeorge | Narrow Boat, N1 | Woodman, SW11 |

# Strippers

Backpacker, N1
Beaufoy Arms, SW11

Browns, E2
Central Station, N1

Crown & Shuttle , E1
Secrets, W6

# Best places for food

All Bar One, Various locations
Alma
Babushka , N1
Beach Blanket Babylon, W11
Belle Vue, SW4
Captain Kidd, E1
Chelsea Ram, SW10
Collection, SW3
Coopers Arms, SW3
Cow, W10
Cross Keys, SW3
Crown, N1
Duke of Cambridge, SW11
Eagle, EC1

Engineer, NW1
Flask, N6
Front Page, SW10
George, SE1
Guinea, W1
Havelock Tavern, W14
Jim Thompson's, SW6
La Perla, WC2
Legless Ladder, SW10
Legless Ladder, SW11
Lord's Tavern, NW8
Masons Arms, SW8
Oblivion, SW4
Prince Bonaparte, W2

Scarsdale, W8
Shoeless Joe's, SW6
Sporting Page, SW10
Stonemasons, W6
Sun, SW4
Three Greyhounds, W1
Trafalgar, SE10
Westbourne, W2
White Horse, SW6
White Swan, Richmond
White Swan, Twickenham
Windsor Castle, W8

# Top 10 coolest places to be seen in

Alphabet, W1
Babushka, W11
Cocktail Bar at
  The Connaught, W1

Collection, SW3
Kemia Bar at Momo, W1
Notting Hill Arts Club, W11
Paradise, W10

Riki Tik, W1
Saint, W1
Windows On The World, W1

# Top 10 naffest places to be seen in

Bluebird, SW10
Cairo Jacks, W1
Coates, EC1
Fashion Cafe, W1

Football Football, SW1
Los Locos Beach Club, W1
MetBar, W1
Mezzo, W1

Quo Vadis, W1
Rat & Parrot – any

# Top 10 easiest places to pull

Atlantic Bar and Grill, W1
Bar Zola's, WC2
Brief Encounter, WC2
Collection, SW3

Fifth Floor Bar,
  Harvey Nichols, SW1
Goat in Boots, SW10
190, SW7

Pals, East Molesey
R Bar, SW3
Zd Bar, NW6

# Top 10 for the wine lovers

Albertine, W12
Cork & Bottle, WC2
Crescent, SW3
Fino's Wine Cellar, W1

Gordon's, WC2
La Grande Marque, EC4
Hanover Square, W1
Olde Wine Shades, EC4

Pavillion, EC2
St Pauls' Wine Vaults, EC4

# Top 10 terrific views

Angel SE16
Corney & Barrow,
  Broadgate Circle
Founders Arms, SE1

Gazebo,
  Kingston-upon-Thames
Oxo Tower
Sun, Barnes

Waterside, N1
Windows on the World
White Cross, Richmond
White Swan, Twickenham

# Top 10 other greats

Elbow Room (pool)
Office Bar (board games)
Le Shaker (cocktails)
O'Hanlon's, EC1, (Irish)
Havana, SW6 (Live Latin
  music)

Filthy McNasty & The Whiskey
  Café (great name)
Lupo, W1 (Stylish and trendy)
Marlborough, Richmond (great
  garden)

Mullins Coffee House, WC2
  (outside seating)
Sports Academy, EC4
  (watching sport)

# International Bars

**Australasian**
  Backpacker, N1
  Bar Oz, W2
  Polar Bear, WC2
  Prince of Teck, SW5
  Sheila's Bar Barbie, WC2
  Walkabout, WC2
  Walkabout, W12

**Canadian**
  Maple Leaf, WC2

**Dutch**
  De Hems, W1

**Irish**
  Brendan O'Grady's, SE1
  The Cow, W2
  The Enterprise, NW3
  Filthy McNasty and the
    Whiskey Cafe, EC1
  Finnegan's Wake – various
    locations, see review
  J J Murphy's, SW3
  O'Hanlon's, EC1

O'Neill's - various locations,
  see review
Scruffy Murphy's - various locations,
  see review
Waxy O'Connor's, W1

**Mexican**
  Cafe Latino, W1
  Cafe Sol Dos, SW4
  Las Fuentes, Purley
  Iberica, SW6
  El Meson de los Barriles, E1
  La Perla, WC2
  Tapas Bars

**South African**
  Springbok, WC2

**Thai**
  Come the Revolution, SW6
  Jim Thompson's, SW6,
  SW15 & Croydon
  Walmer Castle, W11